TWENTIETH-CENTURY LITERARY THEORY

Also by K. M. Newton

THEORY INTO PRACTICE

Twentieth-Century Literary Theory

A Reader

Second Edition

Edited by

K. M. Newton

St. Martin's Press
New York

St. Martin's Press, Scholarly and Reference Division,
175 Fifth Avenue, New York, N.Y. 10010

First edition 1988
Second edition 1997

This book is printed on paper suitable for recycling and
made from fully managed and sustained forest sources.

Printed in Hong Kong

ISBN 0–312–17588–4 cloth
ISBN 0–312–17589–2 paperback

Library of Congress Cataloging-in-Publication Data
Twentieth century literary theory : a reader / edited by K.M. Newton.
 — 2nd ed.
p. cm.
Includes bibliographical references and index.
ISBN 0–312–17588–4 (cloth : alk. paper). — ISBN 0–312–17589–2
(pbk. : alk. paper)
1. Criticism—History—20th century.   I. Newton, K. M.
PN94.T87 1998
801'.95'0904—dc21   97–10704
                                                              CIP

CONTENTS

ACKNOWLEDGEMENTS

The editor and publishers wish to thank the following for permission to use copyright material: Roland Barthes, material from 'Death of the Author' in *Image/Music/Text*, trs. Stephen Heath (1977). English translation copyright © 1977 by Stephen Heath, by permission of Collins Publishers and Hill and Wang, a division of Farrar, Straus & Giroux, Inc; and 'Science versus Literature', *The Times Literary Supplement*, 28 September 1967. Copyright © Times Supplements Ltd, 1967, by permission of Times Newspapers Ltd; Walter Benjamin, material from *Understanding Brecht* (1973), by permission of Verso/NLB; Homi K. Bhabha, material from 'The Other Question', *Screen*, 24:6 (1983), 18–36, by permission of Screen; David Bleich, material from 'The Subjective Character of Critical Interpretation', *College English*, 36 (1975), by permission of the National Council of Teachers of English and the author; Harold Bloom, material from *Poetry and Repression* (1976), by permission of Yale University Press; Cleanth Brooks, material from 'The Formalist Critic', *Kenyon Review*, 13 (1951), by permission of Kenyon Review and the author; Kenneth Burke, material from *Language as Symbolic Action* (1973), by permission of University of California Press; John Casey, material from *The Language of Criticism* (1960), Methuen & Co, by permission of Routledge; Christopher Caudwell, material from *Illusion and Reality* (1946), by permission of Lawrence and Wishart Ltd; Hélène Cixous, material from *Writing Differences: Readings from the Seminar of Hélène Cixous*, ed. Susan Sellers, Open University Press (1988), by permission of Susan Sellers; Rosalind Coward and John Ellis, material from *Language and Materialism* (1977) Routledge and Kegan Paul; by permission of Routledge; Jonathan Culler, material from 'Semiotics as a Theory of Reading' in *In Pursuit of Signs: Semiotics, Literature, Deconstruction* (1981). Copyright © 1981 by Jonathan Culler, by permission of Routledge and Cornell University Press; Paul de Man, material from 'The Resistance to Theory', *Yale French Studies*, 63 (1982), by permission of the editor; Jacques Derrida, material from *The Structuralist Controversy* (1972), by permission of Johns Hopkins University Press; Josephine Donavan, material from 'Beyond the Net: Feminist Criticism as a Moral Criticism', *Denver Quarterly*, 17 (1983), by permission of the editor; Terry Eagleton, material from *Criticism and Ideology* (1976), by permission of Verso/NLB; John M. Ellis, material from *The Theory of Literary Criticism* (1974), by permission of the

University of California Press; Shoshana Felman, material from 'Turning the Screw of Interpretation', *Yale French Studies*, 55/56 (1977), by permission of the editor and author; Stanley Fish, material from *Doing What Comes Naturally: Change, Rhetoric and the Practice of Theory in Literary and Legal Studies.* Copyright © 1989 Duke University Press, by permission of Duke University Press; and from 'Interpreting the *Variorum*', *Critical Inquiry* (1976), by permission of University of Chicago Press; Michel Foucault, material from *Power/Knowledge: Selected Interviews and Other Writings*, ed. Colin Gordon. Text copyright © 1972, 1975, 1976, 1977 by Michel Foucault. This collection copyright © 1980 by The Harvester Press, by permission of Prentice-Hall and Pantheon Books, a division of Random House, Inc; Roger Fowler, material from 'Literature as Discourse' in *Literature as Social Discourse* (1981), by permission of B.T. Batsford Ltd; Gérard Genette, material from 'Structuralism and Literary Criticism' in *Figures of Literary Discourse* (1982). Copyright © 1982 by Columbia University Press, by permission of Blackwell Publishers and Columbia University Press; E. D. Hirsch, Jr, material from 'Three Dimensions of Hermeneutics', *New Literary History*, 3 (1971–2), by permission of Johns Hopkins University Press; Norman N. Holland, material from 'Reading and Identity: A Psychoanalytic Revolution', *Academy Forum (The American Academy of Psychoanalysis)*, 23 (1979), by permission of the author; Linda Hutcheon, material from 'Theorizing the Postmodern' in *A Poetics of Postmodernism* (1988), by permission of Routledge; Wolfgang Iser, material from *Aspects of Narrative*, ed. J. H. Miller (1971). Copyright © 1971 by Columbia University Press, by permission of Columbia University Press; Roman Jakobson, material from *Readings in Russian Poetics*, ed. L. Matejka and K. Pomorska (1978), by permission of University of Michigan; and *Style in Language*, ed. Thomas Sebeok (1960), by permission of MIT Press; Fredric Jameson, material from *The Political Unconscious: Narrative as a Socially Symbolic Act* (1981) Methuen & Co. Copyright © 1981 by Cornell University Press, by permission of Cornell University Press and Routledge; and from 'Postmodernism, or The Cultural Logic of Late Capitalism', *New Left Review*, 146, July–August (1984), by permission of New Left Review; Hans Robert Jauss, material from *Toward an Aesthetic of Reception* (1982), The Harvester Press, by permission of Prentice-Hall and University of Minnesota Press; P. D. Juhl, material from *Interpretation* (1980), by permission of Princeton University Press; Steven Knapp and Walter Benn Michaels, material from 'Against Theory', *Critical Inquiry*, 8 (1982), by permission of The University of Chicago Press; Julia Kristeva, material from 'The System and the Speaking Subject', *The Times Literary Supplement*, 12 October 1973. Copyright © Times

Supplements Ltd, 1973, by permission of TimesNewspapers Ltd; F. R. Leavis, material from *The Common Pursuit* (1962), Chatto & Windus, by permission of Random House UK Ltd; Georg Lukács, material from *The Meaning of Contemporary Realism* (1963), by permission of The Merlin Press Ltd and Humanities Press International, Inc; P. N. Medvedev/M. M. Bakhtin, material from *The Formal Method in Literary Scholarship* (1978), by permission of Johns Hopkins University Press; Elizabeth A. Meese, material from 'Sexual Politics and Critical Judgment' in *After Strange Texts: The Role of Theory in the Study of Literature*, ed. Gregory S. Jay and David L. Miller. Copyright © 1985 The University of Alabama Press, by permission of The University of Alabama Press; Jan Mukařovský, material from *Aesthetic Function, Norm, and Value as Social Facts* (1979), by permission of University of Michigan; Morse Peckham, material from 'The Problem of Interpretation', *College Literature*, 6 (1979), by permission of West Chester University and the author; I. A. Richards, material from *Poetries and Sciences* (1970), Routledge & Kegan Paul, by permission of Routledge; Paul Ricoeur, material from *Freud and Philosophy*, trs. Denis Savage (1970), by permission of Yale University Press; Edward W. Said, material from *Culture and Imperialism* (1993), Chatto & Windus. Copyright © 1993 by Edward Said, by permission of Random House UK Ltd and The Wylie Agency, Inc. on behalf of the author; Victor Shklovsky, material from *Russian Formalist Criticism* (1965), ed. Lee Y. Lemon and Marion J. Reis, by permission of University of Nebraska Press; Elaine Showalter, material from *Women Writing and Women Writing About Women*, ed. Mary Jacobus (1979), by permission of Croom Helm and Barnes and Noble Books; Alan Sinfield, material from *Faultlines: Cultural Materialism and the Politics of Dissident Reading* (1992), Clarendon Press. Copyright © 1992 Alan Sinfield and The Regents of the University of California, by permission of Oxford University Press and University of California Press; William V. Spanos, material from 'Breaking the Circle: Hermeneutics as Disclosure', *boundary 2*, 5 (1977), by permission of the author; Tzvetan Todorov, material from *Introduction to Poetics* (1981), The Harvester Press, by permission of Prentice-Hall and University of Minnesota Press; H. Aram Veeser, material from *The New Historicism* (1989) by permission of Routledge, New York and London; Raymond Williams, material from *Marxism and Literature* (1977). Copyright © 1977 by Oxford University Press, by permission of Oxford University Press.

Every effort has been made to trace the copyright holders but if any have been inadvertently overlooked the publishers will be pleased to make the necessary arrangement at the first opportunity.

INTRODUCTION

No one concerned with developments in literary criticism over the past thirty years or so can ignore the fact that there has been a great revival of interest in questions of theory. Probably the main reason for this has been the impact on literary criticism in the 1960s and 1970s of (structuralism) and (post-structuralism,) which presented a serious challenge both to conventional historically based criticism and to the Anglo-American New Critical tradition. Theoretical issues, apparently dormant in the English-speaking world at least for several decades, were revitalised and new forms of critical approach in which theory and practice were intermingled, such as deconstruction, reception theory, reader-response criticism, feminism, psychoanalytic criticism, various types of Marxist and Marxist-influenced criticism, emerged. One still hears talk of a 'crisis' in literary studies having been created as a consequence of this, though such a crisis is taking a long time to come to a head. However, one clear effect of this was to break down any critical consensus and replace it with warring factions. More recently perhaps, these factions have learned to tolerate each other. But though what have been called the 'theory wars'[1] may be over, theory itself remains central to modern critical practice.

Clearly this situation presents those who are beginning to study literature with serious difficulties since current criticism demands some knowledge of recent theoretical developments. Various literary theory collections and overviews of theory have therefore been published in an attempt to make theoretical issues more accessible to a general literary audience. This book continues in that tradition. Unlike most other theory collections, however, it covers more than just theory since structuralism. It also includes a good deal of material written before 1960 though the greatest part of the book covers later theory. In my view some knowledge of earlier theory is necessary in order to understand later developments. Also most other collections tend to reprint complete essays or articles. This collection adopts a different approach in that it edits the texts selected. This has two major advantages, I believe. Complete essays are difficult for those beginning the study of literary theory to assimilate. In my edited versions I have tried to preserve the structure of the argument of each text, albeit in an abbreviated form, and to present it as sharply and coherently as possible. My aim has been to reprint sufficient material to allow the reader to grasp a particular argument in order either to be persuaded by it or to think of grounds for questioning it. The other major advantage is that this allows me to include a much wider range of material – 54 selections – within one volume of not inordinate length. Of course, I hope that users of this volume will find certain of the selections of sufficient interest that they will take the trouble to read the complete essay, article, chapter or book from which the selections are drawn.

Theory is an area of constant debate and confrontation and, to have an adequate understanding of it, it is necessary to have knowledge not merely of the arguments central to one or two particular standpoints but also of alternative positions explicitly or implicitly in conflict with them. It is also not enough to represent the major theories with only one example for there is conflict and debate not only between different theories but within them. Thus as well as representing a considerable range of theoretical positions, this book tries to show different aspects of or emphases within particular theories. Furthermore, I have tried to strike a balance between authors or particular texts that must be included in any representative collection of twentieth-century literary theory, and work which will be less familiar and not easily available to a general literary audience but which is arguably equally important and interesting. Having some knowledge of the wider context of twentieth-century theory is at the very least a considerable help and in some cases a necessity in understanding current theory. I have tried not only to provide representative examples of particular theoretical perspectives but also to choose texts which highlight the debate between perspectives and which show some of the differences within them.

It may be objected that a book such as this, which is primarily designed to introduce the range of twentieth-century theory to students of literature in higher education and to a non-specialist literary readership, could do more harm than good. Why does one need to burden the mind of students or readers of literature in general with theoretical questions? Can it not be objected that theory merely confuses such readers and has little positive effect on reading? Indeed it has been argued that only mature critics should concern themselves with the theoretical implications of their activity and that readers at a less advanced stage should not be exposed to theory.[2] These objections need to be answered.

The first point to make is that theory or critical principles that have some theoretical base underlie *any* form of reading, even the most naïve, of a literary text. To be unconscious of or uninterested in theory does not mean that it is not present. With virtually all forms of non-literary discourse certain norms and constraints must govern how they are read if such discourses are to serve the interests and purposes that direct our reading. Thus though theoretical questions may be raised in relation to such discourses, theory must take second place to these interests and purposes. This is the case whether one is reading a cooking recipe, a newspaper article, a work of history or philosophy, or a scientific paper. But with literary discourse, there are no practical or logical necessities external to the discourse that determine how it must be read. Theory is therefore always implied in reading literary discourse, since whatever norms and constraints that govern how literary texts are read cannot be seen as an integral part of the discourse itself but are chosen, consciously or unconsciously, from among various possibilities by the reader.

In discussions of different forms of discourse, terms such as 'historical' or 'philosophical' or 'scientific' suggest a range of attributes or characteristics associated with the particular discourse, but the term 'literary' – despite numerous efforts at definition which claim that all texts that have been categorised as 'literary' have at least one common attribute – is empty. It does not refer to qualities that texts have in common but to what appears to be a human need to have a body of texts that exists beyond the pragmatic boundaries within which our reading of other forms of discourse must take place. There is no practical necessity or intrinsic constraint that can stop one using a text that has been categorised as 'literary' for any purpose whatsoever. The category (literature'), therefore, in the narrower, evaluative sense refers to certain of the texts that have been placed in the category of the non-pragmatic which readers and critics over several generations have judged to be particularly effective in serving their various interests.

It follows from what I have said that there could be as many theories of literature as there are readers. Obviously this is not the case. Indeed literary critical discourse exhibits a high degree of order and coherence, and it is perhaps only recently that this has been partially undermined, and many would lay the blame for this on the current literary critical context which has appeared to encourage a proliferation of theories. But even in the present situation there is no sign of complete relativism. Those who have

even tho those on the left are always accused of this

uttered warnings of 'chaos' or 'anarchy' are employing rhetoric designed either to publicise their dislike of changes that have taken place within the literary community or to destabilise literary study for certain political purposes. A more interesting consideration is why there is so much order within literary study when literary discourse does not demand that there be any. ʲⁿ/

Since there are no pragmatic considerations that demand that certain norms and constraints must govern our reading of literary texts, the norms and constraints that do in fact govern our reading of them must have been chosen by us, even if we may not be aware of having made a choice. The reason, then, that literary criticism is comparatively ordered when there would appear to be no intrinsic need for it to be so is that most readers make the same kind of choice from the various options which they perceive to be available. Why so many different theoretical approaches to literature should have emerged in the twentieth century and why readers choose to support one rather than another are interesting questions. This is not the place to try to answer these questions in detail but clearly literary theory cannot be seen in isolation from the political and ideological conflicts which have been such a prominent feature of the twentieth century. Choices about reading, especially in relation to texts which exist beyond the pragmatic limits which govern our reading of other forms of discourse, cannot be ideologically neutral, and the reader may care to bear that in mind in reading the work of the various theorists included in this book.

Before twentieth-century developments in literary criticism the great majority of readers chose to relate literary texts to their historical context and to the intentions of their authors, and this approach still commands great support. But many twentieth-century readers, in contrast, have chosen to pay little or no attention to historical context or authorial intention and allow modern modes of thought, such as psychoanalytic or feminist theory, to govern how they read literary texts. Such readers would argue that the most important consideration in liter-ary study is the text's relation to the concerns of a modern audience. There is also no limit to the number of interests that readers can choose to bring to bear on their reading of literary texts, the most common being aesthetic, historical, linguistic, sociological, biographical, philosophical, psychological, political or combinations of these.

It is important to stress, however, that one cannot do anything other than make a choice. Though there are no intrinsic norms and constraints that determine how we must read literary texts, as soon as we begin to read the text norms and constraints of some sort will come into operation since the very activity of reading cannot take place without them. It is inevitable that readers will make the same kind of choices so that one finds readers and critics forming into groups or, as Stanley Fish calls them, 'interpretive communities'. It is conceivable that an individual may develop an entirely idiosyncratic way of reading literary texts that does not conform to any community of readers that exists or has existed. Markers of certain student essays might find this idea persuasive. But, of course, it is inevitable that the vast majority of readers will accept the norms and constraints that govern the theories which are dominant in the culture at any particular time.

One of the most important arguments in favour of literary theory, therefore, is that since the norms and constraints are not intrinsic but are chosen for particular reasons, there is no justification for ignoring their existence as there might be in reading non-literary forms of discourse, even if this may result, as René Wellek has warned,[3] in the minds of young students being unsettled. It would be bad faith to conceal the fact, even from young students, that no norms or constraints are integral to literary discourse and therefore privileged. Certain norms will, of course, be dominant and there may be justification for stressing their advantages and the dangers of discarding them but there can be no justification for claiming that these norms are intrinsic to the very existence of literary discourse.

An obvious implication of this is that once one knows that the norms and constraints that govern one's reading of literary texts have been chosen, then one may choose to change them. Though some may see such a possibility as a recipe for total relativism, the fact that any change cannot lead to norms being discarded altogether but only to the adoption of a different set of norms suggests that such fears are groundless. Indeed, it may have a positive benefit in that certain readers who have been operating with norms which are alien to their temperament or ideology or world-view may be able to choose a set of norms that they find much more congenial. This book thus has a double purpose: to make readers more aware of the norms and constraints which govern their existing critical approach and to be able to defend it against alternative approaches, and by comparing their present set of norms and interpretative strategies against alternatives to be in a position to adopt a different approach should they find one that is more persuasive.

It would be inaccurate, however, to assert that the current situation of a 'proliferation of theories' has had no fundamental impact on literary criticism. One of the drawbacks of Stanley Fish's notion of 'interpretive communities' is that it implies that once readers of literary texts have chosen, consciously or not, their community there is little point in arguing with those who belong to different(communities)since it is not as if one community is right and all the others wrong. The very word 'community' suggests that one is part of a self-supporting group and that one need bother little with other communities. Yet one cannot but be struck by the constant debate and controversy that takes place in literary studies. Readers of literary texts do not seem content to adopt 'a live and let live' philosophy. This suggests that the 'communities' analogy needs to be modified.

The reason that there is so much controversy and debate in literary studies, I would argue, is that critics and readers feel they belong to a single community, even though they may have made quite different choices as to how they read literary texts. The very fact that they have had to make such a choice links them together with other readers and interpreters of texts. But since they could have chosen differently this will inevitably create the need to justify the choice they have made and encourage the desire to persuade others both that this choice is the right one and that other choices are mistaken. Literary criticism is in consequence an area of continual debate. Even though it is impossible for this debate ever to be resolved finally, the attempt to justify the position one has chosen and to defend it with rational argument against alternative positions is necessary if literary study is to remain vital. Controversy and debate need not be seen, therefore, as signs of crisis or destabilisation but as signs of health and vigour. Ultimately literary criticism is about politics and power, and a sign of crisis is more likely to be a situation in which debate and rational argument are stifled than one in which they are conducted vigorously.

Perhaps the analogy, therefore, that best describes the current situation of literary criticism is not that it is made up of a number of separate 'communities' but, rather, that it is like a parliament. Before the recent explosion in literary theory, that parliament in the English-speaking world resembled one in which two parties dominated and smaller parties were confined to an insignificant role. There was thus relative stability and order with perhaps one party dominating for a period and then the other, but both parties remained at all times sufficiently large not to feel threatened. Debate thus tended to follow predictable lines and there was, except among specialists, relatively little general interest in theoretical questions. These two parties were historical criticism which emphasised such matters as the text in relation to its time, what the author intended, generic considerations, and the New Critical tradition with its anti-intentionalist bias and its emphasis on the text as a self-contained structure.

What has happened to the 'parliament' more recently is that this two-party dominance has been threatened because numerous small parties have entered the parliament, depriving any single party of an overall majority. Most of these parties believe that they have a chance of achieving power and endeavour to persuade those who belong to other parties to join them. There is the likelihood of coalitions and realignments. Debate has become more urgent and acrimonious and theoretical questions have again become central. Literary criticism is thus revealed as a struggle for power among parties which are in a position to use only rational argument and rhetoric as a means of persuading sufficient numbers to support them in order to achieve a majority. The debate also has significance for society in general in that it raises questions that have implications beyond the purely literary sphere. In this anthology of theory, readers can follow the debate with a view to deciding eventually where to cast their votes or they may decide that another new party is needed. But in any case anyone who retains an interest in literature has no option but to vote. *well how damn democratic!*

NOTES

1. See Antony Easthope, *Literary Into Cultural Studies* (London, 1991), p. 11.
2. See René Wellek, 'Respect for Tradition', *The Times Literary Supplement*, 10 December 1982, p. 1356.
3. Ibid.

I RUSSIAN FORMALISM AND PRAGUE STRUCTURALISM

The origins of Russian Formalism date back before the Russian Revolution to the activities of the Moscow Linguistic Circle and the St Petersburg-based group, Opojaz, both of which concerned themselves with the study of poetic language. The major figures were Victor Shklovsky, Roman Jakobson, Boris Eikhenbaum, Osip Brik and Yury Tynyanov. The Russian Formalists rejected the unsystematic and eclectic critical approaches which had previously dominated literary study and endeavoured to create a 'literary science'. As Jakobson put it: 'The subject of literary science is not literature, but literariness, i.e. that which makes a given work a literary work'. The Formalists were uninterested, therefore, in the representational or expressive aspects of literary texts; they focused on those elements of texts which they considered to be uniquely literary in character. Initially they emphasised the differences between literary language and non-literary or practical language. The best known Formalist concept is that of 'defamiliarisation' (*ostranenie*), a concept particularly associated with Shklovsky and discussed in his 'Art as Device', first published in 1917, where he argues that art renews human perception through creating devices which undercut and undermine habitual and automatised forms of perception.

In later Formalism the emphasis shifted from the relation between literary and non-literary language to the linguistic and formal aspects of literary texts themselves. Jakobson and Tynyanov argued that literary devices themselves also became familiar. They shifted the focus to the means by which certain devices become dominant in literary texts and take on a defamiliarising role in relation to other devices or aspects of the text which are perceived in familiar or automatic terms. Jakobson's essay 'The Dominant' represents this aspect of Formalism.

P. N. Medvedev's and Mikhail Bakhtin's *The Formal Method in Literary Scholarship*, excerpts from which are reprinted here, was first published under Medvedev's name in 1928, but was probably written by Bakhtin. It is on the surface a critique of Formalism from a Marxist viewpoint, but it is possible that Marxism was emphasised for reasons of political necessity as Bakhtin seems not to have been a committed Marxist in a

1

doctrinal sense. Fundamental to Bakhtin's thought is his view that language is 'dialogic', that is, any use of language assumes the existence of a listener or addressee. Language must be seen as a social event. The focus for investigation should thus be on language in a social and communicative context. Bakhtin and Medvedev criticise Formalism for refusing to recognise that literary language cannot be discussed in isolation from the sociological context of language. They are, however, clearly unsympathetic to anti-Formalist tendencies in Marxist criticism.

Prague Structuralism was essentially in continuity with Russian Formalism. Jakobson had moved to Czechoslovakia as early as 1920. Indeed, 'The Dominant' was given as a lecture in Czechoslovakia in 1935. Jan Mukařovský, the leading Czech literary theorist, was heavily influenced in his earlier work by Russian Formalism, as, for example, when he described literariness as 'the maximum foregrounding of the utterance', an idea clearly derived from the Formalist concept of the dominant. In Mukařovský's later writings, however, he moves from a strictly Formalist position to one in which the perceiver or reader plays an important role, and he argues that the perceiver of a work of art must be seen in social terms, as a product of society and its ideologies, and not as an isolated individual. In *Aesthetic Function, Norm and Value as Social Facts*, written in 1938, he anticipates semiotic approaches to the study of literature (see 'Structuralism and Semiotics', section V, pp. 112–141).

FURTHER READING

Mikhail Bakhtin, *Problems in Dostoevsky's Poetics*, trans. R.W. Rotsel (Ann Arbor, Mich., 1973).

Tony Bennett, *Formalism and Marxism* (London, 1979).

Paul de Man, 'Dialogue and Dialogism', *Poetics Today*, 4 (1983), 99–107 (Critique of Bakhtin).

Victor Ehrlich, *Russian Formalism: History–Doctrine* (The Hague, 1980).

Paul L. Garvin (ed.), *A Prague School Reader on Esthetics, Literary Structure, and Style* (Washington, DC, 1964).

L. M. O'Toole, Ann Shukman (eds), *Russian Poetics in Translation* (Colchester), Vols 4, 5.

Peter Steiner (ed.), *The Prague School: Selected Writings 1929–1946* (Austin, Texas, 1982).

René Wellek, 'The Literary Theory and Aesthetics of the Prague School', in *Discriminations: Further Concepts of Criticism* (New Haven, Conn., 1970).

1 VICTOR SHKLOVSKY: 'ART AS TECHNIQUE'

'Art is thinking in images.' This maxim, which even high-school students parrot, is nevertheless the starting point for the erudite philologist who is beginning to put together some kind of systematic literary theory. The idea, originated in part by Potebnya, has spread. 'Without imagery there is no art, and in particular no poetry', Potebnya writes. And elsewhere, 'Poetry, as well as prose, is first and foremost a special way of thinking and knowing'. [1]...

Potebnya's conclusion, which can be formulated 'poetry equals imagery', gave rise to the whole theory that 'Imagery equals symbolism', that the image may serve as the invariable predicate of various subjects. ... The conclusion stems partly from the fact that Potebnya did not distinguish between the language of poetry and the language of prose. Consequently, he ignored the fact that there are two aspects of imagery: imagery as a practical means of thinking, as a means of placing objects within categories; and imagery as poetic, as a means of reinforcing an impression. I shall clarify with an example. I want to attract the attention of a young child who is eating bread and butter and getting the butter on her fingers. I call, 'Hey, butterfingers!' This is a figure of speech, a clearly prosaic trope. Now a different example. The child is playing with my glasses and drops them. I call, 'Hey, butterfingers!' This figure of speech is a poetic trope. (In the first example, 'butterfingers' is metonymic; in the second, metaphoric – but this is not what I want to stress.)

Poetic imagery is a means of creating the strongest possible impression. As a method it is, depending upon its purpose, neither more nor less effective than other poetic techniques; it is neither more nor less effective than ordinary or negative parallelism, comparison, repetition, balanced structure, hyperbole, the commonly accepted rhetorical figures, and all those methods which emphasize the emotional effect of an expression (including words or even articulated sounds). ... Poetic imagery is but one of the devices of poetic language.

If we start to examine the general laws of perception, we see that as perception becomes habitual, it becomes automatic. Thus, for example, all of our habits retreat into the area of the un-

Reprinted from *Russian Formalist Criticism: Four Essays*, trans. and ed. Lee T. Lemon and Marion J. Reis (Lincoln, Nebraska, 1965), pp. 5–22.

consciously automatic; if one remembers the sensations of holding a pen or of speaking in a foreign language for the first time and compares that with his feeling at performing the action for the ten thousandth time, he will agree with us. ...
... Habitualization devours works, clothes, furniture, [one's wife,] and the fear of war. ... And art exists that one may recover the sensation of life; it exists to make one feel things, to make the stone *stony*. The purpose of art is to impart the sensation of things as they are perceived and not as they are known. The technique of art is to make objects 'unfamiliar', to make forms difficult, to increase the difficulty and length of perception because the process of perception is an aesthetic end in itself and must be prolonged. *Art is a way of experiencing the artfulness of an object; the object is not important.* ...
After we see an object several times, we begin to recognize it. The object is in front of us and we know about it, but we do not see it – hence we cannot say anything significant about it. Art removes objects from the automatism of perception in several ways. Here I want to illustrate a way used repeatedly by Leo Tolstoy, that writer who ... seems to present things as if he himself saw them, saw them in their entirety, and did not alter them.
Tolstoy makes the familiar seem strange by not naming the familiar object. He describes an object as if he were seeing it for the first time, an event as if it were happening for the first time. In describing something he avoids the accepted names of its parts and instead names corresponding parts of other objects. For example, in 'Shame' Tolstoy 'defamiliarizes' the idea of flogging in this way: 'to strip people who have broken the law, to hurl them to the floor, and to rap on their bottoms with switches', and, after a few lines, 'to lash about on the naked buttocks'. Then he remarks:

Just why precisely this stupid, savage means of causing pain and not any other – why not prick the shoulders or any part of the body with needles, squeeze the hands or the feet in a vise, or anything like that?

I apologize for this harsh example, but it is typical of Tolstoy's way of pricking the conscience. The familiar act of flogging is made unfamiliar both by the description and by the proposal to change its form without changing its nature. Tolstoy uses this technique of 'defamiliarization' constantly. ...
Now, having explained the nature of this technique, let us try to determine the approximate limits of its application. I personally feel that defamiliarization is found almost everywhere form is found. In other words, the difference between Potebnya's point of view and ours is this: An image is not a permanent referent for

those mutable complexities of life which are revealed through it; its purpose is not to make us perceive meaning, but to create a special perception of the object – *it creates a 'vision' of the object instead of serving as a means for knowing it.* ...

Quite often in literature the sexual act itself is defamiliarized; for example the *Decameron* refers to 'scraping out a barrel', 'catching nightingales', 'gay wool-beating work' (the last is not developed in the plot). Defamiliarization is often used in describing the sexual organs.

A whole series of plots is based on such a lack of recognition; for example, in Afanasyev's *Intimate Tales* the entire story of 'The Shy Mistress' is based on the fact that an object is not called by its proper name – or, in other words, on a game of nonrecognition. So too in Onchukov's 'Spotted Petticoats', tale no. 525, and also in 'The Bear and the Hare' from *Intimate Tales*, in which the bear and the hare make a 'wound'. *um... no,*

Such constructions as 'the pestle and the mortar' or 'Old Nick and the infernal regions' (*Decameron*), are also examples of the techniques of defamiliarization in psychological parallelism. Here, then, I repeat that the perception of disharmony in a harmonious context is important in parallelism. The purpose of parallelism, like the general purpose of imagery, is to transfer the usual perception of an object into the sphere of a new perception – that is, to make a unique semantic modification.

In studying poetic speech in its phonetic and lexical structure as well as in its characteristic distribution of words and in the characteristic thought structures compounded from the words, we find everywhere the artistic trademark – that is, we find material obviously created to remove the automatism of perception; the author's purpose is to create the vision which results from that deautomatised perception. A work is created 'artistically' so that its perception is impeded and the greatest possible effect is produced through the slowness of the perception. As a result of this lingering, the object is perceived not in its extension in space, but, so to speak, in its continuity. Thus 'poetic language' gives satisfaction.

NOTE

[Reorganised and renumbered from the original]
1. Alexander Potebnya ([ed.] nineteenth-century Russian philologist and theorist), *Iz zapisok po teorii slovesnosti* [*Notes on the Theory of Language*] (Kharkov, 1905), pp. 83, 97.

2   ROMAN JAKOBSON: 'THE DOMINANT'

The first three stages of Formalist research have been briefly characterized as follows: (1) analysis of the sound aspects of a literary work; (2) problems of meaning within the framework of poetics; (3) integration of sound and meaning into an inseparable whole. During this latter stage, the concept of the *dominant* was particularly fruitful; it was one of the most crucial, elaborated, and productive concepts in Russian Formalist theory. The dominant may be defined as the focusing component of a work of art: it rules, determines, and transforms the remaining components. It is the dominant which guarantees the integrity of the structure.

The dominant specifies the work. The specific trait of bound language is obviously its prosodic pattern, its verse form. It might seem that this is simply a tautology: verse is verse. However, we must constantly bear in mind that the element which specifies a given variety of language dominates the entire structure and thus acts as its mandatory and inalienable constituent dominating all the remaining elements and exerting direct influence upon them. However, verse in turn is not a simple concept and not an indivisible unit. Verse itself is a system of values; as with any value system, it possesses its own hierarchy of superior and inferior values and one leading value, the dominant, without which (within the framework of a given literary period and a given artistic trend) verse cannot be conceived and evaluated as verse. ...

We may seek a dominant not only in the poetic work of an individual artist and not only in the poetic canon, the set of norms of a given poetic school, but also in the art of a given epoch, viewed as a particular whole. For example, it is evident that in Renaissance art such a dominant, such an acme of the aesthetic criteria of the time, was represented by the visual arts. Other arts oriented themselves toward the visual arts and were valued according to the degree of their closeness to the latter. On the other hand, in Romantic art the supreme value was assigned to music. Thus, for example, Romantic poetry oriented itself toward music: its verse is musically focused; its verse intonation imitates

Reprinted from *Readings in Russian Poetics: Formalist and Structuralist Views*, ed. Ladislav Matejka and Krystyna Pomorska (Ann Arbor, Mich., 1978), pp. 82–7.

musical melody. This focusing on a dominant which is in fact external to the poetic work substantially changes the poem's structure with regard to sound texture, syntactic structure, and imagery; it alters the poem's metrical and strophical criteria and its composition. In Realist aesthetics the dominant was verbal art, and the hierarchy of poetic values was modified accordingly.

Moreover, the definition of an artistic work as compared to other sets of cultural values substantially changes, as soon as the concept of the dominant becomes our point of departure. For example, the relationship between a poetic work and other verbal messages acquires a more exact determination. Equating a poetic work with an aesthetic, or more precisely with a poetic, function, as far as we deal with verbal material, is characteristic of those epochs which proclaim self-sufficient, pure art, *l'art pour l'art.* In the early steps of the Formalist school, it was still possible to observe distinct traces of such an equation. However, this equation is unquestionably erroneous: a poetic work is not confined to aesthetic function alone, but has in addition many other functions. Actually, the intentions of a poetic work are often closely related to philosophy, social didactics, etc. Just as a poetic work is not exhausted by its aesthetic function, similarly aesthetic function is not limited to the poetic work; an orator's address, everyday conversation, newspaper articles, advertisements, a scientific treatise – all may employ aesthetic considerations, give expression to aesthetic function, and often use words in and for themselves, not merely as a referential device.

In direct opposition to the straight monistic point of view is the mechanistic standpoint, which recognizes the multiplicity of functions of a poetic work and judges that work, either knowingly or unintentionally, as a mechanical agglomeration of functions. Because a poetic work also has a referential function, it is sometimes considered by adherents of the latter point of view as a straightforward document of cultural history, social relations, or biography. In contrast to one-sided monism and one-sided pluralism, there exists a point of view which combines an awareness of the multiple functions of a poetic work with a comprehension of its integrity, that is to say, that function which unites and determines the poetic work. From this point of view, a poetic work cannot be defined as a work fulfilling neither an exclusively aesthetic function nor an aesthetic function along with other functions; rather, a poetic work is defined as a verbal message whose aesthetic function is its dominant. Of course, the marks disclosing the implementation of the aesthetic function are not unchangeable or always uniform. Each concrete poetic canon, every set of temporal poetic norms, however, comprises indispensable, distinctive elements without which the work cannot be identified as poetic.

The definition of the aesthetic function as the dominant of a poetic work permits us to determine the hierarchy of diverse linguistic functions within the poetic work. In the referential function, the sign has a minimal internal connection with the designated object, and therefore the sign in itself carries only a minimal importance; on the other hand, the expressive function demands a more direct, intimate relationship between the sign and the object, and therefore a greater attention to the internal structure of the sign. In comparison with referential language, emotive language, which primarily fulfils an expressive function, is as a rule closer to poetic language (which is directed precisely toward the sign as such). Poetic language and emotional language often overlap each other, and therefore these two varieties of language are often quite erroneously identified. If the aesthetic function is the dominant in a verbal message, then this message may certainly use many devices of expressive language; but these components are then subject to the decisive function of the work, i.e., they are transformed by its dominant.

Inquiry into the dominant had important consequences for Formalist views of literary evolution. In the evolution of poetic form it is not so much a question of the disappearance of certain elements and the emergence of others as it is the question of shifts in the mutual relationship among the diverse components of the system, in other words, a question of the shifting dominant. Within a given complex of poetic norms in general, or especially within the set of poetic norms valid for a given poetic genre, elements which were originally secondary become essential and primary. On the other hand, the elements which were originally the dominant ones become subsidiary and optional. In the earlier works of Shklovsky, a poetic work was defined as a mere sum of its artistic devices, while poetic evolution appeared nothing more than a substitution of certain devices. With the further development of Formalism, there arose the accurate conception of a poetic work as a structured system, a regularly ordered hierarchical set of artistic devices. Poetic evolution is a shift in this hierarchy. This hierarchy of artistic devices changes within the framework of a given poetic genre; the change, moreover, affects the hierarchy of poetic genres, and, simultaneously, the distribution of artistic devices among the individual genres. Genres which were originally secondary paths, subsidiary variants, now come to the fore, whereas the canonical genres are pushed toward the rear. ...

However, the problems of evolution are not limited to literary history. Questions concerning changes in the mutual relationship between the individual arts also arise, and there the scrutiny of transitional regions is particularly fruitful; for example an analysis of a transitional region between painting and poetry, such as illustration, or an analysis of a border region between music and poetry, such as the *romance*.

Finally, the problem of changes in the mutual relationship between the arts and other closely related cultural domains arises, especially with respect to the mutual relationship between literature and other kinds of verbal messages. Here the instability of boundaries, the change in the content and extent of the individual domains, is particularly illuminating. Of special interest for investigators are the transitional genres. In certain periods such genres are evaluated as extraliterary and extrapoetical, while in other periods they may fulfil an important literary function because they comprise those elements which are about to be emphasized by belles lettres, whereas the canonical literary forms are deprived of these elements. Such transitional genres are, for example, the various forms of *littérature intime* – letters, diaries, notebooks, travelogues, etc. – which in certain periods (for example, in the Russian literature of the first half of the nineteenth century) serve an important function within the total complex of literary values.

In other words, continual shifts in the system of artistic values imply continual shifts in the evaluation of different phenomena of art. That which, from the point of view of the old system, was slighted or judged to be imperfect, dilettantish, aberrant, or simply wrong or that which was considered heretical, decadent, and worthless may appear and, from the perspective of a new system, be adopted as a positive value. ...

The shifting, the transformation, of the relationship between individual artistic components became the central issue in Formalist investigations. This aspect of Formalist analysis in the field of poetic language had a pioneering significance for linguistic research in general, since it provided important impulses toward overcoming and bridging the gap between the diachronic historical method and the synchronic method of chronological cross section. It was the Formalist research which clearly demonstrated that shifting and change are not only historical statements (first there was A, and then A_1 arose in place of A) but that shift is also a directly experienced synchronic phenomenon, a relevant artistic value. The reader of a poem or the viewer of a painting has a vivid awareness of two orders; the traditional canon and the artistic novelty as a deviation from that canon. It is precisely against the background of that tradition that innovation is conceived. The Formalist studies brought to light that this simultaneous preservation of tradition and breaking away from tradition form the essence of every new work of art.

3   P. N. MEDVEDEV/M. M. BAKHTIN: 'THE OBJECT, TASKS, AND METHODS OF LITERARY HISTORY'

The literary work is an immediate part of the literary environment, the aggregate of all the socially active literary works of a given epoch and social group. From a strictly historical point of view the individual literary work is a dependent and therefore actually inseparable element of the literary environment. It occupies a definite place in this environment and is directly determined by its influences. It would be absurd to think that a work which occupies a place in the literary environment could avoid its direct influences or be an exception to its unity and regularity.

But the literary environment itself in its turn is only a dependent and therefore actually inseparable element of the general ideological environment of a given epoch and a given sociological unity. Both in its totality and in each of its elements literature occupies a definite place in the ideological environment, is oriented in it, and defined by its direct influence. In its turn the ideological environment in its totality and in each of its elements is likewise a dependent element of the socioeconomic environment, is determined by it, and is permeated from top to bottom with socioeconomic laws of development.

We thus have a complex system of interconnections and mutual influences. Each element of the system is defined within several unique but interrelated unities.

The work cannot be understood outside the unity of literature. But this whole unity and the individual works which are its elements cannot be understood outside the unity of ideological life. And this last unity, whether it is taken as a whole or

Reprinted from *The Formal Method in Literary Scholarship: A Critical Introduction to Sociological Poetics*, trans. Albert J. Wehrle (Baltimore, 1978), pp. 26–37.

as separate elements, cannot be studied outside the unified socioeconomic laws of development.

Thus, in order to reveal and define the literary physiognomy of a given work, one must at the same time reveal its general ideological physiognomy; one does not exist without the other. And, in revealing the latter, we cannot help revealing its socioeconomic nature as well.

The genuine concrete historical study of the artistic work is only possible when all these conditions are observed. Not one of the links of this complete chain in the conception of the ideological phenomenon can be omitted, and there can be no stopping at one link without going on to the next. It is completely inadmissible to study the literary work directly and exclusively as an element of the ideological environment, as if it were the only example of literature instead of an immediate element of the literary world in all its variety. Without understanding the place of the work in literature and its direct dependence on literature, it is impossible to understand its place in the ideological environment.

It is still more inadmissible to omit two links and attempt to understand the work immediately in the socioeconomic environment, as if it were the only example of ideological creation, instead of being primarily oriented in the socioeconomic environment as an inseparable element of the whole of literature and the whole ideological purview.

The extremely complex aims and methods of literary history are defined by all of the above.

Literary history is concerned with the concrete life of the literary work in the unity of the generating literary environment, the literary environment in the generating ideological environment, and the latter, finally, in the generating socioeconomic environment which permeates it. The work of the literary historian should therefore proceed in unbroken interaction with the history of other ideologies and with socioeconomic history. ...

When literature is studied in living interaction with other domains and in the concrete unity of socioeconomic life, it does not lose its individuality. In fact, its individuality can only be completely discovered and defined in this process of interaction.

The literary historian should not forget for a minute that the literary work is doubly connected to the ideological environment through the reflection of the latter in its content and through direct participation in it as one of its individual parts.

It cannot, and, of course, should not disturb the Marxist literary historian that the literary work is primarily and most directly determined by literature itself. Marxism fully grants the determining influence of other ideologies on literature. What is more, it assumes the return influence of ideologies on the base itself. Consequently, there is all the more reason why it can and should grant the effect of literature on literature.

But this effect of literature on literature is still a sociological effect. Literature, like every other ideology, is social through and through. If the individual work of art does not reflect the base, it does not do so at its own risk, in isolation and detachment from all the rest of literature. And the base does not determine the literary work by 'calling it off to one side', as it were, 'in secret' from the rest of literature. Instead, it acts on all of literature and on the whole ideological environment. It acts on the individual work precisely as a literary work, i.e., as an element of the whole ideological environment which is inseparably joined to the total situation provided by literature. ...

In real fact the socioeconomic laws of development work on all the elements of social and ideological life from both within and without. Science need not cease being science to become a social phenomenon. To do so would be to become bad science. But, incidentally, even when science is bad, it still does not cease being a social phenomenon.

But the literary historian must be careful not to turn the literary environment into an absolutely closed-off, self-sufficient work. The notion of closed and independent cultural systems is completely inadmissible. As we have seen, the individuality of a system (more precisely, an environment) is based exclusively on the interaction of the system as a whole and in each of its elements with all the other systems in the unity of social life. ...

Any external factor which acts on literature evokes a purely literary effect, and this effect becomes a determining intrinsic factor for the subsequent literary development. And this internal factor itself becomes an external factor for other ideological domains, which will bring their own internal languages to bear on it; this reaction, in turn, will become an extrinsic factor for literature.

But, of course, this whole dialectical opposition of factors takes place within the bounds of the unified sociological laws of development. Nothing in ideological creation goes beyond these laws; they are active in every nook and cranny of the ideological construction. Everything in this process of constant dialectical interaction preserves its individuality. Art does not stop being art, science is always science. And, at the same time, the sociological laws of development do not lose their unity and comprehensive determining force.

The truly scholarly study of literary history can only be built on the basis of this dialectical conception of the individuality and interaction of the various ideological phenomena. ...

However, literary scholarship has other aims besides those of literary history. What is more, literary history itself presupposes scholarship which would reveal the individuality of poetic structures, that is, the history of literature presupposes sociological poetics.

What is the literary work? What is its structure? What are the elements of this structure and what are their artistic functions? What is genre, style, plot, theme, motif, hero, meter, rhythm, melody, etc? All these questions and, in particular, the question of the reflection of the ideological horizon in the content of the work and of the functions of this reflection in the whole structure are within the sphere of sociological poetics. ...

Literary history essentially presupposes the answers sociological poetics provides to the problems which have been set. It should begin from definite knowledge of the essence of the ideological structures whose concrete history it traces.

But, at the same time, sociological poetics itself, lest it become dogmatic, must be oriented towards literary history. There should be constant interaction between these two fields. Poetics provides literary history with direction in the specification of the research material and the basic definitions of its forms and types. Literary history amends the definitions of poetics, making them more flexible, dynamic, and adequate to the diversity of the historical material. ...

Sociological poetics must be historically oriented lest it turn into the program of some literary school (the fate of most poetics) or, at best, turn into the program of all literature contemporaneous with it. The dialectical method provides it with an indispensable instrument for the formulation of dynamic definitions, i.e., definitions adequate to the generating system of the development of a given genre, form, etc. Only dialectics can avoid both normativism and dogmatism in definitions and their positivistic atomization into a multiplicity of disconnected facts only conditionally connected.

Therefore, the role of historical poetics is to prepare the historical perspective for the generalizing and synthesizing definitions of sociological poetics. ...

Until, we have a sociological poetics, albeit of a basic, exceedingly simple variety, the productive elaboration of literary history on the monistic basis of the Marxist sociological methods is impossible. ...

It can be said that poetics in the Soviet Union at present is monopolized by the so-called 'formal' or 'morphological' method. In their short history, the formalists have managed to cover a wide range of problems in theoretical poetics. There is hardly a single problem in this area that they have not touched upon somehow in their work. Marxism cannot leave the work of the formalists without exhaustive critical analysis.

Marxism can even less afford to ignore the formal method because the formalists have emerged precisely as specifiers, perhaps the first in Russian literary scholarship. They have succeeded in giving great sharpness and principle to problems of literary specification, which makes them stand out sharply and to advantage against the background of flabby eclecticism and unprincipled academic scholarship.

Specification, as we have seen, is an immediate task of Marxist ideological study and, in particular, of Marxist literary scholarship. However the specifying techniques of our formalism are diametrically opposed to those of Marxism. The formalists consider specification to be the isolation of a given ideological domain, the sealing off of this domain from all other forces and energies of ideological and social life. They see specificity, individuality, as a force that is sluggish and hostile to all other forces; that is, they do not think of individuality dialectically and therefore are not capable of combining it with the living interactions of concrete social and historical life.

The fact that the formalists consistently and totally defend the nonsocial nature of the artistic structure as such makes the meeting of Marxism and formalism particularly productive and important in terms of principle. ...

If the formalists are wrong, then their theory, which is developed so consistently and fully, turns out to be a magnificent *reductio ad absurdum* of principled nonsociological poetics. And this absurdity should first of all be revealed as it pertains to literature and poetry.

For if literature is a social phenomenon, then the formal method, which ignores and denies this, is first of all inadequate to literature itself and provides false interpretations and definitions of its specific characteristics and features.

For this reason Marxist criticism of the formal method cannot and must not be disengaged or disinterested.

4 JAN MUKAŘOVSKÝ: 'AESTHETIC FUNCTION, NORM, AND VALUE AS SOCIAL FACTS'

'Fictionality' in literature is ... something totally different from communicative fiction. All modifications of the material ties of linguistic phenomena which appear in communicative speech can also play a role in literature, and falsehood is one example. But here it acts as an element of structure and not of real-life values having practical importance. Baron Munchausen, if he had really lived, would be a swindler, and his speech would be nothing but lies. But the writer who invented Munchausen and his lies is not a liar but simply a writer, and the statements by Munchausen are, in his presentation, poetic acts.

Well then, given this state of affairs, does the artistic sign lack any direct and necessary contact with reality? Is art in relation to reality less than a shadow which at least tells of the presence of an object, even if the viewer can not see it? One can find, in the history of art, movements which would have answered affirmatively the question thus posed. ...

But these views still do not reveal the true essence of art. In order to explain their error, let us start from a concrete example. Imagine a reader of Dostoevsky's *Crime and Punishment.* The question of whether the story about the student, Raskolnikov, actually happened is, in addition to what we have already stated, outside the pale of the reader's interests. Nevertheless the reader feels the strong relationship of the novel to reality, and not only to that reality which is described in the novel – the events set in Russia in a certain year of the nineteenth century – but to the reality which the reader himself is familiar with, to situations which he has experienced, or, given the circumstances in which he lives, he might experience, to feelings and unrestrained emotions which might – or actually did – accompany the situations, to actions on the part of the reader which might have been caused by the situations. About the novel which has absorbed the reader, there have accumulated not one but many realities. The deeper the work has absorbed the reader, the greater is the area of current and vitally

Reprinted from *Aesthetic Function, Norm, and Value as Social Facts*, trans. M. E. Suino (Ann Arbor, Mich., 1979), pp. 74–90.

important realities of the reader to which the work attaches a material relationship. The change which the material relationship of the work – the sign – has undergone is thus simultaneously its weakening and strengthening. It is weakened in the sense that the work does not refer to the reality which it directly depicts, and strengthened in that the work of art as a sign acquires an indirect (figurative) tie with realities which are vitally important to the perceiver, and through them to the entire universe of the perceiver as a collection of values. Thus the work of art acquires the ability to refer to a reality which is totally different from the one which it depicts, and to systems of values other than the one from which it arose and on which it is founded. ...

We have analysed the sign (semantic) character of the work of art. It was shown that art is closely related to the area of informational signs, but in such a way that it is a dialectical negation of actual concrete reality known to the one who gives the sign, and about which the one to whom the sign is given can be informed. In art, however, the reality about which the work directly provides information (in thematic art)[1] is not the real source of the material connection, but only its intermediary. The real tie in this situation is a variable one, and points to realities known to the viewer. They are not and can in no way be expressed or even indicated in the work itself, because it forms a component of the viewer's intimate experience. This cluster of realities may be very important and the material tie of the art work with each of them is indirect, figurative. ... The indefinite nature of the material tie of the work of art is compensated by the fact that it is paralleled by the perceiving individual who reacts, not partially but with all aspects of his attitude toward the world and reality. The question now arises: is the interpretation of the art work, as sign, only an individual property which differs from one person to the next and which cannot be compared? The answer to this question was anticipated earlier in our statement that the work is a *sign*, and hence at bottom is a social fact. Also, the attitude which the individual takes toward reality is not the exclusive property even of the strongest personalities, for it is to be a considerable extent, and in weaker persons almost totally, determined by the social relationships in which the individual is involved. Thus the result arrived at by the analysis of the sign-like nature of the art work in no way leads to aesthetic subjectivism: we merely concluded that the material ties entered into by the work as sign set in motion the attitude of a viewer toward reality. But the viewer is a social creature, a member of a collective. This affirmation leads us a step closer to our goal; if the material connection introduced by the work affects the manner in which the individual and the collective address themselves to reality, it becomes evident that one important task for us is to treat the question of extra-aesthetic values contained in a work of art.

The work of art, even when it does not overtly or indirectly contain evaluations, is saturated with values. Everything in it, from the medium – even the most material medium (e.g., stone or bronze as used in sculpture) – the most thematic formations, contains values. Evaluation, as we have seen, lies at the very basis of the specific nature of the artistic sign. The material bond of the work involves, by virtue of its multiplicity, not only individual objects but reality as a whole, and thus affects the total attitude of the viewer to reality. It is he who is the source and regulator of evaluation. Since every element of the art work, be it 'content' or 'form', acquires that complex material bond in the context of the work, each element acquires extra-aesthetic values. ...

... The work of art appears, in the final analysis, as an actual collection of extra-aesthetic values and nothing else. The material components of the artistic artefact, and the manner in which they are used as artistic means, assume the role of mere conductors of energies introduced by extra-aesthetic values. If we ask ourselves at this point what has happened to aesthetic value, it appears that it has dissolved into individual extra-aesthetic values, and is really nothing but a general term for the dynamic totality of their mutual interrelationships. The distinction between 'form' and 'content' as used in the investigation of an art work is thus incorrect. The formalism of the Russian school of aesthetic and literary theory was correct in maintaining that all elements of a work are, without distinction, components of form. It must be added that all components are equally the bearers of meaning and extra-aesthetic values, and thus components of content. The analysis of 'form' must not be narrowed to a mere formal analysis. On the other hand, however, it must be made clear that only the *entire* construction of the work, and not just the part called 'content', enters into an active relation with the system of life values which govern human affairs.

The dominance of aesthetic value above all other values, a distinguishing feature of art, is thus something other than a mere external superiority. The influence of aesthetic value is not that it swallows up and represses all remaining values, but that it releases every one of them from direct contact with a corresponding life-value. It brings an entire assembly of values contained in the work as a dynamic whole into contact with a total system of those values which form the motive power of the life practice of the perceiving collective. What is the nature and goal of this contact? Above all it must be borne in mind, as we have already demonstrated, that this contact is rarely idyllically tranquil. As a rule the values contained in the art work are somewhat different, both in their mutual relationships and in the quality of individual values, from the complex system of values which is valid for the collective. There thus arises a mutual tension, and herein lies the particular meaning and effect of art. The constant necessity for practical application of values determines the free movement of the totality of values governing the life practice of the collective. The displacement of individual members of the hierarchy (re-valuation of values) is very difficult here, and is accompanied by strong shocks to the entire life practice of the given collective (slowing the development, uncertainty of values, disintegration of the system, even revolutionary eruptions). On the other hand, values in the art work – of which each by itself is free of actual dependency, but whose totality has potential validity – can, without harm, regroup and transform themselves. They can experimentally crystallize into a new configuration and dissolve an old one, can adapt to the development of the social situation and to new creative facts of reality, or at least seek the possibility of such adaptation.

Viewed in this light, the autonomy of the art work and the dominance of the aesthetic function and value within it appear not as destroyers of all contact between the work and reality – natural and social – but as constant stimuli of such contact. Art is a vital agent of great importance, even in periods of development and forms which stress self-orientation in art plus dominance of aesthetic function and value. Sometimes it is during just such stages which combine development and self-orientation that art may exert considerable influence on the relation of man to reality.

NOTE

1. [Ed.] Mukařovský is making a distinction between arts such as literature and representational painting and nonrepresentational arts such as music or architecture.

II THE NEW CRITICISM AND LEAVISIAN CRITICISM

Though the New Criticism had its origins in Britain in the criticism of T. S. Eliot, the theory of I. A. Richards and the practice of William Empson, its most powerful impact has been in America. John Crowe Ransom, who published a book entitled *The New Criticism* in 1941, was the leading American influence and he acknowledged a debt to Eliot and Richards. The other major American New Critics were Cleanth Brooks, Allen Tate, Robert Penn Warren and W. K. Wimsatt. Indirectly related to the New Criticism are such important figures as Kenneth Burke and R. P. Blackmur. The early New Critics were politically conservative and their attitudes to literature were shaped by their opposition to certain twentieth-century tendencies of thought, such as Marxism.

The fundamental aim of American New Criticism was to create a critical alternative to impressionism and historical scholarship, and thus there are some parallels with Russian Formalism. It advocated 'intrinsic' criticism – an impersonal concern for the literary work as an independent object – and opposed 'extrinsic' critical approaches, which concerned themselves with such matters as authorial intention, historical, moral or political considerations, and audience response. The earlier New Criticism was primarily interested in lyric poetry and regarded most highly forms of poetry in which irony, tension, paradox and ambiguity interact with the semantics of language in such a way, they believed, as to render poetic meaning unique and un-paraphrasable. They claimed, however, that poetry could impart knowledge but a form of knowledge radically different from knowledge in the scientific sense. They particularly admired metaphysical poetry. Because the New Criticism argued that poetic language is semantically different from non-poetic language since it does not refer beyond itself but only functions contextually within the structure of the poem, it is sometimes called, perhaps confusingly, 'contextualism'.

In Richards and in such New Critics as Brooks, there is a similar emphasis on the special nature of poetic language and they also agree that the highest forms of poetry embody heterogeneous or what appear to be contradictory elements, necessitating the use of such critical terms as irony and paradox. But whereas Richards

tends to discuss these aspects of poetry in relation to the reader's
emotions and psychology, Brooks places the greatest emphasis on
the poem as an objective structure, as his essay, 'The Formalist
Critic', shows. Richards's concept of the literary work as 'pseudo-
statement', however, as presented in 'Poetry and Beliefs', first
published in his book *Science and Poetry* (1926), was fundamental
to the New Criticism and this essay also shows how important the
work of T. S. Eliot was to the New Critical approach. Kenneth
Burke might be called the Bakhtin of the New Criticism. He goes
part of the way with Brooks's type of formalism but has some
sympathy with Marxist ideas and argues that one cannot leave out
of account sociological and psychological factors. John M. Ellis is
a more recent theorist who defends fundamental New Critical
concepts from a standpoint influenced by the later philosophy of
Wittgenstein.

F. R. Leavis has a strong claim to be the most influential British
critic of the twentieth century. He had a good deal in common
with the American New Critics in that he attached great importance to language and literary form. In particular he emphasised
the enactive power of literary language. But there is a stronger
moral dimension to his criticism than one finds in the New
Critics. It is perhaps paradoxical, however, to include him in a
book devoted to literary theory since he refused to discuss his
critical position in theoretical terms. The essay 'Literary Criticism
and Philosophy', first published in *Scrutiny* in 1937, was a response
to René Wellek's view that he needed to spell out the theoretical
basis of his criticism. Wellek wrote:

Allow me to sketch your ideal of poetry, your 'norm' with which you
measure every poet: your poetry must be in serious relation to actuality, it
must have a firm grasp of the actual, of the object, it must be in relation
to life, it must not be cut off from direct vulgar living, it should be normally human, testify to spiritual health and sanity, it should not be personal in the sense of indulging in personal dreams and fantasies, there
should be no emotion for its own sake in it ... but a sharp, concrete realization, a sensuous particularity. The language of your poetry must not be
cut off from speech, should not flatter the singing voice, should not be
merely mellifluous. ... I would ask you to defend this position more abstractly and to become conscious that large ethical, philosophical and, of
course, ultimately, also aesthetic *choices* are involved. (*Scrutiny*, 5
[1936–7], p. 376)

Though Leavis in his reply refused to defend his critical position in abstract terms, the arguments he uses to justify his refusal

are of considerable theoretical interest. A theoretical justification of Leavis's position can, however, be formulated, as John Casey shows in his book *The Language of Criticism*. Indeed, Casey argues that the implied theory that underlies Leavis's critical practice is both innovative and cogent, since it embodies a synthesis of expressionist and mimetic theories of art.

FURTHER READING

The New Criticism
Cleanth Brooks, *The Well Wrought Urn: Studies in the Structure of Poetry* (London, 1949).
Kenneth Burke, *The Philosophy of Literary Form* (Berkeley, Calif, 1974).
T. S. Eliot, *The Sacred Wood* (London, 1920).
William Empson, *Seven Types of Ambiguity* (London, 1930).
Gerald Graff, 'On the New Criticism: Literary Interpretation and Scientific Objectivity', *Salmagundi*, 27 (1974), 72–93. (A critical view.)
Murray Krieger, *The New Apologists for Poetry* (Minneapolis, 1956).
John Crowe Ransom, *The New Criticism* (Norfolk, Conn., 1941).
I. A. Richards, *Principles of Literary Criticism* (London, 1924).
William H. Rueckert (ed.), *Critical Responses to Kenneth Burke* (Minneapolis, 1969).
René Wellek, *A History of Modern Criticism: 1750–1950: Vol. 6: American Criticism, 1900–1950* (New Haven, Conn., 1986).
W. K. Wimsatt, Jr, *The Verbal Icon: Studies in the Meaning of Poetry* (New York, 1954). (Contains the essays 'The Intentional Fallacy' and 'The Affective Fallacy', written in collaboration with Monroe K. Beardsley.)

Leavisian Criticism
Michael Bell, *F.R. Leavis* (London and New York, 1988).
F. R. Leavis, *Nor Shall My Sword: Discourses on Pluralism, Compassion and Social Hope* (London, 1972).
——, *The Living Principle: 'English' as a Discipline of Thought* (London, 1975).
Francis Mulhern, *The Moment of 'Scrutiny'* (London, 1979).
William Walsh, *F.R. Leavis* (London, 1980).
René Wellek, *A History of Modern Criticism: 1750–1950: Vol. 5: English Criticism, 1900–1950* (New Haven, Conn., 1986).

5   I. A. RICHARDS: 'POETRY AND BELIEFS'

The business of the poet, as we have seen, is to give order and coherence, and so freedom, to a body of experience. To do so through words which act as its skeleton, as a structure by which the impulses which make up the experience are adjusted to one another and act together. The means by which words do this are many and varied. To work them out is a problem for linguistic psychology, that embarrassed young heir to philosophy. What little can be done shows already that most critical dogmas of the past are either false or nonsense. A little knowledge is not here a danger, but clears the air in a remarkable way.

Roughly and inadequately, even in the light of present knowledge, we can say that words work in the poem in two main fashions. As sensory stimuli and as (in the *widest* sense) symbols. We must refrain from considering the sensory side of the poem, remarking only that it is *not* in the least independent of the other side, and that it has for definite reasons prior importance in most poetry. We must confine ourselves to the other function of words in the poem, or rather, omitting much that is of secondary relevance, to one form of that function, let me call it *pseudo-statement*.

It will be admitted – by those who distinguish between scientific statement, where truth is ultimately a matter of verification as this is understood in the laboratory, and emotive utterance, where 'truth' is primarily acceptability *by* some attitude, and more remotely is the acceptability *of* this attitude itself – that it is *not* the poet's business to make scientific statements. Yet poetry has constantly the air of making statements, and important ones; which is one reason why some mathematicians cannot read it. They find the alleged statements to be *false*. It will be agreed that their approach to poetry and their expectations from it are mistaken. But what exactly is the other, the right, the poetic, approach and how does it differ from the mathematical?

The poetic approach evidently limits the framework of possible consequences into which the pseudo-statement is taken. For the scientific approach this framework is unlimited. Any and every consequence is relevant. If any of the consequences of a

Reprinted from *Poetics and Sciences: A Reissue of 'Science and Poetry'* (*1926, 1935*) *with Commentary* (London, 1970), pp. 57–66.

statement conflicts with acknowledged fact then so much the worse for the statement. Not so with the pseudo-statement when poetically approached. The problem is – just how does the limitation work? One tempting account is in terms of a supposed universe of discourse, a world of make-believe, of imagination, of recognised fictions common to the poet and his readers. A pseudo-statement which fits into this system of assumptions would be regarded as 'poetically true'; one which does not, as 'poetically false'. This attempt to treat 'poetic truth' on the model of general 'coherence theories' is very natural for certain schools of logicians but is inadequate, on the wrong lines from the outset. To mention two objections, out of many; there is no means of discovering what the 'universe of discourse' is on any occasion, and the kind of coherence which must hold within it, supposing it to be discoverable, is not an affair of logical relations. Attempt to define the system of propositions into which

O Rose, thou art sick!

must fit, and the logical relations which must hold between them if it is to be 'poetically true'; the absurdity of the theory becomes evident.

We must look further. In the poetic approach the relevant consequences are not logical or to be arrived at by a partial relaxation of logic. Except occasionally and by accident logic does not enter at all. They are the consequences which arise through our emotional organisation. The acceptance which a pseudo-statement receives is entirely governed by its effects upon our feelings and attitudes. Logic only comes in, if at all, in subordination, as a servant to our emotional response. It is an unruly servant, however, as poets and readers are constantly discovering. A pseudo-statement is 'true' if it suits and serves some attitude or links together attitudes which on other grounds are desirable. This kind of 'truth' is so opposed to scientific 'truth' that it is a pity to use so similar a word, but at the present it is difficult to avoid the malpractice.[1]

This brief analysis may be sufficient to indicate the fundamental disparity and opposition between pseudo-statements as they occur in poetry and statements as they occur in science. A pseudo-statement is a form of words which is justified entirely by its effect in releasing or organising our impulses and attitudes (due regard being had for the better or worse organisations of these *inter se*); a statement, on the other hand, is justified by its truth, i.e., its correspondence, in a highly technical sense, with the fact to which it points.

Statements true and false alike do, of course, constantly touch off attitudes and action. Our daily practical existence is largely guided by them. On the whole true statements are of more service to us than false ones. None the less we do not and, at present, cannot order our emotions and attitudes by true statements alone. Nor is there any probability that we ever shall contrive to do so. This is one of the great new dangers to which civilisation is exposed. Countless pseudo-statements – about God, about the universe, about human nature, the relations of mind to mind, about the soul; its rank and destiny – pseudo-statements which are pivotal points in the organisation of the mind, vital to its well-being, have suddenly become, for sincere, honest and informal minds, impossible to believe as for centuries they have been believed. The accustomed incidences of the modes of believing are changed irrecoverably; and the knowledge which has displaced them is not of a kind upon which an equally fine organisation of the mind can be based.

This is the contemporary situation. The remedy, since there is no prospect of our gaining adequate knowledge, and since indeed it is fairly clear that genuine knowledge cannot meet this need, is to cut our pseudo-statements free from that kind of belief which is appropriate to verified statements. So released they will be changed, of course, but they can still be the main instruments by which we order our attitudes to one another and to the world. This is not a desperate remedy, for, as poetry conclusively shows, even the most important among our attitudes can be aroused and maintained without any believing of a factual or verifiable order entering in at all. We need no such beliefs, and indeed we must have none, if we are to read *King Lear*. Pseudo-statements to which we attach no belief and statements proper, such as science provides, cannot conflict. It is only when we introduce inappropriate kinds of believing into poetry that danger arises. To do so is from this point of view a profanation of poetry...

The long-established and much-encouraged habit of giving to emotive utterances – whether pseudo-statements simple, or looser and larger wholes taken as saying something figuratively – the kind of assent which we give to unescapable facts, has for most people debilitated a wide range of their responses. A few scientists, caught young and brought up in the laboratory, are free from it; but then, as a rule, they pay no *serious* attention to poetry. For most men the recognition of the neutrality of nature brings about – through this habit – a divorce from poetry. ... Over whole tracts of natural emotional response we are to-day like a bed of dahlias whose sticks have been removed. And this effect of the neutralisation of nature is only in its beginnings. However, human nature has a prodigious resilience. Love poetry seems able to out-play psychoanalysis.

A sense of desolation, of uncertainty, of futility, of the groundlessness of aspirations, of the vanity of endeavour, and a thirst for a lifegiving water which seems suddenly to have failed, are the signs in consciousness of this necessary reorganisation of our lives.[2] Our attitudes and impulses are being compelled to become self-supporting; they are being driven back upon their biological justification, made once again sufficient to themselves. And the only impulses which seem strong enough to continue unflagging are commonly so crude that, to more finely developed individuals, they hardly seem worth having. Such people cannot live by warmth, food, fighting, drink, and sex alone. Those who are least affected by the change are those who are emotionally least removed from the animals. ...

It is important to diagnose the disease correctly and to put the blame in the right quarter. ... We are beginning to know too much about the bond which unites the mind to its object in knowledge[3] for that old dream of a perfect knowledge which would guarantee perfect life to retain its sanction. What was thought to be pure knowledge, we see now to have been shot through with hope and desire, with fear and wonder; and these intrusive elements indeed gave it all its power to support our lives. In knowledge, in the 'How?' of events, we can find hints by which to take advantage of circumstances in our favour and avoid mischance. But we cannot get from it a *raison d'être* or a justification of more than a relatively lowly kind of life.

The justification, or the reverse, of any attitude lies, not in the object, but in itself, in its serviceableness to the whole personality. Upon its place in the whole system of attitudes, which is the personality, all its worth depends. This is true equally for the subtle, finely compounded attitudes of the civilised individual as for the simpler attitudes of the child.

In brief, the imaginative life is its own justification; and this fact must be faced, although sometimes – by a lover, for example – it may be very difficult to accept. When it is faced, it is apparent that all the attitudes to other human beings and to the world in all its aspects, which have been serviceable to humanity, remain as they were, as valuable as ever. Hesitation felt in admitting this is a measure of the strength of the evil habit I have been describing. But many of these attitudes, valuable as ever, are, now that they are being set free, more difficult to maintain, because we still hunger after a basis in belief.

NOTES

[From 1935 edition. Reorganised and renumbered from the original]
1. A pseudo-statement, as I use the term, is not necessarily false in any sense. It is merely a form of words whose scientific truth or falsity is irrelevant to the purpose in hand.
'Logic' in this paragraph is, of course, being used in a limited and conventional, or popular, sense.
2. My debt to *The Waste Land* here will be evident.
3. Verifiable scientific knowledge, of course.

6   CLEANTH BROOKS: 'THE FORMALIST CRITIC'

Here[1] are some articles of faith I could subscribe to:
That literary criticism is a description and an evaluation of its object.

That the primary concern of criticism is with the problem of unity – the kind of whole which the literary work forms or fails to form, and the relation of the various parts to each other in building up this whole.

That the formal relations in a work of literature may include, but certainly exceed, those of logic.

That in a successful work, form and content cannot be separated.

That form is meaning.

That literature is ultimately metaphorical and symbolic.

That the general and the universal are not seized upon by abstraction, but got at through the concrete and the particular.

That literature is not a surrogate for religion.

That, as Allen Tate says, 'specific moral problems' are the subject matter of literature, but that the purpose of literature is not to point a moral.

That the principles of criticism define the area relevant to literary criticism; they do not constitute a method for carrying out the criticism.

Such statements as these would not, however, even though greatly elaborated, serve any useful purpose here. The interested reader already knows the general nature of the critical position adumbrated – or, if he does not, he can find it set forth in writings of mine or of other critics of like sympathy. Moreover, a condensed restatement of the position here would probably beget as many misunderstandings as have past attempts to set it forth. It

Reprinted from the *Kenyon Review*, 13 (1951), 72–81.

seems much more profitable to use the present occasion for dealing with some persistent misunderstandings and objections.

In the first place, to make the poem or the novel the central concern of criticism has appeared to mean cutting it loose from its author and from his life as a man, with his own particular hopes, fears, interests, conflicts, etc. A criticism so limited may seem bloodless and hollow...

In the second place, to emphasize the work seems to involve severing it from those who actually read it, and this severance may seem drastic and therefore disastrous. After all, literature is written to be read. Wordsworth's poet was a man speaking to men. ... Moreover, if we neglect the audience which reads the work, including that for which it was presumably written, the literary historian is prompt to point out that the kind of audience that Pope had did condition the kind of poetry that he wrote. The poem has its roots in history, past or present. Its place in the historical context simply cannot be ignored.

I have stated these objections as sharply as I can because I am sympathetic with the state of mind which is prone to voice them. Man's experience is indeed a seamless garment, no part of which can be separated from the rest. Yet if we urge this fact of inseparability against the drawing of distinctions, then there is no point in talking about criticism at all. I am assuming that distinctions are necessary and useful and indeed inevitable.

The formalist critic knows as well as anyone that poems and plays and novels are written by men – that they do not somehow happen – and that they are written as expressions of particular personalities and are written from all sorts of motives – for money, from a desire to express oneself, for the sake of a cause, etc. Moreover, the formalist critic knows as well as anyone that literary works are merely potential until they are read – that is, that they are recreated in the minds of actual readers, who vary enormously in their capabilities, their interests, their prejudices, their ideas. But the formalist critic is concerned primarily with the work itself. Speculation on the mental processes of the author takes the critic away from the work into biography and psychology. There is no reason, of course, why he should not turn away into biography and psychology. Such explorations are very much worth making. But they should not be confused with an account of the work. Such studies describe the process of composition, not the structure of the thing composed, and they may be performed quite as validly for the poor work as for the good one. They may be validly performed for any kind of expression – non-literary as well as literary.

On the other hand, exploration of the various readings which the work has received also takes the critic away from the work into psychology and the history of taste. The various imports of a given work may well be worth studying. ... But such work, valuable and necessary as it may be, is to be distinguished from a criticism of the work itself. The formalist critic, because he wants to criticize the work itself, makes two assumptions: (1) he assumes that the relevant part of the author's intention is what he got actually into his work; that is, he assumes that the author's intention *as realized* is the 'intention' that counts, not necessarily what he was conscious of trying to do, or what he now remembers he was then trying to do. And (2) the formalist critic assumes an ideal reader: that is, instead of focusing on the varying spectrum of possible readings, he attempts to find a central point of reference from which he can focus upon the structure of the poem or novel.

But there *is* no ideal reader, someone is prompt to point out, and he will probably add that it is sheer arrogance that allows the critic, with his own blindsides and prejudices, to put himself in the position of that ideal reader. There is no ideal reader, of course, and I suppose that the practising critic can never be too often reminded of the gap between his reading and the 'true' reading of the poem. But for the purpose of focusing upon the poem rather than upon his own reactions, it is a defensible strategy. Finally, of course, it is the strategy that all critics of whatever persuasion are forced to adopt. (The alternatives are desperate: either we say that one person's reading is as good as another's and equate those readings on a basis of absolute equality and thus deny the possibility of any standard reading. Or else we take a lowest common denominator of the various readings that have been made; that is, we frankly move from literary criticism into socio-psychology. To propose taking a consensus of the opinions of 'qualified' readers is simply to split the ideal reader into a group of ideal readers.) As consequences of the distinction just referred to, the formalist critic rejects two popular tests for literary value. The first proves the value of the work from the author's 'sincerity' (or the intensity of the author's feelings as he composed it). ... Ernest Hemingway's statement in a recent issue of *Time* magazine that he counts his last novel his best is of interest for Hemingway's biography, but most readers of *Across the River and Into the Trees* would agree that it proves nothing at all about the value of the novel – that in this case the judgment is simply pathetically inept. We discount also such tests for poetry as that proposed by A. E. Housman – the bristling of his beard at the reading of a good poem. The intensity of his reaction has critical significance only in proportion as we have already learned to trust him as a reader. Even so, what it tells us is something about Housman – nothing decisive about the poem.

It is unfortunate if this playing down of such responses seems to deny humanity to either writer or reader. The critic may enjoy certain works very much and may be indeed intensely moved by them. I am, and I have no embarrassment in admitting the fact; but a detailed description of my emotional state on reading certain works has little to do with indicating to an interested reader what the work is and how the parts of it are related.

Should all criticism, then, be self-effacing and analytic? I hope that the answer is implicit in what I have already written, but I shall go on to spell it out. Of course not. That will depend upon the occasion and the audience. ...

I have assigned the critic a modest, though I think an important, role. With reference to the help which the critic can give to the practising artist, the role is even more modest. As critic, he can give only negative help. Literature is not written by formula: he can have no formula to offer. Perhaps he can do little more than indicate whether in his opinion the work has succeeded or failed. Healthy criticism and healthy creation do tend to go hand in hand. Everything else being equal, the creative artist is better off for being in touch with a vigorous criticism. But the other considerations are never equal, the case is always special, and in a given case the proper advice *could* be: quit reading criticism altogether, or read political science or history or philosophy – or join the army, or join the church. ...

A literary work is a document and as a document can be analysed in terms of the forces that have produced it, or it may be manipulated as a force in its own right. It mirrors the past, it may influence the future. These facts it would be futile to deny, and I know of no critic who does deny them. But the reduction of a work of literature to its causes does not constitute literary criticism; nor does an estimate of its effects. Good literature is more than effective rhetoric applied to true ideas – even if we could agree upon a philosophical yardstick for measuring the truth of ideas and even if we could find some way that transcended nose-counting for determining the effectiveness of the rhetoric.

NOTE

1. In giving his permission for this article to be reprinted, Cleanth Brooks requested that the following note by him be included:

This is an early essay intended to set forth a rather strict interpretation of a 'literary' criticism. I did not and do not now mean to deny value to other literary studies such as the biographical, historical, those describing the cultural setting of the work, etc. They may prove necessary to an understanding of the text although they cannot of themselves determine literary value. I myself have published such studies from 1946 to the present day.

7 KENNETH BURKE: 'FORMALIST CRITICISM: ITS PRINCIPLES AND LIMITS'

In our essays on the Keats ode,[1] my 'dramatistic' view of form coincided with Mr Brooks's concept of 'dramatic analogues' at those points where we were treating the Urn as a character of the situation in which the 'fair Attitude' was addressed. Thus, above all, when the Urn vatically announces that 'Beauty is truth, truth beauty,' we agreed in viewing this as a statement properly prepared for *within the conditions of the poem*, and not to be read simply as a 'scientific' or 'philosophic' proposition equally valid outside its context.

Our differences arise, I think, from our different ways of interpreting the implications of Mr Brooks's own remarks in 'The Heresy of Paraphrase'[2] when he says: 'Where is the dictionary which contains the terms of a poem? It is a truism that the poet is continually forced to remake language.' *I* take this just observation to imply that a poet is naturally closer to his own particular idiom than his readers can ever hope to be, but that by comparing all available contexts (both poetic and extrapoetic) in which the poet employs a given term, we can get deeper glimpses than were otherwise possible into the functioning of his particular nomenclature. And these possibilities seem to me worth trying to disclose with regard to the nature of symbolic action[3] in general, though many of such speculations may not contribute to Poetics in particular. ...

Underlying my discussion of the Keats ode (and of 'The Ancient Mariner' in *The Philosophy of Literary Form*) there is a procedure of this sort: First, say what can be said of the work if you had nothing but it, and didn't even know who wrote it. Here,

Reprinted from *Language As Symbolic Action: Essays on Life, Literature and Method* (Berkeley, Calif, 1973), pp. 496–500.

necessarily, your analysis would be internal, wholly in the realm of Poetics. Next, if you can place its authorship, and you have other poems written by the same author, examine these on the assumption that the recurrence·of the same terms elsewhere may throw additional light upon their nature as a special nomenclature (the meaning of a given term in a 'Keats Dictionary' as distinct from its meaning in a 'Shelley Dictionary', and so on). Finally, in the attempt *wholly* outside the realm of Poetics proper to study the ways of symbolic action in general, introduce any kind of available evidence (such as letters, diaries, notebooks, biographical data) that might indicate how the terms *within* the poem link up with problematical situations (personal or social) *outside* the poem. ...

Hence, as a major step along our way, I think I can now state precisely what my tactics are with regard to Poetics in particular. I would propose to make the rules in that dimension as strict as possible. Absolutely no biographical reference would be admissible. History itself would be admissible only in the sense that the meaning (and allusiveness) of a term will change through the centuries, and I'd subscribe to Croce's admonition that unless such changes are taken into account, the critic's analysis of an ancient text will be an unintended 'palimpsest'. For the later meaning of a term may cover up its meaning at the time when the poem was written; and a critic's failure to make the appropriate discount (there's 'propriety' again!) is in effect the imposing of a new text upon an old one. ...

The work would be judged not by tests of 'truth', 'scientific' or 'factual' accuracy, but on the basis of 'verisimilitude'. The truth of the 'data' in a literary production by no means guarantees its artistic appeal. But to appeal it *must* have some kind of verisimilitude. Thus, only verisimilitude, not truth, can engage a reader who does not believe in hell, but who derives aesthetic pleasure from Dante's Inferno. Truth enters in a secondary sense, for often accuracy of sheerly factual detail can contribute to our sense of a work's verisimilitude. And regardless of whether or not we believe in the ontological reality of hell, to go along with Dante's poem we must believe beyond all doubt that such unending sufferings really would be hellish.

In analyzing a work strictly in terms of Poetics, one would analyze it solely as a form, without any reference to the personality of the author. Thus, I do think it a notable oversight in Mr Brooks's list of tenets for Formalist criticism that he does not require the ideal Formalist to define works in terms of their *kind*. But in the actual working out of his book on Faulkner, he does propose an overall definition of Faulkner's writing, which in the large he categorizes as a kind of comedy.

But the main point is this: Regardless of what an author may or may not have personally intended, the Formalist critic fulfils his 'proper' task by imputing to the work whatever design, or intention, he thinks is best able to account for the nature of the work. Thus the question of an 'intentional fallacy' becomes quite irrelevant. The *test* of the design is pragmatic. The critic proceeds to substantiate his thesis casuistically, by showing in detail how much the imputed design might account for. If a rival critic can propose different postulates that will account for more aspects of the work, or for more important aspects of it, his job is to offer a different postulate, and to demonstrate pragmatically how much can be accounted for on the basis of his thesis.

A character, let us say, has traits not directly explainable in terms of the intention that a given critic has postulated. A competing critic might propose a postulate that did directly account for these traits. But other possibilities suggest themselves. The problematic traits might be treated as designed to serve some secondary aspect of the plot. Or the critic might argue that though not directly functional so far as the furthering of the plot is concerned, these traits keep the character from being functional in too simple a sense (as with sheer allegory in case the work is not intended as allegory, or with an overly simplified problem play or *Tendenz-roman*).[4] Another way of putting such a case would be for the critic to show why, in order to make a given character seem 'real', the author must endow him with more traits than those most directly needed to account for his actions strictly in terms of his role, as determined by the particular needs of the plot. For the ends of verisimilitude may be shown to require that a character should not be too perfectly adapted to his specific function in furthering the plot, just as one could not design even so simple a tool as a carpenter's hammer that could be used only for the purpose of driving nails.

In any case, as regards strictly Formalist criticism the issue could never lead to such remarks as these by Mr Brooks, when denying that Faulkner regards Gavin Stevens (in *Intruder in the Dust*) 'as a kind of projected image of himself, and means to use him as his mouthpiece': 'Doubtless what he says often represents what many Southerners think and what Faulkner himself – at one time or another – may have thought.' Or above all, it would not involve such a 'sociological' remark as: 'His arguments do reflect a very real cultural situation, and the reader could learn from them a great deal about the problem of the South.'[5]

Let me make myself clear on this point. I am not discussing the truth or falsity of Mr Brooks's comments here. I am merely noting that they are not 'Formalistic'. They could be called 'sociological', and maybe even 'Marxist', in their relation to a book as reflecting a social situation. The first three chapters ('Faulkner, the Provincial'; 'The Plain People: Yeoman Farmers, Sharecroppers, and White Trash'; and 'As Nature Poet') have many valuable things to say about the extrapoetic *situations* from which Faulkner is writing, and which his work takes into account. Despite Mr Wellek's dislike of the term, one might call them 'strategies' for the encompassing of such 'situations'. In any case, one does not convert them into full-blown Formalist criticism simply by an occasional slighting reference to sociology. They are sociological, for they are dealing with 'the Yoknapatawpha Country' *in terms of Mississippi in particular and the South in general.*

True, they also go *beyond* the strictly sociological, quite as in my discussion of 'situations' and 'strategies' in *The Philosophy of Literary Form*, I point out that 'insofar as situations overlap from individual to individual, or from one historical period to another, the strategies possess universal relevance'. But note how readily we slip from the sociological scene to the literary reflection in a passage such as this: 'The South as a whole was wretchedly poor, upper classes as well as lower classes, right on from the Civil War period until the Second World War. The economy of the whole region was basically a colonial economy, manipulated from the outside. Even the so-called aristocracy, as Faulkner depicts them, had little wealth. The Compsons, for example, in 1909 had to sell land in order to send Quentin to Harvard, etc.' Is it not a sheerly *sociological* procedure to show how Faulkner's version of the South reflects an aspect of what the Marxists would call the 'objective situation'? Again let me repeat, to avoid all possibility of mis-understanding: I am not complaining about such 'situational' discussion as such. I am merely asking us to bear in mind that, whatever terms you use, we are here discussing literary *strategies* for confronting *situations*.

NOTES

1. [Ed.] See appendix to Burke's *A Grammar of Motives* (New York, 1945) and Chapter 8 of Brooks's *The Well Wrought Urn*, for their analyses of Keats's 'Ode on a Grecian Urn'.

2. [Ed.] See *The Well Wrought Urn*, Chapter 11.

3. [Ed.] 'Symbolic action' for Burke, in terms of works of art, is the creation of 'strategies for the encompassing of situations'. In his *Attitudes*

towards History Burke writes that 'These strategies size up the situations, name their structure and outstanding ingredients, and name them in a way that contains an attitude towards them.' He defines a symbolic act as 'the dancing of an attitude' that must be distinguished from a real act.
  4. [Ed.] Novel with a purpose.
  5. [Ed.] See Brooks's study *William Faulkner: The Yoknapatawpha Country* (New Haven, Conn., 1963).

8 JOHN M. ELLIS: 'THE RELEVANT CONTEXT OF A LITERARY TEXT'

The question of the relevant context of a literary text is an important one because it is the basis of the more familiar question of what knowledge is necessary for the understanding of a work of literature. It has often been said that criticism should make the literary work more understandable by recreating the original circumstances of its composition: the historical situation in which the author wrote, and the response of the contemporary audience. This view specifies the relevant context: it is the original context of composition – biographical, social, and historical. But in so doing it specifies also relevant information for the understanding of a literary text; we need to know the facts of the original context to understand the work, and criticism should put us in possession of those facts. ...
  When we concern ourselves with a piece of language, it is entirely normal to interpret it in the light of its context: indeed, in most cases not to do so leads to error. We find out what someone means not just from his actual words, but from his actions and the context he is in. ... The question now arises, can we deal with literary texts in this way? That is, can we give an improved version of (correct, add to, delete from, make more specific, or whatever) their meaning by appeal to an intent? And can we infer this intent by knowledge of the biographical context of the author, including both any possible direct comments by him on the text, and his general situation as a man characteristically concerned with certain kinds of things and situations?

Reprinted from *The Theory of Literary Criticism: A Logical Analysis* (Berkeley, Calif, 1974), pp. 104–21.

Literary scholarship had largely assumed an affirmative answer to this question until W. K. Wimsatt and M. C. Beardsley in a celebrated article[1] coined the term 'Intentional Fallacy'; they held that the intent of the author is first of all not available to us (or perhaps even to him) and that even if it were it could not form an adequate basis for judging and interpreting his work. ...

From my discussion of the definition of literary texts, it will be remembered that the defining point for these texts is the use made of them, and the way in which they are treated; and further, that this use was centrally a matter of not taking them as part of the context of their origin in the way in which we normally treat pieces of language. Literary texts are not treated as part of the normal flow of speech, which has a purpose in its original context and is then discarded after that purpose is achieved, and they are not judged according to such limited purposes. These texts are defined as those that outgrow the original context of their utterance, and which function in the community at large. They do not function in that original context, are not dependent on that context for meaning, and are not judged according to their appropriateness or success in achieving what was to be achieved there. Therefore, when we decide to treat a piece of language as literature, that decision is in itself a decision not to refer the text to its originator nor to treat it as a communication from him. ...[2]

The one thing that is different about literary texts, then, is that they are not to be taken as part of the contexts of their origin; and to take them in this way is to annihilate exactly the thing that makes them literary texts. I am not making the point that this use is an inappropriate one, but the stronger point that the texts are actually made into something different by this use: they are not just literature misused, they are no longer literature at all. The process of a text becoming a literary text involves three stages: its originating in the context of its creator, its then being offered for use as literature, and its finally being accepted as such. In the final step, society makes the text into literature. The biographical approach returns the text to its former status, and reverses the process of its becoming a literary text.

This, it appears to me, is the most radical and accurate argument against intentionalism that can be made. ...

In being taken back to its original context, a poem is made more specific, and (as the arguments for and against this operation can both agree) something additional is brought to the poem. But that specificity is a loss, not a gain; what is taken away is the level of generality possessed by the text as a literary text.

Let us assume, for example, that the process of a poet's composing his poem involved as a starting point a situation that he himself experienced; we can immediately see that it must have had much more detail than was eventually put into the text itself. To that extent, much of the original situation was left out. On the other hand, detail and emphasis may have been added which were not in the original situation. There is, then, both more and less in the text than in the original situation and the impact of the text is different from the original situation to the degree that those changes have occurred. To replace everything in the work that was there in the original situation is, in fact, to reverse the process of composition. The work became a work of literature after having been changed from the original situation, so that to put back all that the poet thought was irrelevant and therefore left out is to destroy the structure of the finished work by virtue of which it has its artistic impact and meaning; that meaning was created precisely by the selective operation that so many critics seem to be at pains to reverse and remove. This, then, is the sense in which knowing more, that is, putting back into the work what has been kept out of it, is to end up with less. ... This is nothing less than the demolition of a literary structure.

On occasion, the usefulness of biographical knowledge for literary criticism is argued in a way diametrically opposed to that which I have just considered: in seeking biographical information, the argument runs, we are not trying to reintroduce into the text the details that the poet chose to exclude in order to regard them, too, as part of the meaning of the text, but rather in order to see what choices were made for inclusion or exclusion of detail and emphasis, and thus to learn something about the meaning of the text by our increased awareness of the concerns demonstrated by the process of the literary text taking shape. But this argument fails too; the study of the creative process, in the sense of the development of a work in the hands of its author, contributes nothing whatsoever to our understanding of the meaning of the text; on the contrary, only an understanding of the meaning of the text makes the study of its genesis possible and intelligible (though still not useful from an interpretative standpoint). ...

In the last analysis, arguments from genesis fall foul of a well-known dilemma: either the meaning and emphasis discerned through the genesis of the poem is actually in the poem, in which case it did not need to be sought elsewhere; or it is not in the poem, in which case it is simply not part of the poem at all. In the second case there can never be sufficient reason for writing into the poem something which is not there; in order to make it conform to a statement of intention or to an inferred intent, when in so doing we are going against the best evidence we have of the author's final intent, namely, the text that he finally produced. Whatever his plans may have been, the text is the only evidence we can have of the modification that any previous intent underwent. Even if we grant the intentionalist thesis that the meaning of the poem is what the poet intended, it would still be true that the only reliable evidence of that intent is the poem, and from this it would follow that we should not prefer any other evidence to that of the poem in determining intent.

NOTES

[Reorganised and renumbered from the original]
1. W. K. Wimsatt and M. C. Beardsley, 'The Intentional Fallacy', in *The Verbal Icon* (originally 1946, *Sewanee Review*, 54).
2. [Ed.] For further discussion of this see Chapter 1 of Ellis's *The Theory of Literary Criticism.*

9 F. R. LEAVIS: 'LITERARY CRITICISM AND PHILOSOPHY'

I must thank Dr Wellek for bringing fundamental criticism to my work, and above all for raising in so complete a way an issue that a reviewer or two had more or less vaguely touched on – an issue of which no one can have been more conscious than myself who had seen the recognition of it as an essential constituent of what I naturally (whatever the quality of my performance) hoped for: an appreciation of my undertaking. Dr Wellek points out, justly, that in my dealings with English poetry I have made a number of assumptions that I neither defend nor even state: 'I could wish', he says, 'that you had made your assumptions more explicitly and defended them systematically.' ...

Reprinted from *The Common Pursuit* (London, 1962), pp. 211–16.

I in my turn would ask Dr Wellek to believe that if I omitted to undertake the defence he desiderates it was not from any lack of consciousness: I knew I was making assumptions (even if I didn't – and shouldn't now – state them to myself quite as he states them) and I was not less aware than I am now of what they involve. I am interested that he should be able to say that, for the most part, he shares them with me. But, he adds, he would 'have misgivings in pronouncing them without elaborating a specific defence or a theory in their defence'. That, I suggest, is because Dr Wellek is a philosopher; and my reply to him in the first place is that I myself am not a philosopher, and that I doubt whether in any case I could elaborate a theory that he would find satisfactory. ...

Literary criticism and philosophy seem to me to be quite distinct and different kinds of discipline – at least, I think they ought to be (for while in my innocence I hope that philosophic writing commonly represents a serious discipline, I am quite sure that literary-critical writing commonly doesn't). ...

The difficulty that one who approaches with the habit of one kind of discipline has in duly recognizing the claims of a very different kind – the difficulty of reconciling the two in a working alliance – seems to me to be illustrated in Dr Wellek's way of referring to the business of literary criticism: 'Allow me', he says, 'to sketch your ideal of poetry, your "norm" with which you measure every poet. ...' That he should slip into this way of putting things seems to me significant, for he would on being challenged agree, I imagine, that it suggests a false idea of the procedure of the critic. At any rate, he gives me an excuse for making, by way of reminder, some elementary observations about that procedure.

By the critic of poetry I understand the complete reader: the ideal critic is the ideal reader. The reading demanded by poetry is of a different kind from that demanded by philosophy. I should not find it easy to define the difference satisfactorily, but Dr Wellek knows what it is and could give at least as good an account of it as I could. Philosophy, we say, is 'abstract' (thus Dr Wellek asks me to defend my position 'more abstractly'), and poetry 'concrete'. Words in poetry invite us, not to 'think about' and judge but to 'feel into' or 'become' – to realize a complex experience that is given in the words. They demand, not merely a fuller-bodied response, but a completer respons-iveness – a kind of responsiveness that is incompatible with the judicial, one-eye-on-the-standard approach suggested by

Dr Wellek's phrase: 'your "norm" with which you measure every poet'. The critic – the reader of poetry – is indeed concerned with evaluation, but to figure him as measuring with a norm which he brings up to the object and applies from the outside is to misrepresent the process. The critic's aim is, first, to realize as sensitively and completely as possible this or that which claims his attention; and a certain valuing is implicit in the realizing. As he matures in experience of the new thing he asks, explicitly and implicitly: 'Where does this come? How does it stand in relation to … ? How relatively important does it seem?' And the organization into which it settles as a constituent in becoming 'placed' is an organization of similarly 'placed' things, things that have found their bearings with regard to one another, and not a theoretical system or a system determined by abstract considerations. …

…The business of the literary critic is to attain a peculiar completeness of response and to observe a peculiarly strict relevance in developing his response into commentary; he must be on his guard against any premature or irrelevant generalizing – of it or from it. His first concern is to enter into possession of the given poem (let us say) in its concrete fulness, and his constant concern is never to lose his completeness of possession, but rather to increase it. In making value-judgments (and judgments as to significance) implicitly or explicitly, he does so out of that completeness of possession and with that fulness of response. He doesn't ask, 'How does this accord with these specifications of goodness in poetry?'; he aims to make fully conscious and articulate the immediate sense of value that 'places' the poem. …

From this consistency and this coherence (in so far as I have achieved them) it would, of course, be possible to elicit principles and abstractly formulable norms. Dr Wellek's first criticism of me is (to give it its least exceptionable force) that I haven't proceeded to elicit them: that, having written the book I undertook to write, I haven't gone on to write another book in which I develop the theoretical implications of the first (for it would be essentially a matter of two books, even if there were only one binding). … The cogency I hoped to achieve was to be for other readers of poetry – readers of poetry as such. I hoped, by putting in front of them, in a criticism that should keep as close to the concrete as possible, my own developed 'coherence of response', to get them to agree (with, no doubt, critical qualifications) that the map, the essential order, of English poetry seen as a whole did, when they interrogated their experience, look like that to them also. Ideally I ought perhaps (though, I repeat, I should not put my position in quite the terms Dr Wellek ascribes to me) to be able to complete the work with a theoretical statement. But I am sure that the kind of work that I have attempted comes first, and would, for such a theoretical statement to be worth anything, have to be done first.

If Dr Wellek should still insist that I ought, even if I declined to elaborate the philosophy implicit in my assumptions, at any rate to have been more explicit about them, I can only reply that I think I have gone as far in explicitness as I could profitably attempt to go, and that I do not see what would be gained by the kind of explicitness he demands (though I see what is lost by it). ... My whole effort was to work in terms of concrete judgments and particular analyses: 'This – doesn't it? – bears such a relation to that; this kind of thing – don't you find it so? – wears better than that', etc. If I had to generalize, my generalization regarding the relation between poetry and 'direct vulgar living' or the 'actual' would run rather in the following way than in that suggested by Dr Wellek: traditions, or prevailing conventions or habits, that tend to cut poetry in general off from direct vulgar living and the actual, or that make it difficult for the poet to bring into poetry his most serious interests as an adult living in his own time, have a devitalizing effect. But I cannot see that I should have added to the clarity, cogency or usefulness of my book by enunciating such a proposition (or by arguing it theoretically). Again, I did not say that the language of poetry 'should not flatter the singing voice, should not be merely mellifluous', etc. I illustrated concretely in comparison and analysis the qualities indicated by those phrases, pointed to certain attendant limitations, and tried to show in terms of actual poetic history that there were serious disadvantages to be recognized in a tradition that insisted on such qualities as essential to poetry. In fact, though I am very much aware of the shortcomings of my work, I feel that by my own methods I have attained a relative precision that makes this summarizing seem intolerably clumsy and inadequate. ... There is, I hope, a chance that I may in this way have advanced theory, even if I haven't done the theorizing. I know that the cogency and precision I have aimed at are limited; but I believe that any approach involves limitations, and that it is by recognizing them and working within them that one may hope to get something done.

10 JOHN CASEY: 'OBJECT, FEELING AND JUDGEMENT: F. R. LEAVIS'

In Leavis we have a critic who becomes aware of the paradoxes inherent in romantic expressionism, and whose solution is a remarkably interesting synthesis of expressionist and mimetic theories. In his criticism we have the most thoroughgoing attempt to retain, on the one hand, the emphasis on the emotional importance of literature, and yet to provide, on the other, objective criteria for judging the quality of emotion a poem presents. ...

The first thing to be noticed is that Leavis's critical arguments do not characteristically proceed from the particular to the general. ... To assert this at the outset may seem merely dogmatic. It is, after all, very easy to point to some extremely general terms in Leavis's vocabulary – 'life', 'maturity' and so on – which seem to be paradigms or central criteria, the ultimate premises of a critical 'system'. If we deny the premises we are entitled to deny the conclusion. Hence arises the demand that Leavis 'state his premises' in order that we may first understand his particular judgements and secondly that we may be in the position either to accept or reject them. ...

When Leavis describes de la Mare's poetry[1] as predominantly 'glamorous' and 'dream-like' one is tempted, particularly if one admires de la Mare, to retort, 'But what is wrong with the poetry of day-dream?' However, we soon notice that his attitude to 'dream' poetry is more complex than that. ... Leavis is himself trying to distinguish between 'dream' and 'day-dream'. A day-dream is a 'yielding', a shutting off of intelligence. ...

It is easy to see how the groupings are developing; intelligence, self-knowledge, maturity, reality stand together against immaturity, self-dramatization, sentimentality, day-dream, self-indulgence. It is obvious that there is a large set of terms in Leavis's criticism which are closely interrelated, and sometimes even equated. We quickly see what the paradigmatic terms are. ... Leavis's 'key' terms are so thickly interrelated that it is at any rate misleading to talk about his 'premises' – as though 'life', 'maturity', etc. existed in isolation and *a priori*, to be accepted or rejected entirely in their own right. ...

Reprinted from *The Language of Criticism* (London, 1966), pp. 153–77.

Leavis's attitude to expressionism is characterized by a similar tendency to connect apparently distinct concepts. Much of Leavis's critical terminology can be seen in terms of a tension between expressionism and its opposite. Overwhelmingly his language is the sort which normally characterizes an 'expressionist' rather than a 'mimetic' theory of literature. ... Leavis, although finding it natural to use expressionist language, tries to avoid the usual expressionist difficulties, by denying the expressionist distinction between the thing expressed and the expression of it. We may schematize the procedure as follows: the expressionist asserts that 'behind' the words on the page is an emotion or idea which the words express, or for the expression of which the words are a 'medium'. (For a relevant comment see Leavis's 'Tragedy and the Medium'.[2]) This, however, leads to the difficulties I have diagnosed in the earlier chapters. Broadly speaking, there is no way of inferring the 'thing expressed' from the passage which 'expresses' it. One response to the dilemma is to insist that nothing about the author can be inferred from his work. ... Words like 'sincerity' are to be avoided, as are all phrases that have moral overtones. Biographical criticism is impermissible. ...

Another solution is to reduce the 'thing expressed' to the 'expression' of it, and this is something like the position Leavis adopts. It is a position which can easily lead to an extreme formalism, and formalism hardly goes with an emphasis on moral criteria in criticism. ...

We can best begin to illustrate by examining Leavis's attacks upon Milton.

...Milton is using only a small part of the resources of the English language. The remoteness of his poetic idiom from his own speech is to be considered here ... *a man's most vivid emotional and sensuous experience is inevitably bound up with the language that he actually speaks.* [My italics.][3]

Leavis wishes to characterize Milton's defects as failures of intelligence, of awareness. ... C. S. Lewis suggests that he and Dr Leavis 'see the same things' in *Paradise Lost* but 'He sees and hates the very same that I see and love'.[4] ... Leavis is strenuously attempting to make it impossible to see the same things in Milton but value them differently. ... That is, he is trying to 'build in' to his description of Milton's verse terms which, from the very beginning, would be accepted by almost everybody as in some sense 'evaluative'. However – a central point – this *could* be denied. ...

This is not just to say that a critic opposed to Leavis's opinions about Milton could invoke 'the fact/value distinction'. ... Rather he could say something like this: 'I grant Leavis's (or Eliot's or Pound's or Murry's) description of Milton's verse, but I insist that the verse can have all these qualities and still be the vehicle of intelligence, awareness and so on'. ... Leavis's rejoinder is, as I have suggested, to equate the terms. A lack of concrete grasp *is* a failure of imagination, which *is* a failure of intelligence.

But it is in the 'versification' everywhere that the essential inaptitude [for justifying 'the ways of God to men'] appears: *the man who uses words in this way* has (as Mr Eliot virtually says) no 'grasp of ideas' and, whatever he may suppose, *is not really interested in the achievement of precise thought of any kind* ... [My italics.][5]

Enough has now been said to show first how Leavis's 'key' terms are related to each other, and, in connection with this, secondly how the central questions of expressionism are dealt with. We may take, as a final example of this second point, the question of 'sincerity'. To call a poem insincere is not to make an inference to the state of mind of the author, nor is it to say something of the effect on the audience. For instance, an insincere poem may betray a lack of any real interest in the subject it is supposed to be presenting: to show this we may point to the language which may all be on the level of the vaguely emotional cliché with no precision of expression. Such a use of language *cannot* be the sincere expression of genuine feeling, no matter what facts we may discover about the poet's life, his spiritual struggles and so on. The way the poet uses language is the central criterion of how he feels, and the condition of his having certain feelings is his capacity to use language in a certain way. ... But similarly, where the poem is sincere in expression, no facts about the poet can of themselves make it insincere. To use an example of Eliot's, if we discovered that Dante wrote the *De Rerum Natura* as well as the *Divina Commedia*, and that he left notebooks scoffing at religion and ridiculing St Thomas, then we would not know what to say. This would be especially true if none of this new information enabled us to *see* elements of insincerity in the *Divina Commedia* which before we had been blind to. ... But the very difficulty of even imagining with any concreteness such a situation points to what we mean when we say that the sincerity of a poem does not depend upon facts about its author. ...

...I distinguished earlier ... between two ways in which Leavis seeks to compel critical agreement. The first was to connect – practically to equate – the initial description with further descriptions which almost anyone would admit carried pejorative implications of value. The second ... is to equate certain descriptions with certain evaluations: 'and a certain valuing is implicit in the realizing'. But we are now in a position to see that there is really no distinction between these two procedures. For the same scepticism that would permit someone to refuse to call a certain family of activities in which he has just taken part 'evaluating unfavourably' would equally permit him to accept certain descriptions of a poem and yet refuse to call it 'sentimental' or 'morbid' or 'unintelligent'. And the two replies to these moves are, in fact, the same reply. That is, respectively: 'But this just *is* evaluating', and 'But maturity *involves* intelligence'. This is the only way of convicting the denier of contradiction. I have suggested that this may be a move which Leavis makes; it is certainly a move towards which he is tempted when he is trying hardest to convince. ...

The sense in which Leavis has produced a synthesis of mimeticism and expressionism should now be clear. Inner states are essentially expressed and judged in terms of objective qualities; there is no room for essentially private emotions, subjective responses. And in the same way valuing is not the arbitrary addition of an 'attitude' to neutral facts, but is involved in the way we see and know the facts. All this amounts to a rejection of certain presuppositions about 'facts' and 'emotions' which are very deeply ingrained in the empiricist tradition and which have generally dominated critical theory since Wordsworth. For a critic to have arrived at such a theoretical position is a very remarkable achievement.

NOTES

[Reorganised and renumbered from the original]
1. *New Bearings in English Poetry* (London, 1932), pp. 50–6.
2. [Ed.] See *Scrutiny*, 12 (1944–5), 249–60.
3. *Revaluation* (London, 1936), p. 54.
4. *A Preface to Paradise Lost* (Oxford, 1942), p. 130.
5. *The Common Pursuit* (Harmondsworth, 1962), p. 23.

III   HERMENEUTICS

Hermeneutics, the science of interpretation, had its origins in the work of sixteenth-century German theologians. Literary critics tend to regard the German Romantic, Friedrich Schleiermacher (1768–1834) as the first major contributor to modern hermeneutic theory. The basic problem that hermeneutics confronts is that while the words of a text written in the past, such as the Bible, remain constant, the context that produced those words no longer exists. Schleiermacher argued that the purpose of hermeneutics was to reconstruct the original context so that the words of the text could be properly understood. Hermeneutics was further developed later in the nineteenth century by Wilhelm Dilthey (1833–1911), who attempted to found hermeneutics on a more scientific basis for the purpose of studying the 'human sciences', that is, the humanities and the social sciences as opposed to the natural sciences. Hermeneutics would thus focus on 'understanding' (*Verstehen*) rather than on 'explanation' (*Erklären*), which operated in the natural sciences, since in natural science interpretation was directed at the non-human world. In the 'human sciences', in contrast, interpretation was directed at what had been produced by human beings, so that 'understanding' had to operate in order to bring humanly produced objects, such as texts written in the past, to life. Dilthey also confronted the problem of the 'hermeneutic circle', that is, that in order to understand a text one must have a prior idea of its whole meaning, yet one can know the meaning of the whole only through knowing the meaning of its parts. Dilthey believed that this circularity could be overcome by a constant interplay and feedback between the parts and the whole.

A major change in hermeneutic thinking took place in this century as a result of the impact of the philosophy of Martin Heidegger, whose work was a major influence on one of the most important figures in modern hermeneutics, Hans-Georg Gadamer. Gadamer developed Heidegger's contention that the historical and temporal situation of the interpreter can never be excluded from hermeneutics, and thus there is no escape from the hermeneutic circle. In his major work, *Truth and Method*, he argues that the past can be grasped only through relating it to the present. Understanding the past, therefore, involves a 'fusion of horizons' between the text as the embodiment of past experiences and the

45

interests and even prejudices of its interpreter in the present and not, as Schleiermacher and Dilthey believed, the reconstruction of the text's original context in its own terms with the interests and prejudices of its interpreter eliminated as far as possible. Some more recent theorists have, however, gone much further than Gadamer and have argued that hermeneutics should not only reject the view that the purpose of hermeneutics is to restore a text's past meaning in its own terms but should use modern concepts to question and undermine that meaning.

E. D. Hirsch, probably the most important defender of the traditional hermeneutic approach of Schleiermacher and Dilthey, opposes Heidegger and Gadamer because he believes that their form of hermeneutics leads to total relativism. He argues that the interpreter of a text has a moral duty to understand it in relation to its original context. But he seeks to preserve some role for the interests of the interpreter by drawing a distinction between meaning and significance. Whereas the meaning of a text remains constant, its significance will change in relation to the interests of its interpreters.

P. D. Juhl in his book *Interpretation* also favours traditional hermeneutics but unlike Hirsch he does so on a radically intentionalist basis. He argues that we can only begin to interpret a text if we assume that it was created as a result of human intentionality. It is therefore absurd to interpret texts as if they were authorless. What hermeneutics should consist in is the attempt to reconstruct the original author's intention from whatever evidence remains available.

Paul Ricoeur, primarily a philosopher in the phenomenological tradition, but also an important influence on literary critics and theorists, discusses hermeneutics 'as reduction of the illusions and lies of consciousness'. It is, he claims, in this hermeneutic context that the importance of Marx, Nietzsche and Freud for modern thought is to be found. William V. Spanos was the first editor of *boundary 2*, a journal which is committed to a 'destructive' poetics and hermeneutics based on a radical interpretation of Heidegger's phenomenology. He argues that even Derridian deconstructive criticism has not freed itself from the inbuilt tendency of Western thinking to spatialise temporality.

FURTHER READING

E. D. Hirsch Jr, *The Aims of Interpretation* (Chicago, 1976).
——, *Validity in Interpretation* (New Haven, Conn., 1967).

Don Ihde, *Hermeneutic Phenomenology: The Philosophy of Paul Ricoeur* (Evanston, Ill., 1971).

Theodore Kisiel, 'The Happening of Tradition: The Hermeneutics of Gadamer and Heidegger', *Man and World*, 2, 3 (1969), 358–85.

Richard E. Palmer, *Hermeneutics: Interpretation Theory in Schleiermacher, Dilthey, Heidegger, and Gadamer* (Evanston, Ill., 1969).

Paul Ricoeur, *Hermeneutics and the Human Sciences*, ed. and trans. John B. Thompson (Cambridge, 1981).

———, *Interpretation Theory: Discourse and the Surplus of Meaning* (Fort Worth, Texas, 1976).

T. K. Seung, *Semiotics and Thematics in Hermeneutics* (New York, 1982).

William V. Spanos (ed.), *Martin Heidegger and the Question of Literature* (Bloomington, Ind., 1979).

11 HANS-GEORG GADAMER: 'LANGUAGE AS DETERMINATION OF THE HERMENEUTIC OBJECT'

Writing involves self-alienation. Its overcoming, the reading of the text, is thus the highest task of understanding. Even the pure signs of an inscription can be seen properly and articulated correctly only if the text can be transformed back into language. This transformation, however, always establishes ... a relationship to what is meant, to the object that is being spoken about. Here the process of understanding moves entirely in the sphere of a meaning mediated by the linguistic tradition. Thus the hermeneutical task with an inscription starts only after it has been deciphered. Only in an extended sense do non-literary monuments present a hermeneutical task, for they cannot be understood of themselves. What they mean is a question of the interpretation, not of the deciphering and understanding of what they say.

In writing, language gains its true intellectual quality, for when confronted with a written tradition understanding consciousness acquires its full sovereignty. Its being does not depend on anything. Thus reading consciousness is in potential possession of its history. It is not for nothing that with the emergence of a literary culture the idea of 'philology', 'love of speech', was transferred

Reprinted from *Truth and Method*, trans. William Glen-Doepel (London, 1979), pp. 352–7.

entirely to the all-embracing art of reading, losing its original connection with the cultivation of speech and argument. A reading consciousness is necessarily historical and communicates freely with historical tradition. Thus it has some historical justification if, with Hegel, one says that history begins with emergence of a will to hand things down, to make memory last. Writing is not merely chance or extra addition that qualitatively changes nothing in the development of oral tradition. Certainly, there can be a will to make things continue, a will to permanency without writing. But only a written tradition can detach itself from the mere continuance of fragments left over from the life of the past, remnants from which it is possible to reconstruct life.

From the start, the tradition of inscriptions does not share in the free form of tradition that we call literature, inasmuch as it depends on the existence of the remains, whether of stone or whatever material. But it is true of everything that has come down to us that here a will to permanence has created the unique forms of continuance that we call literature. It presents us not only with a stock of memorials and signs. Literature, rather, has acquired its own simultaneity with every present. To understand it does not mean primarily to reason one's way back into the past, but to have a present involvement in what is said. It is not really about a relationship between persons, between the reader and the author (who is perhaps quite unknown), but about sharing in the communication that the text gives us. This meaning of what is said is, when we understand it, quite independent of whether we can gain from the tradition a picture of the author and of whether or not the historical interpretation of the tradition as a literary source is our concern.

Let us here recall that the task of hermeneutics was originally and chiefly the understanding of texts. Schleiermacher was the first to see that the hermeneutical problem was not raised by words alone, but that oral utterance also presented – and perhaps in its fullest form – the problem of understanding. We have outlined above how the psychological dimension that he gave to hermeneutics blocked its historical one. In actual fact, writing is central to the hermeneutical phenomenon, insofar as its detachment both from the writer or author and from a specifically addressed recipient or reader has given it a life of its own. What is fixed in writing has raised itself publicly into a sphere of meaning in which everyone who can read has an equal share.

Certainly, in relation to language, writing seems a secondary phenomenon. The sign language of writing refers back to the actual language of speech. But that language is capable of being written is by no means incidental to its nature. Rather, this capacity of being written down is based on the fact that speech itself shares in the pure ideality of the meaning that communicates itself in it. In writing, this meaning of what is spoken exists purely for itself, completely detached from all emotional elements of expressions and communication. A text is not to be understood as an expression of life, but in what it says. Writing is the abstract ideality of language. Hence the meaning of something written is fundamentally identifiable and reproducible. What is identical in the reproduction is only that which was formulated. This indicates that 'reproduction' cannot be meant here in its strict sense. It does not mean referring back to some original source in which something is said or written. The understanding of something written is not a reproduction of something that is past, but the sharing of a present meaning.

Writing has the methodological advantage that it presents the hermeneutical problem in all its purity, detached from everything psychological. What is, however, in our eyes and for our purposes a methodological advantage is at the same time the expression of a specific weakness that is characteristic of writing even more than of language. The task of understanding is seen with particular clarity when we recognise this weakness of all writing. We need only to think again of what Plato said, namely that the specific weakness of writing was that no one could come to the aid of the written word if it falls victim to misunderstanding, intentional or unintentional. ...

All writing is, as we have said, a kind of alienated speech, and its signs need to be transformed back into speech and meaning. Because the meaning has undergone a kind of self-alienation through being written down, this transformation back is the real hermeneutical task. The meaning of what has been said is to be stated anew, simply on the basis of the words passed on by means of the written signs. In contrast to the spoken word there is no other aid in the interpretation of the written word. Thus the important thing here is, in a special sense, the 'art' of writing. The spoken word interprets itself to an astonishing degree, by the way of speaking, the tone of voice, the tempo etc., but also by the circumstances in which it is spoken. ...

All writing claims that it can be awakened into spoken language, and this claim to autonomy of meaning goes so far that even an authentic reading, e.g. the reading of a poem by the poet, becomes questionable if the direction of our listening takes us away from what our understanding should really be concerned with. ... What is stated in the text must be detached from all contingent factors and grasped in its full ideality, in which alone it has validity. Thus, precisely because it entirely detaches the sense of what is said from the person saying it, the written word makes the reader, in his understanding of it, the arbiter of its claim to truth. The reader experiences in all its validity what is addressed to him and what he understands. What he understands is always more than an alien meaning: it is always possible truth. This is what emerges from the detachment of what is spoken from the speaker and from the permanence that writing bestows. This is the deeper hermeneutical reason for the fact ... that it does not occur to people who are not used to reading that what is written down could be wrong, since, anything written seems to them like a document that is self-authenticating.

Everything written is, in fact, in a special way the object of hermeneutics. What we found in the extreme case of a foreign language and the problems of translation is confirmed here by the autonomy of reading: understanding is not a psychic transposition. The horizon of understanding cannot be limited either by what the writer had originally in mind, or by the horizon of the person to whom the text was originally addressed.

It sounds at first like a sensible hermeneutical rule, generally recognised as such, that nothing should be put into a text that the writer or the reader could not have intended. But this rule can be applied only in extreme cases. For texts do not ask to be understood as a living expression of the subjectivity of their writers. This, then, cannot define the limits of a text's meaning. However, it is not only the limiting of the meaning of a text to the 'actual' thoughts of the author that is questionable. Even if we seek to determine the meaning of a text objectively by seeing it as a contemporary document and in relation to its original reader, as was Schleiermacher's basic procedure, such limitation is a very chancy affair. The idea of the contemporary addressee can claim only a restricted critical validity. For what is contemporaneity? Listeners of the day before yesterday as well as of the day after tomorrow are always among those to whom one speaks as a contemporary. Where are we to draw the line that excludes a reader from being addressed? What are contemporaries and what is a text's claim to truth in the face of this multifarious mixture of past and future? The idea of the original reader is full of unexamined idealisation.

Furthermore, our concept of the nature of literary tradition contains a fundamental objection to the hermeneutical legitimisation of the idea of the original reader. We saw that literature is defined by the will to hand on. But a person who copies and passes on is doing it for his own contemporaries. Thus the reference to the original reader, like that to the meaning of the author, seems to offer only a very crude historico-hermeneutical criterion which cannot really limit the horizon of a text's meaning. What is fixed in writing has detached itself from the contingency of its origin and its author and made itself free for new relationships. Normative concepts such as the author's meaning or the original reader's understanding represent in fact only an empty space that is filled from time to time in understanding.

12 E. D. Hirsch, Jr: 'Three Dimensions of Hermeneutics'

Stated bluntly, the nature of interpretation is to construe from a sign-system (for short, 'text') something more than its physical presence. That is, the nature of a text is to mean whatever we construe it to mean. I am aware that theory should try to provide normative criteria for discriminating good from bad, legitimate from illegitimate constructions of a text, but mere theory cannot change the nature of interpretation. Indeed, we need a norm precisely because the nature of a text is to have no meaning except that which an interpreter wills into existence. We, not our texts, are the makers of the meanings we understand, a text being only an occasion for meaning, in itself an ambiguous form devoid of the consciousness where meaning abides. One meaning of a text can have no higher claim than another on the grounds that it derives from the 'nature of interpretation', for all interpreted meanings are ontologically equal; they are all equally read. ... This ontological equality of all interpreted meaning shows forth in the fact that hermeneutic theory has sanctioned just about every conceivable norm of legitimacy in interpretation. From this historical fact I infer that interpretive norms are not really derived from theory, and that theory codifies *ex post facto* the interpretive norms we already prefer. ...

...Under Schleiermacher's canon, no text can legitimately mean at a later time what it could not have meant originally, but logic alone hardly supports this inference. The medieval interpreters were well aware that Homer and Vergil had been pagans

Reprinted from *New Literary History*, 3 (1971–2), 246–60.

who could not consciously have intended or communicated Christian meanings. The exegetes of the Middle Ages implicitly held to another principle which can be stated as follows: 'Everything in a given text which requires fuller interpretation need *not* be explained and determined exclusively from the linguistic domain common to the author and his original public.' Which principle is logically the more compelling, this implicit medieval one, or that of Schleiermacher? The answer is easy. The medieval principle is logically stronger because self-evidently a text can mean anything it has been understood to mean. If an ancient text has been interpreted as a Christian allegory, that is unanswerable proof that it can be so interpreted. Thus, the illegitimacy of anachronistic allegory, implied by Schleiermacher's canon, is deduced neither from empirical fact nor logic. His norm of legitimacy is not, of course, deduced at all; it is chosen. It is based upon a value-preference, and not on theoretical necessity. His preference for original meaning over anachronistic meaning is ultimately an ethical choice. I would confidently generalize from this example to assert that the normative dimension of interpretation is always in the last analysis an ethical dimension. ...

If the normative dimension of hermeneutics belongs, as I have argued, to the domain of ethical choice, is it nevertheless possible to discover truly universal principles of the sort Schleiermacher envisioned, principles that do not depend on the value-preferences of individual interpreters? Is there in hermeneutics an analytical dimension which, in contrast to the normative, is logically deductive, empirically descriptive, and neutral with respect to values and ethical choices?. ...

One example of a purely descriptive theoretical conception, and one that seems to me potentially fruitful is the distinction between meaning and significance. When I first proposed this distinction my motivation was far from neutral; I equated meaning simply with original meaning, and I wished to point up the integrity and permanence of original meaning.[1] This earlier discussion I now regard as being only a special application of a conception that is in principle universal. For the distinction between meaning and significance (and the clarifications it provides) is not limited to instances where meaning is equated with the author's original meaning; it holds as well for any and all instances of 'anachronistic meaning'.[2]

This universality in the distinction is readily seen if meaning is defined *tout court* as that which a text is taken to represent. No normative limitations are imported into the definition, since under it, meaning is simply meaning-for-an-interpreter. Moreover, the definition does not (and did not in my earlier discussion) limit itself merely to a paraphrasable or translatable 'message', but embraces every aspect of representation, including the typographical and phonemic, which an interpreter construes. My earlier definition of meaning was too narrow and normative only in that it restricted meaning to those constructions where the interpreter is governed by his conception of the author's will. The enlarged definition now comprises constructions where authorial will is partly or totally disregarded.

The important feature of meaning as distinct from significance is that meaning is the determinate representation of a text for an interpreter. An interpreted text is always taken to represent something, but that something can always be related to something else. Significance is meaning-as-related-to-something-else. If an interpreter did not conceive a text's meaning to be *there* as an occasion for contemplation or application, he would have nothing to think or talk about. Its there-ness, its self-identity from one moment to the next allows it to be contemplated. Thus, while meaning is a principle of stability in an interpretation, significance embraces a principle of change. Meaning-for-an-interpreter can stay the same although the meaningfulness (significance) of that meaning can change with the changing contexts in which that meaning is applied. ... Meaning is what an interpreter actualizes from a text; significance is that actual speaking as heard in a chosen and variable context of the interpreter's experiential world. ...

I have dwelt on meaning and significance because I believe this purely analytical distinction can help resolve some of the disagreements in hermeneutics, particularly certain disagreements involving the concept of historicity. This concept belongs to a third dimension of hermeneutics – the metaphysical. Adherents to Heidegger's metaphysics take the view that all attempts accurately to reconstruct past meanings are doomed to failure since not just our texts but also our understandings are historical. ... Interpreters make the best of our historicity not by reconstructing an alien world from our texts but by interpreting them within our own world and making them speak to us. ...

It is a notable irony that Heidegger's metaphysics itself depends upon a purely analytical principle taken directly from hermeneutic theory – namely the hermeneutic circle. This principle holds that the process of understanding is necessarily circular, since we cannot know a whole without knowing some of its constituent parts, yet we cannot know the parts as such without knowing the whole which determines their functions. (This principle can be easily grasped by self-consciously construing a sentence.) In *Sein und Zeit*, Heidegger expands the circumference of the hermeneutic circle beyond textual interpretation to embrace all knowing. ... We cannot escape the fact that our historical world is a pre-given of our experience and is therefore constitutive of any textual interpretation.

This generalized version of the hermeneutic circle seems at first glance to support the position that accurate reconstruction of past meaning is impossible. It is futile to project ourselves into the historical past where our texts arose, since our own present world is already pre-given in our attempted projection. Our reconstruction can never be authentic because we can never exclude our own world through which alone the past was disclosed. If Heidegger's version of the hermeneutic circle is correct, it follows that the traditional aims of historical scholarship are largely illusory.

The direct application of this metaphysical argument to textual interpretation seems to be premature on at least two grounds. First, the metaphysical principle says nothing about subtle questions of degree. It argues that some degree of anachronism is necessarily present in any historical reconstruction, but as to whether a particular reconstruction is severely or trivially compromised the principle says nothing. ...

The second and more important objection to carrying Heidegger's metaphysics directly into the theory of interpretation is that his expanded version of the hermeneutic circle is in crucial respects probably wrong. The principle of the hermeneutic circle does not lead inevitably to dogmatic historical skepticism. If an interpretation is grounded in the interpreter's entire *Welt*, it will no doubt be different from any past meaning, since undoubtedly a person's entire spiritual world will be different from any that existed in the past. Yet it is open to question whether the whole that prestructures meaning must be conceived in this comprehensive way. The very introduction of 'historicity' as a chief characteristic of *Welt* means that a boundary has been drawn, since historicity is not the chief component of a person's spiritual world. It is, rather, a limited domain of shared cultural experience apart from the bigger domain of unshared experience that makes up a person's world. The Heideggerian concept of *Welt* is at times undistinguishable from what used to be called *Zeitgeist*, and is just as problematical as the earlier concept. To limit the circumference of *Welt* (after having insisted upon its expansion) at the vague boundary between shared and private experience is entirely arbitrary. ...

If one resists confusing meaning and significance one gets the impression that most controversies in interpretation do not really involve a conflict over original meaning versus anachronistic meaning. Usually the debates can be readily transposed into disagreement over the proper *emphasis* of an interpretation, over whether it is better to explain original meaning or to bring out some aspect of the significance of meaning, for the interpreter or for present-day readers. ...

But the ethical problem is not to be solved quite that simply. Even if some interpretive disagreements turn out to reside in choice of emphasis rather than choice of meaning, still a choice of emphasis is ultimately an ethical choice. Many of us have felt at one time or other a distinct preference for anachronistic over original meaning, although nothing in the analytical or metaphysical dimension of hermeneutics compels us to choose one over the other. ... It is not rare that anachronistic meaning on *some* ground or other is undoubtedly the best meaning.

Therefore, let me state what I consider to be a fundamental ethical maxim for interpretation, a maxim that claims no privileged sanction from metaphysics or analysis, but only from general ethical tenets, generally shared. *Unless there is a powerful overriding value in disregarding an author's intention (i.e. original meaning), we who interpret as a vocation should not disregard it.* Mere individual preference would not be such an overriding value, nor would be the mere preferences of many persons. The possible exception is mentioned only because every ethical maxim requires such an escape clause. (Example: unless there is a powerful overriding value in lying, a person should tell the truth. Yet there are times when a lie is ethically better than to tell the truth, so the maxim cannot be an absolute one.) Similarly, one might fudge on original meaning for the sake of young, impressionable children, and so on. But except in these very special cases there is a strong ethical presumption against anachronistic meaning. When we simply use an author's words for our own purposes without respecting his intention, we transgress what Charles Stevenson in another context called 'the ethics of language', just as we transgress ethical norms when we use another person merely for our own ends. Kant held it to be a foundation of moral action that men should be conceived as ends in themselves, and not as instruments of other men. This imperative is transferable to the words of men because speech is an extension and expression of men in the social domain, and also because when we fail to conjoin a man's intentions to his words we lose the soul of speech, which is to convey meaning and to understand what is intended to be conveyed.

I am not impressed with the view that this ethical imperative of speech, to which we all submit in ordinary discourse, is not applicable to written speech or, in particular, to literary texts. No literary theorist from Coleridge to the present has succeeded in formulating a viable distinction between the nature of ordinary written speech and the nature of literary written speech. ... Moreover, if it is seen that there is no viable distinction between 'literature' and other classifications of written speech, it will also come to be recognized that the ethics of language hold good in all language, oral and written, in poetry as well as in philosophy. All are ethically governed by the intentions of the author. To treat an author's words merely as grist for one's own mill is ethically analogous to using another man merely for one's own purposes. I do not say such ruthlessness of interpretation is never justifiable in principle, but I cannot imagine an occasion where it would be justifiable in the professional practice of interpretation.

NOTES

[Reorganised and renumbered from the original]
1. The structure of this distinction I owe to the writings of Husserl and Frege, whose influence I acknowledge in the earlier piece alluded to, 'Objective Interpretation', *PMLA*, 75 (Sept. 1960).
2. This is a shorthand, not a pejorative term which comprises all non-authorial meaning, whether or not such meaning was possible within 'the linguistic domain common to the author and his original public'. I use the term in preference to 'non-authorial meaning' because the chief disputes have centered, as Schleiermacher's canon suggests, on the question of historicity. Either term would serve.

13   P. D. JUHL: 'THE APPEAL TO THE TEXT: WHAT ARE WE APPEALING TO?'

When we appeal to the text in support of an interpretation, we also invoke some general criterion such as, most commonly, coherence or, less frequently, complexity. We say that the text, or a certain part of the text, supports this interpretation rather than that because under the former the text is more coherent, or more complex, than under the latter.

Consider an example based on the following poem by Wordsworth.

> A slumber did my spirit seal;
>   I had no human fears:
> She seemed a thing that could not feel
>   The touch of earthly years.
>
> No motion has she now, no force;
>   She neither hears nor sees.
> Rolled round in earth's diurnal course,
>   With rocks, and stones, and trees.

One might argue that the words 'in earth's diurnal course' which qualify 'rolled round' suggest that the woman's motion is relatively 'slow and gentle ... since one revolution takes twenty-four hours' and that it is 'an orderly motion, since it follows a simple circular path'.[1] One might claim, therefore, that on the assumption that 'rolled round' connotes slow and gentle motion, the line is more coherent than on the assumption that the woman is 'being whirled about'[2] – that is, that the words 'rolled round' connote 'violent motion'.[3] I shall not argue for or against this claim; rather, I shall try to show what it involves.

Let us call the interpretation according to which the words 'rolled round' suggest slow and gentle motion I_1, and the interpretation according to which they connote violent motion I_2. The question then is: What could it mean to say that on I_1, the line is more coherent than on I_2? Someone defending I_1 might say: 'On the assumption that I_2 is correct, it would be odd that the phrase

Reprinted from *Interpretation: An Essay in the Philosophy of Literary Criticism* (Princeton, NJ, 1980), pp. 69–76.

"rolled round" should be qualified by words which suggest slow and gentle motion rather than by words suggesting violent motion'. In other words, what is being claimed is that I_1, but not I_2, *can account for* the fact that 'rolled round' is qualified by words connoting gentle motion rather than by words which would suggest that the woman is being violently whirled about. As Beardsley has put it: 'A proposed explication may be regarded as a hypothesis that is tested by its capacity to account for the greatest quantity of data in the words of the poem...'[4]

What, then, is the explanation which I_1 provides for the fact – let us call it f – that 'rolled round' is qualified by the words 'in earth's diurnal course'? It is this: On the assumption that 'rolled round' connotes slow and gentle motion, it would be natural or plausible to suppose that the phrase is qualified by the words 'in earth's diurnal course' *because* they are an appropriate means to suggest a slow and gentle motion. ...

Now suppose that the poem I have quoted above is not in fact by Wordsworth but has been accidentally typed out by a monkey randomly depressing keys on a typewriter. (Or suppose that we found the lines as marks – on, say, a large rock – produced by water erosion.) It is immediately obvious that we can no longer say that the words 'in earth's diurnal course' – rather than some other words which suggest violent motion – qualify 'rolled round' *because* they are an appropriate means to suggest gentle motion (or because they suggest gentle motion). We can no longer explain f in functional terms at all, in terms of some purpose for which the words 'in earth's diurnal course' are an appropriate linguistic means. All we can now say is: The words 'in earth's diurnal course' rather than some other words, qualify 'rolled round' because the monkey just happened to hit that series of keys there (or because the water just happened to erode the rock in such a way that those marks, rather than some others, were produced there).

Consequently, given any interpretation (I), it would not be possible for I to account for f more adequately than any other interpretation; that is, on no interpretation of the words 'rolled round' could we understand any more or any less than on any other interpretation of those words why they should be qualified by 'in earth's diurnal course' rather than by some other words. No matter what interpretation we choose, *there could be nothing odd*, on that interpretation, about the fact that 'in earth's diurnal course' qualifies 'rolled round'; for regardless of which interpretation we assume, it would simply be an 'accident' that 'rolled round' is qualified by the words 'in earth's diurnal course' rather than being followed by a meaningless jumble of letters.

What is odd (when there is something odd) on the assumption that I_2, is correct – that 'rolled round' connotes violent motion – is not that the words 'in earth's diurnal course' qualify the phrase 'rolled round', but that *the author* should have *used them to qualify* (or in qualifying) the phrase 'rolled round'; for that is the only relevant difference between the 'poem' produced by the monkey or by water erosion and the poem written by Wordsworth. Thus only if the words 'in earth's diurnal course' have been used to qualify 'rolled round', only if the qualification is the result of a person's (intentional) action, could it be odd on I_2 that the latter words are qualified by the former. Hence it is logically possible for I_1 to account more adequately than I_2 for f only if f is the result of a person's action, only if what is to be accounted for is the fact that *the author used* the words 'in earth's diurnal course' to qualify 'rolled round'. ...

These considerations shed light on what it is to say that 'rolled round' connotes gentle motion. For the only kind of explanation appropriate to the fact to be accounted for (a person's use of certain words rather than others) is an explanation referring to the agent's (the author's) motive, reason, purpose, or intention. ...

Hence the fact that the words 'in earth's diurnal course' connote, or are an appropriate means to suggest, gentle motion could in principle explain f (that the author used them to qualify 'rolled round') only under the assumption that *the author had a certain purpose or intention.* Thus if it is logically possible for an interpretation of 'rolled round' to provide this kind of explanation of f, an explanation in terms of the function for which the words 'in earth's diurnal course' are appropriate, then that interpretation must be, or logically imply, a statement about the author's intention. ...

Furthermore, it cannot plausibly be argued that what we are concerned with is only what the *speaker*, not the author, means. For the question 'Why, if I_2 is correct and "rolled round" connotes violent motion, is that phrase qualified by "in earth's diurnal course", rather than by words suggesting violent motion?' is clearly a request for an explanation, not (or not just) of the speaker's action, but of the author's. Moreover, would it make sense to suppose that a 'poem' (that is, the corresponding physical marks) produced by water erosion has a speaker?...

I have argued that unless an interpretation is a statement about the author's intention, it cannot in principle account for f. To what extent can we generalize from this example? It is clear, I think, that what I have shown for f holds for any textual feature which can be described in terms of what the author has done. This is fairly obvious for facts about the use of language in a work – that, for example, a certain event is described in terms of such-and-such imagery, that a certain sentence is in the passive, or that it is in the subjunctive, that this word, rather than such-and-such a word, occurs here, or that a certain word is in a curious position, and so on. For by the same argument I have given above one can easily show that an interpretation can account for such facts only if it is a statement about the author's intention.

NOTES

[Reorganised and renumbered from the original]

1. Monroe Beardsley, *The Possibility of Criticism* (Detroit, 1970), p. 46.

2. Cleanth Brooks, 'Irony as a Principle of Structure', in *Literary Opinion in America*, ed. Morton D. Zabel (New York, 1951), p. 736.

3. Ibid.

4. Monroe Beardsley, *Aesthetics: Problems in the Philosophy of Criticism* (New York, 1958), p. 145.

14 PAUL RICOEUR: 'THE CONFLICT OF INTERPRETATIONS'

The difficulty – it initiated my research in the first place – is this: there is no general hermeneutics, no universal canon for exegesis, but only disparate and opposed theories concerning the rules of interpretation. The hermeneutic field, whose outer contours we have traced, is internally at variance with itself.

I have neither the intention nor the means to attempt a complete enumeration of hermeneutic styles. The most enlightening course, it seems to me, is to start with the polarized opposition that creates the greatest tension at the outset of our investigation. According to the one pole, hermeneutics is understood as the manifestation and restoration of a meaning addressed to me in the manner of a message, a proclamation, or as is sometimes said,

Reprinted from *Freud and Philosophy: An Essay on Interpretation*, trans. Denis Savage (New Haven, Conn., 1970), pp. 26–35.

a kerygma; according to the other pole, it is understood as a demystification, as a reduction of illusion. Psychoanalysis, at least on a first reading, aligns itself with the second understanding of hermeneutics.

From the beginning we must consider this double possibility: this tension, this extreme polarity, is the truest expression of our 'modernity'. The situation in which language today finds itself comprises this double possibility, this double solicitation and urgency: on the one hand, purify discourse of its excrescences, liquidate the idols, go from drunkenness to sobriety, realize our state of poverty once and for all; on the other hand, use the most 'nihilistic', destructive, iconoclastic movement so as to *let speak* what once, what each time, was *said*, when meaning appeared anew, when meaning was at its fullest. Hermeneutics seems to me to be animated by this double motivation: willingness to suspect, willingness to listen; vow of rigor, vow of obedience. In our time we have not finished doing away with *idols* and we have barely begun to listen to *symbols*. It may be that this situation, in its apparent distress, is instructive: it may be that extreme iconoclasm belongs to the restoration of meaning. ...

Over against interpretation as restoration of meaning we shall oppose interpretation according to what I collectively call the school of suspicion. A general theory of interpretation would thus have to account not only for the opposition between two interpretations of interpretation, the one as recollection of meaning, the other as reduction of the illusions and lies of consciousness; but also for the division and scattering of each of these two great 'schools' of interpretation into 'theories' that differ from one another and are even foreign to one another. This is no doubt truer of the school of suspicion than of the school of reminiscence. Three masters, seemingly mutually exclusive, dominate the school of suspicion: Marx, Nietzsche, and Freud. It is easier to show their common opposition to a phenomenology of the sacred, understood as a propaedeutic to the 'revelation' of meaning, than their interrelationship within a single method of demystification. It is relatively easy to note that these three figures all contest the primacy of the object in our representation of the sacred, as well as the fulfilling of the intention of the sacred by a type of analogy of being that would engraft us onto being through the power of an assimilating intention. It is also easy to recognize that this contesting is an exercise of suspicion in three different ways; 'truth as lying' would be the negative heading under which one might place these three exercises of suspicion. But we are still far from having assimilated the positive meaning of the enterprises of these three thinkers. ...

If we go back to the intention they had in common, we find in it the decision to look upon the whole of consciousness primarily as 'false' consciousness. They thereby take up again, each in a different manner, the problem of the Cartesian doubt, to carry it to the very heart of the Cartesian stronghold. The philosopher trained in the school of Descartes knows that things are doubtful, that they are not such as they appear; but he does not doubt that consciousness is such as it appears to itself; in consciousness, meaning and consciousness of meaning coincide. Since Marx, Nietzsche, and Freud, this too has become doubtful. After the doubt about things, we have started to doubt consciousness.

These three masters of suspicion are not to be misunderstood, however, as three masters of skepticism. They are, assuredly, three great 'destroyers'. But that of itself should not mislead us; destruction, Heidegger says in *Sein und Zeit*, is a moment of every new foundation, including the destruction of religion, insofar as religion is, in Nietzsche's phrase, a 'Platonism for the people'. It is beyond destruction that the question is posed as to what thought, reason, and even faith still signify.

All three clear the horizon for a more authentic word, for a new reign of Truth, not only by means of a 'destructive' critique, but by the invention of an art of *interpreting*. Descartes triumphed over the doubt as to things by the evidence of consciousness; they triumph over the doubt as to consciousness by an exegesis of meaning. Beginning with them, understanding is hermeneutics: henceforward, to seek meaning is no longer to spell out the consciousness of meaning, but to *decipher its expressions*. What must be faced, therefore, is not only a threefold guile. If consciousness is not what it thinks it is, a new relation must be instituted between the patent and the latent; this new relation would correspond to the one that consciousness had instituted between appearances and the reality of things. For Marx, Nietzsche, and Freud, the fundamental category of consciousness is the relation hidden-shown or, if you prefer, simulated-manifested. ... What is essential is that all three create with the means at hand, with and against the prejudices of their times, a *mediate* science of meaning, irreducible to the immediate *consciousness* of meaning. What all three attempted, in different ways, was to make their 'conscious' methods of deciphering coincide with the 'unconscious' *work* of ciphering which they attributed to the will to power, to social being, to the unconscious psychism. *Guile will be met by double guile.*

Thus the distinguishing characteristic of Marx, Freud, and Nietzsche is the general hypothesis concerning both the process of false consciousness and the method of deciphering. The two go together, since the man of suspicion carries out in reverse the work of falsification of the man of guile. Freud entered the problem of false consciousness via the double road of dreams and neurotic symptoms; his working hypothesis has the same limits as his angle of attack, which was ... an economics of instincts. Marx attacks the problem of ideologies from within the limits of economic alienation, now in the sense of political economy. Nietzsche, focusing on the problem of 'value' – of evaluation and transvaluation – looks for the key to lying and masks on the side of the 'force' and 'weakness' of the will to power.

Fundamentally, the *Genealogy of Morals* in Nietzsche's sense, the theory of ideologies in the Marxist sense, and the theory of ideals and illusions in Freud's sense represent three convergent procedures of demystification.

Yet there is perhaps something they have even more in common, an underlying relationship that goes even deeper. All three begin with suspicion concerning the illusions of consciousness, and then proceed to employ the stratagem of deciphering; all three, however, far from being detractors of 'consciousness', aim at extending it. What Marx wants is to liberate *praxis* by the understanding of necessity; but this liberation is inseparable from a 'conscious insight' which victoriously counterattacks the mystification of false consciousness. What Nietzsche wants is the increase of man's power, the restoration of his force; but the meaning of the will to power must be recaptured by mediating on the ciphers 'superman', 'eternal return', and 'Dionysus', without which the power in question would be but worldly violence. What Freud desires is that the one who is analyzed, by making his own the meaning that was foreign to him, enlarge his field of consciousness, live better, and finally be a little freer and, if possible, a little happier. ...

This last reference to Freud's 'reality principle' and to its equivalents in Nietzsche and Marx – eternal return in the former, understood necessity in the latter – brings out the positive benefit of the ascesis required by a reductive and destructive interpretation: confrontation with bare reality, the discipline of Ananke, of necessity.

While finding their positive convergence, our three masters of suspicion also present the most radically contrary stance to the phenomenology of the sacred and to any hermeneutics understood as the recollection of meaning and as the reminiscence of being.

15 WILLIAM V. SPANOS: 'BREAKING THE CIRCLE: HERMENEUTICS AS DIS-CLOSURE'

Martin Heidegger's phenomenological de-struction (*Destruktion*) of the Western onto-theo-logical tradition has shown that modern philosophy from Descartes to Kant, Hegel, and Nietzsche, in completing the imperatives of a metaphysical or 'logocentric' (and representational) concept of truth, constitutes the 'end of philosophy'.[1] Simultaneously, in disclosing the temporality of being which the *logos* as Word or Presence encloses, i.e., covers over and forgets, his destruction of the tradition points to a hermeneutics of being which is capable of the 'surpassing of metaphysics' (*Überwindung*), a post-modern hermeneutics of dis-covery, in which a dis-closed temporality is given ontological priority over Being.[2] What I wish to suggest in this essay is that a destruction or – in Jacques Derrida's more recent, and, in literary studies, more familiar term – deconstruction of the Western literary/critical tradition will reveal an analogous significance: that the American New Criticism (and its recent extension in French Structuralism), in aestheticizing the literary text or, what really is the same thing, in coercing the experience of the text into a metaphysical hermeneutic framework, constitutes the completion of the Western literary tradition and thus the 'end of criticism'. To put it in a more immediate way, it will suggest that Modernist criticism, in fulfilling the traditional formal imperative to *see* the work of literary art from the *end* – i.e., as an autonomous and inclusive object or, in the phrase adopted by most recent critics to characterize 'Modern' literature, as a spatial form[3] – has 'accomplished' the forgetting of the processual nature and thus the temporal/historical being – the be-ing – of the experience it projects.

As Derrida has suggested in his deconstruction of Heidegger's thought, Heidegger's late quest for originary language – 'the one word' – tends to reappropriate the metaphysics he intended to overcome. His 'hermeneutic' project in the essays on poetry, language, and thought, therefore, does not suggest an interpretive method radical enough to accomplish the task of breaking out of the impasse – the enclosure – into which the New Critical and Structuralist formalism has driven modern literary studies. It is,

Reprinted from *boundary 2*, 5 (1977), pp. 421–48.

rather, his existential analytic in *Being and Time*, by which (through its hermeneutical violence) he intends to gain access into being, that points to a hermeneutics of literature commensurate with the crisis of contemporary criticism. In retrieving or, what is the same thing, in dis-covering the temporality of being that a recollective metaphysics covers over and forgets, it points to a hermeneutics of literature equivalent in its potentialities to that inhering in the open-ended post-Modern literature, which, in its iconoclasm, its breaking of closed form, is attempting to release time from form and being from Being and thus to activate the being of the reader as being-in-the-world. The quest for a new hermeneutics, therefore, requires a rethinking of Heidegger's existential analytic. This analytic, it must be remembered throughout, is a project in fundamental ontology, not in ethics. It is intended not to reveal the moral limitations of man but to provide access into the *Seinfrage*, the being question or, better, the question of what it means to be.

In thus drawing this analogy between Western literature and Western philosophy, I am, it will be seen, in significant disagreement with Paul de Man's influential fundamental assumption – derived from Nietzsche's notion of art as the will to power and Derrida's apotheosis of writing over speech (*écriture* over *parole*) – about the literary tradition: that *literary* texts, unlike critical texts – and myths – have never been self-deceived: that they have always been 'fictional', i.e., characterized by a deliberate 'play' that consciously takes the void and the radical differences between sign and meaning, language and empirical reality, for granted. Indeed, this essay is implicitly an effort to bring this assumption, which might be called a mystification of literary texts in reverse into question, not to revalorize the authorless, the logocentric myth, but to demystify the literary text and the text of the literary tradition for the sake of hermeneutic dialogue. ...

...What Heidegger discovers ... is that the Western ontotheological tradition, from Plato and St Thomas to Descartes, Kant, Hegel, Nietzsche, and modern science, has been essentially a *metaphysical* tradition, in which, according to its familiar medieval formulation, essence precedes (is ontologically prior to) existence. ... As such, it has been a tradition that has reified being, transformed verbal being into nominal Being, into a super thing (*summum ens*) at rest, which contains and determines all other things (*Seiende*), thus 'relegating becoming to the realm of the apparent'.[4]...

This fundamental disclosure of Heidegger's phenomenological destruction of the ontotheological tradition has, of course, often been noted. What needs to be thematized, however, especially in the context of the question of the relation between Heidegger's thought and the Western literary tradition and its hermeneutics, is that *this reification of existence is a spatialization of time or, as the etymology of 'metaphysics' clearly suggests, constitutes a coerced metamorphosis of temporality into image or picture, i.e., an aesthetic structure the model or prototype of which is the plastic or architectonic – visual – arts.* It is no accident, as Heidegger implies, that the Western tradition has valued the eyes over the other senses ever since Plato gave them ontological priority. ...

To put it succinctly, then, Heidegger's destruction of the Western ontotheological tradition discovers that its metaphysical orientation manifests itself in a coercive 'permanentizing' of being (*Bestandsicherung*), and this discovery reveals the platonic reality to be appearance, *eidos* (Idea), to be, in fact an *eidolon*, an idol or image. In 'seeing' existence *meta-ta-physika*, in grounding temporal existence in *presence*, the beginning and the middle in the *end*, being in *Being*, the tradition's spatialization of time, we may add, *assumes its ultimate iconic form in the auto-telic and inclusive circle, whose center is the logos as presence.* Put in terms of this extension of the destruction, the assumption by the tradition of the ontological priority of Being over temporality recalls, of course, Plato's abiding circular image of history ('The Great Year').[5] ... But it also evokes the circular image of time and history of Modernists like Yeats, Joyce, Proust, Woolf, and Eliot (and of the 'new' critics, who modelled their poetics on it) – and, by contrast, the essential strategy of the postmodern literary imagination: the formal effort by contemporary writers like Sartre, Ionesco, Beckett, William Carlos Williams, and Charles Olson to break out of the symbolic circle. In so doing it also makes explicit the logocentric parallel between the philosophic and literary traditions and suggests in what sense both are 'coming to the end'.

In spatializing time, the metaphysical perspective closes off the possibilities of existence and thus transforms the hermeneutic process into a vicious circle. The metaphysical is a genealogical perspective, the circle of which provides a spatial 'insight' that at the same time shuts off – 'blinds' – the interpreter to the more primordial and problematic temporality of being. ...

...Indeed, it is precisely the historical hardening of the impulse to spatialize time and the consequent 'forgetting' of the primordial temporality of the being of the literary text that constitutes the 'Western literary tradition' ... Modernism – and especially its critical/hermeneutic counterpart, i.e., the New Criticism and, more recently, Structuralism – can be seen to constitute a 'fulfillment' – and end – of the Western literary tradition analogous to that arrived at by modern philosophy. ...

...We begin to understand ... that the New Critical and Structuralist assumption that a poem is an *object (Seiendes)* or, to put it in terms of its best known formulation, that 'A poem should not mean/But *be*',[6] demands a hermeneutics which begins the interpretive process from the end – meta-ta-physika – and thus a methodological suspension, a *making present* or *presenting*, of the temporality of a text (its words) similar to that demanded by the metaphysical orientation of the Western ontotheological tradition. ...

Thus, like its philosophical counterpart, the 'objective' or 'disinterested' hermeneutics of Modernism inevitably becomes, from a destructive phenomenological standpoint, a privileged 'awaiting which forgets', a 'deliberative' or 'calculating' awaiting, which, grounded as it is in *certain* expectation that the 'whole picture' will emerge tends to coerce a temporal medium into an 'inclusive' object or a closed circle, and thus *closes off*, becomes 'blind' to, the possibility of a more original – a phenomenological – understanding of the text, whether particular work or the tradition – an understanding that is, in which meaning would be infinitely open. ... To be truer to *Being and Time*, perhaps, the reification of language, the transformation of words into image, by the mystified logocentric hermeneutics of Modernist criticisms – The New Criticism, the myth criticism of Northrop Frye, the 'phenomenological' criticism of consciousness of Georges Poulet, and the structuralism of Todorov and Barthes – closes off the possibility of *hearing* the temporality of words, in which the real 'being' of a literary text inheres. ...

... According to a phenomenological hermeneutics, then, it is not, as it has been 'from ancient times', the static, presentational – and coercive – language of assertion that constitutes the 'locus of truth'.[7] It is, rather, the *kinetic, explorative – and generous – language* of human speech, i.e., not the mystified orality of the Word of mythic man that Derrida restricts speech to but the always potential 'dialogic' process, which, in being temporal, precludes a definitive revelation of any being. ...

Further, as I have been trying to suggest, temporal reading of particular texts must constitute the first stage, the beginning, the *point de départ*, of that destruction or deconstruction of the Western literary tradition which promises the paradoxically liberating double retrieval (*Wiederholen*). I mean the dis-covering not only of texts 'buried' in and by the hardened tradition (i.e., their 'meaning' for us in the present), but also of a stance before the

Western literary tradition, especially as it has been formulated by the ontotheological New Critics and Structuralists, that opens up the possibility of a perpetually new – a postModern or an authentically modern – literary history, a history that, in focusing on dis-closure, both validates the inexhaustibility of literary texts (i.e., literary history as misreading) and commits literature to the difficult larger task of 'overcoming metaphysics' – a history, in other words, that puts literature at the service of being rather than being at the service of literature. ...

...The literary application of the Derridian version of Heidegger's destruction, i.e., deconstruction, has indeed yielded provocative and fruitful initial results concerning the question of literary history. However ... it is subject to significant error – or blindness – in interpretation and even lends itself to willful misreading *because it continues to begin the hermeneutic process from the end, i.e., to ground its deconstruction of the tradition on an unexamined tendency to read particular historical texts or oeuvres spatially.* ...

It is, further – and more important – this spatializing tendency in reading particular texts that seems also to blind de Man to the essentially mystified nature of the imaginative literature of the Western tradition – to the pervasive teleological structure, the logocentricism of literary texts from Sophocles to the 'Modern' period – and thus leads him to conclude that literature has never been self-deceived, that it begins with an awareness 'that sign and meaning can never coincide',[8] that it 'knows and names itself as fiction' (CC, 18), that in other words, in imaginative literature 'the human self has experienced the void within itself and the invented fiction, far from filling the void, asserts itself as a pure nothingness, our nothingness stated and restated by a subject that is the agent of its own instability' (CC, 19), and that, finally, 'as knowing and naming itself as fiction', it is 'demystified from the start' (CC, 18) and thus not in need of deconstruction.

Temporal reading, that is, dis-covers phenomenologically that, like the philosophical and historiological texts in the ontotheological tradition, the literary text in the history of Western literature has, by and large – and increasingly until quite recently – been intent on holding a mirror up to one form of logocentric metaphysical universe or another. And it has done this not as de Man insists, to create 'fiction' that, aware of the 'presence of nothingness', 'names this void with ever-renewed understanding' (CC, 18), but, like myth, to mediate, i.e., to spatialize immediate temporal experience for the purpose of securing its readers' always flagging faith in the logocentric order of that experience.

To put it another way, temporal reading discovers that Western literature has by and large existed to fulfill, to certify and strengthen, the teleological expectations (the logocentric hermeneutics) of the readers, not to demystify them. This, in fact, is the *essential* testimony of postmodern literature at large – of the fiction of Beckett, Robbe-Grillet, Barth, Pynchon; of the drama of Ionesco and Pinter; and of the poetry of Wallace Stevens, William Carlos Williams, and Charles Olson – a literature that in playing havoc with both the sense of an ending (i.e., linear narrative) and of symbolic form (circular narrative), exists primarily to deconstruct and demystify the logocentric or, as I prefer to put it, spatialized literary texts of the tradition, especially its Modernist allotrope, and thus to deconstruct, to phenomenologically reduce by violence, the traditional privileged logocentric or spatial frame of reference of the modern reader.

NOTES

[Reorganised and renumbered from the original]
1. Martin Heidegger, *The End of Philosophy*, trans. Joan Stambaugh (New York, 1973).
2. I use the conventional capitalization only when I refer to the word 'Being' as a substantive, i.e., as it is understood by the Western ontotheological tradition.
3. See Joseph Frank, 'Spatial Form in Modern Literature', *Sewanee Review*, 53 (1945), 221–40, 433–45, 643–65; reprinted in *The Widening Gyre: Crisis and Mastery in Modern Literature* (New Brunswick, NJ, 1963), pp. 3–62.
4. Theodore Kisiel, 'Translator's Introduction' to Werner Marx, *Heidegger and the Tradition* (Evanston, Ill., 1971), p. xxiv.
5. [Ed.] See Plato's *Timaeus*.
6. This passage is, of course, from Archibald MacLeish's 'Ars Poetica' (1926), which may have its source in I. A. Richards' statement that 'it is never what a poem says that matters, but what it is'. Quoted in Cleanth Brooks, *Modern Poetry and the Tradition* (New York, 1965), p. 48. (My emphasis)
7. Martin Heidegger, *Being and Time*, trans. John Macquarrie and Edward Robinson (New York, 1962), pp. 33, 196.
8. Paul de Man, 'Criticism and Crisis', *Blindness and Insight: Essays in the Rhetoric of Contemporary Criticism* (New York, 1971), p. 17. Further references to this essay will be abbreviated as CC and incorporated in the text.

IV LINGUISTIC CRITICISM

Linguistics has had a major impact on twentieth-century literary theory, primarily through the influence of the Swiss linguist, Ferdinand de Saussure (1857–1913). Saussure argued that linguistics should move from a diachronic study of language, that is, how language develops historically, to a synchronic study, that is, treating language as a system within one temporal plane. He divided language into 'langue', the underlying system that governs linguistic usage, and 'parole', how language is actually used in practice. The basis of 'langue' is that words are arbitrary signs in that the relation between a word and what it signifies is arbitrary, that is, almost entirely determined by convention. What determines meaning is not that a word refers to the world or to ideas or concepts that exist outside of language; it is the differences between linguistic signs themselves that create meaning. Saussure's shift of linguistic emphasis to language as a signifying system paralleled developments in formalistic criticism and his work has been most influential on those who favour a formalist approach.

Roman Jakobson, a central figure in both Russian Formalism and Prague Structuralism, in his later career developed a theory of literature that had its basis in linguistics. He believes that the difference between the poetic and the non-poetic is fundamentally a linguistic question and can therefore be described in linguistic terms. Poetry does not have unique linguistic attributes but is distinguished from non-poetry by the fact that the dominant focus is on the message for its own sake and not on such factors as what the message refers to or its effect on the person to whom it is addressed. Jakobson's poetics is founded on the Saussurian linguistic principle that language as a system is governed by two relationships: the syntagmatic – the relations between linguistic elements in sequence and combination – and the paradigmatic – the vertical plane of language which creates the differential relations between words of the same type, so that 'cat' in any sentence differs from 'dog' or 'fish' or any word that could be substituted for it. Jakobson's famous but compressed definition of the poetic function is based on this distinction between syntagmatic and paradigmatic: 'The poetic function projects the principle of equivalence from the axis of selection into the axis of combination.' In poetry, unlike other forms of language use, syntagmatic relations are interpreted as if they are paradigmatic. That is, the horizontal relations of language have to be considered as if they are vertical. One therefore considers the relationships between the words of a poem in a non-linear, differential way, as if they existed together in the one temporal plane.

Other linguistic approaches have also influenced literary criticism. Roger Fowler criticises Jakobson's theory because of its formalist bias and its lack of social dimension. In 'Literature as Discourse' he makes use of the work of M. A. K. Halliday and of speech-act theory to formulate an alternative linguistic approach to that of Jakobson.

FURTHER READING

Jonathan Culler, *Saussure* (London, 1976).

Roger Fowler, *Linguistic Criticism* (Oxford, 1986).

Roman Jakobson and Morris Halle, *Fundamentals of Language* (The Hague, 1956).

David Lodge, *The Modes of Modern Writing: Metaphor, Metonymy, and the Typology of Modern Literature* (London, 1977). (Applies Jakobsonian theory to prose texts.)

Mary Louise Pratt, *Toward a Speech Act Theory of Literary Discourse* (Bloomington, Indiana, 1977).

Ferdinand de Saussure, *Course in General Linguistics*, trans. Roy Harris (London, 1983).

16 ROMAN JAKOBSON: 'LINGUISTICS AND POETICS'

I have been asked for summary remarks about poetics in its relation to linguistics. Poetics deals primarily with the question, *What makes a verbal message a work of art?* Because the main subject of poetics is the *differentia specifica* of verbal art in relation to other arts and in relation to other kinds of verbal behavior, poetics is entitled to the leading place in literary studies.

Poetics deals with problems of verbal structure, just as the analysis of painting is concerned with pictorial structure. Since linguistics is the global science of verbal structure, poetics may be regarded as an integral part of linguistics. ...

Reprinted from 'Closing Statement: Linguistics and Poetics', in *Style in Language*, ed. Thomas Sebeok (Cambridge, Mass., 1960), pp. 350–9.

Literary studies, with poetics as their focal portion, consist like linguistics of two sets of problems: synchrony and diachrony. The synchronic description envisages not only the literary production of any given stage but also that part of the literary tradition which for the stage in question has remained vital or has been revived. Thus, for instance, Shakespeare on the one hand and Donne, Marvell, Keats, and Emily Dickinson on the other are experienced by the present English poetic world, whereas the works of James Thomson and Longfellow, for the time being, do not belong to viable artistic values. The selection of classics and their reinterpretation by a novel trend is a substantial problem of synchronic literary studies. Synchronic poetics, like synchronic linguistics, is not to be confused with statics; any stage discriminates between more conservative and more innovatory forms. Any contemporary stage is experienced in its temporal dynamics, and, on the other hand, the historical approach both in poetics and in linguistics is concerned not only with changes but also with continuous, enduring, static factors. A thoroughly comprehensive historical poetics or history of language is a superstructure to be built on a series of successive synchronic descriptions. ...

Language must be investigated in all the variety of its functions. Before discussing the poetic function we must define its place among the other functions of language. An outline of these functions demands a concise survey of the constitutive factors in any speech event, in any act of verbal communication. The ADDRESSER sends a MESSAGE to the ADDRESSEE. To be operative the message requires a CONTEXT referred to ('referent' in another, somewhat ambiguous, nomenclature), seizable by the addressee, and either verbal or capable of being verbalized; a CODE fully, or at least partially, common to the addresser and addressee (or in other words, to the encoder and decoder of the message); and, finally, a CONTACT, a physical channel and psychological connection between the addresser and the addressee, enabling both of them to enter and stay in communication. All these factors, inalienably involved in verbal communication may be schematized as follows:

CONTEXT

ADDRESSER   MESSAGE   ADDRESSEE

....

CONTACT

CODE

Each of these six factors determines a different function of language. Although we distinguish six basic aspects of language, we could, however, hardly find verbal messages that would fulfill only one function. The diversity lies not in a monopoly of some one of these several functions but in a different hierarchical order of functions. The verbal structure of a message depends primarily on the predominant function. But even though a set (*Einstellung*) towards the referent, an orientation towards the CONTEXT – briefly the so-called REFERENTIAL, 'denotative', 'cognitive' function – is the leading task of numerous messages, the accessory participation of the other functions in such messages must be taken into account by the observant linguist.

The so-called EMOTIVE or 'expressive' function, focused on the ADDRESSER, aims a direct expression of the speaker's attitude towards what he is speaking about. It tends to produce an impression of a certain emotion whether true or feigned; therefore, the term 'emotive', launched and advocated by Marty[1] has proved to be preferable to 'emotional'. The purely emotive stratum in language is presented by the interjections. They differ from the means of referential language both by their sound pattern (peculiar sound sequences or even sounds elsewhere unusual) and by their syntactic role (they are not components but equivalents of sentences). '*Tut! Tut!* said McGinty': the complete utterance of Conan Doyle's character consists of two suction clicks. The emotive function, laid bare in the interjections, flavors to some extent all our utterances, on their phonic, grammatical, and lexical level. If we analyze language from the standpoint of the information it carries, we cannot restrict the notion of information to the cognitive aspect of language. ...

Orientation toward the ADDRESSEE, and the CONATIVE function, finds its purest grammatical expression in the vocative and imperative, which syntactically, morphologically, and often even phonemically deviate from other nominal and verbal categories. The imperative sentences cardinally differ from declarative sentences: the latter are and the former are not liable to a truth test. When in O'Neill's play *The Foundation*, Nano '(in a fierce tone of command)', says 'Drink!' – the imperative cannot be challenged by the question 'is it true or not?' which may be, however, perfectly well asked after such sentences as 'one drank', 'one will drink', 'one would drink'. In contradistinction to the imperative sentences, the declarative sentences are convertible into interrogative sentences: 'did one drink?' 'will one drink?' 'would one drink?'

The traditional model of language as elucidated particularly by Bühler[2] was confined to these three functions – emotive, conative, and referential – and the three apexes of this model – the first person of the addresser, the second person of the addressee, and the 'third person', properly – someone or something spoken of. ... We observe, however, three further constitutive factors of verbal communication and three corresponding functions of language.

There are messages primarily serving to establish, to prolong, or to discontinue communication, to check whether the channel works ('Hello, do you hear me?'), to attract the attention of the interlocutor or to confirm his continued attention ('Are you listening?' or in Shakespearean diction, 'Lend me your ears!' and on the other end of the wire 'Um-Hum!'). This set for CONTACT, or in Malinowski's terms PHATIC function,[3] may be displayed by a profuse exchange of ritualized formulas, by entire dialogues with the mere purport of prolonging communication. Dorothy Parker caught eloquent examples: '"Well!" the young man said. "Well!" she said. "Well, here we are," he said. "Here we are," she said, "Aren't we?" "I should say we were," he said, "Eeyop! Here we are." "Well!" she said. "Well!" he said, "well".' The endeavor to start and sustain communication is typical of talking birds; thus the phatic function of language is the only one they share with human beings. It is also the first verbal function acquired by infants; they are prone to communicate before being able to send or receive informative communication.

A distinction has been made in modern logic between two levels of language, 'object language' speaking of objects and 'metalanguage' speaking of language. But metalanguage is not only a necessary scientific tool utilized by logicians and linguists; it plays also an important role in our everyday language. ... Whenever the addresser and/or the addressee need to check up whether they use the same code, speech is focused on the CODE: it performs a METALINGUAL (i.e., glossing) function. ...

We have brought up all the six factors involved in verbal communication except the message itself. The set (*Einstellung*) toward the MESSAGE as such, focus on the message for its own sake, is the POETIC function of language. This function cannot be productively studied out of touch with the general problems of language, and, on the other hand, the scrutiny of language requires a thorough consideration of its poetic function. Any attempt to reduce the sphere of poetic function to poetry or to confine poetry to poetic function would be a delusive oversimplification. Poetic function is not the sole function of verbal art but only its dominant, determining function, whereas in all other verbal activities it acts as a subsidiary, accessory constituent. This function, by promoting the palpability of signs, deepens the fundamental dichotomy of signs and objects. Hence, when dealing with poetic function, linguistics cannot limit itself to the field of poetry. ...

As we said, the linguistic study of the poetic function must overstep the limits of poetry, and, on the other hand, the linguistic scrutiny of poetry cannot limit itself to the poetic function. The particularities of diverse poetic genres imply a differently ranked participation of the other verbal functions along with the dominant poetic function. Epic poetry, focused on the third person, strongly involves the referential function of language; the lyric, oriented toward the first person, is intimately linked with the emotive function; poetry of the second person is imbued with the conative function and is either supplicatory or exhortative, depending on whether the first person is subordinated to the second one or the second to the first.

Now that our cursory description of the six basic functions of verbal communication is more or less complete, we may complement our scheme of the fundamental factors by a corresponding scheme of the functions:

REFERENTIAL

EMOTIVE   POETIC   CONATIVE
               PHATIC

METALINGUAL

What is the empirical linguistic criterion of the poetic function? In particular, what is the indispensable feature inherent in any piece of poetry? To answer this question we must recall the two basic modes of arrangement used in verbal behavior, *selection* and *combination*. If 'child' is the topic of the message, the speaker selects one among the extant, more or less similar, nouns like child, kid, youngster, tot, all of them equivalent in a certain respect, and then, to comment on this topic, he may select one of the semantically cognate verbs – sleeps, dozes, nods, naps. Both chosen words combine in the speech chain. The selection is produced on the base of equivalence, similarity and dissimilarity, synonymity and antonymity, while the combination, the build up of the sequence, is based on contiguity. *The poetic function projects the principle of equivalence from the axis of selection into the axis of combination.* Equivalence is promoted to the constitutive device of the sequence. In poetry one syllable is equalized with any other syllable of the same sequence; word stress is assumed to equal word stress, as unstress equals unstress; prosodic long is matched with long, and short with short; word boundary equals word boundary, no boundary equals no boundary; syntactic pause equals syntactic pause, no pause equals no pause. Syllables are converted into units of measure, and so are morae or stresses.

It may be objected that metalanguage also makes a sequential use of equivalent units when combining synonymic expressions into an equational sentence: $A=A$ (*'Mare* is *the female of the horse'*). Poetry and metalanguage, however, are in diametrical opposition to each other: in metalanguage the sequence is used to build an equation, whereas in poetry the equation is used to build a sequence.

In poetry, and to a certain extent in latent manifestations of poetic function, sequences delimited by word boundaries become commensurable whether they are sensed as isochronic or graded. ... Without its two dactylic words the combination *'innocent bystander'* would hardly have become a hackneyed phrase. The symmetry of three disyllabic verbs with an identical initial consonant and identical final vowel added splendor to the laconic victory message of Caesar: *'Veni, vidi, vici'*.

Measure of sequences is a device which, outside of poetic function, finds no application in language. Only in poetry with its regular reiteration of equivalent units is the time of the speech flow experienced, as it is – to cite another semiotic pattern – with musical time. Gerard Manley Hopkins, an outstanding searcher in the science of poetic language, defined verse as 'speech wholly or partially repeating the same figure of sound'. Hopkins' subsequent question, 'but is all verse poetry?' can be definitely answered as soon as poetic function ceases to be arbitrarily confined to the domain of poetry. Mnemonic lines cited by Hopkins (like 'Thirty days hath September'), modern advertising jingles, and versified medieval laws, mentioned by Lotz, or finally Sanscrit scientific treatises in verse which in Indic tradition are strictly distinguished from true poetry (*kavya*) – all these metrical texts make use of poetic function without, however, assigning to this function the coercing, determining role it carries in poetry. Thus verse actually exceeds the limits of poetry, but at the same time verse always implies poetic function. ...

To sum up, the analysis of verse is entirely within the competence of poetics, and the latter may be defined as that part of linguistics which treats the poetic function in its relationship to the other functions of language. Poetics in the wider sense of the word deals with the poetic function not only in poetry, where this function is superimposed upon the other functions of language, but also outside of poetry, when some other function is superimposed upon the poetic function.

NOTES

[Reorganised and renumbered from the original]
1. A. Marty, *Untersuchungen zur Grundlegung der allgemeinen Grammatik und Sprachphilosophie*, Vol. (Hallen, 1908).
2. K. Bühler, 'Die Axiomatik der Sprachwissenschaft', *Kant-Studien* 38, 19–90 (Berlin, 1933).
3. B. Malinowski, 'The Problem of Meaning in Primitive Languages', in C. K. Ogden and I. A. Richards, *The Meaning of Meaning* (New York, 1953), pp. 296–336.

17 ROGER FOWLER: 'LITERATURE AS DISCOURSE'

Adopting a linguistic approach to literature, as I do, it is tempting to think of and describe the literary text as a *formal* structure, an object whose main quality is its distinctive syntactic and phonological shape. This is a common approach, adopted by, for instance, the most famous of the linguistic stylisticians, Roman Jakobson.[1] It also happens to agree with the dominant formalist tendency of the more conservative schools of modern criticism. I argue that linguistic formalism is of limited significance in literary studies, and educationally restrictive. As an alternative I shall employ some linguistic techniques which emphasize the *interactional* dimensions of texts. To treat literature as discourse is to see the text as mediating relationships between language-users: not only relationships of speech, but also of consciousness, ideology, role and class. The text ceases to be an object and becomes an action or process.

This anti-formalist approach is pretty much at odds with received opinion in conventional literary aesthetics. Among my heresies, from this point of view, are willingness for literary works to be kinetic; denial of their alleged formal autonomy; acceptance

Reprinted from *Literature as Social Discourse: The Practice of Linguistic Criticism* (London, 1981), pp. 80–94.

of the relevance of truth-values to literature. It is not my purpose in this paper to argue a collision of linguistics and aesthetics, however – as I said, my immediate object is methodological. Furthermore, I shall assert, without offering any formal justification, one other assumption implicit in my position – that is, that no plausible essentialist or intrinsic definition of literature has been or is likely to be devised. For my purpose, no such theory is necessary. What literature is, can be stated empirically, within the realm of sociolinguistic fact. It is an open set of texts, of great formal diversity, recognised by a culture as possessing certain institutional values and performing certain functions. (Of course, 'recognition' in this context doesn't mean that members of the society are capable of describing these values and functions accurately or willing to acknowledge them truthfully.) The values are neither universal, though they are subject to a small range of types of historical explanation, nor stable, although they change slowly. They derive from the economic and social structures of particular societies, and I am sure you can think of any number of Marxist and historicist interpretations which illustrate the causal process to which I refer. My aim here is not to promulgate Marxist explanations, but to suggest that once we start looking at literature as a part of social process then texts are opened to the same kinds of causal and functional interpretations as are found in the sociology of language generally.

Now I must talk a little bit about linguistic metatheory. It is obvious that my approach requires what might be called a 'functional' theory of language. Not all schools of linguistics pay any attention to linguistic functions, to the various kinds of work language performs in actual communicative situations. ... A functional grammar would be concerned to pose and answer the question *why* languages like English provide a choice between *John threw the ball* and *The ball was thrown by John* as different ways of talking about the same event. One explanation seems to be that active and passive equivalents tend to be used in texts and situations with different information structures. *John threw the ball* seems an appropriate answer to the question 'What did John do?' whereas *The ball was thrown by John* responds to 'What happened to the ball?' Also, it has been suggested that the passive provides for deletion of agency in descriptions of transitive events – *The ball was thrown, The window was broken.* Such deletion could occur for any of a number of reasons: anonymity, impersonality, mystification, ignorance. It is clear that a rich set of motivations could be supplied for the active/passive choice, that it is not a case of arbitrary syntactic variation. Similarly, the functionalist would claim, all other aspects of linguistic structure are to be explained by reference to their communicative purposes. This is the position of the Prague linguistic school and of the English linguist M. A. K. Halliday.[2] ... Halliday posits three functions, which he calls *ideational, interpersonal* and *textual.* The ideational function has to do with the transmission of a world-view, a structuring of experience; the interpersonal, with communicative intercourse, the establishment and maintenance of personal and group relationships; the textual, with the completeness and shape of a communicative unit, a text or utterance, within its context of situation. Textually, we recognise that a piece of language is a well-formed communication rather than inconsequential gibberish; interpersonally, that it is addressed by our interlocutor to us, that it is a question or an assertion, etc., that it signals the interlocutor's status relative to us, and so on; ideationally, that this discourse is a series of propositions conveying structured judgements on some topic or topics. Each of these functions relates to some definite aspects of language structure. The ideational func-tion explains such structural features as the distinction between nouns and predicates, the semantics of quantification, logical connectives between propositions, etc. ...

Note that Halliday's three functions of language are conceived of as *simultaneous,* not *alternative:* any complete piece of language working in a communicative context is structured to serve all three needs. ... I. A. Richards's 'two uses of language', 'scientific' versus 'poetic', otherwise 'referential' versus 'emotive', provide an excellent example of the absurdity of exclusively alternative general functions.[3] A purely scientific, inexpressive language is as absurd as a contentless poem of total expression. And I don't think it helps to make it a relative, more-or-less, choice, as Roman Jakobson tries to do. ...

Despite his concession that no linguistic event obeys only one function of language, Jakobson's theory implies a potent suppression of functions other than the one chosen for designating a particular text or corpus. The practical analyses of poetry which he has published bear out this impression. Jakobson has decided that poetry is dominated by phonetic and syntactic features of repetition, parallelism and antithesis, and his analyses concentrate on the way these features contribute to the concreteness, perceptibility, of the texts discussed. Other aspects of language are neglected. ... I think it is clear that Jakobson's concentration on formal structure is determined not by the nature of the material but by his decision to treat it in such a way. This decision has its causes and its consequences. The causes I would locate historically in Jakobson's own intellectual maturation during the high period of European modernism, and, more specifically, Russian formalism. Jakobson's definition of literature is in fact a way of looking at literature which reflects the classicist and formalist goals of the precisely historical culture within which he was educated. The consequences of his definition are to perpetuate the value of that culture, to insist that literature is a contained quiet, socially unresponsive object outside of history.

One can see the attraction of these values to a society which favours stability and closure above change and openness. Such predilections are prominent in both Jakobson's culture and our own. But our culture is also – as Jakobson's was also – a society of verbal violence – advertising, abuse, rant – and verbal intimacy – the solidarity of shared class languages. To define literature as patterned form is to cover one's ears against the presence of these actional and kinetic potentialities in all language. Literature isn't exempt from language's general responsibility to work in the real world of conflicts and sympathies. Being language, literature can't shed its interpersonal function. The theorist and critic, obeying his ideology, may choose (without knowing he is choosing) to downgrade the interpersonal in favour of the less committing formal-textual-poetic function. I choose, perhaps for equally ideological reasons, to redress the balance by drawing attention to the inevitable and important interpersonal-interactional-discursive dimension of literary texts.

I now make my way towards analysis by way of a little more theory. John Searle's revision of Austin's speech acts is relevant to my thesis. ...[4] Austin divided speech acts into performative and constative utterances, and concentrated on the latter. Searle, though still much interested in performative speech acts like promising, maintains what seems to be the correct general position, namely, that every utterance is simultaneously three language acts. It is a locutionary act, that is, an utterance in the words and sounds of English, French, etc.; it is a propositional act, i.e. it attributes a property to a referent outside of language; and it is an illocutionary act, e.g. an act of stating, promising, questioning, marrying, or whatever. ...

... As far as literary criticism is concerned, the priority is to investigate the implications of both marked and, particularly, unmarked illocutionary determinants of the discourse structure of texts. ... To give a quick example of my own ... consider William Blake's poem *Tyger*. The text is dense with morphological and punctuational indicators of illocutionary actions – exclamations and questions – so a speech act approach is *prima facie* appropriate. Application of the Austin–Searle theory is immediately rewarded. Felicity conditions are obviously and functionally broken. In general, the requirement of a normal communicative channel is not fulfilled. You can't expect a civil answer if you put questions to a tiger, and if you don't expect an answer, it is arguable that you are not asking a question at all. There are also more specific infelicities; the speaker asks, among other things:

> What the hammer? what the chain?
> In what furnace was thy brain?
> What the anvil? what dread grasp
> Dare its deadly terrors clasp?

No creature, cat or man, can be expected to give a reliable first-hand report on the circumstances of its creation. These unanswerable questions bounce off the tiger towards the implied reader of the poem, and so a discourse is established. The reader recognises rhetorical questions which are really directed to persuading him of the error and the inscrutability of power and beauty. Speech act theory in this case initiates a formal explanation of our recognition of the force of the question, our creative disorientation in the face of a battery of infelicitous illocutions. These facts about illocution (which could be elaborated) do not take the critic very far towards an interpretation, but an understanding of them is prerequisite to interpretation. ...

I will sum up very briefly. I have tried to demonstrate the value of analysing texts in a way which differs from the emphasis on objective, formal structure found in received literary education, and which yet stays close to actual regularities of language. A text is treated as a *process*, the communicative interaction of implied speakers and thus of consciousnesses and of communities. So we focus on those features of language – usually suppressed in criticism – which signal the interaction of consciousnesses, the awareness by a speaker of the voice of another. The consequences of this approach, for literary criticism, are very considerable. Literature seen as discourse is inevitably *answerable, responsible;* it cannot be cocooned from an integral and mobile relationship with society by evasive critics' strategies such as 'implied author', 'persona', 'fiction'; or 'stasis', 'objectivity', 'depersonalization', 'tradition'. This is *not* to deny the applicability of such concepts in the analysis of literature, of course; only, to demand that they should not be invoked as compositional principles setting literature aloof from other communicative transactions.

NOTES

[Notes reorganised and renumbered from the original]
1. See Jakobson's 'Closing Statement: Linguistics and Poetics'; Jakobson and Claude Lévi-Strauss, 'Les Chats de Charles Baudelaire', *L'Homme*, 2, 5–21; Jakobson and L. Jones, *Shakespeare's Verbal Art in 'Th'Expence of Spirit'* (The Hague, 1970).
2. M. A. K. Halliday, 'Language Structure and Language Function' in *New Horizons in Linguistics*, ed. John Lyons (Harmondsworth, 1970), pp. 140–65.
3. I. A. Richards, *Principles of Literary Criticism* (London, 1924), Ch. 34.
4. J. L. Austin, *How To Do Things With Words* (London, 1962); John R. Searle, *Speech Acts* (London, 1969).

V STRUCTURALISM AND SEMIOTICS

Structuralism rose to prominence in France through the application by the French anthropologist, Claude Lévi-Strauss, of Saussurian structural linguistics to the study of such phenomena as myths, rituals, kinship relations, eating conventions. (For a discussion of Saussure, see the introduction to 'Linguistic Criticism'.) These were understood as signifying systems and therefore open to a linguistic type of analysis in which attention was focused not on empirical or functional matters but on myth or ritual as a set of relations in which meaning was created by differences between signifying elements. This use of language as a model for understanding aspects of reality that are predominantly non-linguistic in character established structuralism, particularly in the 1960s, as a powerful alternative to positivistic or empiricist methods of analysis.

Literature seemed especially appropriate to a structuralist approach since it was wholly made up of language. Thus structuralist literary criticism tends to emphasise the system of conventions which makes literature possible and to attach little importance to authorial or historical considerations or to questions of meaning or reference. As language from a Saussurian point of view is seen as a signifying system in which the relations between the elements that make up the system are crucial, so literature could also be seen as embodying systematic sets of rules and codes which enable literature to signify. By considering literary texts as 'paroles' which must be understood in relation to 'langue' or the underlying signifying system, structuralist literary criticism inevitably concerned itself predominantly with poetics as a general science of literature. Individual texts were used mainly to exemplify general characteristics of literature as a whole.

Semiotics is closely related to structuralism. The term 'semiotic' was coined in the late nineteenth century by the American pragmatist philosopher, C. S. Peirce (1839–1914), to denote 'the formal doctrine of signs', and Saussure in his *Cours de Linguistique Générale* (1915) argued that linguistics was only part of a general science of signs, which he called semiology. The terms are more or less interchangeable. The basis of semiotics is the sign, that is, any configuration to which there is a conventionalised response. Not only are languages and communication systems such as morse code constituted by signs but, radical semioticians would argue, the world itself as it relates to the human mind consists entirely of signs since there can be no unmediated relationship with reality. Semiotics investigates the various systems of signs that create the shared meanings that constitute any culture. Language being the fundamental sign system for human beings, non-verbal signs such as gestures, forms of dress, numerous conventionalised social practices like eating, can be seen as akin to language in that they are constituted by signs which take on meaning and communicate by virtue of the relations between signs.

Tzvetan Todorov and Gérard Genette are most associated with structuralism as poetics as can be seen in the selections from their work reprinted here. The most famous structuralist critic was Roland Barthes though Barthes gradually moved away from a strictly structuralist position, as later works such as S/Z indicate. His article 'Science versus Literature' exemplifies the overwhelming emphasis on language which structuralism ushered in. Jonathan Culler, a critic whose strongest sympathies are with structuralism, has attempted to continue structuralist criticism in the post-structuralist era by reformulating it in semiotic terms. He argues that a semiotics of literature should concern itself with the signifying practices and interpretative conventions that make it possible for literary texts to communicate with readers. Literary criticism should concern itself not with literary meaning as such but with how that meaning is produced. There is obvious continuity between this concept of semiotics and structuralism's concern with poetics.

An interesting development in recent literary theory was the emergence in the Soviet Union of critics and theorists who restored links with Russian Formalism, formalist criticism having been forbidden during the Stalinist period. Yury M. Lotman of the Tartu school of semiotics is generally seen as the most important of these theorists. His concept of semiotics develops particularly the work of Bakhtin and the Prague structuralists. He argues that literary texts have to be seen as doubly coded. They are part of natural language and can be decoded accordingly, but as soon as a text is categorised as literary numerous supplementary codes come into operation. Morse Peckham is a theorist in the American pragmatist tradition of semiotics that would include – in addition to Peirce – G. H. Mead and Charles Morris. Though he adopts the radical position that the meaning of a sign is any response to it whatsoever, he nevertheless holds that the only tenable form of literary interpretation is historical and philological in basis.

FURTHER READING

Structuralism

Roland Barthes, *Critical Essays*, trans. Richard Howard (Evanston, Ill., 1972).

Jonathan Culler, *Barthes* (London, 1983).

———, *Structuralist Poetics: Structuralism, Linguistics and the Study of Literature* (London, 1975).

Jacques Ehrmann (ed.), *Structuralism* (New York, 1970).

Terence Hawkes, *Structuralism and Semiotics* (London, 1977).

Fredric Jameson, *The Prison-House of Language: A Critical Account of Structuralism and Russian Formalism* (Princeton, NJ, 1972).

Michael Lane (ed.), *Structuralism: A Reader* (London, 1970).

Robert Scholes, *Structuralism in Literature: An Introduction* (New Haven, Conn., 1974).

Susan Sontag (ed.), *A Barthes Reader* (London, 1972).

John Sturrock (ed.), *Structuralism and Since: From Lévi-Strauss to Derrida* (Oxford, 1979).

Semiotics

Umberto Eco, *The Role of the Reader: Explorations in the Semiotics of Texts* (Bloomington, Indiana, 1979).

Julia Kristeva, *Desire in Language: A Semiotic Approach to Literature and Art* (Oxford, 1980).

Yury M. Lotman, *The Analysis of the Poetic Text*, trans. D. B. Johnson (Ann Arbor, Mich., 1976).

L. M. O'Toole and Ann Shukman (eds), *Russian Poetics in Translation* (Colchester), Vols 2, 3, 6, 8.

Morse Peckham, *Romanticism and Ideology: Essays and Addresses, 1971–80* (Greenwood, Fl., 1985).

Michael Riffaterre, *Semiotics of Poetry* (Bloomington, Indiana, 1978).

Robert Scholes, *Semiotics and Interpretation* (New Haven, Conn., 1982).

Ann Shukman, *Literature and Semiotics: A Study of the Writings of Yu. M. Lotman* (Amsterdam, 1977).

18   TZVETAN TODOROV: 'DEFINITION OF POETICS'

To understand what poetics is, we must start from a general and of course a somewhat simplified image of literary studies. It is unnecessary to describe actual schools and tendencies; it will suffice to recall the positions taken with regard to several basic choices. Initially there are two attitudes to be distinguished: one sees the literary text itself as a sufficient object of knowledge; the other considers each individual text as the manifestation of an abstract structure. (I herewith disregard biographical studies, which are not literary, as well as journalistic writings, which are not 'studies'.) These two options are not, as we shall see, incompatible; we can even say that they achieve a necessary complementarity; nonetheless, depending on whether we emphasize one or the other, we can clearly distinguish between the two tendencies.

Let us begin with a few words about the first attitude, for which the literary work is the ultimate and unique object, and which we shall here and henceforth call *interpretation*. Interpretation, which is sometimes also called *exegesis, commentary, explication de texte, close reading, analysis,* or even just *criticism* (such a list does not mean we cannot distinguish or even set in opposition some of the terms), is defined, in the sense we give it here, by its aim, which is *to name the meaning of the text examined.* This aim forthwith determines the ideal of this attitude – which is to make the text itself speak; i.e., it is a fidelity to the object, to the *other*, and consequently an effacement of the subject – as well as its drama, which is to be forever incapable of realizing *the* meaning, but only *a* meaning subject to historical and psychological contingencies. This ideal, this drama will be modulated down through the history of commentary, itself coextensive with the history of humanity.

In effect, it is impossible to interpret a work, literary or otherwise, for and in itself, without leaving it for a moment, without projecting it elsewhere than upon itself. Or rather, this task is possible, but then description is merely a word-for-word repetition of the work itself. It espouses the forms of the work so closely that the two are identical. And, in a certain sense, every work constitutes its own best description. ...

Reprinted from *Introduction to Poetics*, trans. Richard Howard (Brighton, 1981), pp. 3–11.

If *interpretation* was the generic term for the first type of analysis to which we submit the literary text, the second attitude remarked above can be inscribed within the general context of *science*. By using this word, which the 'average literary man' does not favor, we intend to refer less to the degree of precision this activity achieves (a precision necessarily relative) than to the general perspective chosen by the analyst: his goal is no longer the description of the particular work, the designation of its meaning, but the establishment of general laws of which this particular text is the product.

Within this second attitude, we may distinguish several varieties, at first glance very remote from one another. Indeed, we find here, side by side, psychological or psychoanalytic, sociological or ethnological studies, as well as those derived from philosophy or from the history of ideas. All deny the autonomous character of the literary work and regard it as the manifestation of laws that are external to it and that concern the psyche, or society, or even the 'human mind'. The object of such studies is to transpose the work into the realm considered fundamental: it is a labor of decipherment and translation; the literary work is the expression of 'something', and the goal of such studies is to reach this 'something' through the poetic code. Depending on whether the nature of this object to be reached is philosophical, psychological, sociological, or something else, the study in question will be inscribed within one of these types of discourse (one of these 'sciences'), each of which possesses, of course, many subdivisions. Such an activity is related to science insofar as its object is no longer the particular phenomenon but the (psychological, sociological, etc.) law that the phenomenon illustrates.

Poetics breaks down the symmetry thus established between interpretation and science in the field of literary studies. In contradistinction to the interpretation of particular works, it does not seek to name meaning, but aims at a knowledge of the general laws that preside over the birth of each work. But in contradistinction to such sciences as psychology, sociology, etc., it seeks these laws within literature itself. Poetics is therefore an approach to literature at once 'abstract' and 'internal'.

It is not the literary work itself that is the object of poetics: what poetics questions are the properties of that particular discourse that is literary discourse. Each work is therefore regarded only as the manifestation of an abstract and general structure, of which it is but one of the possible realizations. Whereby this science is no longer concerned with actual literature, but with a possible literature, in other words with that abstract property that constitutes the singularity of the literary phenomenon: *literariness*. The goal of this study is no longer to articulate a paraphrase, a descriptive résumé of the concrete work, but to propose a theory of the structure and functioning of literary discourse, a theory that affords a list of literary possibilities, so that existing literary works appear as achieved particular cases. The work will then be projected upon something other than itself, as in the case of psychological or sociological criticism; this *something other* will no longer be a heterogeneous structure, however, but the structure of literary discourse itself. The particular text will be only an instance that allows us to describe the properties of literature. ...

The fact that this essay was originally intended for a series of structuralist studies raises a new question: what is structuralism's relation to poetics? The difficulty of answering is proportional to the polysemy of the term 'structuralism'.

Taking this word in its broad acceptation, all poetics, and not merely one or another of its versions, is structural: since the object of poetics is not the sum of empirical phenomena (literary works) but an abstract structure (literature). But then, the introduction of a scientific point of view into any realm is always and already *structural*.

If on the other hand this word designates a limited corpus of hypotheses, one that is historically determined – thereby reducing language to a system of communication, or social phenomena to the products of a code – poetics, as presented here, has nothing particularly structuralist about it. We might even say that the literary phenomenon and, consequently, the discourse that assumes it (poetics), by their very existence, constitute an objection to certain instrumentalist conceptions of language formulated at the beginnings of 'structuralism'.

Which leads us to specify the relations between poetics and linguistics. ... [L]iterature is, in the strongest sense of the term, a product of language. (Mallarmé had said: 'The book, total expansion of the letter ...'.) For this reason, any knowledge of language will be of interest to the poetician. But formulated this way, the relation unites poetics and linguistics less than it does literature and language: hence poetics and *all* the sciences of languages. Now, no more than poetics is the only science to take literature as its object is linguistics (at least as it exists today) the unique science of language. Its object is a certain type of linguistic structure (phonological, grammatical, semantic) to the exclusion of others, which are studied in anthropology, in psychoanalysis, or in 'philosophy of language'. Hence poetics might find a certain assistance in each of these sciences, to the degree that language constitutes part of their object. Its closest relatives will be the other disciplines that deal with *discourse* – the group forming the field of *rhetoric*, understood in the broadest sense as a general science of discourses.

It is here that poetics participates in the general semiotic project that unites all investigations whose point of departure is the *sign*.

19 GÉRARD GENETTE: 'STRUCTURALISM AND LITERARY CRITICISM'

In a new chapter of *La Pensée sauvage*, Claude Lévi-Strauss defines mythical thought as 'a kind of intellectual *bricolage*'.[1] The nature of *bricolage* is to make use of materials and tools that, unlike those of the engineer, for example, were not intended for the task in hand. ... But there is another intellectual activity, peculiar to more 'developed' cultures, to which this analysis might be applied almost word for word: I mean criticism, more particularly literary criticism, which distinguishes itself formally from other kinds of criticism by the fact that it uses the same materials – writing – as the works with which it is concerned; art criticism or musical criticism are obviously not expressed in sound or in color, but literary criticism speaks the same language as its object: it is a metalanguage, 'discourse upon a discourse'.[2] It can therefore be a metaliterature, that is to say, 'a literature of which literature itself is the imposed object'.[3]...

... If the writer questions the universe, the critic questions literature, that is to say, the universe of signs. But what was a sign for the writer (the work) becomes meaning for the critic (since it is the object of the critical discourse), and in another way what was meaning for the writer (his view of the world) becomes a sign for the critic, as the theme and symbol of a certain literary nature. ... If such a thing as 'critical poetry' exists, therefore, it is in the sense in which Lévi-Strauss speaks of a 'poetry of *bricolage*': just as the *bricoleur* 'speaks through things', the critic speaks – in the full

Reprinted from *Figures of Literary Discourse*, trans. Alan Sheridan (Oxford, 1982), pp. 3–21.

sense, that is to say, speaks up – through books, and we will paraphrase Lévi-Strauss once more by saying that 'without ever completing his project he always puts something of himself into it'.
In this sense, therefore, one can regard literary criticism as a
'structuralist activity'; but it is not – as is quite clear – merely an
implicit, unreflective structuralism. The question posed by the
present orientation of such human sciences as linguistics or
anthropology is whether criticism is being called upon to organize its structuralist vocation explicitly in a structural method. My
aim here is simply to elucidate the meaning and scope of this
question, suggesting the principal ways in which structuralism
could reach the object of criticism, and offer itself to criticism as
a fruitful method.

Literature being primarily a work of language, and structuralism, for its part, being preeminently a linguistic method, the
most probable encounter should obviously take place on the
terrain of linguistic material: sounds, forms, words, and sentences
constitute the common object of the linguist and the philologist
to such an extent that it was possible, in the early enthusiasm of
the Russian Formalist movement, to define literature as a mere
dialect, and to envisage its study as an annex of general dialect-
ology. ... But, like other 'excesses' committed by Formalism, this
particular one had cathartic value: by temporarily ignoring
content, the provisional reduction of literature's 'literary being'
to its linguistic being made it possible to revise certain traditional
'verities' concerning the 'truth' of literary discourse, and to study
more closely the system of its conventions. Literature had long
enough been regarded as a message without a code for it to
become necessary to regard it for a time as a code without a
message.

Structuralist method as such is constituted at the very moment
when one rediscovers the message in the code, uncovered by an
analysis of the immanent structures and not imposed from the
outside by ideological prejudices. This moment was not to be long
in coming, for the existence of the sign, at every level, rests on
the connection of form and meaning. ... Between pure
Formalism, which reduces literary 'forms' to a sound material that
is ultimately formless, because nonsignifying, and traditional
realism, which accords to each form an autonomous, substantial
'expressive value', structural analysis must make it possible to
uncover the connection that exists between a system of forms and
a system of meanings, by replacing the search for term-by-term
analogies with one for overall homologies. ...

The structural study of 'poetic language' and of the forms of literary expression in general cannot, in fact, reject the analysis of the relations between code and message. ... The ambition of structuralism is not confined to counting feet and to observing the repetitions of phonemes: it must also attack semantic phenomena which, as Mallarmé showed us, constitute the essence of poetic language, and more generally the problems of literary semiology. In this respect one of the newest and most fruitful directions that are now opening up for literary research ought to be the structural study of the 'large unities' of discourse, beyond the framework – which linguistics in the strict sense cannot cross – of the sentence. ... One would thus study systems from a much higher level of generality, such as narrative, description, and the other major forms of literary expression. There would then be a linguistics of discourse that was a *translinguistics*, since the facts of language would be handled by it in great bulk, and often at one remove – to put it simply, a rhetoric, perhaps that 'new rhetoric' which Francis Ponge once called for, and which we still lack.

The structural character of language at every level is sufficiently accepted by all today for the structuralist 'approach' to literary expression to be adopted as it were without question. As soon as one abandons the level of linguistics (or that 'bridge thrown between linguistics and literary history', as Leo Spitzer called studies of form and style) and approaches the domain traditionally reserved for criticism, that of 'content', the legitimacy of the structural point of view raises very serious questions of principle. *A priori*, of course, structuralism as a method is based on the study of structures wherever they occur; but to begin with, structures are not directly encountered objects – far from it; they are systems of latent relations, conceived rather than perceived, which analysis constructs as it uncovers them, and which it runs the risk of inventing while believing that it is discovering them. Furthermore, structuralism is not only a method; it is also what Ernst Cassirer calls a 'general tendency of thought', or as others would say (more crudely) an ideology, the prejudice of which is precisely to value structures at the expense of substances, and which may therefore overestimate their explanatory value. ...

Apparently, structuralism ought to be on its own ground whenever criticism abandons the search for the conditions of existence or the external determinations – psychological, social, or other – of the literary work, in order to concentrate its attention on that work itself, regarded no longer as an effect, but as an absolute being. In this sense, structuralism is bound up with the general movement away from positivism, 'historicizing history' and the 'biographical illusion', a movement represented in various ways by the critical writings of a Proust, an Eliot, a Valéry, Russian Formalism, French 'thematic criticism' or Anglo-American 'New Criticism'. ... Any analysis that confines itself to a work without considering its sources or motives would, therefore, be implicitly structuralist, and the structural method ought to intervene in order to give to this immanent study a sort of rationality of understanding that would replace the rationality of explanation abandoned with the search for causes. A somewhat spatial determinism of structure would thus take over, but in a quite modern spirit, from the temporal determinism of genesis, each unit being defined in terms of relations, instead of filiation. 'Thematic' analysis, then, would tend spontaneously to culminate and to be tested in a structural synthesis in which the different themes are grouped in *networks*, in order to extract their full meaning from their place and function in the system of the work. ...

Structuralism, then, would appear to be a refuge for all immanent criticism against the danger of fragmentation that threatens thematic analysis: the means of reconstituting the unit of a work, its principle of coherence, what Spitzer called its spiritual *etymon*. ...

...Structural criticism is untainted by any of the transcendent reductions of psychoanalysis, for example, or Marxist explanation, but it exerts, in its own way, a sort of internal reduction, traversing the substance of the work in order to reach its bone-structure: certainly not a superficial examination, but a sort of radioscopic penetration, and all the more external in that it is more penetrating. ...

...What Merleau-Ponty wrote of ethnology as a discipline can be applied to structuralism as a method: 'It is not a specialty defined by a particular object, "primitive societies". It is a way of thinking, the way which imposes itself when the object is different, and requires us to transform ourselves. We also become the ethnologists of our own society if we set ourselves at a distance from it.'

Thus the relation that binds structuralism and hermeneutics together might not be one of mechanical separation and exclusion, but of complementarity: on the subject of the same work, hermeneutic criticism might speak the language of the resumption of meaning and of internal recreation, and structural criticism that of distant speech and intelligible reconstruction. They would thus bring out complementary significations, and their dialogue would be all the more fruitful, on condition that one could never speak these two languages at once. In any case, literary criticism has no reason to refuse to listen to the new significations that structuralism can obtain from the works that are apparently closest and most familiar by 'distancing' their speech; for one of the most profound lessons of modern anthropology is that the distant is also close to us, by virtue of its very distance. ...

The structuralist idea ... is to follow literature in its overall evolution, while making synchronic cuts at various stages and comparing the tables one with another. Literary evolution then appears in all its richness, which derives from the fact that the system survives while constantly altering. Here, again, the Russian Formalists showed the way by paying special attention to the phenomena of structural dynamics, and by isolating the notion of *change of function*. Noting the presence or absence, in isolation, of a literary form or theme at a particular point in diachronic evolution is meaningless until the synchronic study has shown the function of this element in the system. An element can remain while changing function, or on the contrary disappear while leaving its function to another. ...

In this sense literary history becomes the history of a system: it is the evolution of the functions that is significant, not that of the elements, and knowledge of the synchronic relations necessarily precedes that of the processes.

NOTES

[Reorganised and renumbered from the original]
1. Claude Lévi-Strauss, *The Savage Mind* (Chicago, 1966), p. 17.
2. Roland Barthes, *Critical Essays*, p. 258.
3. Paul Valéry, 'Albert Thibaudet', *Nouvelle revue française* (July 1936), 6.

20   ROLAND BARTHES: 'SCIENCE VERSUS LITERATURE'

As far as science is concerned language is simply an instrument, which it profits it to make as transparent and neutral as possible; it is subordinate to the matter of science (workings, hypotheses, results) which, so it is said, exists outside language and precedes it. On the one hand and *first* there is the content of the scientific message, which is everything, on the other hand and *next*, the verbal form responsible for expressing that content, which is nothing. ...

For literature on the other hand, or at any rate that literature which has freed itself from classicism and humanism, language can no longer be the convenient instrument or the superfluous back-cloth of a social, emotional or poetic 'reality' which pre-exists it, and which it is language's subsidiary responsibility to express, by means of submitting itself to a number of stylistic rules. Language is litera-ture's Being, its very world; the whole of literature is contained in the act of writing, and no longer in those of 'thinking', 'portraying', 'telling' or 'feeling'. Technically, as Roman Jakobson has defined it, the 'poetic' (i.e., the literary) refers to that type of message which takes as its object not its content but its own form. Ethically, it is only by its passage through language that literature can continue to shake loose the essential concepts of our culture, one of the chief among which is the 'real'. Politically, it is by professing and illustrat-ing that no language is innocent, by practising what might be called 'integral language', that literature is revolutionary. Thus today literature finds itself bearing unaided the entire responsibility for language, for although science has a certain need of language it is not, like literature, in language. ...

Since it turns essentially on a certain way of taking language, conjured away into thin air in one case and assumed in the other, the opposition between science and literature is of particular im-portance for structuralism. Agreed that this word, most often imposed from outside, is today applied to projects that are very diverse, sometimes divergent and sometimes even antagonistic, and no one can arrogate the right to speak in its name. The present writer does not claim to be doing so, but retains contem-

Reprinted from *The Times Literary Supplement*, 28 September 1967, pp. 897–8.

porary 'structuralism' only in its most specialized and consequently most relevant version, using it to mean a certain mode of analysis of cultural artefacts, insofar as this mode originates in the methods of contemporary linguistics. This is to say that structuralism, itself developed from a linguistic model, finds in literature, which is the work of language, an object that has much more than an affinity with it; the two are homogeneous. Their coincidence does not exclude a certain confusion or even cleavage, according to whether structuralism sets out to maintain a scientific distance between itself and its object or whether, on the other hand, it agrees to compromise and abandon the analysis of which it is the bearer in that infinitude of language that today passes through literature; in short, whether it elects to be science or writing.

As a science, structuralism can be said to 'find itself' at each level of the literary work. First, at the level of the content or, to be more exact, of the form of the content, since it seeks to establish the 'language' of the stories that are told, their articulation, their units and the logic which links these together; in short, the general mythology in which each literary work shares. Secondly, at the level of the forms of discourse. By virtue of its method structuralism gives special attention to classification, hierarchies and arrangements: its essential object is the taxonomy or distributive model which every human creation, be it institution or book, inevitably establishes, since there can be no culture without classification. Now the discourse, or the complex of words superior to the phrase, has its own forms of organization; it too is a classification and a classification which signifies. In this respect structuralism has an august forbear whose historical role has generally been underestimated or discredited for ideological reasons – Rhetoric, that impressive attempt by a whole culture to analyse and classify the forms of speech, and to make the world of language intelligible. And, finally, at the level of the words. The phrase does not only have a literal or indicative sense, it is crammed with additional meanings. The literary word is at once a cultural reference, a rhetorical model, a deliberately ambiguous utterance and a simple indicative unit; it has three dimensions, within which lies the field of structural analysis, whose aims are much wider than those of the old stylistics, based as they were on an erroneous idea of 'expressivity'. At every level, therefore, be it that of the argument, the discourse or the words, the literary work offers structuralism the picture of a structure perfectly homological (present-day research is tending to prove this) with that of language itself. Structuralism has emerged from linguistics and in literature it finds an object which has itself emerged from language.

We can understand then why structuralism should want to found a science of literature or, to be more exact, a linguistics of discourse, whose object is the 'language' of literary forms, grasped on many levels. ...

But although it may be a new aim it is not a satisfactory, or at least not a sufficient one. It does nothing to solve the dilemma we spoke of at the beginning and which is suggested allegorically by the opposition between science and literature, insofar as the latter assumes its language under the name of writing, whereas the former evades it, by pretending to believe that this language is merely instrumental. In short, structuralism will be just one more 'science' (several are born each century, some of them only ephemeral) if it does not manage to place the actual subversion of scientific language at the centre of its programme, that is to 'write itself'. How could it fail to question the very language it uses in order to know language? The logical continuation of structuralism can only be to rejoin literature, no longer as an 'object' of analysis but as the activity of writing, to do away with the distinction derived from logic which turns the work itself into a language-object and science into a metalanguage, and thus to forgo that illusory privilege which science attaches to the possession of a captive language.

It remains therefore for the structuralist to turn himself into a 'writer', certainly not in order to profess or practise 'fine style', but in order to rediscover the crucial problems involved in every utterance, once it is no longer wrapped in the beneficent cloud of strictly *realist* illusions, which see language simply as the medium of thought. This transformation, still pretty theoretical it must be admitted, requires that certain things should be made clear or recognized. In the first place, the relationship between subjectivity and objectivity or, if one prefers, the place of the subject in his own work, can no longer be thought of as in the halcyon days of positivist science. ... Every utterance implies its own subject, whether this subject be expressed in an apparently direct fashion, by the use of 'I', or indirectly, by being referred to as 'he', or avoided altogether by means of impersonal constructions. These are purely grammatical decoys, which do no more than vary the way in which the subject is constituted within the discourse, that is the way he gives himself to others, theatrically or as a phantasm; they all refer therefore to forms of the imaginary. ...

Only writing, again, and this is a first step towards defining it, can practise language in its totality. To resort to scientific discourse as if to an instrument of thought is to postulate that there exists a neutral state of language, from which a certain number of specialized languages, the literary or poetic languages for example, have derived, as so many deviants or embellishments. It is held that this neutral state would be the referential code for all the 'excentric' languages, which themselves would be merely its sub-codes. By identifying itself with this referential code, as the basis of all normality, scientific discourse is arrogating to itself a right which it is writing's duty precisely to contest. The notion of 'writing' implies indeed that language is a vast system, none of whose codes is privileged or, if one prefers, central, and whose various departments are related in a 'fluctuating hierarchy'. Scientific discourse believes itself to be a superior code; writing aims at being a total code, including its own forces of destruction. It follows that writing alone can smash the theological idol set up by a paternalistic science, refuse to be terror-stricken by what is wrongly thought of as the 'truth' of the content and of reasoning, and open up all three dimensions of language to research, with its subversions of logic, its mixing of codes, its shifts of meaning, dialogues and parodies. ...

There is, finally between science and literature, a third margin which science must reconquer, that of pleasure. In a civilization entirely brought up by monotheism to the idea of sin, where every value is attained through suffering, the word 'pleasure' has an unfortunate ring; there is something frivolous, trivial and incomplete about it. ... Yet 'pleasure', as we are readier to admit these days, implies an experience much vaster and more meaningful than the mere satisfaction of a 'taste. ... Only the baroque, a literary experiment which has never been more than tolerated by our society, at least in France, has dared to explore to some extent what might be called the Eros of language. ...

What we must perhaps ask for today is a mutation in the consciousness, the structure and the objectives of scientific discourse, at a time, however, when the human sciences, now firmly established and flourishing, seem to be leaving less and less room for a literature commonly charged with being unreal and inhuman. To be precise: the role of literature is actively to *represent* to the scientific establishment what the latter denies, to wit the sovereignty of language. And structuralism ought to be in a strong position to cause such a scandal because, being acutely aware of the linguistic nature of human artefacts, it alone today can reopen the question of the linguistic status of science. Its subject-matter being language – all language – it has come to define itself very quickly as the metalanguage of our culture. But this stage must be transcended, because the opposition of language-objects and their meta-languages is still subject in the end to the paternalistic model of a science without a language. The task confronting structuralist discourse is to make itself entirely homogenous with its object. There are two ways in which this task can be successfully tackled, both equally radical; by an exhaustive formalization or else by 'integral writing'. In the second of these hypotheses, the one we are defending here, science will become literature, to the same extent as literature, growingly subject as it is to an overturning of the traditional genres of poetry, narrative, criticism and essay, already is and always has been a science. What the human sciences are discovering today, in whatever field it may be, sociological, psychological, psychiatric, linguistic, etc., literature has always known. The only difference is that literature has not *said* it, but *written* it. In contrast to the integral truth of literature, the human sciences, belatedly formulated in the wake of bourgeois positivism, appear as the technical alibis proffered by our society in order to maintain within itself the fiction of a theological truth proudly, and improperly, freed from language. .

21   JONATHAN CULLER: 'SEMIOTICS AS A THEORY OF READING'

The fact that people engaged in the study of literature are willing to read works of criticism tells us something important about the nature of our discipline. ... Our assumptions that significant things will be said in critical writings may be an expectation more frequently defeated than fulfilled but its presence, indeed its extraordinary persistence in the face of defeat, suggests that we see literary criticism as a discipline that aims at knowledge.

Of course, it may be difficult to explain how our discipline does move toward knowledge. Ever since literary studies turned from erudition to interpretation it has been easy to question the notion of a cumulative discipline. Acts of interpretation do not necessarily seem to bring us closer to a goal such as a more accurate understanding of all the major works of European literature. ...

Reprinted from *The Pursuit of Signs: Semiotics, Literature, Deconstruction* (London, 1981), pp. 47–51.

One strategy popular in these circumstances is to legislate against the proliferation of interpretations by proposing a theory declaring that each work has *a* meaning and that the critic's quest for knowledge is an attempt to discover that meaning. If the meaning of a work is what its author meant by it, or what it would have meant to an ideal audience of its day, or what accounts for its every detail without violating the historical norms of the genre, then the critic knows what he is attempting to discover. But such theories do not persuade readers and critics to restrict themselves to interpretations of the preferred kind, and the very existence of competing theories of the meaning of works encourages and re-produces the proliferation each theory was designed to cure. To make the goal of literary studies knowledge of the meaning of each individual literary work involves the futile attempt to impose a particular standard and a single goal upon the activity of reading.

The question then becomes: what sort of knowledge is possible? Instead of taking the proliferation of interpretations as an obstacle to knowledge, can one attempt to make it an object of knowledge, asking how it is that literary works have the meaning they do for readers? The institution of literature involves interpretive practices, techniques for making sense of literary works, which it ought to be possible to describe. Instead of attempting to legislate solutions to interpretive disagreements, one might attempt to analyze the interpretive operations that produce these disagreements – discord which is part of the literary activity of our culture. Such a program falls under the aegis of semiotics, which seeks to identify the conventions and operations by which any signifying practice (such as literature) produces its observable effects of meaning.

A signal virtue of semiotics (and perhaps in these early days its principal virtue) is the methodological clarity it can introduce into literary studies by explicit identification of assumptions and goals. Semiotic investigation is possible only when one is dealing with a mode of signification or communication. One must be able to identify effects of signification – the meanings objects and events have for participants and observers. Then one can attempt to construct models of signifying processes to account for these effects. A semiotics of literature is thus based on two assumptions, both of which can be questioned: first, that literature should be treated as a mode of signification and communication, in that a proper description of a literary work must refer to the meanings it has for readers; second, that one can identify the effects of signification one wants to account for.

Objections to the first assumption insist on the importance of attempting to separate the work itself from interpretations of it: interpretations vary in unpredictable ways; they are determined by factors external to the work and should not be seen either as part of it or as reliable guides to it. Instead of adopting the semiotic perspective and treating interpretations as the completion of a work, this argument would run, one should seek ways of analyzing the work as an objective artifact. Debates on this point have now become familiar, and there is little reason to believe that either side will discover a decisive argument.

But even if one accepts the first assumption, that literature is a mode of communication, one might still be skeptical of the possibility of identifying and collecting effects of signification. Any technique for ascertaining the meanings works have for readers, one might argue, will produce massive distortions, either because the questions asked will provoke reflections that did not belong to the 'original' response, or else because the procedure will collect only certain kinds of responses and interpretations. One cannot deny that works do have an impact on readers and do produce effects of signification, but these effects, one can argue, are not a content that could be grasped, catalogued, and studied.

These are reasonable grounds for disputing the assumptions of semiotics. When confronted with such objections, the semiotician must choose between two strategies. He may disagree, asserting that literature is a form of communication and that what it communicates cannot be ignored even if one wishes to. Or else he may grant the objections and modestly claim the reduced role that remains. Even if interpretations and responses do not belong to the structure of the work, they are an important cultural activity that should be studied; and even if responses are not objects that can be collected and analyzed, there are still numerous records of responses and interpretations that semiotics can use. Since communication does take place, since interpretations are recorded, one can study literary signification by attempting to describe the conventions and semiotic operations responsible for these interpretations...

Such a semiotics would be a theory of reading and its object would not be literary works themselves but their intelligibility: the ways in which they make sense, the ways in which readers have made sense of them. Indeed, the semiotic program may be better expressed by the concepts of 'sense' and 'making sense' than by the concept of 'meaning', for while 'meaning' suggests a property of a text (a text 'has' meaning), and thus encourages one to distinguish an intrinsic (though perhaps ungraspable) meaning from the interpretations of readers, 'sense' links the qualities of a text to the operations one performs upon it. A text can make sense and someone can make sense of a text. If a text which at first did not make sense comes to make sense, it is because someone has made sense of it. 'Making sense' suggests that to investigate literary signification one must analyze interpretive operations.

The most common objection to a semiotics of reading, especially one that invokes the example of linguistics and speaks of its project as an attempt to describe 'literary competence',[1] is that it wrongly assumes agreement among readers or posits as a norm a 'competent' reading which other readers ought to accept. It is crucial to insist that a semiotics of reading leaves entirely open the question of how much readers agree or disagree in their interpretations of literature. It attempts to account for facts about interpretation, whatever one takes those facts to be. It is interested in the range of readings for a given work, whether one takes that range to be wide or narrow. Where there seems to be agreement among readers – that *King Lear* has tragic impact – this is an important fact about interpretation; where disagreement seems clearly focused – is Marvell's 'Horatian Ode' a celebration or an ironic critique of Cromwell? – that is of interest; when there is a much wider spread of interpretations, as in readings of Wordsworth's 'A Slumber did my Spirit Seal', that also needs to be accounted for. In general, divergence of readings is more interesting than convergence, though of course it must be defined in relation to convergence. In any event, since facts of interpretation constitute the point of departure and the data to be explained, a semiotic discussion will simply be judged irrelevant if it starts from a blatantly unrepresentative range of interpretations.

One could, of course, scrap the term 'literary competence' to avoid the appearance of presuming agreement among readers on the existence of a normative, 'competent' interpretation, but this would involve a loss, since 'competence' does indicate that one is dealing with an ability involving norms. Not only does interpretation employ repeatable operations, but in one's attempt to interpret a text one is always implicitly appealing to norms. When one wonders whether a particular line of thought will work out, whether one will succeed in elucidating an obscure passage, one posits norms of successful interpretations, adequate clarity, sufficient coherence. These norms may remain vague and they may vary greatly from one situation to another and from one interpretive community to another, but the process of interpretation is incomprehensible without them, and one is usefully reminded of this by the allusion to norms implicit in the concept of 'literary competence'.

NOTE

1. [Ed.] For a full discussion of 'literary competence' see Culler's *Structuralist Poetics* (London, 1975), Ch. 6.

22   YURY M. LOTMAN: 'THE CONTENT AND STRUCTURE OF THE CONCEPT OF "LITERATURE"'

If we regard literature as a specific body of texts, then it must be noted first that these texts constitute only a part of the general system of culture. The existence of literary texts implies both the simultaneous presence of non-literary texts and the ability, on the part of the group which uses them, to distinguish between them. The inevitable oscillations in borderline cases only strengthen the principle itself: when we are in doubt as to whether to assign the mermaid to woman or fish, or free verse to poetry or prose, we proceed from these classificatory divisions as given. In this sense, our conception of literature logically, although not historically, precedes literature itself.

There are two different points of view from which one may differentiate between works of literature and the entire mass of other texts which function as components of a given culture:

1. DIFFERENTIATION IN TERMS OF FUNCTION

From this point of view, any verbal text which is capable, within the limits of the culture in question, of fulfilling an aesthetic function can be counted as literature. Since it is in principle possible (and historically this occurs frequently) that the conditions required for the fulfilment of the aesthetic function differ between the time of creation of the text and the time of its study, a text which, for the author, does not come into the sphere of art can, in the view of the researcher, belong to it, and vice versa.

Reprinted from *PTL: A Journal for Descriptive Poetics and Literature*, 1 (1976), 339–43.

One of the basic tenets of the Formalist school was that aesthetic function is realized when the text is closed in upon itself and when its functioning is determined by orientation towards expression; consequently, whereas in the non-literary text the question 'what' is foremost in importance, the aesthetic function is realized in orientation towards the question 'how'. Therefore the plane of expression becomes a kind of immanent sphere, which acquires independent cultural value. The most recent semiotic research, however, leads to quite opposite conclusions. The aesthetically functioning text now emerges as a text whose semantic weighting is greater, not smaller than that of non-literary texts. It means more, and not less than normal speech. When decoded with the aid of the normal mechanisms of natural language, the literary text reveals a certain level of meaning, but it is not totally exposed by this means. As soon as the recipient of information becomes aware that he is dealing with a literary communication, he approaches it in a special way. The text stands before him as, at minimum doubly encoded; the first encoding is the system of the natural language (let us say, Russian). To the extent that this code system is given in advance and the addresser and addressee possess it to an equal degree of fluency, the decoding on this level is carried out automatically. Its mechanism becomes, in a sense, transparent; its users cease to notice it. However, the recipient of the information knows that this text is encoded in some other way as well. Part of the condition on which a text functions aesthetically is the recipient's knowledge of this double coding and his ignorance (or, more likely, his incomplete knowledge) as to the actual secondary code used for this purpose. Since the recipient of the information does not know which elements in the text perceived by him are significant on this level and which are not, he 'suspects' that all the elements of expression are content elements. Once we approach a text as a literary one, then in principle any element, right down to misprints, as E. T. A. Hoffmann perceptively remarked in the foreword to *Lebensansichten des Katers Murr*, may turn out to be significant. In applying to the work of literature a whole hierarchy of supplementary codes (those of epoch, of genre, or of style), which function within an entire national body or a narrowly delimited group (right down to individuals), we are faced in one and the same text with the most varied sets of significant elements and, consequently, a complicated hierarchy of strata of meanings additional to those of the non-literary text.

The Formalist school was undoubtedly right in its observation that, in texts which function as literature, attention is often fastened upon elements which, in other cases, are perceived automatically and are not registered by the consciousness. However, the explanation which it gave for this was radically wrong. Literary functioning does not produce a text which is 'purged' of meanings, but, on the contrary, a text which is to a maximum degree overloaded with meanings. As soon as we detect a certain ordering in the sphere of expression, we immediately attribute to it a specific content or postulate the presence of content as yet unknown to us. ...

2. DIFFERENTIATION IN TERMS OF THE INTERNAL ORGANIZATION OF THE TEXT

In order for the text to be able to behave in the manner indicated above, it must be constructed in a specific way: the sender of the information *actually* encodes it many times and in several different codes (in individual instances, however, it is possible for the sender to create a text as non-literary, i.e., only singly encoded, while the recipient *attributes* to it a literary function, thereby envisaging subsequent encodings and an additional concentration of meaning). The recipient must also know that the text with which he is concerned is to be regarded as literary. Consequently, the text must be semantically organized in some definite way and must contain signals which direct attention to this organization. This means that the literary text may be described not only as functioning in a given way within the general system of texts belonging to the culture in question, but also as being arranged in some particular way. Where in the first instance we are dealing with the structure of culture, in the second we are concerned with the structure of the text.

Function and Internal Structure in their Diachronic Correlation

There is no simple, automatic relationship between the function of a text and its internal organization: the formula of the relationship between these two structural principles takes shape differently in each type of culture, depending on the most general ideological models. This correlation may be defined in the following very general and inevitably schematic form: the emergence of any system of culture entails the formation of a definite structure of functions, which is peculiar to that culture, and the establishment of a system of relationships between functions and texts.

Thus for example, Russian literature of the 1740s to the 1750s experienced a regularization at the most varied levels: metre, genre, style, etc. The same period saw the establishment both of a system of relationships between these organizations and of their general hierarchy of values. Then the period of organization comes to an end. The indeterminacy of the correlation between the links in the chain is replaced by a simple ordered relationship. But this signifies a diminution in the information capacity of the system, its ossification. This is the time when, as a rule aesthetic theories change and if, as is often the case, the literary ossification turns out to be only a partial manifestation of wider, social processes of stagnation, then deep-seated ideological conceptions will also undergo change. At this stage, the system of functions and the system of the internal constructions of texts may become liberated from their existing ties and enter into new combinations: value characteristics change, and the 'bottom' and 'top' of the culture functionally change places. During this period, those texts which serve an aesthetic function do their best to resemble literature as little as possible in their immanent structure. The very words 'art' and 'literature' take on a pejorative connotation. But it would be naïve to think that the iconoclasts of art abolish the aesthetic function as such. It is simply that, as a rule, the literary texts turn out to be incapable, in the new conditions, of fulfilling the literary function, which is served successfully by texts which signalize by their type of organization an inherently non-literary orientation. Thus, folklore, excluded by the theory of Classicism from the domain of art, became for the men of the Enlightenment and the pre-Romantics an ideal aesthetic norm. ...

There follows a phase in which a new system of ideological-artistic codifications is formed, as a result of which there emerges a new system sufficiently flexible in its initial stages, of correlations between the structure of texts and their function.

Thus, it is not just literary texts which take part in the development of literature. Art, being a part of culture, needs non-art for its development, just as culture, being only a part of human existence, needs the dynamic process of correlation with the sphere of non-culture exterior to it – the non-sign, non-text, non-semiotic life of man. There is a constant exchange, a complex system of entries and exits, between the external and the internal spheres. Moreover, the very fact of the introduction of a text into the sphere of art signifies a transcoding of it into the language of literary perception, i.e., a definite reinterpretation.

23   MORSE PECKHAM: 'THE PROBLEM OF INTERPRETATION'

Any theory of the interpretation of literature is necessarily sub-sumed by a theory of interpretation in ordinary, mundane, spoken verbal interaction. But we must dig deeper than this. One cannot stop with words, or verbal behavior, because verbal behavior always takes place in some kind of situational context, and that context obviously plays a part in the act of interpretation. A theory of verbal behavior, therefore, must be subsumed by a more general theory, a theory of signs, or a semiotic theory. And here a further difficulty arises. Signs are said to have something called significance, or meaning. A sign, as the French say, wants to say something. Yet it can scarcely say something unless there is some-body to receive and respond to what it wants to say. Unless there is response on the part of somebody, there is no significance, no meaning. Clearly, a theory of signs must be subsumed by a theory of meaning. And if without response there is no meaning, then meaning can scarcely be immanent. And if it is not immanent, then the meaning is the response. ...

All of us have asked thousands of times what is meant by some statement or word or sign. When we shift to literary interpreta-tion, the problem is not, then, why there are different interpreta-tions of the same work, often totally inconsistent with one another. Nor is it enough to say, as most students of the question have said, and as Hirsch tried to say, and failed, that one interpre-tation is right and others are wrong.[1] We cannot say that because, in fact, we have no criteria of rightness and wrongness in interpre-tation, nor, as I shall point out later, can we have. Rather, the question is, Why is interpretational variety possible? But if we locate meaning in the response, and reflect upon the endless oc-casions in which we are uncertain of meaning, that is, uncertain of how we ought to respond, it becomes clear that uncertainty is the very condition of interpretation.

Let me put this in the form of two corollaries to the proposition that meaning is response. The first is, that all possible signs are capable of eliciting in a single individual but one response; the second is that any sign is capable of eliciting from an individual any of all possible responses. Clearly, it is only in extreme situations, such as psychosis, that either of these possibilities actually occurs. It follows that there are factors which prevent such extremes, which control response; that is, control meanings. Thus, when we are uncertain of the meaning of some semiotic configuration and request further information so that we might respond, we are asking that our response be controlled by the individual responsible for presenting the semiotic configuration, or – and this is the crux of the matter for literary interpretation – if the generator of the sign configuration is not present, it is necessary for us to seek elsewhere for that control.

For the full importance of this condition, it is useful to begin at the simplest and fundamental level of sign response. A sign, then, is any perceptual configuration to which there is a response. ... A further factor in the response is to be noticed. In the case of each response there [is] a transfer of a response, that is, of a meaning from configurations already experienced and identified to the configuration new in experience. Behaviorally, then, categorization is the transfer of response in the individual's repertory to a novel configuration. This leads us to a fuller description of sign response. It is categorization, by means of perceptual attributes. A sign, then, is always categorial: a sign response is subsumed by the explanatory term, analogy; and of highest importance, the identification of the unidentifiable configuration is some individual's analogical *determination* of a categorial meaning. ...

Let us now consider an example of semiotic behavior in which both verbal and non-verbal signs are clearly present and identifiable.

I walk into a restaurant and sit down at a table. A waiter approaches. I ask him for a cup of coffee. He goes off to the kitchen, returns with the cup of coffee, and places it in front of me. What has been the waiter's semiotic behavior? ... I think what the waiter has done can be described in the following rather formulaic and abstract proposition. The waiter has performed *a perceptual disengagement of an analogically determined recurrent semiotic pattern from an analogically determined series of semiotic matrices*. The pattern he disengages is the request for coffee, a request which can be given in a variety of ways. The waiter responds to all such requests in the same way, analogically determining that each such request is a variant of a single pattern. The matrix is the semiotic configuration of restaurant plus customer plus request. The controlling interest of the waiter, that which controls his interpretation of pattern plus matrix, is his desire to keep his job. But that economic interest is also the matrix for the pattern of restaurant-plus-customer-plus-request. ... Let us change the situation. I ask for coffee, but the waiter says that he's sorry: he can't provide it for me. The reason is that it is exactly 11:00 A.M., and at that precise time all the waiters in the city are going on strike. Here the waiter is controlling his response by a completely different matrix, and his economic control has an opposite effect. ...

From this example we may take several further steps. It is now possible to grasp what we are doing when we raise questions about the interest or the intention of an utterance, that is, it is ordinarily believed, about the intention of the generator of an utterance. ... When we use the word 'intention' ... we are limiting our possible responses and setting out to generate what we judge will be an appropriate response. When we say that Dickens' intention in writing *Oliver Twist* was to protest against the treatment of orphans (or whatever intention we choose), all that we are doing is constructing a matrix which will serve to control our interpretation of the text. The establishment of a literary intention is not a discovery; it is, as in all verbal interaction, the construction of a matrix. ...

This insight permits us to take the next step. Just as the meaning of any pattern is not immanent, so the subsumption of any pattern by a matrix is not immanent. That subsumption, it needs to be emphasized, is a matter of determination, and a determination is a judgment that the response generated is an appropriate response. Hence the subsumption of a pattern by a matrix is a judgment of appropriateness. It is for this reason that we cannot speak of a right or wrong response to any utterance, we can only speak of its appropriateness, and moreover only of its appropriateness in the judgment of some actual living individual. ...

However, if human interaction is to take place with any smoothness, as it must for fundamentally economic reasons, meaning must be stabilized. If semiotic behavior, found in animals far lower on the evolutionary scale than the human animal, is adaptive, it is, like any adaptation, also a mal-adaptation. Culture, then, we may judge profitably to be a counter-adaptation to semiosis. Culture stabilizes performance, that is, it stabilizes responses to signs. ... But it is also equally obvious that with the emergence of the New Criticism and the untenable doctrine of the semiotic autonomy of literature, that stabilization has ceased to be the task of at least many of the most active publishing members of our profession. What has been going on for several decades is the spread of interpretational deviance, following the principle that I proposed in my book on pornography,[2] that to the degree that any behavior pattern is badly transmitted, to that degree there will be a spread of that pattern into a delta of deviancy. We have seen why that has been possible, and the explanation may be put in this form. *Any analogically determined series of semiotic matrices can be used to control the interpretation of any analogically determined recurrent semiotic pattern.* That is, any work of literature can be interpreted any way you want to. By that I mean, what controls the interpreter's interest, his way of limiting his response to a work of literature, can be any cultural control, highly stabilized or highly innovative. ...

I am not concerned here with why this should have happened. From one point of view there is nothing odd about it. The history of interpretation is a history of re-interpretations of canonical texts. ... But from another point of view it is very odd. By that I mean that there has long been established, for nearly 400 years, a model for the interpretation of literature. And that model is the norm of interpretational behavior; that is, when I ask the waiter for a cup of coffee, he does not refuse, he does not pour it on my head, but he brings it to me. My claim is that *interpretation in the presence of the generator of an utterance and judged by him to be appropriate is the proper model for the interpretation of an utterance in the absence of the generator of that utterance.* If in the presence of the speaker you are uncertain of the appropriate response, you can ask for further instructions. You mediate your response by those instructions. In his absence you mediate your response by constructing as best you can what you judge to have been the matrix that controlled the generation of the utterance. ...

The model for the interpretation of literature I proposed above is what Frank Kermode in his interesting book *The Classic* has called historical-philological interpretation. He asserts that it really got under way in the early 17th century, but to my mind it got under way in the interpretation of non-literary historical documents in the early 15th. At that time several Florentine historians claimed that the medieval negation of the value of the historical figure Cicero was an error. That negation had been based on his opposition to Augustus and the establishment of the empire. But since the Roman empire had been established by the will of God to provide secular support and an arm of force for the Christian church, Cicero was certainly to be condemned. The new historians, however, claimed that Cicero could not be blamed for his opposition to Augustus because, living before Christianity, and having been brought up in the ideal of the Republic, he could not possibly know what God's purpose was in establishing the Empire. He was not then a bad man, but a good man.

At about the same time and in the same place a radical change was introduced into painting – perspective. Mountains and trees were no longer emblems of mountains and trees without consideration of the scale of the human beings acting in the foreground. Rather the background was constructed as it might have been seen at the time of the event by an individual standing at a particular fixed spot. What was in common to both of these radical changes, that in historiography and that in painting was the effort to place the historical event in a situation in which it might have taken place. The questions now were, What was the semiotic matrix of Cicero? What was the semiotic matrix of the episode in the saint's legend? Shortly, the old medieval device of presenting two or more episodes of the same legend within a single emblematic landscape was abandoned and for the same reason. There emerged what might be called situational thinking. Within two hundred years there had appeared the basic theory of modern science. ... The basic scientific sentence is 'If you do so and so, then such and such will happen'. And that sentence is the basic sentence of all our instructions for interacting with the non-verbal, for it is the only way the inadequacy of the verbal instructions, or scientific theory, can be uncovered, located, and corrected. It seems clear to me that the historical-philological interpretation of literature is, like science, based upon the norm of interpretation, and that both are culturally convergent, emerging from the matrix of situational thinking.

Moreover for a long time, for science until the late 19th century and for historical-philological interpretation still, it was assumed that both could arrive at a certainty. However, as I have pointed out, interpretation at a distance is inherently uncertain. And as for science, scientific experimentation always produces more data than the directing theory can subsume and data of a kind it cannot subsume at all. ... Likewise the uncertainty inherent in historical-philological interpretation at a distance is responsible for the endlessness of historical-philological research, the endlessness of its effort to construct the situation or matrix which controlled the generation of the literary text in question.

Nevertheless, though the use of the term 'research' is justifiable for both scientific behavioral and historical interpretation, there are profound differences. The first is that science gets outside of the verbal but historical-philological interpretation as the second term shows does not. ... The second difference is of considerably greater importance. It has been realized for some time that successful scientific theory construction depends upon the principles of parsimony and elegance. But the student of literature is faced with an entirely different problem. Extravagance of vocabulary and inelegance, or shagginess, of possible relation among the terms of that vocabulary is the characteristic of literature, and the higher the cultural level at which the literature is generated the more true this is. ... Not semantic continuity but discontinuity is the character of literary art. For example, the more important the character in a work of fiction, the more frequently the reader has to change the attributes which the proper name of that character subsumes. ... The lesson of this is that no single matrix can be successfully used to control the interpretation of a work of literature of even slight complexity, of one that exhibits neither parsimony nor elegance. Again, the higher the cultural level the truer this is.

To conclude, then, my position is that since literature only selects and intensifies, and makes more incoherent, according to its cultural level, the semantic functions of ordinary face-to-face verbal interaction, the most appropriate model for the interpretation of literature is the model offered by interpretation in such interaction. I think that the *historical-philological*, or *situational* interpretation of literature has almost as solid a theoretical base as does science, the difference, of course, being that literature interpretation does not move out of the realm of verbal signs, and though the interpretation of the non-literary arts does, it does not move beyond the realm of man-produced signs, or man-arranged signs, as in gardens. ... As for the current fashion of deviant interpretation, that is, interpretation not interested in what controlled the generation of the work of literature but only in using the work to exemplify an interest of the interpreter, it is not, I think a serious rival to historical-philological interpretation, or even a serious alternative. Rather, it is governed by an ideology of which the practitioners are themselves unaware, and which, as a cultural phenomenon, I am very interested in interpreting and explaining. But that is another story.

NOTES

1. [Ed.] See E.D. Hirsch, Jr, *Validity in Interpretation* (New Haven, Conn., 1967).

2. [Ed.] See Morse Peckham, *Art and Pornography: An Experiment in Explanation* (New York, 1969).

VI POST-STRUCTURALISM

Structuralism was founded on the Saussurian principle that language as a system of signs must be considered synchronically, that is, within a single temporal plane. The diachronic aspect of language, how it develops and changes over time, was seen as being of secondary importance. In post-structuralist thinking temporality again becomes central.

The major influence on post-structuralist literary theory is the French philosopher Jacques Derrida, though the work of the psychoanalyst Jacques Lacan and the cultural theorist Michel Foucault is also important in the emergence of post-structuralism. Derrida emphasises the 'logocentrism' of Western thinking, that is, that meaning is conceived as existing independently of the language in which it is communicated and is thus not subject to the play of language. Derrida accepts Saussure's position that meaning is the product of the differential relations between signifiers, but he goes beyond Saussure in claiming that the temporal dimension cannot be left out of account. Language is seen as a never-ending chain of words in which there is no extralinguistic origin or end to the chain. He argues that Saussure was not able to free himself from 'logocentric' thinking since, by elevating speech above writing, he indicated that he believed signifier and signified could be fused within the same temporal plane in the act of speaking. Derrida attacks such 'logocentrism' and claims that writing is a better model for understanding how language functions. In writing the signifier is always productive, thus introducing a temporal aspect into signification which undermines any fusion between signifier and signified. Written signs enjoy a semiotic independence in that though meaning is created by the differential relations between signs, as Saussure had argued, the semiotic independence of writing entails that meaning is always deferred, since writing will produce meaning in an unlimited number of potential contexts which may exist in the future. Derrida's basic formulation 'différance', by punning on the French word 'différence', which can mean both 'difference' and 'deferment', undermines 'logocentrism' by implying that meaning can never be fully present since it is always deferred. His 'deconstructive' practice with regard to the texts he analyses has also been a major influence on literary critics since, in contrast, for example, to the

New Criticism, he does not set out to demonstrate the structural coherence or organic unity of the text but to show how the text undermines its own assumptions and is thus divided against itself. His essay, 'Structure, Sign, and Play in the Discourse of the Human Sciences', first delivered as a lecture at Johns Hopkins University in 1966, has been especially influential on literary theory.

Roland Barthes' essay, 'The Death of the Author', first published in 1968, adopts a radically textual view of language and meaning and clearly shows his shift towards a post-structuralist position. It has close connections with his *S/Z*, first published in 1970, generally regarded as the first important work of post-structuralist literary criticism.

Julia Kristeva, though associated with structuralism, like Barthes eventually moved beyond it. For her, like Derrida, the emphasis is on the signifier rather than the signified in language, as the signifying process undermines all stability of meaning. The signifying process both creates and undermines systems of signs. Influenced by both psychoanalysis and Bakhtin, she stresses the role of the 'speaking subject' in language with the subject being always divided because the 'other' cannot be eliminated from discourse. She suggests that in modernist literary writing language can be a force for renewal since modernist literary language both creates and calls into question systematisation.

Like Kristeva, Michel Foucault was initially seen as a structuralist, but his later work is usually characterised as post-structuralist, though he rejected such labels. Though his main focus was on social practices or systems of thought these were treated like 'langues' in the Saussurian sense, that is, as sign systems in which meaning was produced through the operation of rules and codes of signification. Since Foucault claimed the human subject was also produced by such rules and codes, he proclaimed the 'death of Man', the concept of the human individual having been generated by a previous cultural epoch now superseded. Works of art or literature should thus not be thought of as individual creations but as emanations of a cultural system and have to be understood in relation to the codes that operate to create meaning within that cultural system. His later writing is predominantly concerned with power and a critique of totalities. By adopting a 'genealogical' method, hierarchies can be undermined by exposing discontinuities, 'subjugated' or 'buried' forms of knowledge that resist such hierarchies. Foucault's work underlies much of the theorised historical criticism associated with such critical approaches as New Historicism and Cultural Materialism.

Post-structuralist thinking had a major impact on American criticism in the 1970s, particularly on a group of critics who were based at Yale, the 'Yale deconstructionists'. The leading Yale theorist was Paul de Man, who argued that literary texts already incorporated Derridian 'différance'. De Man argues that there is a radical division in literary texts between the grammatical or logical structure of language and its rhetorical aspects. This creates a play of signification in literary texts which is finally undecidable. De Man argues that literature is constituted by this undecidable play between the grammatical and the rhetorical in texts and not by aesthetic considerations. Any text which by deconstructive analysis can be shown to exhibit such characteristics, de Man suggests, functions as literature.

FURTHER READING

Roland Barthes, *S/Z*, trans. Richard Miller (London, 1975).

Harold Bloom et al., *Deconstruction and Criticism* (London, 1979).

Jonathan Culler, *On Deconstruction: Theory and Criticism after Structuralism* (London, 1983).

Paul de Man, *Allegories of Reading: Figural Language in Rousseau, Nietzsche, Rilke, and Proust* (New Haven, Conn., 1979).

——, *Blindness and Insight: Essays in the Rhetoric of Contemporary Criticism* (London, 1983).

Jacques Derrida, *Of Grammatology*, trans. Gayatri C. Spivak (Baltimore, 1976).

——, *Acts of Literature*, ed. Derek Attridge (London, 1992).

Michel Foucault, *Language, Counter-Memory, Practice: Selected Essays and Interviews*, ed. D. F. Bouchard (Oxford, 1977).

Gerald Graff, *Literature Against Itself: Literary Ideas in Modern Society* (Chicago, 1979). (A critical view.)

Geoffrey H. Hartman, *Saving the Text: Literature/Derrida/Philosophy* (Baltimore, 1981).

Barbara Johnson, *The Critical Difference: Essays in the Contemporary Rhetoric of Reading* (Baltimore, 1980).

Vincent B. Leitch, *Deconstructive Criticism: An Advanced Introduction* (London, 1983).

J. Hillis Miller, *Theory Now and Then* (Hemel Hempstead, 1991).

Christopher Norris, *Deconstruction: Theory and Practice* (London, 1982).

Edward W. Said, *The World, the Text, and the Critic* (London, 1984).

T. K. Seung, *Structuralism and Hermeneutics* (New York, 1982). (Contains critique of Derrida.)

Robert Young (ed.), *Untying the Text: A Post-Structuralist Reader* (London, 1981).

24 JACQUES DERRIDA: 'STRUCTURE, SIGN, AND PLAY¹ IN THE DISCOURSE OF THE HUMAN SCIENCES'

Perhaps something has occurred in the history of the concept of structure that could be called an 'event', if this loaded word did not entail a meaning which it is precisely the function of structural – or structuralist – thought to reduce or to suspect. But let me use the term 'event' anyway, employing it with caution and as if in quotation marks. In this sense, this event will have the exterior form of a *rupture* and a *redoubling*.

It would be easy enough to show that the concept of structure and even the word 'structure' itself are as old as the *épistémé* – that is to say, as old as western science and western philosophy – and that their roots thrust deep into the soil of ordinary language, into whose deepest recesses the *épistémé* plunges to gather them together once more, making them part of itself in a metaphorical displacement. Nevertheless, up until the event which I wish to mark out and define, structure – or rather the structurality of structure – although it has always been involved, has always been neutralized or reduced, and this by a process of giving it a center or referring it to a point of presence, a fixed origin. The function of this center was not only to orient, balance, and organize the structure – one cannot in fact conceive of an unorganized structure – but above all to make sure that the organizing principles of the structure would limit what we might call the *freeplay* of the structure. No doubt that by orienting and organizing the coherence of the system, the center of a structure permits the freeplay of its elements inside the total form. And even today the notion of a structure lacking any center represents the unthinkable itself.

Nevertheless, the center also closes off the freeplay it opens up and makes possible. *Qua* center, it is the point at which the substitution of contents, elements, or terms is no longer possible. At the center, the permutation or the transformation of elements (which may of course be structures enclosed within a structure) is forbidden. At least this permutation has always remained *interdicted* ²

Reprinted from *The Structuralist Controversy: The Languages of Criticism and the Sciences of Man*, ed. Richard Macksey and Eugenio Donato (Baltimore, 1972), pp. 247–65.

(I use this word deliberately). Thus it has always been thought that the center, which is by definition unique, constitutes that very thing within a structure which governs the structure, while escaping structurality. This is why classical thought concerning structure could say that the center is, paradoxically, *within* the structure and *outside* it. The center is at the center of the totality, and yet, since the center does not belong to the totality (is not part of the totality), the totality *has its center elsewhere.* The center is not the center. The concept of centered structure – although it represents coherence itself, the condition of the *épistémé* as philosophy or science – is contradictorily coherent. And, as always, coherence in contradiction expresses the force of a desire. The concept of centered structure is in fact the concept of a freeplay based on a fundamental ground, a freeplay which is constituted upon a fundamental immobility and a reassuring certitude, which is itself beyond the reach of the freeplay. With this certitude anxiety can be mastered, for anxiety is invariably the result of a certain mode of being implicated in the game, of being caught by the game, of being as it were from the very beginning at stake in the game. ...

The event I called a rupture, the disruption I alluded to at the beginning of this paper, would presumably have come about when the structurality of structure had to begin to be thought, that is to say, repeated, and this is why I said that this disruption was repetition in all of the senses of this word. From then on it became necessary to think the law which governed, as it were, the desire for the center in the constitution of structure and the process of signification prescribing its displacements and its substitutions for this law of the central presence – but a central presence which was never itself, which has always already been transported outside itself in its surrogate. The surrogate does not substitute itself for anything which has somehow pre-existed it. From then on it was probably necessary to begin to think that there was no center, that the center had no natural locus, that it was not a fixed locus but a function, a sort of non-locus in which an infinite number of sign-substitutions came into play. This moment was that in which language invaded the universal problematic; that in which, in the absence of a center or origin, everything became discourse – provided we can agree on this word – that is to say, when everything became a system where the central signified, the original or transcendental signified, is never absolutely present outside a system of differences. The absence of the transcendental signified extends the domain and the interplay of signification *ad infinitum.*

Where and how does this decentering, this notion of the structurality of structure, occur? It would be somewhat naïve to refer to an event, a doctrine, or an author in order to designate this occurrence. It is no doubt part of the totality of an era, our own, but still it has already begun to proclaim itself and begun to *work*. Nevertheless, if I wished to give some sort of indication by choosing one or two 'names', and by recalling those authors in whose discourses this occurrence has most nearly maintained its most radical formulation, I would probably cite the Nietzschean critique of metaphysics, the critique of the concepts of being and truth, for which were substituted the concepts of play, interpretation, and sign (sign without truth present); the Freudian critique or self-presence, that is, the critique of consciousness, of the subject, of self-identity and of self-proximity or self-possession; and, more radically, the Heideggerean destruction of metaphysics, of ontotheology, of the determination of being as presence. But all these destructive discourses and all their analogues are trapped in a sort of circle. This circle is unique. It describes the form of the relationship between the history of metaphysics and the destruction of the history of metaphysics. *There is no sense* in doing without the concepts of metaphysics in order to attack metaphysics. We have no language – no syntax and no lexicon – which is alien to this history; we cannot utter a single destructive proposition which has not already slipped into the form, the logic, and the implicit postulations of precisely what it seeks to contest. To pick out one example from many: the metaphysics of presence is attacked with the help of the concept of the *sign*. But from the moment anyone wishes this to show, as I suggested a moment ago, that there is no transcendental or privileged signified and that the domain or the interplay of signification has, henceforth, no limit, he ought to extend his refusal to the concept and to the word sign itself – which is precisely what cannot be done. For the signification 'sign' has always been comprehended and determined, in its sense, as sign-of, signifier referring to a signified, signifier different from its signified. If one erases the radical difference between signifier and signified, it is the word signifier itself which ought to be abandoned as a metaphysical concept. … But we cannot do without the concept of the sign, we cannot give up this metaphysical complicity without also giving up the critique we are directing against this complicity, without the risk of erasing difference [altogether] in the self-identity of a signified reducing into itself its signifier, or, what amounts to the same thing, simply expelling it outside itself. For there are two heterogeneous ways of erasing the difference between the signifier and the signified: one, the classic way, consists in reducing or deriving the signifier, that is to say, ultimately in *submitting* the sign to thought; the other, the one we are using here against the first one, consists in putting into question the system in which the preceding reduction functioned: first and foremost, the opposition between the sensible and the intelligible. The paradox is that the metaphysical reduction of the sign needed the opposition it was reducing. The opposition is part of the system, along with the reduction. And what I am saying here about the sign can be extended to all the concepts and all the sentences of metaphysics, in particular to the discourse on 'structure'. But there are many more ways of being caught in this circle. They are all more or less naïve, more or less empirical, more or less systematic, more or less close to the formulation or even to the formalization of this circle. It is these differences which explain the multiplicity of destructive discourses and the disagreement between those who make them. ...

... Freeplay is the disruption of presence. The presence of an element is always a signifying and substitutive reference inscribed in a system of differences and the movement of a chain. Freeplay is always an interplay of absence and presence, but if it is to be radically conceived, freeplay must be conceived of before the alternative of presence and absence; being must be conceived of as presence or absence beginning with the possibility of freeplay and not the other way around. If Lévi-Strauss, better than any other, has brought to light the freeplay of repetition and the repetition of freeplay, one no less perceives in his work a sort of ethic of presence, an ethic of nostalgia for origins, an ethic of archaic and natural innocence, of a purity of presence and self-presence in speech – an ethic, nostalgia, and even remorse which he often presents as the motivation of the ethnological project when he moves towards archaic societies – exemplary societies in his eyes. These texts are well known.

As a turning toward the presence, lost or impossible, of the absent origin, this structuralist thematic of broken immediateness is thus the sad, *negative*, nostalgic, guilty, Rousseauist facet of the thinking of freeplay of which the Nietzschean *affirmation* – the joyous affirmation of the freeplay of the world and without truth, without origin, offered to an active interpretation – would be the other side. *This affirmation then determines the non-center otherwise than as loss of the center.* And it plays the game without security. For there is a *sure* freeplay: that which is limited to the *substitution* of *given and existing*, *present*, pieces. In absolute chance, affirmation also surrenders itself to *genetic* indetermination, to the *seminal* adventure of the trace.

There are thus two interpretations of interpretation, of structure, of sign, of freeplay. The one seeks to decipher, dreams of deciphering, a truth or an origin which is free from freeplay and from the order of the sign, and lives like an exile the necessity of interpretation. The other, which is no longer turned toward the origin, affirms freeplay and tries to pass beyond man and humanism, the name man being the name of that being who, throughout the history of metaphysics or of ontotheology – in other words, through the history of all of his history – has dreamed of full presence, the reassuring foundation, the origin and the end of the game. The second interpretation of interpretation, to which Nietzsche showed us the way, does not seek in ethnography, as Lévi-Strauss wished, the 'inspiration of a new humanism' (again from the 'Introduction to the Work of Marcel Mauss').

There are more than enough indications today to suggest we might perceive that these two interpretations of interpretation – which are absolutely irreconcilable even if we live them simultaneously and reconcile them in an obscure economy – together share the field which we call, in such a problematic fashion, the human sciences.

For my part, although these two interpretations must acknowledge and accentuate their difference and define their irreducibility, I do not believe that today there is any question of *choosing* – in the first place because here we are in a region (let's say, provisionally, a region of historicity) where the category of choice seems particularly trivial; and in the second, because we must first try to conceive of the common ground, and the *différance* of this irreducible difference.[3] Here there is a sort of question, call it historical, of which we are only glimpsing today the *conception, the formulation, the gestations, the labor.* I employ these words, I admit, with a glance toward the business of childbearing – but also with a glance toward those who, in a company from which I do not exclude myself, turn their eyes away in the face of the as yet unnameable which is proclaiming itself and which can do so, as is necessary whenever a birth is in the offing, only under the species of the non-species, in the formless, mute, infant, and terrifying form of monstrosity.

NOTES

[Reorganised and renumbered from the original]

1. The word 'jeu' is variously translated here as 'play', 'interplay', 'game', and 'stake', besides the normative translation 'freeplay'. All footnotes to this article are additions by the translator [Richard Macksey].

2. *Interdite*: 'forbidden', 'disconcerted', 'confounded', 'speechless'.

3. From *différer*, in the sense of 'to postpone', 'put off', 'defer'.
Elsewhere Derrida uses the word as a synonym for the German *Aufschub*:
'postponement', and relates it to the central Freudian concepts of
Verspätung, Nachträglichkeit, and to the '*detours* to death' of *Beyond the
Pleasure Principle* by Sigmund Freud (Standard Edition, ed. James
Strachey, vol. XIX, London, 1961), Chap. V.

25   ROLAND BARTHES: 'THE DEATH OF THE AUTHOR'

In his story *Sarrasine*[1] Balzac, describing a castrato disguised as a
woman, writes the following sentence: *'This was woman herself, with
her sudden fears, her irrational whims, her instinctive worries, her impetu-
ous boldness, her fussings, and her delicious sensibility.'* Who is speaking thus? Is it the hero of the story bent on remaining ignorant of
the castrato hidden beneath the woman? Is it Balzac the individual, furnished by his personal experience with a philosophy of
Woman? Is it Balzac the author professing 'literary' ideas on femininity? Is it universal wisdom? Romantic psychology? We shall
never know, for the good reason that writing is the destruction of
every voice, of every point of origin. Writing is that neutral, com-
posite, oblique space where our subject slips away, the negative
where all identity is lost, starting with the very identity of the body
writing.

No doubt it has always been that way. As soon as a fact is
narrated no longer with a view to acting directly on reality but
intransitively, that is to say, finally outside of any function other
than that of the very practice of the symbol itself, this disconnection occurs, the voice loses its origin, the author enters into
his own death, writing begins. The sense of this phenomenon,
however, has varied; in ethnographic societies the responsibility
for a narrative is never assumed by a person but by a mediator,
shaman or relator whose 'performance' – the mastery of the
narrative code – may possibly be admired but never his 'genius'.
The author is a modern figure, a product of our society insofar
as, emerging from the Middle Ages with English empiricism,
French rationalism and the personal faith of the Reformation, it

Reprinted from *Image–Music–Text*, trans. Stephen Heath (London,
1977), pp. 142–8.

discovered the prestige of the individual, of, as it is more nobly put, the 'human person'. It is thus logical that in literature it should be this positivism, the epitome and culmination of capitalist ideology, which has attached the greatest importance to the 'person' of the author. ...

Though the sway of the Author remains powerful (the new criticism[2] has often done no more than consolidate it), it goes without saying that certain writers have long since attempted to loosen it. In France, Mallarmé was doubtless the first to see and to foresee in its full extent the necessity to substitute language itself for the person who until then had been supposed to be its owner. For him, for us too, it is language which speaks, not the author; to write is, through a prerequisite impersonality (not at all to be confused with the castrating objectivity of the realist novelist), to reach that point where only language acts, 'performs', and not 'me'. Mallarmé's entire poetics consists in suppressing the author in the interests of writing (which is, as will be seen, to restore the place of the reader). ... Linguistically, the author is never more than the instance writing, just as *I* is nothing other than the instance saying *I*: language knows a 'subject', not a 'person', and this subject, empty outside of the very enunciation which defines it, suffices to make language 'hold together', suffices, that is to say, to exhaust it.

The removal of the Author (one could talk here with Brecht of a veritable 'distancing', the Author diminishing like a figurine at the far end of the literary stage) is not merely an historical fact or an act of writing; it utterly transforms the modern text (or – which is the same thing – the text is henceforth made and read in such a way that at all its levels the author is absent). The temporality is different. The Author, when believed in, is always conceived of as the past of his own book: book and author stand automatically on a single line divided into a *before* and an *after*. The Author is thought *to nourish* the book, which is to say that he exists before it, thinks, suffers, lives for it, is in the same relation of antecedence to his work as a father to his child. In complete contrast, the modern scriptor is born simultaneously with the text, is in no way equipped with a being preceding or exceeding the writing, is not the subject with the book as predicate; there is no other time than that of the enunciation and every text is eternally written *here and now*. The fact is (or, it follows) that *writing* can no longer designate an operation of recording, notation, representation, 'depiction' (as the Classics would say); rather, it designates exactly what linguists, referring to Oxford philosophy, call a performative, a rare verbal form (exclusively given in the first person and in the present tense) in which the enunciation has no other content (contains no other proposition) than the act by which it is uttered – something like the *I declare* of kings or the *I sing* of very ancient poets. Having buried the Author, the modern scriptor can thus no longer believe, as according to the pathetic view of his predecessors, that this hand is too slow for his thought or passion and that consequently, making a law of necessity, he must emphasize this delay and indefinitely 'polish' his form. For him, on the contrary, the hand, cut off from any voice, borne by a pure gesture of inscription (and not of expression), traces a field without origin – or which, at least, has no other origin than language itself, language which ceaselessly calls into question all origins.

We know now that a text is not a line of words releasing a single 'theological' meaning (the 'message' of the Author-God) but a multi-dimensional space in which a variety of writing, none of them original, blend and clash. The text is a tissue of quotations drawn from the innumerable centres of culture. Similar to Bouvard and Pécuchet,[3] those eternal copyists, at once sublime and comic and whose profound ridiculousness indicates precisely the truth of writing, the writer can only imitate a gesture that is always anterior, never original. His only power is to mix writings, to counter the ones with the others, in such a way as never to rest on any one of them. Did he wish to *express himself*, he ought at least to know that the inner 'thing' he thinks to 'translate' is itself only a ready-formed dictionary, its words only explainable through other words, and so on indefinitely. ... Succeeding the Author, the scriptor no longer bears within him passions, humours, feelings, impressions, but rather this immense dictionary from which he draws a writing that can know no halt: life never does more than imitate the book, and the book itself is only a tissue of signs, an imitation that is lost, infinitely deferred.

Once the Author is removed, the claim to decipher a text becomes quite futile. To give a text an Author is to impose a limit on that text, to furnish it with a final signified, to close the writing. Such a conception suits criticism very well, the latter then allotting itself the important task of discovering the Author (or its hypostases: society, history, psyche, liberty) beneath the work: when the Author has been found, the text is 'explained' – victory to the critic. Hence there is no surprise in the fact that, historically, the reign of the Author has also been that of the

Critic, nor again in the fact that criticism (be it new) is today undermined along with the Author. In the multiplicity of writing, everything is to be *disentangled*, nothing *deciphered*; the structure can be followed, 'run' (like the thread of a stocking) at every point and at every level, but there is nothing beneath: the space of writing is to be ranged over, not pierced; writing ceaselessly posits meaning ceaselessly to evaporate it, carrying out a systematic exemption of meaning. In precisely this way literature (it would be better from now to say *writing*), by refusing to assign a 'secret', an ultimate meaning, to the text (and to the world as text), liberates what may be called an anti-theological activity, an activity that is truly revolutionary since to refuse to fix meaning is, in the end, to refuse God and his hypostases – reason, science, law.

Let us come back to the Balzac sentence. No one, no 'person', says it: its source, its voice, is not the true place of the writing, which is reading. ... The reader is the space on which all the quotations that make up a writing are inscribed without any of them being lost; a text's unity lies not in its origin but in its destination. Yet this destination cannot any longer be personal: the reader is without history, biography, psychology; he is simply that *someone* who holds together in a single field all the traces by which the written text is constituted. Which is why it is derisory to condemn the new writing in the name of a humanism hypocritically turned champion of the reader's rights. Classic criticism has never paid any attention to the reader; for it, the writer is the only person in literature. We are now beginning to let ourselves be fooled no longer by the arrogant antiphrastical recriminations of good society in favour of the very thing it sets aside, ignores, smothers, or destroys; we know that to give writing its future, it is necessary to overthrow the myth: the birth of the reader must be at the cost of the death of the Author.

NOTES

1. [Ed.] Balzac's *Sarrasine* is discussed in detail in Barthes' *S/Z*.
2. [Ed.] Barthes is referring to the French 'la nouvelle critique' not Anglo-American New Criticism.
3. [Ed.] See Flaubert's novel *Bouvard et Pécuchet*.

26   JULIA KRISTEVA: 'THE SYSTEM AND THE SPEAKING SUBJECT'

However great the diversity, the irregularity, the disparity even of current research in semiotics, it is possible to speak of a specifically semiotic *discovery*. What semiotics has discovered in studying 'ideologies' (myths, rituals, moral codes, arts, etc.) as sign-systems is that the *law* governing or, if one prefers, the *major constraint* affecting any social practice lies in the fact that it signifies; i.e., that it is articulated *like* a language. Every social practice, as well as being the object of external (economic, political, etc.) determinants, is also determined by a set of signifying rules, by virtue of the fact that there is present an order of language; that this language has a double articulation (signifier/signified), that this duality stands in an arbitrary relation to the referent; and that all social functioning is marked by the split between referent and symbolic and by the shift from signified to signifier coextensive with it.

One may say, then, that what semiotics had discovered is the fact that there is a general social law, that this law is the symbolic dimension which is given in language, and that every social practice offers a specific expression of that law.

A discovery of this order cuts short the speculations characteristic of idealism, which throughout its history has claimed the domain of meaning as subordinate to itself, refusing to allow it both external determination and internal adjustment. But it is no less unkind to vulgar sociologism or those mechanistic assumptions which, under the ill-defined general term of 'ideology', define superstructures which are without exception externally determined. The semiological approach identifies itself, from Hjelmslev on; as an anti-humanism which outmodes those debates – still going on even now – between philosophers, where one side argues for a transcendence with an immanent 'human' causality, while the other argues for an 'ideology' whose cause is external and therefore transcendent; but where neither shows any awareness of the linguistic and, at a more general level, semiotic, logic of the sociality in which the (speaking, historical) subject is embedded.

Reprinted from *The Times Literary Supplement*, 12 October 1973, pp. 1249–50.

And yet semiotics, by its attempt to set itself up as a theory of practices using language as its model, restricts the value of its discovery to the field of practices which do no more than subserve the principle of social cohesions, of the social contract. In other words, in so far as linguistics has established itself as the science of an object ('language', 'speech' or 'discourse') so obedient to the necessity for social communication as to be inseparable from sociality, any semiotics which adopts this linguistic model can speak only of those social practices (or those aspects of social practices) which subserve such social exchange: a semiotics that records the systematic, systematizing, or informational aspect of signifying practices. ...

... Semiotics must not be allowed to be a mere application to signifying practices of the linguistic model – or any other model, for that matter. Its *raison d'être*, if it is to have one, must consist in its identifying the systematic constraint within each signifying practice (using for that purpose borrowed or original 'models') but above all in going beyond that to specifying just what, within the practice, falls outside the system and characterizes the specificity of the practice as such.

One phase of semiology is now over: that which runs from Saussure and Peirce to the Prague School and structuralism, and has made possible the systematic description of the social and/or symbolic constraint within each signifying practice. To criticize this phase for its 'ideological bias' – whether phenomenological or more specifically phonological or linguistic – without recognizing the truth it has contributed by revealing and characterizing the immanent causality and/or the presence of a social-systematic constraint in each social functioning, leads to a rejection of the symbolic and/or social *thesis* (in Husserl's sense of the word) indispensable to every practice. This rejection is shared both by idealist philosophy, with its neglect of the historical socializing role of the symbolic, and by the various sociological dogmatisms, which suppress the specificity of the symbolic and its logic in their anxiety to reduce them to an 'external' determinant.

In my view, a critique of this 'semiology of systems' and of its phenomenological foundations is possible only if it starts from a theory of meaning which must necessarily be a theory of the speaking subject. It is common knowledge that the linguistic revival which goes by the name of Generative Grammar – whatever its variants and mutations – is based on the rehabilitation of the Cartesian conception of language as an *act* carried out by a *subject*.[1] On close inspection, as certain linguists (from Jakobson to Kuroda) have shown in recent years, this 'speaking subject' turns out in fact to be that *transcendental ego* which, in Husserl's view, underlies any and every predicative synthesis, if we 'put in brackets' logical or linguistic externality. Yet this transcendental subject is not the essential concern of the semiological revival, and if it bases itself on the conception of language proper to Generative Grammar, semiology will not get beyond the reduction – still commonly characteristic of it – of signifying *practices* to their systematic aspect.

In respect of the subject and of signifying, it is the Freudian revolution which seems to me to have achieved the definitive displacement of the western *épistémé* from its presumed centrality. ... The theory of meaning now stands at a cross-roads: either it will remain an attempt at formalizing meaning-systems by increasing sophistication of the logico-mathematical tools which enable it to formulate models on the basis of a conception (already rather dated) of meaning as the act of a *transcendental ego*, cut off from its body, its unconscious, and also its history; or else it will attune itself to the theory of the speaking subject as a divided subject (conscious/unconscious) and go on to attempt to specify the types of operation characteristic of the two sides of this split; thereby exposing them, that is to say, on the one hand, to bio-physiological processes (themselves already inescapably part of signifying processes; what Freud labelled 'drives'), and, on the other hand, to social constraints (family structures, modes of production, etc.).

In following this latter path, semiology, or, as I have suggested calling it, *semanalysis* conceives of meaning not as a sign-system but as a *signifying process*. Within this process one might see the release and subsequent articulation of the drives as constrained by the social code yet not reducible to the language system as a *geno-text*; and the signifying system as it presents itself to phenomenological intuition as a *pheno-text*; describable in terms of structure, or of competence/performance, or according to other models. The presence of the *geno-text* is indicated by what I have called a *semiotic disposition*. In the case, for example, of a signifying practice such as 'poetic language', the *semiotic disposition* will be the various deviations from the grammatical rules of the language: articulatory effects which shift the phonemative system back towards its articulatory, phonetic base and consequently towards the drive-governed bases of sound-production; the over-determination of a lexeme by multiple meanings which it does not carry in ordinary usage but which accrue to it as a result of its occurrence in other texts; syntactic irregularities such as ellipses, non-recoverable deletions, indefinite embeddings, etc.; the replacement of the relationship between the protagonists of any enunciation as they function in a locutory act – see here the work of J. L. Austin and John Searle – by a system of relations based on fantasy; and so forth. ...

The moment of transgression is the key moment in practice: we can speak of practice wherever there is a transgression of systematicity, i.e., a transgression of the unity proper to the *transcendental ego*. The subject of the practice cannot be the transcendental subject, who lacks the shift, the split in logical unity brought about by language which separates out, within the signifying body, the symbolic order from the workings of the libido (this last revealing itself by the *semiotic disposition*). Identifying the semiotic disposition means in fact identifying the shift in the speaking subject, his capacity for renewing the order in which he is inescapably caught up; and that capacity is, for the *subject*, the capacity for enjoyment.

It must however, be remembered that although it can be described in terms of operations and concepts, this logic of shifts, splits, and the infinitization of the symbolic limit leads us towards operations heterogeneous to meaning and its system. By that I mean that these 'operations' are *pre-meaning* and *pre-sign* (or *trans-meaning, trans-sign*), and that they bring us back to processes of division in the living matter of an organism subject to biological constraints as well as social norms. Here it seems indispensable that Melanie Klein's theory of drives should be refined and extended, together with the psycholinguistic study of the acquisition of language. ...

The point is not to replace the semiotics of signifying systems by considerations on the biological code appropriate to the nature of those employing them – a tautological exercise, after all, since the biological code has been modelled on the language system. It is rather to postulate the *heterogeneity* of biological operations in respect of signifying operations, and to study the dialectics of the former (that is, the fact that, though invariably subject to the signifying and/or social codes, they infringe the code in the direction of allowing the subject to get pleasure from it, renew it, even endanger it; where, that is, the processes are not blocked by him in repression or 'mental illness').

But since it is itself a metalanguage, semiotics can do no more than postulate this heterogeneity: as soon as it speaks about it, it homogenizes the phenomenon, links it with a system, loses hold of it. Its specificity can be preserved only in the signifying practices which set off the heterogeneity at issue: thus poetic language making free with the language code. ...

... It is only now, and only on the basis of a theory of the speaking subject as subject of a heterogeneous process, that semiotics can show that what lies outside its metalinguistic mode of operation – the 'remainder', the 'waste' – is what, in the process of the speaking subject, represents the moment in which it is set in action, put on trial, put to death: a heterogeneity with respect to system, operating within the practice and one which is liable if not seen for what it is, to be reified into a transcendence.

We can now grasp all the ambiguities of *semanalysis*: on the one hand it demystifies the logic at work in the elaboration of every transcendental reduction and, for this purpose, requires the study of each signifying system as a practice. Thus intent on revealing the negativity which Hegel had seen at work beneath all rationality but which, by a masterly stroke, he subordinated to absolute knowledge, *semanalysis* can be thought of as the direct successor of the dialectical method; but the dialectic it continues will be one which will at last be genuinely materialist since it recognizes the *materiality* – the *heterogeneity* – of that negativity whose concrete base Hegel was unable to see and which mechanistic Marxists have reduced to a merely economic externality. ...

As 'classical' semiotics was already aware, discourse receives its meanings from the person(s) to whom it is addressed. The semiotics of signifying practices is addressed to all those who, committed to a practice of challenge, innovation or personal experiment, are frequently tempted to abandon their discourse as a way of communicating the logic of that practice, since the dominant forms of discourse (from positivist grammar to sociologism) have no room for it, and to go into voluntary exile in what Mallarmé called an 'indicible qui ment', for the ultimate benefit of a practice that shall remain silent.

The semiology of signifying practices, by contrast, is ready to give a hearing to any or all of those efforts which, ever since the elaboration of a new position for the speaking subject, have been renewing and reshaping the status of meaning within social exchange to a point where the very order of language is being renewed: Joyce, Burroughs, Sollers.

This is a moral gesture, inspired by a concern to make intelligible, and therefore socializable, what rocks the foundations of sociality. In this respect *semanalysis* carries on the semiotic discovery of which we spoke at the outset: it places itself at the service of the social law which requires systematization, communication, exchange. But if it is to do this, it must inevitably respect a further, more recent requirement – and one which neutralizes the phantom of 'pure science': the subject of the semiotic meta-language must, however, briefly, call himself in question, must emerge from the protective shell of a transcendental ego within a logical system, and so restore his connexion with that negativity – drive-governed, but also social, political and historical – which rends and renews the social code.

NOTE

1. [Ed.] See Noam Chomsky, *Cartesian Linguistics: A Chapter in the History of Rationalist Thought* (New York, 1966).

27   MICHEL FOUCAULT: 'LECTURE: 7 JANUARY 1976'

I would say, then, that what has emerged in the course of the last ten or fifteen years is a sense of the increasing vulnerability to criticism of things, institutions, practices, discourses. A certain fragility has been discovered in the very bedrock of existence – even, and perhaps above all, in those aspects of it that are most familiar, most solid and most intimately related to our bodies and to our everyday behaviour. But together with this sense of instability and this amazing efficacy of discontinuous, particular and local criticism, one in fact also discovers something that perhaps was not initially foreseen, something one might describe as precisely the inhibiting effect of global, *totalitarian theories*. It is not that these global theories have not provided nor continue to provide in a fairly consistent fashion useful tools for local research: Marxism and psychoanalysis are proofs of this. But I believe these tools have only been provided on the condition that the theoretical unity of these discourses was in some sense put in abeyance, or at least curtailed, divided, overthrown, caricatured, theatricalised, or what you will. In each case, the attempt to think in terms of a totality has in fact proved a hindrance to research. ...

It is here that we touch upon another feature of these events that has been manifest for some time now: it seems to me that this local criticism has proceeded by means of what one might

Reprinted from *Power/Knowledge: Selected Interviews and Other Writings 1972–1977* (New York: 1980), pp. 80–92.

term 'a return of knowledge'. What I mean by that phrase is this: it is a fact that we have repeatedly encountered, at least at a superficial level, in the course of most recent times, an entire thematic to the effect that it is not theory but life that matters, not knowledge but reality, not books but money etc.; but it also seems to me that over and above, and arising out of this thematic, there is something else to which we are witness, and which we might describe as an *insurrection of subjugated knowledges*.

By subjugated knowledges I mean two things: on the one hand, I am referring to the historical contents that have been buried and disguised in a functionalist coherence or formal systemisation. Concretely, it is not a semiology of the life of the asylum, it is not even a sociology of delinquency, that has made it possible to produce an effective criticism of the asylum and likewise of the prison, but rather the immediate emergence of historical contents. And this is simply because only the historical contents allow us to rediscover the ruptural effects of conflict and struggle that the order imposed by functionalist or systematising thought is designed to mask. Subjugated knowledges are thus those blocs of historical knowledge which were present but disguised within the body of functionalist and systematising theory and which criticism – which obviously draws upon scholarship – has been able to reveal.

On the other hand, I believe that by subjugated knowledges one should understand something else, something which in a sense is altogether different, namely, a whole set of knowledges that have been disqualified as inadequate to their task or insufficiently elaborated: naïve knowledges, located low down on the hierarchy, beneath the required level of cognition or scientificity. I also believe that it is through the re-emergence of these low-ranking knowledges, these unqualified, even directly disqualified knowledges (such as that of the psychiatric patient, of the ill person, of the nurse, of the doctor – parallel and marginal as they are to the knowledge of medicine – that of the delinquent etc.), and which involve what I would call a popular knowledge (*le savoir des gens*) though it is far from being a general commonsense knowledge, but is on the contrary a particular, local, regional knowledge, a differential knowledge incapable of unanimity and which owes its force only to the harshness with which it is opposed by everything surrounding it – that it is through the re-appearance of this knowledge, of these local popular knowledges, these disqualified knowledges, that criticism performs its work.

However, there is a strange kind of paradox in the desire to assign to this same category of subjugated knowledges what are on the one hand the products of meticulous, erudite, exact historical knowledge, and on the other hand local and specific knowledges which have no common meaning and which are in some fashion allowed to fall into disuse whenever they are not effectively and explicitly maintained in themselves. Well, it seems to me that our critical discourses of the last fifteen years have in effect discovered their essential force in this association between the buried knowledges of erudition and those disqualified from the hierarchy of knowledges and sciences.

In the two cases – in the case of the erudite as in that of the disqualified knowledges – with what in fact were these buried, subjugated knowledges really concerned? They were concerned with a *historical knowledge of struggles*. In the specialised areas of erudition as in the disqualified, popular knowledge there lay the memory of hostile encounters which even up to this day have been confined to the margins of knowledge.

What emerges out of this is something one might call a genealogy, or rather a multiplicity of genealogical researches, a painstaking rediscovery of struggles together with the rude memory of their conflicts. And these genealogies, that are the combined product of an erudite knowledge and a popular knowledge, were not possible and could not even have been attempted except on one condition, namely that the tyranny of globalising discourses with their hierarchy and all their privileges of a theoretical *avant-garde* was eliminated.

Let us give the term *genealogy* to the union of erudite knowledge and local memories which allows us to establish a historical knowledge of struggles and to make use of this knowledge tactically today. This then will be a provisional definition of the genealogies which I have attempted to compile with you over the last few years.

You are well aware that this research activity, which one can thus call genealogical, has nothing at all to do with an opposition between the abstract unity of theory and the concrete multiplicity of facts. It has nothing at all to do with a disqualification of the speculative dimension which opposes to it, in the name of some kind of scientism, the rigour of well established knowledges. It is not therefore via an empiricism that the genealogical project unfolds, nor even via a positivism in the ordinary sense of that term. What it really does is to entertain the claims to attention of local, discontinuous, disqualified, illegitimate knowledges against the claims of a unitary body of theory which would filter, hierarchise and order them in the name of some true knowledge and some arbitrary idea of what constitutes a science and its objects. Genealogies are therefore not positivistic returns to a more careful or exact form of science. They are precisely anti-sciences. Not that they vindicate a lyrical right to ignorance or non-knowledge: it is not that they are concerned to deny knowledge or that they esteem the virtues of direct cognition and base their practice upon an immediate experience that escapes encapsulation in knowledge. It is not that with which we are concerned. We are concerned, rather, with the insurrection of knowledges that are opposed primarily not to the contents, methods or concepts of a science, but to the effects of the centralising powers which are linked to the institution and functioning of an organised scientific discourse within a society such as ours. Nor does it basically matter all that much that this institutionalisation of scientific discourse is embodied in a university, or, more generally, in an educational apparatus, in a theoretical-commercial institution such as psychoanalysis or within the framework of reference that is provided by a political system such as Marxism; for it is really against the effects of the power of a discourse that is considered to be scientific that the genealogy must wage its struggle.

To be more precise, I would remind you how numerous have been those who for many years now, probably for more than half a century, have questioned whether Marxism was, or was not, a science. One might say that the same issue has been posed, and continues to be posed, in the case of psychoanalysis, or even worse, in that of the semiology of literary texts. But to all these demands of: 'Is it or is it not a science?', the genealogies or the genealogists would reply: 'If you really want to know, the fault lies in your very determination to make a science out of Marxism or psychoanalysis or this or that study'. If we have any objection against Marxism, it lies in the fact that it could effectively be a science. ...

By comparison, then, and in contrast to the various projects which aim to inscribe knowledges in the hierarchical order of power associated with science, a genealogy should be seen as a kind of attempt to emancipate historical knowledges from that subjection, to render them, that is, capable of opposition and of struggle against the coercion of a theoretical, unitary, formal and scientific discourse. It is based on a reactivation of local knowledges – of minor knowledges, as Deleuze might call them – in opposition to the scientific hierarchisation of knowledges and the effects intrinsic to their power: this, then, is the project of these disordered and fragmentary genealogies. If we were to characterise it in two terms, then 'archaeology' would be the appropriate methodology of this analysis of local discursivities, and 'genealogy' would be the tactics whereby, on the basis of the descriptions of these local discursivities, the subjected knowledges which were thus released would be brought into play. ...

What is at stake in all these genealogies is the nature of this power which has surged into view in all its violence, aggression and absurdity in the course of the last forty years, contemporaneously, that is, with the collapse of Fascism and the decline of Stalinism. What, we must ask, is this power – or rather, since that is to give a formulation to the question that invites the kind of theoretical coronation of the whole which I am so keen to avoid – what are these various contrivances of power, whose operations extend to such differing levels and sectors of society and are possessed of such manifold ramifications? What are their mechanisms, their effects and their relations? The issue here can, I believe, be crystallised essentially in the following question: is the analysis of power or of powers to be deduced in one way or another from the economy? ...

Well then, the problem involved in the researches to which I refer can, I believe, be broken down in the following manner: in the first place, is power always in a subordinate position relative to the economy? Is it always in the service of, and ultimately answerable to, the economy? Is its essential end and purpose to serve the economy? Is it destined to realise, consolidate, maintain and reproduce the relations appropriate to the economy and essential to its functioning? In the second place, is power modelled upon the commodity? Is it something that one possesses, acquires, cedes through force or contract, that one alienates or recovers, that circulates, that voids this or that region? Or, on the contrary, do we need to employ varying tools in its analysis – even, that is, when we allow that it effectively remains the case that the relations of power do indeed remain profoundly enmeshed in and with economic relations and participate with them in a common circuit? If that is the case, it is not the models of functional subordination or formal isomorphism that will characterise the interconnection between politics and the economy. Their indissolubility will be of a different order, one that it will be our task to determine.

What means are available to us today if we seek to conduct a non-economic analysis of power? Very few, I believe. We have in the first place the assertion that power is neither given, nor exchanged, nor recovered, but rather exercised, and that it only exists in action. Again, we have at our disposal another assertion to the effect that power is not primarily the maintenance and reproduction of economic relations, but is above all a relation of force. The questions to be posed would then be these: if power is exercised, what sort of exercise does it involve? In what does it consist? What is its mechanism? There is an immediate answer that many contemporary analyses would appear to offer: power is essentially that which represses. Power represses nature, the instincts, a class, individuals. Though one finds this definition of power as repression endlessly repeated in present day discourse, it is not that discourse which invented it – Hegel first spoke of it, then Freud and later Reich. In any case, it has become almost automatic in the parlance of the times to define power as an organ of repression. So should not the analysis of power be first and foremost an analysis of the mechanisms of repression?

Then again, there is a second reply we might make: if power is properly speaking the way in which relations of forces are deployed and given concrete expression, rather than analysing it in terms of cession, contract or alienation, or functionally in terms of its maintenance of the relations of production, should we not analyse it primarily in terms of *struggle, conflict and war?*...

So, no sooner do we attempt to liberate ourselves from economistic analyses of power, than two solid hypotheses offer themselves: the one argues that the mechanisms of power are those of repression. For convenience sake, I shall term this Reich's hypothesis. The other argues that the basis of the relationship of power lies in the hostile engagement of forces. Again for convenience, I shall call this Nietzsche's hypothesis.

These two hypotheses are not irreconcilable; they even seem to be linked in a fairly convincing manner. After all, repression could be seen as the political consequence of war, somewhat as oppression, in the classic theory of political right, was seen as the abuse of sovereignty in the juridical order. ...

Thus we have two schemes for the analysis of power. The contract – oppression schema, which is the juridical one, and the domination – repression or war – repression schema for which the pertinent opposition is not between the legitimate and illegitimate, as in the first schema, but between struggle and submission.

It is obvious that all my work in recent years has been couched in the schema of struggle–repression, and it is this – which I have hitherto been attempting to apply – which I have now been forced to reconsider, both because it is still insufficiently elaborated at a whole number of points, and because I believe that these two notions of repression and war must themselves be considerably modified if not ultimately abandoned. In any case, I believe that they must be submitted to closer scrutiny.

I have always been especially diffident of this notion of repression: it is precisely with reference to those genealogies of which I was speaking just now – of the history of penal right, of psychiatric power, of the control of infantile sexuality etc. – that I have tried to demonstrate to you the extent to which the mechanisms that were brought into operation in these power formations were something quite other, or in any case something much more, than repression. The need to investigate this notion of repression more thoroughly springs therefore from the impression I have that it is wholly inadequate to the analysis of the mechanisms and effects of power that it is so pervasively used to characterise today.

28 PAUL DE MAN: 'THE RESISTANCE TO THEORY'

Literary theory can be said to come into being when the approach to literary texts is no longer based on non-linguistic, that is to say historical and aesthetic, considerations or, to put it somewhat less crudely, when the object of discussion is no longer the meaning or the value but the modalities of production and of reception of meaning and of value prior to their establishment – the implication being that this establishment is problematic enough to require an autonomous discipline of critical investigation to consider its possibility and its status. ...

The advent of theory, the break that is now so often being deplored and that sets it aside from literary history and from literary criticism, occurs with the introduction of linguistic terminology in the metalanguage about literature. By linguistic terminology is meant a terminology that designates reference prior to designating the referent and takes into account, in the consideration of the world, the referential function of language or, to be somewhat more specific, that considers reference as a function of language and not necessarily as an intuition. Intuition implies perception, consciousness, experience, and leads at once into the world of logic and understanding with all its correlatives, among which aesthetics occupies a prominent place. The assumption that there can be a science of language

Reprinted from *Yale French Studies*, 63 (1982), 7–17.

which is not necessarily a logic leads to the development of a terminology which is not necessarily aesthetic. Contemporary literary theory comes into its own in such events as the application of Saussurian linguistics to literary texts. ...

... By considering language as a system of signs and of signification rather than as an established pattern of meanings, one displaces or even suspends the traditional barriers between literary and presumably non-literary uses of language and liberates the corpus from the secular weight of textual canonization. ...

Literariness, however, is often misunderstood in a way that has provoked much of the confusion which dominates today's polemics. It is frequently assumed, for instance, that literariness is another word for, or another mode of, aesthetic response. The use, in conjunction with literariness, of such terms as style and stylistics, form or even 'poetry' (as in 'the poetry of grammar'), all of which carry strong aesthetic connotations, helps to foster this confusion, even among those who first put the term in circulation. Roland Barthes, for example, in an essay properly and revealingly dedicated to Roman Jakobson, speaks eloquently of the writer's quest for a perfect coincidence of the phonic properties of a word with its signifying function. 'We would also wish to insist on the Cratylism of the name (and of the sign) in Proust ... Proust sees the relationship between signifier and signified as motivated, the one copying the other and representing in its material form the signified essence of the thing (and not the thing itself). ...'[1] To the extent that Cratylism[2] assumes a convergence of the phenomenal aspects of language as sound, with its signifying function as referent, it is an aesthetically oriented conception ... Barthes and Jakobson often seem to invite a purely aesthetic reading, yet there is a part of their statement that moves in the opposite direction. For the convergence of sound and meaning celebrated by Barthes in Proust and, as Gérard Genette has decisively shown,[3] later dismantled by Proust himself as a seductive temptation to mystified minds, is also considered here to be a mere *effect* which language can perfectly well achieve, but which bears no substantial relationship, by analogy or by ontologically grounded imitation, to anything beyond the particular effect. It is a rhetorical rather than an aesthetic function of language, an identifiable trope (paranomasis) that operates on the level of the signifier and contains no responsible pronouncement on the nature of the world – despite its powerful potential to create the opposite illusion. The phenomenality of the signifier, as sound, is unquestionably involved in the correspondence between the name and the thing named, but the link, the relationship between word and thing is not phenomenal but conventional.

This gives the language considerable freedom from referential restraint, but it makes it epistemologically highly suspect and volatile, since its use can no longer be said to be determined by considerations of truth and falsehood, good and evil, beauty and ugliness, or pleasure and pain. Whenever this autonomous potential of language can be revealed by analysis, we are dealing with literariness and, in fact, with literature as the place where this negative knowledge about the reliability of linguistic utterance is made available. The ensuing foregrounding of material, phenomenal aspects of the signifier creates a strong illusion of aesthetic seduction at the very moment when the actual aesthetic function has been, at the very least, suspended. It is inevitable that semiology or similarly oriented methods be considered formalistic, in the sense of being aesthetically rather than semantically valorized, but the inevitability of such an interpretation does not make it less aberrant. Literature involves the voiding, rather than the affirmation, of aesthetic categories. One of the consequences of this is that, whereas we have traditionally been accustomed to reading literature by analogy with the plastic arts and with music, we now have to recognize the necessity of a non-perceptual, linguistic moment in painting and in music, and learn to *read* pictures rather than to *imagine* meaning.

If literature is not an aesthetic quality, it is also not primarily mimetic. Mimesis becomes one trope among others, language choosing to imitate a non-verbal entity just as paranomasis 'imitates' a sound without any claim to identity (or reflection on difference) between the verbal and non-verbal elements. ... Literature is fiction not because it somehow refuses to acknowledge 'reality', but because it is not *a priori* certain that language functions according to principles which are those, or which are *like* those, of the phenomenal world. It is therefore not *a priori* certain that literature is a reliable source of information about anything but its own language.

It would be unfortunate, for example, to confuse the materiality of the signifier with the materiality of what it signifies. ... This does not mean that fictional narratives are not part of the world and of reality; their impact upon the world may well be all too strong for comfort. What we call ideology is precisely the confusion of linguistic with natural reality, of reference with phenomenalism. It follows that, more than any other mode of inquiry, including economics, the linguistics of literariness is a powerful

and indispensable tool in the unmasking of ideological aberrations, as well as a determining factor in accounting for their occurrence. Those who reproach literary theory for being oblivious to social and historical (that is to say ideological) reality are merely stating their fear at having their own ideological mystifications exposed by the tool they are trying to discredit. They are, in short, very poor readers of Marx's *German Ideology*. ...
...The resistance to theory is a resistance to the use of language about language. It is therefore a resistance to language itself or to the possibility that language contains factors or functions that cannot be reduced to intuition. But we seem to assume all too readily that, when we refer to something called 'language', we know what it is we are talking about, although there is probably no word to be found in the language that is as overdetermined, self-evasive, disfigured and disfiguring as 'language'. ... The most familiar and general of all linguistic models, the classical *trivium*, which considers the sciences of language as consisting of grammar, rhetoric and logic (or dialectics), is in fact a set of unresolved tensions powerful enough to have generated an infinitely prolonged discourse of endless frustration of which contemporary literary theory, even at its most self-assured, is one more chapter. ... For even if one assumes, for the sake of argument and against a great deal of historical evidence, that the link between logic and the natural sciences is secure, this leaves open the question, within the confines of the *trivium* itself, of the relationship between grammar, rhetoric and logic. And this is the point at which literariness, the use of language that foregrounds the rhetorical over the grammatical and the logical function, intervenes as a decisive but unsettling element which, in a variety of modes and aspects, disrupts the inner balance of the model and, consequently, its outward extension to the nonverbal world as well.

Logic and grammar seem to have a natural enough affinity for each other and, in the tradition of Cartesian linguistics, the grammarians of Port-Royal experienced little difficulty at being logicians as well. ... A. J. Greimas disputes the right to use the dignity of 'grammar' to describe a reading that would not be committed to universality . ...[4] It is clear that, for Greimas as for the entire tradition to which he belongs, the grammatical and the logical function of language are co-extensive. Grammar is an isotope of logic.

It follows that, as long as it remains grounded in grammar, any theory of language, including a literary one, does not threaten what we hold to be the underlying principle of all cognitive and aesthetic linguistic systems. Grammar stands in the service of logic which, in turn, allows for the passage to the knowledge of the world. The study of grammar, the first of the *artes liberales*, is the necessary precondition for scientific and humanistic knowledge. As long as it leaves this principle intact, there is nothing threatening about literary theory. The continuity between theory and phenomenalism is asserted and preserved by the system itself. Difficulties occur only when it is no longer possible to ignore the epistemological thrust of the rhetorical dimension of discourse, that is, when it is no longer possible to keep it in its place as a mere adjunct, a mere ornament within the semantic function.

The uncertain relationship between grammar and rhetoric (as opposed to that between grammar and logic) is apparent, in the history of the *trivium*, in the uncertain status of figures of speech or tropes, a component of language that straddles the disputed borderlines between the two areas. Tropes used to be part of the study of grammar but were also considered to be the semantic agent of the specific function (or effect) that rhetoric performs as persuasion as well as meaning. Tropes, unlike grammar, pertain primordially to language. They are text-producing functions that are not necessarily patterned on a non-verbal entity, whereas grammar is by definition capable of extra-linguistic generalization. The latent tension between rhetoric and grammar precipitates out in the problem of reading, the process that necessarily partakes of both. It turns out that the resistance to theory is in fact a resistance to reading, a resistance that is perhaps at its most effective, in contemporary studies, in the methodologies that call themselves theories of reading but nevertheless avoid the function they claim as their object.

What is meant when we assert that the study of literary texts is necessarily dependent on an act of reading, or when we claim that this act is being systematically avoided? ... To stress the by no means self-evident necessity of reading implies at least two things. First of all, it implies that literature is not a transparent message in which it can be taken for granted that the distinction between the message and the means of communication is clearly established. Second, and more problematically, it implies that the grammatical decoding of a text leaves a residue of indetermination that has to be, but cannot be, resolved by grammatical means, however extensively conceived. ... It is equally clear, however, that this extension is always strategically directed towards the replacement of rhetorical figures by grammatical codes. The tendency to replace a rhetorical by a grammatical terminology ... is part of an explicit program, a program that is entirely admirable in its intent since it tends towards the mastering and the clarification of meaning. The replacement of a hermeneutic by a semiotic model, of interpretation by decoding, would represent, in view of the baffling historical instability of textual meanings (including, of course, those of canonical texts) a considerable progress. Much of the hesitation associated with 'reading' could thus be dispelled.

The argument can be made, however, that no grammatical decoding, however refined, could claim to reach the determining figural dimensions of a text. There are elements in all texts that are by no means ungrammatical, but whose semantic function is not grammatically definable, neither in themselves nor in context. Do we have to interpret the genitive in the title of Keats' unfinished epic *The Fall of Hyperion* as meaning 'Hyperion's fall', the case story of the defeat of an older by a newer power, the very recognizable story from which Keats indeed started out but from which he increasingly strayed away, or as 'Hyperion falling', the much less specific but more disquieting evocation of an actual process of falling, regardless of its beginning, its end or the identity of the entity to whom it befalls to be falling. This story is indeed told in the later fragment entitled *The Fall of Hyperion*, but it is told about a character who resembles Apollo rather than Hyperion. ... Both readings are grammatically correct, but it is impossible to decide from the context (the ensuing narrative) which version is the right one. The narrative context suits neither and both at the same time, and one is tempted to suggest that the fact that Keats was unable to complete either version manifests the impossibility, for him as for us, of reading his own title. One could then read the word 'Hyperion' in the title *The Fall of Hyperion* figurally, or, if one wishes, intertextually, as referring not to the historical or mythological character but as referring to the title of Keats' own earlier text (*Hyperion*). But are we then telling the story of the failure of the first text as the success of the second, the Fall of *Hyperion* as the Triumph of *The Fall of Hyperion*? Manifestly, yes, but not quite, since the second text also fails to be concluded. Or are we telling the story of why all texts, as texts, can always be said to be falling? Manifestly yes, but not quite, either, since the story of the fall of the first version, as told in the second, applies to the first version only and could not legitimately be read as meaning also the fall of *The Fall of Hyperion*. The undecidability involves the figural or literal status of the proper name Hyperion as well as of the verb falling, and is thus a matter of figuration and not of grammar. In 'Hyperion's Fall', the word 'fall' is plainly figural, the representation of a figural fall and we, as readers, read this fall standing up. But in 'Hyperion falling', this is not so clearly the case, for if Hyperion can be Apollo and Apollo can be Keats, then he can also be us and his figural (or symbolic) fall becomes his and our literal falling as well. The difference between the two readings is itself structured as a trope. And it matters a great deal how we read the title, as an exercise not only in semantics, but in what the text actually does to us. Faced with the ineluctable necessity to come to a decision, no grammatical or logical analysis can help us out. Just as Keats had to break off his narrative, the reader has to break off his understanding at the very moment when he is most directly engaged and summoned by the text. One could hardly expect to find solace in this 'fearful symmetry' between the author's and the reader's plight since, at this point, the symmetry is no longer a formal but an actual trap, and the question no longer 'merely' theoretical.

This undoing of theory, this disturbance of the stable cognitive field that extends from grammar to logic to a general science of man and of the phenomenal world, can in its turn be made into a theoretical project of theoretical analysis that will reveal the inadequacy of grammatical models of non-reading. Rhetoric, by its actively negative relationship to grammar and to logic, certainly undoes the claims of the *trivium* (and by extension, of language) to be an epistemologically stable construct. The resistance to theory is a resistance to the rhetorical or tropological dimension of language, a dimension which is perhaps more explicitly in the foreground in literature (broadly conceived) than in other verbal manifestations or – to be somewhat less vague – which can be revealed in any verbal event when it is read textually. Since grammar as well as figuration is an integral part of reading, it follows that reading will be a negative process in which the grammatical cognition is undone, at all times, by its rhetorical displacement. The model of the *trivium* contains within itself the pseudo-dialectic of its own undoing and its history tells the story of this dialectic.

NOTES

[Reorganised and renumbered from the original]
1. 'Gérard Genette, "Proust et les noms"', in *To Honor Roman Jakobson* (The Hague, 1967), part I, pp. 157ff.
2. [Ed.] See the dialogue by Plato, *Cratylus*, which is concerned with the philosophy of language.
3. 'Proust et le langage indirect' in *Figures II* (Paris, 1969).
4. A. J. Greimas, *Du Sens* (Paris, 1970), p. 13.

VII   PSYCHOANALYTIC CRITICISM

Most psychoanalytic criticism has tended to concentrate on the relation between a literary text and the psychology of its creator. Contemporary psychoanalytic criticism has either shifted the focus to the reader or seen the author's relation to his text in a radically new context.

Norman N. Holland is the best known representative of the 'Buffalo school', a group of critics who teach or have taught at the State University of New York-Buffalo. He applies 'ego-psychology' to the study of literature. Reading is seen as fundamentally a re-creation of identity by means of a 'transactive' relation between reader and text. Holland goes further than almost any other theorist in his rejection of the 'affective fallacy', a concept associated with the New Critics, who used it to dismiss the reader's subjectivity as irrelevant because they regarded the text as an object, that is, independent of both author and reader. Holland, in contrast, argues that the meaning and significance of a literary text need to be seen in relation to the identity-structure of the reader of that text.

Harold Bloom is a critic who has been associated with both Freudian ideas and the Yale school of deconstruction, but he has distanced himself from a radically textualist position. For him the author or 'strong poet' is still central, but he uses the Freudian concept of repression to introduce a temporal dimension into the study of poetry since he believes that no poet can create in isolation from his predecessors. Poetic 'presence', intrinsic to the New Critical concept of the poem as organic or spatial in form, is thus undermined. Yet 'strong poets' must believe that they can achieve liberation from their predecessors, therefore their dependence on them must be repressed. It is the critic's task to uncover repressed influences and show their role in determining the form of the poem.

Shoshana Felman is a post-structuralist critic, strongly influenced by Derrida and Lacanian psychoanalysis. She attacks traditional psychoanalytical criticism from a post-structuralist point of view and argues that what psychoanalysis calls into question is the reader's drive to interpretative mastery of the literary text.

FURTHER READING

Harold Bloom, *A Map of Misreading* (New York, 1975).
——, *The Anxiety of Influence: A Theory of Poetry* (New York, 1973).
'French Freud', *Yale French Studies*, 48 (1973). (Contains essay by Lacan on Poe's *The Purloined Letter*.)
Norman N. Holland, *5 Readers Reading* (New Haven, Conn., 1975).
——, The Miller's Wife and the Professors: Questions about the Transactive Theory of Reading', *New Literary History*, 17 (1986), 423–47.
Joseph H. Smith (ed.), *The Literary Freud: Mechanisms of Defense and the Poetic Will* (New Haven, Conn., 1980). (Contains essay by Shoshana Felman on poetry and psychoanalysis.)
Elizabeth Wright, *Psychoanalytic Criticism: Theory in Practice* (London, 1984).

29 NORMAN N. HOLLAND: 'READING AND IDENTITY: A PSYCHOANALYTIC REVOLUTION'

The revolution began as an inquiry into the way readers read. It has become a re-thinking from the roots up of what psychoanalysis can say about the ways people sense and know things.

We theorists of literature used to think that a given story or poem evoked some 'correct' or at least widely shared reponse. When, however, I began (at Buffalo's Center for the Psychological Study of the Arts) to test this idea, I rather ruefully found a much subtler and more complex process at work. Each person who reads a story, poem, or even a single word construes it differently. These differences evidently stem from personality. But how?

The key concept is identity (as developed by Heinz Lichtenstein). I see it as forming the latest of the four characterologies that psychoanalysis has evolved. First there are diagnostic categories like hysteric, manic, or schizophrenic. Second, Freud and his followers added the libidinal types: anal, phallic, oral, genital, and urethral. Although these terms could bring larger segments of someone's behavior together in a significant way, they pointed toward childhood; necessarily they infantalized adult achievements. A third, ego-psychological, notion of character was Fenichel's: 'the

Reprinted from *Academy Forum (American Academy of Psychoanalysis)*, 23 (1979), 7–9.

ego's habitual mode of bringing into harmony' the demands of the external world and the internal world of personal drives and needs. Lichtenstein suggests a way to conceptualize Fenichel's central term, 'habitual'. We are each constantly doing new things, yet we stamp each new thing with the same personal style as our earlier actions. Think of the individual as embodying a dialectic of sameness and difference. We detect the sameness by seeing what persists within the constant change of our lives. We detect the difference by seeing what has changed against the background of sameness.

The easiest way to comprehend that dialectic of sameness and difference is Lichtenstein's concept of identity as a theme and variations – like a musical theme and variations. Think of the sameness as a theme, an 'identity theme'. Think of the difference as variations on that identity theme. I can arrive at an identity theme by sensing the recurring patterns in someone's life, just as I would arrive at the theme of a piece of music. I would express it, not in terms from elsewhere (either diagnostic words like 'hysteric' or structural words like 'ego'), but in words as descriptive as possible of that person's behavior.

For example, I phrased an identity theme for a subject I'll call Sandra: 'she sought to avoid depriving situations and to find sources of nurture and strength with which she could exchange and fuse.' Similarly, 'Saul sought from the world balanced and defined exchanges, in which he would not be the one overpowered.' 'Sebastian wanted to unite himself with forces of control, to which he would give something verbal or intellectual, hoping to sexualize them.' Thus, Sandra's thoughts about the need for equal strengths in marriage were one variation on her identity theme, and Sebastian's desire to please an aristocracy or Saul's fear of me as an interviewer were variations on theirs, just as their various readings were.

For instance, these three read this clause in Faulkner's 'A Rose for Emily' describing Colonel Sartoris: 'he who fathered the edict that no Negro woman should appear on the streets without an apron.' Sandra adjusted the phrase to just the amount of strength she could identify with ... Sebastian discovered an aristocratic, sexualized master–slave relationship ... Saul, however, had to reduce the force and cruelty of the original. ...

One could have labeled Saul, Sandra, and Sebastian hysterics or obsessionals (in diagnostic categories) or oral, anal, or phallic (in libidinal stage characterology) or as identifiers, reversers, or deniers (in a characterology of defense and adaptation). But these categories would have lumped together and blurred the particular details of their readings of stories, and that is what reading involves – responses to detail. Saul, Sandra, Sebastian, and the many other readers and writers we have studied led us to a general principle: we actively transact literature so as to re-create our identities.

We can refine that principle further, however. I see Sandra bringing to this sentence both the general expectations I think she has toward any other (that it will nurture or protect) and also specific expectations toward Faulkner or the south or short stories. She also brings to bear on the text what I regard as her characteristic pattern of defensive and adaptive strategies ('defenses', for short) so as to shape the text until, to the degree she needs that certainty, it is a setting in which she can gratify her wishes and defeat her fears about closeness and distance: 'a great little touch'. Sandra also endows the text with what I take to be her characteristic fantasies, that is, her habitual wishes for some strong person who will balance closeness, nurture, and strength, here, 'the voice in the story' which undercuts the bigot. Finally, as a social, moral, and intellectual being, she gives the text a coherence and significance that confirm her whole transaction of the clause. She reads it ethically.

These four terms: defense, expectation, fantasy, and transformation (DEFT, for short) connect to more than clinical experience. One can understand *expectation* as putting the literary work in the sequence of a person's wishes in time, while *transformation* endows the work with a meaning beyond time. Similarly, I learn of *defenses* as they shape what the individual lets in from outside; while *fantasies* are what I see the individual putting out from herself into the outside world. Thus these four terms let me place a person's DEFTing at the intersection of the axes of human experience, between time and timelessness, between inner and outer reality.

Our readings of readers imply still more. We may extend what we have found out about the perception of texts to other kinds of perception. If Sandra uses Faulkner's words to re-create her identity, will she not use The New York Times or, indeed, any words the same way? If she DEFTs the narrator or Colonel Sartoris, characters in fiction, will she not DEFT characters in real life?

Freud seemed to believe in 'immaculate perception'. He assumed that eyes and ears faithfully transmit the real world into the mind, where later these originally sound percepts may be distorted by unconscious or neurotic needs. Few, if any, twentieth century students of perception would agree. Hundreds of their experiments have shown that perception is a constructive act. ...

Psychologists who study sensing, knowing, or remembering, have long recognized the importance of the person who senses, knows, or remembers. They have asked for a 'top-level theory of motivation' to take that whole person into account. That is, a person's needs, motivation, and character shape even small details of perception, cognition, and memory. But how can we articulate that relationship?

I believe identity theory provides the necessary top-level theory. That is, we can conceptualize sensing, knowing or remembering – indeed, the whole human mind (as William T. Powers has done) as a hierarchy of feedback networks, each set to a reference level from the loop above it. At the lowest level, the outer world triggers signals from the cells of retina or cochlea which, if they are big enough by the reference standards set from above, stimulate movements of eyeball or ear canal to vary and test those signals. Higher loops will deal with intensities, sensations, configurations, objects, positioning, tracking, sequencing, changing sequences, and will look more like DEFTings. The highest reference level will be set by the identity loop: we transact the world through all these particular transactions so as to re-create our individual identities.

Because identity theory lets us integrate psychoanalysis with at least some kinds of experimental psychology and psycholinguistics, we have begun to teach psychoanalytic theory at our Center in new ways. We see identity theory as moving psychoanalysis definitively into a third phase. ...

We believe that identity enriches the psychoanalytic theory of motivation. Freud began with a two-level theory. The pleasure principle (really, the avoidance of unpleasure) was the dominant human motive except as it became modified by the reality principle (we learned to delay gratification so as to achieve a net increase in pleasure). Later he provided a third, deeper level, 'beyond' the pleasure principle, a death instinct or perhaps a drive toward a constant or zero level of excitation, an idea questioned by many psychoanalysts. Lichtenstein suggests replacing it with an identity principle: the organism's most basic motivation is to maintain its identity. Indeed, we will even die to be true to what we hold fundamental to our being. So deep and strong is identity, it defines what the pleasure and the reality of the other principles are.

... Ego, id, superego, reality, and the compulsion to repeat all exist as functions of identity. Hence, instead of structures, they can be better understood as questions about a total transaction by a self with an identity. One can ask, What in this transaction looks like an integrating, synthesizing activity? What looks like an incorporated parental voice? These questions will lead to a picture of the whole person acting, rather than five 'agencies'.

Similarly, in teaching development through the familiar oral, anal, phallic, etc., stages, we avoid giving the idea that the child is 'done to' by drives, parents, environment, or society. Rather, an active child with a developing identity marches through an 'epigenetic landscape' of questions posed by his own biology, his parents, and the social and environmental structures they embody. In effect, we can read the development of any given individual as the particular answers he chooses (because they re-create his identity) to questions that his particular body or family poses or that he shares with other children who have his biology and culture. And, of course, the answers he arrives at become part of the identity he brings to the questions he gets thereafter. ...

Finding the principle of identity re-creation has changed the method as well as the substance of our teaching. More and more we use the Delphi ('know thyself') seminar to help students discover how they each bring a personal style (identity) to reading, writing, learning, and teaching. Students and faculty read imaginative or even theoretical texts and pre-circulate to one another written free associations. The seminar discusses both texts and associations, but eventually turns entirely to the associations as the texts to be responded to. Students master the subject matter and also see how people in the seminar use that subject matter to re-create their identities. Most important, each student gains insight into his own characteristic ways with texts and people – that is why we feel this method is particularly valuable for all teaching of psychoanalysis, psychiatry, and psychology.

In a Delphi seminar we come face to face with the ultimate implication of identity theory. If any reading of a story or another person or psychological theory is a function of the reader's identity, then my reading of your identity must be a function of my own. Identity, then, is not a conclusion but a relationship: the potential, transitional, in-between space in which I perceive someone as a theme and variations. Just as in most psychoanalytic thinking about human development, the existence of a child constitutes a mother and the existence of a mother constitutes a child, so, in identity theory, all selves and objects constitute one another. The hard and fast line between subjective and objective blurs and dissolves. Instead of simple dualism, we try for a detailed inquiry into the potential space of that DEFT feedback in which self and other mutually constitute each other.

That inquiry is part of science, so that it no longer makes sense to ask: Is psychoanalysis 'scientific'? That is, is it independent of the personality of the scientist? Rather, psychoanalysis is the science that tells us how to inquire into that very question: How does a person doing science thereby re-create identity?

The question applies most pointedly to those in the human sciences. Traditionally psychologists have tried to understand new human events by impersonal if-then generalizations about countable categories. Few large-scale generalizations have resulted, however. If we define a science as yielding understanding, psychology, as we have known it so far, has not been scientific.

Identity theory suggests a more promising method: one should bring not generalizations but questions to the new event, questions to be asked by a scientist acknowledging and actively using his involvement with what he is studying. That is – I now understand – what I was doing when I set out to study reading. It is also the method shared by all psychoanalytic psychologists, be they clinical or theoretical.

30   HAROLD BLOOM: 'POETRY, REVISIONISM, AND REPRESSION'

Jacques Derrida asks a central question in his essay on Freud and the Scene of Writing: 'What is a text, and what must the psyche be if it can be represented by a text?' My narrower concern with poetry prompts the contrary question: 'What is a psyche, and what must a text be if it can be represented by a psyche?' Both Derrida's question and my own require exploration of three terms: 'psyche', 'text', 'represented'.

'Psyche' is ultimately from the Indo-European root *bhes*, meaning 'to breathe', and possibly was imitative in its origins. 'Text' goes back, to the root *teks*, meaning 'to weave', and also 'to fabricate'. 'Represent' has its root *es*: 'to be'. My question thus can be rephrased: 'What is a breath, and what must a weaving or a fabrication be so as to come into being again as a breath?'

Reprinted from *Poetry and Repression: Revisionism from Blake to Stevens* (New Haven, 1976), pp. 1–26.

In the context of post-Enlightenment poetry, a breath is at once a *word*, and a *stance* for uttering that word, a word and a stance *of one's own*. In this context, a weaving or a fabrication is what we call a poem, and its function is to represent, to bring back into being again, as individual stance and word. The poem, as text, is represented or seconded by what psychoanalysis calls the psyche. But the text *is* rhetoric, and as a persuasive system of tropes can be carried into being again only by another system of tropes. Rhetoric can be seconded only by rhetoric, for all that rhetoric can *intend* is more rhetoric. If a text and a psyche can be represented by one another, this can be done only because each is a departure from proper meaning. Figuration turns out to be our only link between breathing and making.

The strong word and stance issue only from a strict will, a will that dares the error of reading all of reality as a text, and all prior texts as opening for its own totalizing and unique interpretations. Strong poets present themselves as looking for truth *in the world*, searching in reality and in tradition, but such a stance, as Nietzsche said, remains under the mastery of desire, of instinctual drives. So, in effect, the strong poet wants pleasure and not truth: he wants what Nietzsche named as 'the belief in truth and the pleasurable effects of this belief'. No strong poet can admit that Nietzsche was accurate in this insight, and no critic need fear that any strong poet will accept and so be hurt by demystification. ...

A poetic 'text', as I interpret it, is not a gathering of signs on a page, but is a psychic battlefield upon which authentic forces struggle for the only victory worth winning, the divinating triumph over oblivion, or as Milton sang it:

> Attir'd with Stars, we shall for ever sit,
> Triumphing over Death, and Chance, and thee O Time.

Few notions are more difficult to dispel than the 'commonsensical' one that a poetic text is self-contained, that it has an ascertainable meaning or meaning without reference to other poetic texts. Something in nearly every reader wants to say: '*Here* is a poem and *there* is a meaning, and I am reasonably certain that the two can be brought together.' Unfortunately, poems are not things but only words that refer to other words, and *those* words refer to still other words, and so on, into the densely overpopulated world of literary language. Any poem is an inter-poem, and any reading of a poem is an inter-reading. A poem is not writing, but *rewriting*, and though a strong poem is a fresh start, such a start is a starting-again.

In some sense, literary criticism has known always this reliance of texts upon texts, but the knowing changed (or should have changed) after Vico, who uncovered the genuine scandal of poetic origins, in the complex defensive trope or troping defense he called 'divination'. ...

Language for Vico, particularly poetic language, is always and necessarily a revision of previous language. Vico, so far as I know, inaugurated a crucial insight that most critics still refuse to assimilate, which is that every poet is belated, that every poem is an instance of what Freud called *Nachträglichkeit* or 'retroactive meaningfulness'. Any poet (meaning even Homer, if we could know enough about his precursors) is in the position of being 'after the Event', in terms of literary language. His art is necessarily an *altering*, and so at best he strives for a selection, through repression, out of the traces of the language of poetry; that is, he represses some of the traces, and remembers others. This remembering is a misprision, or creative misreading, but no matter how strong a misprision, it cannot achieve an autonomy of meaning, or a meaning *fully* present, that is, free from all literary context. Even the strongest poet must take up his stance *within* literary language. If he stands *outside* it, then he cannot begin to write poetry. The caveman who traced the outline of an animal upon the rock always retraced a precursor's outline. ...

...Vico's insight is that poetry is born of our ignorance of causes, and we can extend Vico by observing that if any poet knows too well what causes his poem, then he cannot write it, or at least will write it badly. He must repress the causes, including the precursor-poems, but such forgetting ... itself is a condition of a particular exaggeration of style or hyperbolical figuration that tradition has called the Sublime. ...

... A strong poem does not *formulate* poetic facts any more than strong reading or criticism formulates them, for a strong reading is the only poetic fact, the only revenge against time that endures, that is successful in canonizing one text as opposed to a rival text.

There is no textual authority without an act of imposition, a declaration of property that is made figuratively rather than properly or literally. For the ultimate question a strong reading asks of a poem is: Why? Why should it have been written? Why must we read it, out of all the too many other poems available? Who does the poet think he is, anyway? Why is his poem?

By defining poetic strength as usurpation or imposition, I am offending against civility, against the social conventions of literary scholarship and criticism. But poetry, when it aspires to strength, is necessarily a competitive mode, indeed an obsessive mode, because poetic strength involves a self-representation that is reached only through trespass, through crossing a daemonic threshold. ...

... Since poetry, unlike the Jewish religion, does not go back to a truly divine origin, poetry is always at work *imagining its own origin*, or telling a persuasive lie about itself, to itself. Poetic strength ensues when such lying persuades the reader that his own origin has been reimagined by the poem. Persuasion, in a poem, is the work of rhetoric, and again Vico is the best of guides, for he convincingly relates the origins of rhetoric to the origins of what he calls poetic logic, or what I would call poetic misprision. ... Vico's profundity as a philosopher of rhetoric, beyond all others ancient and modern except for his true son, Kenneth Burke, is that he views tropes as defenses. ...

Vico is asking a crucial question, which could be interpreted reductively as, What is a poetic image, or what is a rhetorical trope, or what is a psychic defense? Vico's answer can be read as a formula: poetic image, trope, defense are all forms of a ratio between human ignorance making things out of itself, and human self-identification moving to transform us into the things we have made. When the human ignorance is the trespass of a poetic repression of anteriority, and the transforming movement is a new poem, then the ratio measures a rewriting or an act of revision. ...

... For a strong poet in particular, rhetoric is also what Nietzsche saw it as being, a mode of interpretation that is the will's revulsion against time, the will's revenge, its vindication against the necessity of passing away. Pragmatically, a trope's revenge is against an earlier trope, just as defenses tend to become operations against one another. We can define a strong poet as one who will not tolerate words that intervene between him and the Word, or precursors standing between him and the Muse. ...

The hyperbole or intensified exaggeration that such boundlessness demands exacts a psychic price. To 'exaggerate' etymologically means 'to pile up, to heap', and the function of the Sublime is to heap us, as Moby Dick makes Ahab cry out 'He heaps me!' Precisely here I locate the difference between the strong poets and Freud, since what Freud calls 'repression' is, in the greater poets, the imagination of a Counter-Sublime. By attempting to show the poetic ascendancy of 'repression' over 'sublimation' I intend no revision of the Freudian trope of 'the Unconscious', but rather I deny the usefulness of the Unconscious, as opposed to repression, as a literary term. ...

...To say that a poem's true subject is its repression of the precursor poem is not to say that the later poem reduces to the process of that repression. On a strict Freudian view, a good poem is a sublimation, and not a repression. Like any work of substitution that replaces the gratification of prohibited instincts, the poem, as viewed by the Freudians, may contain antithetical effects but not unintended or counterintended effects. In the Freudian valorization of sublimation, the survival of those effects would be flaws in the poem. But poems are actually stronger when their counterintended effects battle most incessantly against their overt intentions.

Imagination, as Vico understood and Freud did not, is the faculty of self-preservation, and so the proper use of Freud, for the literary critic, is not so to apply Freud (or even revise Freud) as to arrive at an Oedipal interpretation of poetic history. I find such to be the usual misunderstanding that my own work provokes. In studying poetry we are not studying the mind, nor the Unconscious, even if there is an unconscious. We are studying a kind of labor that has its own latent principles, principles that can be uncovered and then taught systematically. ...

Poems are not psyches, nor things, nor are they renewable archetypes in a verbal universe, nor are they architectonic units of balanced stresses. They are defensive processes in constant change, which is to say that poems themselves are *acts of reading*. A poem is, as Thomas Frosch says, a fierce, proleptic debate *with itself*, as well as with precursor poems. Or, a poem is a dance of substitutions, a constant breaking-of-the-vessels, as one limitation undoes a representation, only to be restituted in its turn by a fresh representation. Every strong poem, at least since Petrarch, has known implicitly what Nietzsche taught us to know explicitly: that there is only interpretation, and that every interpretation answers an earlier interpretation, and then must yield to a later one.

31 SHOSHANA FELMAN: 'THE MADNESS OF INTERPRETATION: LITERATURE AND PSYCHOANALYSIS'

Let us return ... to Wilson's reading [of Henry James's *The Turn of the Screw*][1] which will be considered here not as a model 'Freudian reading', but as the illustration of a prevalent tendency as well as an inherent temptation of psychoanalytical interpretation as it undertakes to provide an 'explanation', or an 'explication' of a literary text. In this regard, Wilson's later semi-retraction of this thesis is itself instructive: convinced by his detractors that for James the ghosts were real, that James's *conscious* project or intention was to write a simple ghost story and not a madness story, Wilson does not, however, give up his theory that the ghosts consist of the neurotic hallucinations of the governess, but concedes in a note:

One is led to conclude that, in *The Turn of the Screw*, not merely is the governess self-deceived, but that James is self-deceived about her. (*Wilson*, note added 1948, p. 143)

This sentence can be seen as the epitome, and as the verbal formulation, of the desire underlying psychoanalytical interpretation: the desire to be *non-dupe*, to interpret, i.e., at once uncover and avoid, the very traps of the unconscious. James's text, however, is made of traps and dupery: in the first place, from an analytical perspective the governess is *self-deceived*; duping us, she is equally herself a *dupe* of her own unconscious; in the second place, in Wilson's view, James himself is self-deceived: the author also is at once our duper and the dupe of his unconscious; the reader, in the third place, is in turn duped, deceived, by the very rhetoric of the text, by the author's 'trick', by the ruse of his narrative technique which consists in presenting 'cases of self-deception' 'from their own point of view' (*Wilson*, p. 142). Following Wilson's suggestions, there seems to be only one exception to this circle of universal dupery and deception: the so-called Freudian literary critic himself. By avoiding the double trap set at once by the unconscious and by rhetoric, by remaining himself *exterior* to the reading-errors which delude and blind both characters and

Reprinted from *Yale French Studies*, 55/56 (1977), 187–200.

author, the critic thus becomes the sole agent and the exclusive mouthpiece of the *truth* of literature.

This way of thinking and this state of mind, however, strikingly resemble those of the governess herself, who is equally preoccupied by the desire, above all, not to be made a dupe, by the determination to avoid, detect, demystify, the cleverest of traps set for her credulity. ... Like Wilson, the governess is *suspicious* of the ambiguity of signs and of their rhetorical reversibility; like Wilson, she thus proceeds to *read* the world around her, to *interpret* it, not by looking at it but by seeing *through* it, by demystifying and *reversing* the values of its outward signs. In each case, then, it is *suspicion* which gives rise as such to *interpretation*.

But isn't James's reader-trap, in fact, a *trap set for suspicion?* The *Turn of the Screw* thus constitutes a trap for psychoanalytical interpretation to the extent that it constructs a trap, precisely, for suspicion. ... Psychoanalysis ... is strictly speaking a 'school of suspicion' to the extent that it is, in effect, a *school of reading.* Practiced by Wilson as well as by the governess, but quite unknown to Mrs Grose, 'suspicion' is directed, first and foremost, toward the non-transparent, arbitrary nature of the sign: it feeds on the discrepancy and distance which separates the signifier from its signified. While suspicion constitutes, thereby, the very motive of the process of interpretation, the very moving force behind the 'wit' of the discriminating reader, we should not forget, however, that the reader is here 'caught' or trapped, not *in spite of* but *by virtue of, because of* his intelligence and his sophistication. ... Like faith (naïve or 'witless' reading), suspicion (the intelligence of reading) is here a *trap.*

The trap, indeed, resides precisely in the way in which these two opposing types of reading are themselves inscribed and comprehended in the text. The reader of *The Turn of the Screw* can choose either to *believe* the governess, and thus to behave like Mrs Grose, or *not to believe the governess,* and thus to behave precisely *like the governess.* Since it is the governess who, within the text, plays the role of the suspicious reader, occupies the *place* of the interpreter, to *suspect* that place and that position is, thereby, *to take it.* To demystify the governess is only possible on one condition: the condition of *repeating* the governess's very gesture. The text thus constitutes a reading of its two possible readings, both of which, in the course of that reading, it deconstructs. James's trap is then the simplest and the most sophisticated in the world: the trap is but a text, that is, an invitation to the reader, a simple invitation to undertake its reading. But in the case of *The Turn of the*

Screw, the invitation to undertake a reading of the text is perforce an invitation to *repeat* the text, to enter into its labyrinth of mirrors, from which it is henceforth impossible to escape.

It is in just the same manner as the governess that Wilson, in his reading, seeks to avoid above all being duped: to avoid, precisely, being the governess's dupe. Blind to his own resemblance with the governess, he repeats, indeed, one after the other, the procedures and delusions of her reading strategy. 'Observe', writes Wilson, 'from a Freudian point of view, the significance of the governess's interest in the little girl's pieces of wood' (*Wilson*, p. 104). But to 'observe' the *signified* behind the wooden *signifier*, to observe the meaning, or the significance, of the very *interest* shown for that signifier, is precisely what the governess herself does, and invites others to do, when she runs crying to Mrs Grose, 'They know – it's too monstrous: they know, they know!' (ch. 7, p. 30).[2] In just the same manner as the governess, Wilson equally *fetishizes* the phallic simulacrum, delusively raises the mast in Flora's boat to the status of Master-Signifier. Far from following the incessant slippage, the unfixable movement of the signifying chain from link to link, from signifier to signifier, the critic, like the governess, seeks to *stop* the meaning, to *arrest* signification, by a grasp, precisely, of the Screw (or of the 'clue'), by a firm hold on the Master-Signifier. ... In their attempt to elaborate a speech of mastery, a discourse of *totalitarian* power, what Wilson and the governess both *exclude* is nothing other than the threatening power of rhetoric itself – of sexuality as *division* and as meaning's *flight*, as contradiction and as ambivalence; the very threat, in other words, of the unmastery, of the impotence, and of the unavoidable castration which inhere in *language*. From his very *grasp* of meaning and from the grasp of his interpretation, Wilson thus excludes, *represses*, the very thing which led to his analysis, the very subject of his study: the role of language in the text. ...

Here, then, is the crowning aberration which psychoanalysis sometimes unwittingly commits in its mêlées with literature. In seeking to 'explain' and *master* literature, in refusing, that is, to become a *dupe* of literature, in killing within literature that which makes it literature – its reserve of silence, that which, within speech, is incapable of speaking, the literary silence of a discourse *ignorant of what it knows* – the psychoanalytic reading, ironically enough, turns out to be a reading which *represses the unconscious*, which represses, paradoxically, the unconscious which it purports to be 'explaining'. To *master*, then (to become the Master) is, here as elsewhere, to *refuse to read* the letters; here as elsewhere, to 'see it all' is in effect to 'shut one's eyes as tight as possible to the truth'; once more, 'to see it all' is in reality to *exclude*; and to exclude, specifically, the unconscious. ...

'It is not by locking up one's neighbor,' as Dostoievsky once said, 'that one can convince oneself of one's own soundness of mind.' This, however, is what Wilson seems precisely to be doing, insofar as he is duplicating and *repeating* the governess's gesture. This, then, is what psychoanalytical interpretation might be doing, and indeed is doing whenever it gives in to the temptation of *diagnosing* literature, of indicating and of *situating madness* in a literary text. For in shutting madness up in literature, in attempting not just to explain the literary symptom, but to explain away the very symptom of literature itself, psychoanalysis, like the governess, only diagnoses literature so as to *justify itself*, to insure its own *control* of meaning, to deny or to negate the lurking possibility of its own madness, to convince itself of its own incontrovertible soundness of mind. ...

Thus it is that *The Turn of the Screw* succeeds in *trapping* the very analytical interpretation it in effect *invites* but whose authority it at the same time *deconstructs*. In inviting, in *seducing* the psychoanalyst, in tempting him into the quicksand of its rhetoric, literature, in truth, only invites him to *subvert himself*, only lures psychoanalysis into its necessary self-subversion. ...

...That psychoanalytical theory itself occupies precisely a symmetrical, and hence a specular, position with respect to the madness it observes and faces, is in fact a fundamental given of psychoanalysis, acknowledged both by Freud and by Lacan. Lacan as well as Freud recognize indeed that the very value – but equally the risk – inherent in psychoanalysis, its insightfulness but equally its blindness, its truth but also its error, reside precisely in this turn of the screw. ...

... In its efforts to master literature, psychoanalysis ... can thus but blind itself: blind itself in order to deny its own castration, in order not to see, and not to read, literature's subversion of the very possibility of psychoanalytical mastery. The irony is that, in the very act of judging literature from the height of its masterly position, psychoanalysis – like Wilson – in effect rejoins within the structure of the text the masterly position, the specific place of the Master of *The Turn of the Screw*: the place, precisely, of the textual *blind spot.*

Now, to occupy a blind spot is not only to be blind, but in particular, to be blind to one's own blindness; it is to be unaware of the fact that one occupies a spot *within* the very blindness one seeks to demystify, that one is *in* the madness, that one is always, necessarily, *in* literature; it is to believe that one is on the *outside*, that one *can* be outside: outside the traps of literature, of the unconscious, or of madness. James's reader-trap thus functions by precisely luring the reader into attempting to avoid the trap, into believing that there *is* an outside to the trap. This belief, of course, is itself one of the trap's most subtle mechanisms: the very act of trying to escape the trap is the proof that one is caught in it. 'The unconscious,' writes Lacan, 'is most effectively misleading when it is caught in the act.' This, precisely, is what James suggests in *The Turn of the Screw.* And what James in effect *does* in *The Turn of the Screw,* what he undertakes through the performative action of his text, is precisely to mislead us, and to catch us, by on the contrary inviting us to *catch the unconscious in the act.* In attempting to escape the reading-error constitutive of rhetoric, in attempting to escape the rhetorical error constitutive of literature, in attempting to master literature in order *not to be its dupe,* psychoanalysis, in reality, is *doubly duped*: unaware of its own inescapable participation *in* literature and *in* the errors and the traps of rhetoric, it is blind to the fact that it itself exemplifies no less than the *blind spot* of rhetoricity, the spot where any affirmation of mastery in effect amounts to a self-subversion and to a self-castration. '*Les non-dupes errent*' [non-dupes err], says Lacan. If James's text does not explicitly make such a statement, it enacts it, and acts it out, while also dramatizing at the same time the suggestion that this very sentence – which entraps us in the same way as does the 'turn of the screw' – this very statement, which cannot be affirmed without thereby being negated, whose very diction is in fact its own contradiction, constitutes, precisely, the position *par excellence* of *meaning* in the *literary utterance*: a rhetorical position, implying a relation of mutual subversion and of radical, dynamic contradiction between utterance and statement.

NOTES

1. [Ed.] See Edmund Wilson, 'The Ambiguity of Henry James', in *The Triple Thinkers* (Harmondsworth, 1962). Page numbers in the text are to this edition.

2. [Ed.] Page references are to Henry James, *The Turn of the Screw,* ed. Robert Kimbrough (New York, 1966).

VIII   MARXIST AND NEO-MARXIST CRITICISM

Marxist literary theory starts from the assumption that literature must be understood in relation to historical and social reality as interpreted from a Marxist standpoint. The fundamental Marxist postulate is that the economic base of a society determines the nature and structure of the ideology, institutions and practices (such as literature) that form the superstructure of that society. The most direct form of Marxist criticism, what has been called 'vulgar' Marxism, takes the view that there is a straightforward deterministic relation between base and superstructure, so that literary texts are seen as causally determined by the economic base. The selection from Christopher Caudwell's *Illusion and Reality* adopts this position in discussing Victorian poetry.

The Hungarian theorist, Georg Lukács, a Marxist in the Hegelian tradition, also sees literature as reflecting socio-economic reality, but he rejected the view that there was a simple deterministic relationship between the two. He argues that the greatest literary works do not merely reproduce the dominant ideologies of their time but incorporate in their form a critique of these ideologies. Thus in his view the realism of the realistic nineteenth-century novel, the literary genre he was most sympathetic to, what he calls 'critical realism', is not merely mimetic but incorporates a recognition of the contradictions within bourgeois society. To achieve this, it sometimes has to break with realism in the mimetic sense, as for example in the exaggeration of Balzac's characters. Lukács's artistic criterion is 'typicality'. Realistic or naturalistic works which focus on what he regards as the untypical or the bizarre, or works in which technique is emphasised more than content, are criticised by him. He thus tends to be unsympathetic to modernist literature, as 'Critical Realism and Socialist Realism' shows.

Lukács's anti-modernism was criticised by such Marxists as Bertolt Brecht, Theodor Adorno and Walter Benjamin. Benjamin in 'The Artist as Producer' argues that a truly revolutionary art must break radically with traditional forms since even works which use conventional techniques to attack capitalism will tend merely to be consumed by a bourgeois audience. Socialist artists must place the emphasis on production rather than consumption by using radical techniques, as Brecht does in his epic theatre, to uncover the relations of production and compel the audience to adopt a political standpoint towards them. Whereas Marxist criticism until the 1960s was mainly of interest to those committed to Marxism as a system, more recent Marxist criticism has had a much wider influence. The main reason for this is that Marxist thinking has entered into fruitful relationships with other sets of ideas. Louis Althusser has been a particularly significant figure as he was a Marxist philosopher who had clearly been influenced by structuralism and psychoanalysis. He criticised Hegelian-influenced Marxist theories which were attracted to notions of totality and instead emphasised the 'decentred' nature of the 'social formation' which was made of various levels. This led him to reject the so-called 'vulgar' Marxist view that works of art are wholly determined by socio-economic forces and to argue that they have 'relative autonomy' and are 'overdetermined', that is, determined by a complex network of factors. Althusser's work created mental space for critics who were sympathetic to the political aims of Marxism but unhappy at the restrictive nature of most earlier Marxist criticism.

Althusserian influence has affected all contemporary Marxist critics to a greater or lesser degree. Terry Eagleton is a Marxist critic of long standing but his more recent work has engaged with Althusserian Marxism and post-structuralism without rejecting traditional Marxian concepts. Thus in the essay included here he retains the Marxian concept of ideology but modifies traditional Marxian formulations and argues that the relation of the literary text to ideology should be seen in terms of 'overdetermination'. Ellis and Coward attempt a more far-reaching alignment between Marxian concepts and other sets of ideas – structuralism and post-structuralism, Lacanian psychoanalysis, Kristevan semiology, discourse theory, feminist theory – and create what has been called a 'syncretist' form of criticism in which Marxism is only one element among many, as their discussion of Roland Barthes's book *S/Z* indicates. Fredric Jameson, the leading American Marxist critic, has been influenced by Althusserian concepts and also favours aligning Marxism with contemporary theories such as post-structuralism and psychoanalysis, but he has strong connections with traditional Marxism of the Hegelian totalising type since, for him, Marxism can subsume and incorporate within itself all other forms of thought. In contrast to the anti-interpretative tendency of much structuralist and post-structuralist influenced criticism, he supports an interpretative critical approach in which Marxism functions as the 'master code'.

FURTHER READING

Walter Benjamin, *Illuminations*, ed. Hannah Arendt and trans. Harry Zohn (London, 1970).

Peter Demetz, *Marx, Engels, and the Poets: Origins of Marxist Criticism*, trans. Jeffrey L. Sammons (Chicago, 1967).

William C. Dowling, *Jameson, Althusser, Marx: An Introduction to 'The Political Unconscious'* (London, 1984).

Terry Eagleton, *Marxism and Literary Criticism* (London, 1976).

———, *The Function of Criticism* (London, 1984).

———, *Walter Benjamin or Towards a Revolutionary Criticism* (London, 1981).

Fredric Jameson, *Marxism and Form: Twentieth-Century Dialectical Theories of Literature* (Princeton, NJ, 1971).

———, 'Marxism and Historicism', *New Literary History*, 11 (1979), 41–73.

Georg Lukács, *The Historical Novel*, trans. Hannah and Stanley Mitchell (London, 1962).

Pierre Macherey, *A Theory of Literary Production*, trans. Geoffrey Wall (London, 1978).

Ronald Taylor (ed.), *Aesthetics and Politics* (London, 1977).

René Wellek, *Four Critics: Croce, Valéry, Lukács, and Ingarden* (Seattle, 1981).

Raymond Williams, *Marxism and Literature* (Oxford, 1977).

32   CHRISTOPHER CAUDWELL: 'ENGLISH POETS: THE DECLINE OF CAPITALISM'

Arnold, Swinburne, Tennyson and Browning, each in his own way, illustrate the movement of the bourgeois illusion in this 'tragic' stage of its history.

Tennyson's Keatsian world is shattered as soon as he attempts to compromise between the world of beauty and the real world of misery which will not let him rest. Only the elegiac *In Memoriam*, with its profound pessimism, the most genuinely pessimistic poem in English up to this date, in any way successfully mirrors contemporary problems in contemporary terms.

Like Darwin, and even more Darwin's followers, he projects the conditions of capitalist production into Nature (individual struggle for existence) and then reflects this struggle, intensified by its instinctive and therefore unalterable blindness, back into society, so that God – symbol of the internal forces of society – seems captive to Nature – symbol of the external environment of society. ...

Reprinted from *Illusion and Reality* (London, 1946), pp. 114–19.

The unconscious ruthlessness of Tennyson's 'Nature' in fact only reflects the ruthlessness of a society in which capitalist is continually hurling down fellow capitalist into the proletarian abyss. ... Browning revolts from the drab present not to the future but to the glories of the virile Italian springtime of the bourgeoisie. Never before had that vigour been given in English poetry so deep a colouring. But his vocabulary has a foggy verbalism which is a reflection of his intellectual dishonesty in dealing with real contemporary problems. To Tennyson the Keatsian world of romance, to Browning the Italian springtime; both are revolting backwards, trying to escape from the contradiction of the class for whom they speak. Browning dealing with contemporary problems, can produce no higher poetry than that of Mr Sludge or Bishop Blougram. ...

Swinburne's poetry is Shelley's world of immanent light and beauty made more separate by being stiffened with something of the materiality and hypnotic heaviness of Keats' world. Fate, whether as Hertha or the Nemesis of *Atalanta in Calydon*, is no longer tragic, but sad, sad as the death of Baudelaire. Swinburne is profoundly moved by the appeal of the contemporary bourgeois-democratic revolutions taking place all over Europe (1848–1871), but the purely verbal and shallow character of his response reflects the essential shallowness of all such movements in this late era when, owing to the development of the proletariat, they almost instantly negate themselves.

Arnold's poems breathe the now characteristic 'pessimism' of the bourgeois illusion, which is now working out its final and (to itself) tragic stages. Arnold battles against the Philistine, but he has an uneasy suspicion that he is doomed to lose. And in fact he is, for he fights his mirror reflection. As long as he moves within the categories of bourgeois society his own movement produces the Philistine; he drives on the movement which generates Philistine and poet, by separating the poet from society.

The next phase of bourgeois poetry is therefore that of 'commodity-fetishism' – or 'art for art's sake' – and is given in the false position of the bourgeois poet as producer for the market, a position forced on him by the development of bourgeois economy. As soon as the pessimism of Arnold and the young Tennyson, and the even sadder optimism of Browning and Swinburne and the old Tennyson when dealing with the contemporary scene, made it inevitable that the poet quit the contemporary scene, it was equally inevitable that the poet should fall a victim to commodity-fetishism. This meant a movement which would completely separate the world of art from the world of reality and, in doing so, separate it from the source of art itself so that the work would burst like a bubble just when it seemed most self-secure.

Engels in *Anti-Dühring* very clearly explains the characteristic of every society based on commodity production:

[It] has the peculiarity that in it the producers have lost control of their own social relationships. Each produces for himself, with the means of production which happen to be at his disposal and in order to satisfy his individual needs through the medium of exchange. No one knows how much of the article he produces is coming on the market, or how much demand there is for it; no one knows whether his individual product will meet a real need, whether he will cover his costs or even be able to sell at all. Anarchy reigns in social production. ... *The product dominates the producers.*

Engels contrasts this with the older and more universal method of production for use instead of exchange. Here the origin and end of production are clearly seen. All are part of the one social act, and the product is only valued in so far as it is of use to the society which produces it. In such a society the poem as such derives its value from its collective appearance, from the effect it has on the hearts of its hearers and the impact, direct and evident, on the life of the tribe.

In capitalist production, which is commodity production *in excelsis*, all this is altered. Everyone produces blindly for a market whose laws are unfathomable, although they assert themselves with iron rigidity. The impact of the commodity upon the life of society cannot be measured or seen. 'Man has lost control of his social relationships.' The whole elaborate warp and woof of capitalism, a complex web spun in anarchy, makes this helplessness inevitable.

To the poet the bourgeois market appears as the 'public'. The invention and development of printing and publishing was part of the development of the universal bourgeois free market. Just as the development of this market (by the extension of colonisation and transport and exchange facilities) made it possible for a man to produce for places whose very names he did not know, much less their location, so the poet now writes for men of whose existence he is ignorant, whose social life, whose whole mode of being is strange to him. The market is for him 'The Public' – blind, strange, passive.

This leads to what Marx called 'commodity-fetishism'. The social character of the art-process, so evident in the collective festival, now disappears. ...

But the poet is not a capitalist. He does not exploit labour. To the capitalist commodity-fetishism takes the form of sacralisation of the common market-denominator of all commodities – money. Money acquires for him a high, mystic, *spiritual* value. But the writer is himself exploited. In so far as he 'writes for money' of course he acquires a purely capitalist mentality. He may even himself exploit labour by means of secretaries and hacks who do his 'donkeywork' for him. But the man who writes for money is not an artist, for it is the characteristic of the artist that his products are adaptative, that the artistic illusion is begotten of the tension between instinct and consciousness, between productive forces and productive relations, the very tension which drives on all society to future reality. In bourgeois society this tension is that between the productive forces (the socially organised power of capitalist technique in the factories) and the social relations (production for private profit and the resulting anarchy in the market as a whole indicated by the universality of the money or 'exchange' relation instead of the direct or 'use' relation). Because this is the fundamental contradiction, the poet 'revolts' against the system of profit-making or production for exchange-value as crippling the meaning and significance of art. But as long as he revolts within the categories of bourgeois thought – that is, as long as he cannot cast off the basic bourgeois illusion – his revolt takes a form made necessary by the system of commodity production.

33 GEORG LUKÁCS: 'CRITICAL REALISM AND SOCIALIST REALISM'

Socialist realism differs from critical realism, not only in being based on a concrete socialist perspective, but also in using this perspective to describe the forces working towards socialism *from the inside*. Socialist society is seen as an independent entity, not simply as a foil to capitalist society, or as a refuge from its dilemmas – as with those critical realists who have come closest to embracing socialism. Even more important is the treatment of those social forces leading towards socialism; scientific, as against utopian, socialism aims to locate those forces scientifically, just as socialist realism is concerned to locate those human qualities which make for the creation of a new social order. ...

Reprinted from *The Meaning of Contemporary Realism*, trans. John and Necke Mander (London, 1963), pp. 93–127.

The perspective of socialism enables the writer to see society and history for what they are. This opens a fundamentally new, and highly fruitful, chapter in literary creation. Let us take two points. Socialist realism is a possibility rather than an actuality; and the effective realization of the possibility is a complex affair. A study of Marxism (not to speak of other activity in the Socialist movement, even Party membership) is not of itself sufficient. A writer may acquire useful experience in this way, and become aware of certain intellectual and moral problems. But it is no easier to translate 'true consciousness' of reality into adequate aesthetic form than it is bourgeois 'false consciousness'.

Again, while it is true that a correct theoretical approach and a correct aesthetic (i.e. the creation of a typology) may often coincide, the methods and the results are not really identical. Their coincidence derives from the fact that both reflect the same reality. A correct aesthetic understanding of social and historical reality is the precondition of realism. A merely theoretical understanding – whether correct or incorrect – can only influence literature if completely absorbed and translated into suitable aesthetic categories. Whether the theory is correct or not is immaterial, since for a writer no theory, no conceptual understanding, can be more than a general guide. ...

Our account of the similarities between socialist and critical realism would be incomplete if the alliance between both these movements, and its historical necessity, were to be disregarded. The theoretical basis of this alliance is socialism's concern for the truth. In no other aesthetic does the truthful depiction of reality have so central a place as in Marxism. This is closely tied up with other elements in Marxist doctrine. For the Marxist, the road to socialism is identical with the movement of history itself. There is no phenomenon, objective or subjective, that has not its function in furthering, obstructing or deviating this development. A right understanding of such things is vital to the thinking socialist. Thus, *any* accurate account of reality is a contribution – whatever the author's subjective intention – to the Marxist critique of capitalism, and is a blow in the cause of socialism. ...

But the alliance between critical and socialist realism is implicit also in the nature of art. It is impossible to work out the principles of socialist realism without taking into account the opposition between realism and modernism. In regard to the past, theoreticians of socialist realism are well aware of this; they have always considered the great critical realists allies in their struggle to establish the supremacy of realism in aesthetics. But the alliance is not merely theoretical. The historical insights in these writers' works, and the methods they used to achieve these insights, are vital to an understanding of the forces shaping the present and the future. They may help us to understand the struggle between the forces of progress and reaction, life and decay, in the modern world. To ignore all this is to throw away a most important weapon in our fight against the decadent literature of anti-realism. ...

As socialism develops, critical realism, as a distinct literary style, will wither away. We have pointed out some of the limitations, and the problems, facing the critical realist in a socialist society. We have shown that the scope of critical realism will narrow as a society comes into being the portrayal of which is beyond the grasp of the critical realist. The critical realist will increasingly apply perspectives approximating to socialist realism. This will gradually lead to a withering-away of critical realism. ...

All this argues the superiority – historically speaking – of socialist realism (I cannot sufficiently emphasize that this superiority does not confer automatic success on each individual work of socialist realism). The reason for this superiority is the insights which socialist ideology, socialist perspective, make available to the writer: they enable him to give a more comprehensive and deeper account of man as a social being than any traditional ideology. ...

We have already touched on the problem of typology. What is the key to these 'typical' heroes of literature? The *typical* is not to be confused with the *average* (though there are cases where this holds true), nor with the *eccentric* (though the typical does as a rule go beyond the normal). A character is typical, in this technical sense, when his innermost being is determined by objective forces at work in society. Vautrin or Julien Sorel,[1] superficially eccentric, are *typical* in their behaviour: the determining factors of a particular historical phase are found in them in concentrated form. Yet, though typical, they are never crudely 'illustrative'. There is a dialectic in these characters linking the individual – and all accompanying accidentals – with the typical. Levin[2] was typical of the Russian land-owning class at a period when everything was 'being turned upside down'. The reader learns his personal peculiarities and is sometimes tempted to consider him, not wholly wrongly, as an outsider and an eccentric – until he realizes that such eccentricities are the mark of an age in transition.

The heroes of that schematic literature I have described altogether lack these features. They are not typical, but topical. Their features are prescribed by a specific political intention. I should add that it is always extremely difficult to isolate 'typical' features.

The typical hero reacts with his entire personality to the life of his age. Whenever socialist realism produces authentic types – Fadejev's Levinson, or Sholokhov's Grigory Melyekov – there is present this organic unity of profound individuality and profound typicality. The characters produced by the schematists, on the other hand, are both above and beneath the level of typicality. The individual characterization is beneath it (whereas Natasha Rostova's[3] 'tripping step', say, or Anna Karenina's ball costume are unquestionably typical), whereas what is intended to establish their typicality may be irrelevant to their psychological make-up. This weakness is common, of course, to all naturalistic literature – Zola's 'typical' characters have similar shortcomings. ...

Naturalism, socialist or otherwise, deprives life of its poetry, reduces all to prose. Naturalism's schematic methods are incapable of grasping the 'slyness' of reality, its wealth and beauty. That naturalism destroys the poetry of life is widely recognized, even by those critics and writers who have helped to bring about this state of affairs. Characteristically, public opinion in the socialist countries was never as vain of socialist naturalism as were bourgeois intellectuals of their modernism. But during the Stalinist period, as we know, many crucial Marxist doctrines were misrepresented. Literary theoreticians, therefore, thought up a poetical substitute for naturalism, 'revolutionary romanticism', instead of attempting an ideologically correct aesthetic solution. ...

The theoreticians of revolutionary romanticism often refer to Lenin's saying, in his early work *What is to be done?*, that revolutionaries 'must dream'. Mistakenly. For Lenin always distinguished sharply between perspective and reality, even while pointing out their interdependence. ... Lenin's 'dreaming' is simply that profound, passionate vision of a future which it is in the power of realistic revolutionary measures to construct. This 'dreaming' adds a new dimension to every revolutionary act, however insignificant. But only if that act is based on a correct understanding of objective reality, taking into account the complexity, the 'slyness' of reality. ... Again, it is no accident that Lenin, like Marx, should regard Tolstoy's realism – in spite of its apparent ideological shortcomings – as a model for the literature of the future.

NOTES

1. [Ed.] Characters in Balzac's series of novels *La Comédie Humaine* and Stendhal's *The Red and the Black* respectively.
2 [Ed.] Character in Tolstoy's *Anna Karenina*.
3. [Ed.] Character in Tolstoy's *War and Peace*.

34   WALTER BENJAMIN: 'THE AUTHOR AS PRODUCER'[1]

You will remember how Plato, in his project for a Republic, deals with writers. In the interests of the community, he denies them the right to dwell therein. Plato had a high opinion of the power of literature. But he thought it harmful and superfluous – in a *perfect* community, be it understood. Since Plato, the question of the writer's right to exist has not often been raised with the same emphasis; today, however, it arises once more. Of course it only seldom arises in this *form*. But all of you are more or less conversant with it in a different form, that of the question of the writer's autonomy: his freedom to write just what he pleases. You are not inclined to grant him this autonomy. You believe that the present social situation forces him to decide in whose service he wishes to place his activity. The bourgeois author of entertainment literature does not acknowledge this choice. You prove to him that, without admitting it, he is working in the service of certain class interests. A progressive type of writer does acknowledge this choice. His decision is made upon the basis of the class struggle: he places himself on the side of the proletariat. And that's the end of his autonomy. He directs his activity towards what will be useful to the proletariat in the class struggle. This is usually called pursuing a tendency, or 'commitment'. ...

... I hope to be able to show you that the concept of commitment, in the perfunctory form in which it generally occurs in the debate I have just mentioned, is a totally inadequate instrument of political literary criticism. I should like to demonstrate to you that the tendency of a work of literature can be politically correct only if it is also correct in the literary sense. That means that the tendency which is politically correct includes a literary tendency. And let me add at once: this literary tendency, which is implicitly or explicitly included in every correct political tendency, this and nothing else makes up the quality of a work. It is because of this that the correct political tendency of a work extends also to its literary quality: because a political tendency which is correct comprises a literary tendency which is correct. ...

Reprinted from *Understanding Brecht*, trans. Anna Bostock (London, 1973), pp. 85–101.

... Social relations, as we know, are determined by production relations. And when materialist criticism approached a work, it used to ask what was the position of that work *vis-à-vis* the social production relations of its times. This is an important question. But also a very difficult one. ... Before I ask: what is a work's position *vis-à-vis* the production relations of its time, I should like to ask: what is its position *within* them? This question concerns the function of a work within the literary production relations of its time. In other words, it is directly concerned with literary *technique*.

By mentioning technique I have named the concept which makes literary products accessible to immediate social, and therefore materialist, analysis. At the same time, the concept of technique represents the dialectical starting-point from which the sterile dichotomy of form and content can be surmounted.

... If, then, we were entitled earlier on to say that the correct political tendency of a work includes its literary quality because it includes its literary tendency, we can now affirm more precisely that this literary tendency may consist in a progressive development of literary technique, or in a regressive one. ...

... And so we come back to the thesis we proposed at the beginning: the place of the intellectual in the class struggle can only be determined, or better still chosen, on the basis of his position within the production process. ...

... Here I should like to confine myself to pointing out the decisive difference between merely supplying a production apparatus and changing it. I should like to preface my remarks on the New Objectivity[2] with the proposition that to supply a production apparatus without trying, within the limits of the possible, to change it, is a highly disputable activity even when the material supplied appears to be of a revolutionary nature. For we are confronted with the fact – of which there has been no shortage of proof in Germany over the last decade – that the bourgeois apparatus of production and publication is capable of assimilating, indeed of propagating, an astonishing amount of revolutionary themes without ever seriously putting into question its own continued existence or that of the class which owns it. In any case this remains true so long as it is supplied by hacks, albeit revolutionary hacks. And I define a hack as a man who refuses as a matter of principle to improve the production apparatus and so prise it away from the ruling class for the benefit of Socialism. I further maintain that an appreciable part of so-called left-wing literature had no other social function than that of continually extracting new effects or sensations from this situation for the public's entertainment. Which brings me to the New Objectivity. It launched the fashion for reportage. Let us ask ourselves whose interests were advanced by this technique.

For greater clarity let me concentrate on photographic reportage. Whatever applies to it is transferable to the literary form. Both owe their extraordinary development to publication techniques – radio and the illustrated press. Let us think back to Dadaism. The revolutionary strength of Dadaism lay in testing art for its authenticity. You made still-lifes out of tickets, spools of cotton, cigarette stubs, and mixed them with pictorial elements. You put a frame round the whole thing. And in this way you said to the public: look, your picture frame destroys time; the smallest authentic fragment of everyday life says more than painting. ... But now let us follow the subsequent development of photography. What do we see? It has become more and more subtle, more and more modern, and the result is that it is now incapable of photographing a tenement or a rubbish-heap without transfiguring it. Not to mention a river dam or an electric cable factory: in front of these, photography can now only say, 'How beautiful'. ... It has succeeded in turning abject poverty itself, by handling it in a modish, technically perfect way, into an object of enjoyment. For if it is an economic function of photography to supply the masses, by modish processing, with matter which previously eluded mass consumption – Spring, famous people, foreign countries – then one of its political functions is to renovate the world as it is from the inside, i.e. by modish techniques.

Here we have an extreme example of what it means to supply a production apparatus without changing it. Changing it would have meant bringing down one of the barriers, surmounting one of the contradictions which inhibit the productive capacity of the intelligentsia. What we must demand from the photographer is the ability to put such a caption beneath his picture as will rescue it from the ravages of modishness and confer upon it a revolutionary use value. ...

... Turning to the New Objectivity as a literary movement, I must go a step further and say that it has turned *the struggle against misery* into an object of consumption. In many cases, indeed, its political significance has been limited to converting revolutionary reflexes, in so far as these occurred within the bourgeoisie, into themes of entertainment and amusement which can be fitted without much difficulty into the cabaret life of a large city. The characteristic feature of this literature is the way it transforms political struggle so that it ceases to be a compelling motive for decision and becomes an object of comfortable contemplation; it ceases to be a means of production and becomes an article of consumption. ...

... Commitment is a necessary, but never a sufficient, condition for a writer's work acquiring an organizing function. For this to happen it is also necessary for the writer to have a teacher's attitude. And today this is more than ever an essential demand. *A writer who does not teach other writers teaches nobody.* The crucial point, therefore, is that a writer's production must have the character of a model: it must be able to instruct other writers in their production and, secondly, it must be able to place an improved apparatus at their disposal. This apparatus will be the better, the more consumers it brings in contact with the production process – in short, the more readers or spectators it turns into collaborators. We already possess a model of this kind, of which, however, I cannot speak here in any detail. It is Brecht's epic theatre.

... Epic theatre does not reproduce conditions; rather, it discloses, it uncovers them. This uncovering of the conditions is effected by interrupting the dramatic processes; but such interruption does not act as a stimulant; it has an organizing function. It brings the action to a standstill in mid-course and thereby compels the spectator to take up a position towards the action, and the actor to take up a position towards his part. Let me give an example to show how Brecht, in his selection and treatment of gestures, simply uses the method of montage – which is so essential to radio and film – in such a way that it ceases to be a modish technique and becomes a human event. Picture to yourself a family row: the wife is just about to pick up a bronze statuette and hurl it at the daughter; the father is opening a window to call for help. At this moment a stranger enters. The process is interrupted; what becomes apparent in its place is the condition now exposed before the stranger's view: disturbed faces, open window, a devastated interior. There exists, however, a viewpoint from which even the more normal scenes of present-day life do not look so very different from this. That is the viewpoint of the epic dramatist.

He opposes the dramatic laboratory to the finished work of art. He goes back, in a new way, to the theatre's greatest and most ancient opportunity: the opportunity to expose the present. ...

You may have noticed that the reflections whose conclusions we are now nearing make only one demand on the writer: the demand to *think*, to reflect upon his position in the production process. We can be sure that such thinking, *in the writers who matter* – that is to say the best technicians in their particular branches of the trade – will sooner or later lead them to confirm very soberly their solidarity with the proletariat.

NOTES

1. Address delivered at the Institute for the Study of Fascism, Paris, on 27 April 1934.
2. [Ed.] *Die neue Sachlichkeit*: A post-expressionist artistic movement of the mid-1920s in Germany that included such figures as George Grosz.

35 TERRY EAGLETON: 'TOWARDS A SCIENCE OF THE TEXT'

The literary text is not the 'expression' of ideology, nor is ideology the 'expression' of social class. The text, rather, is a certain *production* of ideology, for which the analogy of a dramatic production is in some ways appropriate. A dramatic production does not 'express', 'reflect', or 'reproduce' the dramatic text on which it is based; it 'produces' the text, transforming it into a unique and irreducible entity. ... The relation between text and production is a relation of *labour*: the theatrical instruments (staging, acting skills and so on) transform the 'raw materials' of the text into a specific product, which cannot be mechanically extrapolated from an inspection of the text itself. ...

The parallel I am pursuing, then, may be schematised as follows:

history/ideology → dramatic text → dramatic production
history → ideology → literary text

The literary text, that is to say, produces ideology (itself a production) in a way analogous to the operations of dramatic production on dramatic text. And just as the dramatic production's relation to its text reveals the text's internal relations to its 'world' under the form of its own *constitution* of them, so the literary text's relation to ideology so constitutes that ideology as to reveal something of its relations to history.

Reprinted from *Criticism and Ideology: A Study in Marxist Literary Theory* (London, 1976), pp. 64–99.

Such a formulation instantly raises several questions, the first of which concerns the relation of the text to 'real' history. In what sense is it correct to maintain that *ideology*, rather than *history*, is the object of the text? Or, to pose the question slightly differently: In what sense, if any, do elements of the historically 'real' enter the text? Georg Lukács, in his *Studies in European Realism*, argues that Balzac's greatness lies in the fact that the 'inexorable veracity' of his art drives him to transcend his reactionary ideology and perceive the real historical issues at stake. Ideology, here, clearly signifies a 'false consciousness' which blocks true historical perception, a screen interposed between men and their history. As such, it is a simplistic notion: it fails to grasp ideology as an inherently complex formation which, by inserting individuals into history in a variety of ways, allows of multiple kinds and degrees of access to that history. It fails, in fact, to grasp the truth that some ideologies, and levels of ideology, are more false than others. ...

It is not that the text, in allowing us access to ideology, swathes us in simple illusion. Commodities, money, wage-relations are certainly 'phenomenal forms' of capitalist production, but they are nothing if not 'real' for all that. ...

History, then, certainly 'enters' the text, not least the 'historical' text; but it enters it precisely *as ideology*, as a presence determined and distorted by its measurable absences. This is not to say that real history is present in the text but in disguised form, so that the task of the critic is then to wrench the mask from its face. It is rather that history is 'present' in the text in the form of a *double-absence*. The text takes as its object, not the real, but certain significations by which the real lives itself – significations which are themselves the product of its partial abolition. Within the text itself, then, ideology becomes a dominant structure, determining the character and disposition of certain 'pseudo-real' constituents. This inversion, as it were, of the real historical process, whereby in the text itself ideology seems to determine the historically real rather than *vice versa*, is itself naturally determined in the last instance by history itself. History, one might say, is the *ultimate* signifier of literature, as it is the ultimate signified. For what else in the end could be the source and object of any signifying practice but the real social formation which provides its material matrix? The problem is not that such a claim is false, but that it leaves everything exactly as it was. For the text presents itself to us less as historical than as a sportive flight from history, a reversal and resistance of history, a momentarily liberated zone in which the exigencies of the real seem to evaporate, an enclave of freedom enclosed within the realm of necessity. We know that such freedom is largely illusory – that the text is *governed*; but it is not illusory merely in the sense of being a false perception of our own. The text's illusion of freedom is part of its very nature – an effect of its peculiarly *overdetermined* relation to historical reality. ...

History, then, operates upon the text by an ideological determination which within the text itself privileges ideology as a dominant structure determining its own imaginary or 'pseudo' history. This 'pseudo' or 'textual' real is not related to the historical real as an imaginary 'transposition' of it. Rather than 'imaginatively transposing' the real, the literary work is the production of certain produced representations of the real into an imaginary object. If it distantiates history, it is not because it transmutes it to fantasy, shifting from one ontological gear to another, but because the significations it works into fiction are already representations of reality rather than reality itself. The text is a tissue of meanings, perceptions and responses which inhere in the first place in that imaginary production of the real which is ideology. The 'textual real' is related to the historical real, not as an imaginary transposition of it, but as the product of certain signifying practices whose source and referent is, in the last instance, history itself...

It is true that some texts seem to approach the real more closely than others. The level of the 'textual real' in *Bleak House* is considerably more predominant than it is in, say, Burns's lyric, *My love is like a red, red rose*. The former seeks to illuminate, among other things, a highly localised history; the latter has an extremely abstract referent. Yet whereas it is obvious that Burns's poem refers us to certain modes of ideological signification rather than to a 'real' object, so that whether he had a lover at all is, of course, entirely irrelevant (and is *intimated* to be so by the poem's very form), the same is true, if not so obviously, of Dickens's novel. It is simply that Dickens deploys particular modes of signification (realism) which entail a greater foregrounding of the 'pseudo-real'; but we should not be led by this to make direct comparisons between the imaginary London of his novel and the real London. The imaginary London of *Bleak House* exists as the product of a representational process which signifies, not 'Victorian England' as such, but certain of Victorian England's ways of signifying itself. ...

... No text literally 'conforms itself to its content', adequates its signifiers to some signified distinct from them; what is in question is not the relation between the text and some separable signified, but the relation between textual signification (which is both 'form' and 'content') and those more pervasive significations we name ideology. This is not a relation which can be gauged simply by the degree to which the text *overtly* foregrounds its significations, even though such a practice in particular texts may well produce, and be produced by, a peculiar relation to ideology. For ... even the 'prosaic' text reproduces – although not in its every phrase – that dominance of signifier over signified paraded by the poem. It reproduces it in its entire structure – in that internal distribution of its elements, characterised by a high degree of relative autonomy, which is possible only because it has no real particular referent.

It remains to resolve a possible ambiguity as to what precisely constitutes the literary work's 'signified'. The signified *within the text* is what I have termed its 'pseudo-real' – the imaginary situations which the text is 'about'. But this pseudo-real is not to be directly correlated with the historically real; it is, rather, an effect or aspect of the text's whole process of signification. What that whole process signifies is ideology, which is itself a signification of history. The relations in question here can be clarified by a simple diagram:

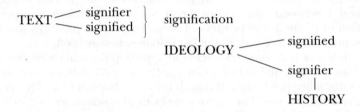

...Ideology pre-exists the text; but the *ideology of the text* defines, operates and constitutes that ideology in ways unpremeditated, so to speak, by ideology itself. The particular production of ideology which we may term the 'ideology of the text' has no pre-existence: it is identical with the text itself. What is in question here, indeed, is a double relation – not only the objectively determinable relation between text and ideology, but also (and simultaneously) that relation as 'subjectively' flaunted, concealed, intimated or mystified by the text itself. ...

It is essential, then, to examine in conjuncture two mutually constitutive formations: the nature of the ideology worked by the text and the aesthetic modes of that working. For a text may operate an ideology which contains elements of the real and simultaneously 'dissolve' those elements, in whole or part, by the manner of its working. Conversely, a notably 'impoverished' ideology may be transmuted by aesthetic forms into something approximating to knowledge. ...

The guarantor of a scientific criticism is the science of ideological formations. It is only on the basis of such a science that such a criticism could possibly be established – only by the assurance of a knowledge of ideology that we can claim a knowledge of literary texts. This is not to say that scientific criticism is merely an 'application' of historical materialism to literature. Criticism is a specific element of the theory of superstructures, which studies the particular laws of its proper object; its task is not to study the laws of ideological formations, but the laws of the production of ideological discourses as literature. ...

This complex relation of text to ideology, whereby the text is neither an epiphenomenon of ideology nor a wholly autonomous element, is relevant to the question of the text's 'structure'. The text can be spoken of as having a structure, even if it is a structure constituted not by symmetry but by rupture and decentrement. For this itself, in so far as the distances and conflicts between its diverse elements are determinate rather than opaque, constitutes a structure of a specific kind. Yet this structure is not to be seen as a microcosm or cryptogram of ideology; ideology is not the 'truth' of the text, any more than the dramatic text is the 'truth' of the dramatic performance. The 'truth' of the text is not an essence but a practice – the practice of its relation to ideology, and in terms of that to history. On the basis of this practice, the text constitutes itself as a structure: it destructures ideology in order to reconstitute it on its own relatively autonomous terms, in order to process and recast it in aesthetic production, at the same time as it is itself destructured to variable degrees by the effect of ideology upon it. In this destructuring practice, the text encounters ideology as a relatively structured formation which presses upon its own particular valencies and relations, confronts it with a 'concrete logic' which forms the outer perimeter of the text's own self-production. The text works, now with, now against the variable pressure of these valencies, finding itself able to admit one ideological element in relatively unprocessed form but finding therefore the need to displace or recast another, struggling against its recalcitrance and producing, in that struggle, new problems for itself. In this way the text disorders ideology to produce an internal order which may then occasion fresh disorder both in itself and in the ideology. This complex movement cannot be imaged as the 'structure of the text' transposing or reproducing the 'structure of the ideology': it can only be grasped as a ceaseless reciprocal *operation* of text on ideology and ideology on text, a mutual structuring and destructuring in which the text constantly overdetermines its own determinations. The structure of the text is then the *product* of this process, not the reflection of its ideological environs. The 'logic of the text' is not a discourse which doubles the 'logic of ideology'; it is, rather, a logic constructed '*athwart*' that more encompassing logic.

36 ROSALIND COWARD AND JOHN ELLIS: '*S/Z*'

S/Z aims to demonstrate how language produces the realist text as natural. It examines not the structure of the text but its structuration. The text is seen as a productivity of meaning which is carried on within a certain regime of sense: realism. The productivity of language which is dramatically revealed in the unconscious and in *avant-garde* texts is given a fixity, a positionality, so that it functions to 'denote' a 'reality'. Thus realism is more than a 'natural attitude', it is a practice of signification which relies upon the limits that society gives itself: certain realist texts, like the novella analysed in *S/Z* are consequently capable of dramatising these limits at certain moments. ...

Sarrasine[1] is a 'limit-text' of realism, a text which uses all the mechanisms of realism to produce a narrative which dramatises its very founding presuppositions. So, basing his aesthetic on the practice of writing (*écriture*), Barthes reveals realism as a social practice of representation which exploits the plurality of language in a limited way. ...

To understand *S/Z* as anything other than a superior formal method (and every indication is that this is how it has been received in Britain), it is necessary to understand what linguistic and ideological practices produce these various kinds of text. We must first understand the relation between realism and the plurality of language.

First, realism stresses the product and not the production. It represses production in the same way that the mechanism of the market, of general exchangeability, represses production in capitalist society. It does not matter where a product comes from, how it was made, by whom or for what purpose it was intended. All that matters is its value measured against the general medium of

Reprinted from *Language and Materialism: Developments in Semiology and the Theory of the Subject* (London, 1977), pp. 45–60.

exchange, money. In the same way, it does not matter that realism is produced by a certain use of language, by a complex production; all that matters is the illusion, the story, the content. What we value is its truth to life, the accuracy of its vision. ... We do not look at the production, but the product; hence the shock of reading an unusual book like *S/Z*, which goes against the 'natural' way of reading realist texts, and looks precisely at the way in which the illusion is produced. It treats realism as an effect of language, and not language as a (rhetorical) effect of realism.

This repression of production takes place because realism has as its basic philosophy of language not a production (signification being the production of a signified through the action of the signifying chain), but an identity: the signifier is treated as identical to a (pre-existent) signified. The signifier and signified are seen as caught up together in a process of production, they are treated as equivalents: the signifier is merely the equivalent of its pre-established concept. It seems as though it is not the business of language to establish this concept, but merely to express or communicate it. 'Not only do signifier and signified seem to unite, but in this confusion, the signifier seems to be erased or to become transparent so as to let the concept present itself, just as if it were referring to nothing but its own presence' (Derrida, *Positions*, pp. 32–3).[2] Language is treated as though it stands in for, is identical with, the real world. The business of realist writing is, according to its philosophy, to be the equivalent of a reality, to imitate it. This 'imitation' is the basis of realist literature, and its technical name is *mimesis*, mimicry. The whole basis of mimesis is that writing is a mere transcription of the real, carrying it over into a medium that exists only as a parasitic practice because the word is identical to, the equivalent of, the real world. Realism naturalises the arbitrary nature of the sign; its philosophy is that of an identity between signifier and signified on the level of an entire text as much as that of a single word. ...

The identity between signifier and signified which is established in realist writing is the precondition of its ability to represent a *vraisemblable*, an accepted natural view of the world. It does not mean that all writing is absolutely transparent, but rather that the narration, the dominant discourse, is able to establish itself as Truth. The narration does not appear to be the voice of an author; its source appears to be a true reality which speaks. The value of other discourses in the text (the speech of various characters, descriptions of subjective processes, etc.) is measured against this voice of truth. Thus a general evaluation of the discourses of the writing is established. The absolute value is that of reality itself, and the discourse of the narration attains this through the creation of an identity between signifier and signified. The other discourses of the text then contain varying degrees of truth or even none at all. Through this position of dominance, based on its equivalence with reality, the narration can then attribute points of origin for subsidiary discourses, appearing itself to have a point of origin in reality. So fragments of writing are confidently attributable to one character or another. And as we shall see with the analysis of *S/Z*, the narration also establishes the basic positionality for these characters, by setting up antithetical oppositions between them, creating a system of mutually-defining, separated spaces.

The realist narrative functions to uncover a world of truth, a world without contradictions, a homogeneous world of appearance supported by essences. But as Stephen Heath has pointed out in his seminal analysis of the film *Touch of Evil* (*Screen*, vol. 16, nos 1, 2), the process of narration is itself necessarily a statement of contradiction and heterogeneity: although the narrative-as-product displays a harmonious world of reality, the process of unfolding is the continuous statement of contradiction which will be more or less closed at the end. ...

This process of narration, a process that opens and closes with homogeneity, depends on 'the inscription of the subject as the place of its intelligibility' (ibid., no. 2, p. 98). The whole process is directed towards the place of a reader: in order that it should be intelligible, the reader has to adopt a certain position with regard to the text. This position is that of homogeneity, of truth. The narration calls upon the subject to regard the process of the narrative as a provisional openness, dependent upon the closure which the subject expects as the very precondition of its pleasure. In order that the narrative is intelligible at all, it is necessary that the subject regards the discourse of narration as the discourse of the unfolding of truth. The subject must operate the identity between signifier and signified: and as we shall see, the construction of the subject as homogeneous in ideology places it in an imaginary position of transcendence to this system. So the subject is constructed in such a way that it is not questioned by the flux of the text (something that is regarded as an 'aberrant reaction'); neither is it thrown into process by the sliding of signifiers which disestablish social positionality, as with the *avant-garde* text. Narration rather sets the subject in place as the point of intelligibility of its activity: the subject is then in a position of observation, understanding, synthesising. The subject of narration is a homogeneous subject, fixed in a relation of watching. ...

Thus realism has two basic features: mimesis, the imitation of reality based on fixing the signifier/signified identity, and the stratification of discourses around this which set the subject in a place of mastery. But these mechanisms take place over a multitude of different texts, and are supported by a practice of reading and writing. So how does realism find its social hold, how does it appear multiple and always changing, as the immediate 'spontaneous' mode of writing and reading? The practices of reading and writing are determined by the widest forms of behaviour, the basic attitude of capitalist society: reading is a consumption, writing is a purely instrumental use of language. Reading as consumption presupposes that a text is read once, for its imitation of reality. ...

The way of writing complementary to this mode of consumerist reading is that of *écrivance,* instrumental use of language. It is a use of language that calls up a vast reserve of echoes from similar texts, similar phrasing, remarks, situations, characters. This process is not one of pure repetition therefore, but, rather, a limited exploitation of the plurality of language, through a controlled process of echoing, re-calling. Kristeva introduced the term *intertextuality* for this process. ...

Barthes sees five forms of connotation, five codes that organise the intelligibility of *Sarrasine.* ... Two of the codes are responsible for giving the text its forward impulsion, moving it from point to point, towards its inevitable end. These are the *proiaretic* code and the *hermeneutic* code. ... Three other codes provide the vital information, produce the connotations necessary to complete the intelligibility of the text. These are the cultural, semic and symbolic codes. Of these, the symbolic code is the most difficult for us to understand, both because it is the source of the troubling in *Sarrasine* and because it depends on Lacanian psychoanalysis.

The *cultural code* is the way in which the text refers outwards to general knowledge (of art, medicine, politics, literature, etc., as well as to proverb and cliché). It is the realm of 'mythology', of ideology when it is considered as a system of ideas. ... The interweaving of the references in this code forms the sense of reality of the book; for these ideas themselves form the natural, the *vraisemblable* of their culture. They are what everybody knows, naturally.

The *semic code* deals in characteristics, whether they are psychological, of character or of atmosphere. Their naming is an important moment in the closure of the play of meaning. ...

These characteristics are sown throughout the text; they are fixed to a character by grouping themselves around a name. ...

The *symbolic code* is the field in which the basic positionality of the text and the reader is charted. In the realist text, positions are inevitably constituted according to psychoanalytic principles. At the beginning of *S/Z*, Barthes shows how certain semes (inside/outside; hot/cold) are organised into an antithesis that gives the basic positionality of the text: either masculine or feminine. No position is possible between or outside them: they are the normal (ideologically constructed) positions of society. Thus the shock of Zambinella's castration: the introduction of a castrato, straddling the division between these irreconcilable elements of the antithesis masculine/feminine, disturbs both language and the positions it constructs.

But it is not only the rhetorical device that provides the positionality. Usually, this is the textual expression 'of the biological axis of the sexes (which would force us, quite pointlessly, to put all women in this story in the same class)' (*S/Z*, p. 35). This relationship of positions is defined around the 'to have' or 'to have not' of the phallus, which according to Lacan is the sign around which the dialectic of identifications of the subject is made. For the phallus functions as a signifier whose reference is the cultural order. It is by taking up positions around it that accession to the symbolic is achieved. Sexual relations are grouped around the phallic symbol, and positions of exchange are established by identifications made by the ego in relation to it. ...

S/Z demonstrates how a 'limit-text' disturbs the positionalities upon which the representations of bourgeois society depend, positionalities towards which these representations contribute. However, such a limit-text can only dramatise the existence of positionality and representation. It is the discourse of Marxism and psychoanalysis which can unveil them as arrangements of an activity of production. Psychoanalysis demonstrates how the positions of the subject that are necessary for predication are constructed in the interaction of somatic drives and the contradictory outside of sociality. It shows how the accession to language is the crucial moment in the formation of this subject who is able to participate in the social processes of exchange, communication and reproduction. Marxism demonstrates how the positionality of exchange is a necessary fixity (a 'contractual relation') within a social process formed by the articulation of economic, political and ideological practices. Furthermore, ideological practice shows that this positionality is produced for a subject within a mode of representation. This fixing of positions for the subject can be seen to be a part of the process analysed in psychoanalysis. It has been the research into language (the key to both ideology and to the simultaneous construction of conscious and unconscious) which had made it possible to develop this crucial area in theory.

NOTES

1. [Ed.] Novella by Balzac analysed by Roland Barthes in *S/Z.* Page numbers are to the translation by Richard Miller (London, 1970).
   2. [Ed.] Reference is to Jacques Derrida, *Positions* (Paris, 1972).

37   FREDRIC JAMESON: 'ON INTERPRETATION: LITERATURE AS A SOCIALLY SYMBOLIC ACT'

This book will argue the priority of the political interpretation of literary texts. It conceives of the political perspective not as some supplementary method, not as an optional auxiliary to other interpretive methods current today – the psychoanalytic or the myth-critical, the stylistic, the ethical, the structural – but rather as the absolute horizon of all reading and all interpretation.

This is evidently a much more extreme position than the modest claim, surely acceptable to everyone, that certain texts have social and historical – sometimes even political – resonance. Traditional literary history has, of course, never prohibited the investigation of such topics as the Florentine political background in Dante, Milton's relationship to the schismatics, or Irish historical allusions in Joyce. I would argue, however, that such information – even where it is not recontained, as it is in most instances, by an idealistic conception of the history of ideas – does not yield interpretation as such, but rather at best its (indispensable) preconditions.

Today this properly antiquarian relationship to the cultural past has a dialectical counterpart which is ultimately no more satisfactory; I mean the tendency of much contemporary theory to rewrite selected texts from the past in terms of its own aesthetic and, in particular, in terms of a modernist (or more properly post-modernist) conception of language. ...

This unacceptable option, or ideological double bind, between antiquarianism and modernizing 'relevance' or projection

Reprinted from *The Political Unconscious: Narrative as a Socially Symbolic Act* (London, 1981), pp. 17–102.

demonstrates that the old dilemmas of historicism – and in particular, the question of the claims of monuments from distant and even archaic moments of the cultural past on a culturally different present – do not go away just because we choose to ignore them. Our presupposition, in the analyses that follow, will be that only a genuine philosophy of history is capable of respecting the specificity and radical difference of the social and cultural past while disclosing the solidarity of its polemics and passions, its forms, structures, experiences, and struggles, with those of the present day. ...

My position here is that only Marxism offers a philosophically coherent and ideologically compelling resolution to the dilemma of historicism evoked above. Only Marxism can give us an adequate account of the essential *mystery* of the cultural past, which, like Tiresias drinking the blood, is momentarily returned to life and warmth and allowed once more to speak, and to deliver its long-forgotten message in surroundings utterly alien to it. This mystery can be reenacted only if the human adventure is one; only thus – and not through the hobbies of antiquarianism or the projections of the modernists – can we glimpse the vital claims upon us of such long-dead issues as the seasonal alternation of the economy of a primitive tribe, the passionate disputes about the nature of the Trinity, the conflicting models of the *polis* of the universal Empire, or, apparently closer to us in time, the dusty parliamentary and journalistic polemics of the nineteenth-century nation states. These matters can recover their original urgency for us only if they are retold within the unity of a single great collective story; only if, in however disguised and symbolic a form, they are seen as sharing a single fundamental theme – for Marxism, the collective struggle to wrest a realm of Freedom from a realm of Necessity; only if they are grasped as vital episodes in a single vast unfinished plot: 'The history of all hitherto existing society is the history of class struggles: freeman and slave, patrician and plebeian, lord and serf, guild-master and journeyman – in a word, oppressor and oppressed – stood in constant opposition to one another, carried on an uninterrupted, now hidden, now open fight, a fight that each time ended, either in a revolutionary reconstitution of society at large or in the common ruin of the contending classes.'[1] It is in detecting the traces of that uninterrupted narrative, in restoring to the surface of the text the repressed and buried reality of this fundamental history, that the doctrine of a political unconscious finds its function and its necessity.

From this perspective the convenient working distinction between cultural texts that are social and political and those that are not becomes something worse than an error: namely, a symptom and a reinforcement of the reification and privatization of contemporary life. ... To imagine that, sheltered from the omnipresence of history and the implacable influence of the social, there already exists a realm of freedom – whether it be that of the microscopic experience of words in a text or the ecstasies and intensities of the various private religions – is only to strengthen the grip of Necessity over all such blind zones in which the individual subject seeks refuge, in pursuit of a purely individual, a merely psychological, project of salvation. The only effective liberation from such constraint begins with the recognition that there is nothing that is not social and historical – indeed, that everything is 'in the last analysis' political.

The assertion of a political unconscious proposes that we undertake just such a final analysis and explore the multiple paths that lead to the unmasking of cultural artifacts as socially symbolic acts. It projects a rival hermeneutic to those already enumerated; but it does so, as we shall see, not so much by repudiating their findings as by arguing its ultimate philosophical and methodological priority over more specialized interpretive codes whose insights are strategically limited as much by their own situational origins as by the narrow or local ways in which they construe or construct their objects of study.

Still, to describe the readings and analyses contained in the present work as so many *interpretations*, to present them as so many exhibits in the construction of a new *hermeneutic*, is already to announce a whole polemic program, which must necessarily come to terms with a critical and theoretical climate variously hostile to these slogans. It is, for instance, increasingly clear that hermeneutic or interpretive activity has become one of the basic polemic targets of contemporary post-structuralism in France, which – powerfully buttressed by the authority of Nietzsche – has tended to identify such operations with historicism, and in particular with the dialectic and its valorization of absence and the negative, its assertion of the necessity and priority of totalizing thought. I will agree with this identification, with this description of the ideological affinities and implications of the ideal of the interpretive or hermeneutic act; but I will argue that the critique is misplaced. ...

... Leaving aside for the moment the possibility of any genuinely immanent criticism, we will assume that a criticism which asks the question 'What does it mean?' constitutes something like an allegorical operation in which a text is systematically *rewritten* in terms of some fundamental master code or 'ultimately determining instance'. On this view, then, all 'interpretation' in the narrower sense demands the forcible or imperceptible transformation of a given text into an allegory of its particular master code or 'transcendental signified': the discredit into which interpretation has fallen is thus at one with the disrepute visited on allegory itself.

Yet to see interpretation this way is to acquire the instruments by which we can force a given interpretive practice to stand and yield up its name, to blurt out its master code and thereby reveal its metaphysical and ideological underpinnings. It should not, in the present intellectual atmosphere, be necessary laboriously to argue the position that every form of practice, including the literary-critical kind, implies and presupposes a form of theory; that empiricism, the mirage of an utterly nontheoretical practice, is a contradiction in terms; that even the most formalizing kinds of literary or textual analysis carry a theoretical charge whose denial unmasks it as ideological. ... I will here go much further than this, and argue that even the most innocently formalizing readings of the New Criticism have as their essential and ultimate function the propagation of this particular view of what history is. Indeed, no working model of the functioning of language, the nature of communication or of the speech act, and the dynamics of formal and stylistic change is conceivable which does not imply a whole philosophy of history. ...

Interpretation proper – what we have called 'strong' rewriting, in distinction from the weak rewriting of ethical codes, which all in one way or another project various notions of the unity and the coherence of consciousness – always presupposes, if not a conception of the unconscious itself, then at least some mechanism of mystification or repression in terms of which it would make sense to seek a latent meaning behind a manifest one, or to rewrite the surface categories of a text in the stronger language of a more fundamental interpretive code. This is perhaps the place to answer the objection of the ordinary reader, when confronted with elaborate and ingenious interpretations, that the text means just what it says. Unfortunately, no society has ever been quite so mystified in quite so many ways as our own, saturated as it is with message and information, the very vehicles of mystification (language, as Talleyrand put it, having been given us in order to conceal our thoughts). If everything were transparent, then no ideology would be possible, and no domination either: evidently that is not our case. But above and beyond the sheer fact of mystification, we must point to the supplementary problem involved in the study of cultural or literary texts, or in other words, essentially, of narratives:

for even if discursive language were to be taken literally, there is always, and constitutively, a problem about the 'meaning' of narrative as such; and the problem about the assessment and subsequent formulation of the 'meaning' of this or that narrative is the hermeneutic question, which leaves us as deeply involved in our present inquiry as we were when the objection was raised. ...

...The type of interpretation here proposed is more satisfactorily grasped as the rewriting of the literary text in such a way that the latter may itself be seen as the rewriting or restructuration of a prior historical or ideological *subtext*, it being always understood that the 'subtext' is not immediately present as such, not some common-sense external reality, nor even the conventional narrative of history manuals, but rather must itself always be (re)constructed after the fact. The literary or aesthetic act therefore always entertains some active relationship with the Real: yet in order to do so, it cannot simply allow 'reality' to persevere inertly in its own being, outside the text and at distance. It must rather draw the Real into its own texture, and the ultimate paradoxes and false problems of linguistics, and most notably of semantics, are to be traced back to this process, whereby language manages to carry the Real within itself as its own intrinsic or immanent subtext. Insofar, in other words, as symbolic action – what Burke will map as 'dream', 'prayer', or 'chart'[2] – is a way of doing something to the world, to that degree what we are calling 'world' must inhere within it, as the content it has to take up into itself in order to submit it to the transformation of form. The symbolic act therefore begins by generating and producing its own context in the same moment of emergence in which it steps back from it, taking its measure with a view toward its own projects of transformation. The whole paradox of what we have here called the subtext may be summed up in this, that the literary work or cultural object, as though for the first time, brings into being that very situation to which it is also, at one and the same time, a reaction. It articulates its own situation and textualizes it, thereby encouraging and perpetuating the illusion that the situation itself did not exist before it, that there is nothing but a text, that there never was any extra- or con-textual reality before the text itself generated it in the form of a mirage. One does not have to argue the reality of history: necessity, like Dr Johnson's stone, does that for us. That history – Althusser's 'absent cause', Lacan's 'Real' – is *not* a text, for it is fundamentally non-narrative and nonrepresentational; what can be added, however, is the proviso that history is inaccessible to us except in textual form, or in other words, that it can be

approached only by way of prior (re)textualization. Thus, to insist
on either of the two inseparable yet incommensurable dimensions
of the symbolic act without the other: to overemphasize the active
way in which the text reorganizes its subtext (in order, presumably, to reach the triumphant conclusion that the 'referent' does
not exist); or on the other hand to stress the imaginary status of
the symbolic act so completely as to reify its social ground, now no
longer understood as a subtext but merely as some inert given
that the text passively or fantasmatically 'reflects' – to overstress
either of these functions of the symbolic act at the expense of the
other is surely to produce sheer ideology, whether it be, as in the
first alternative, the ideology of structuralism, or, in the second,
that of vulgar materialism. ...

   History is therefore the experience of Necessity, and it is this
alone which can forestall its thematization or reification as a mere
object of representation or as one master code among many
others. Necessity is not in that sense a type of content, but rather
the inexorable *form* of events; it is therefore a narrative category in
the enlarged sense of some properly narrative political unconscious which has been argued here, a retextualization of History
which does not propose the latter as some new representation or
'vision', some new content, but as the formal effects of what
Althusser, following Spinoza, calls an 'absent cause'. Conceived in
this sense, History is what hurts, it is what refuses desire and sets
inexorable limits to individual as well as collective praxis, which its
'ruses' turn into grisly and ironic reversals of their overt intention.
But this History can be apprehended only through its effects, and
never directly as some reified force. This is indeed the ultimate
sense in which History as ground and untranscendable horizon
needs no particular theoretical justification: we may be sure that
its alienating necessities will not forget us, however much we
might prefer to ignore them.

NOTES

[Reorganised and renumbered from the original]
   1. Karl Marx and Friedrich Engels, 'The Communist Manifesto', in
Karl Marx, *On Revolution*, ed. and trans. S.K. Padover (New York, 1971),
p. 81.
   2. Kenneth Burke, *The Philosophy of Literary Form* (Berkeley, Calif.,
1973), pp. 5–6; and see my 'Symbolic Inference; or, Kenneth Burke and
Ideological Analysis', *Critical Inquiry*, 4 (1978), 507–23.

IX RECEPTION THEORY AND READER-RESPONSE CRITICISM

A major difference between recent literary theory and earlier critical approaches such as Russian Formalism, the New Criticism, and the first phase of French structuralism is that there has been a shift of emphasis towards the reader in much recent theory. In both reception theory (*Rezeptionsästhetik*) and reader-response criticism the role of the reader is seen as particularly crucial. Though reception theory has had its greatest impact in Germany and reader-response criticism is associated mainly with American criticism, there is some continuity between the two, particularly through the work of Wolfgang Iser, who is commonly included in both.

The leading figure in reception theory, however, Hans Robert Jauss, does not fit easily into a reader-response framework. Gadamer's hermeneutics is a strong influence on his work (see 'Hermeneutics', (section III, pp. 45–69). Jauss criticises two opposite extremes in literary theory: formalism, with its lack of a historical dimension, and Marxist criticism with its view of the literary text as a purely historical product. He uses Gadamer's concept of a 'fusion of horizons', in which a fusion takes place between the past experiences that are embodied in the text and the interests of its present-day readers, to discuss the relation between the original reception of a literary text and how it is perceived at different stages in history up until the present. Jauss argues that literary texts are inadequately understood if one focuses only on how they were produced without taking any account of their original reception. He advocates a new type of literary history in which the role of the critic is to mediate between how the text was perceived in the past and how it is perceived in the present. This relation needs continually to be rethought. Jauss believes that one of the most important justifications for literary study is that it allows one not only to perceive the fundamental difference between past and present but also partially to overcome that difference through being able to achieve direct contact with texts as human products even if they have emanated from strange and alien cultures.

Whereas Gadamer is Jauss's major influence, Iser's theory relies considerably on the phenomenology of the Polish theorist and philosopher Roman Ingarden. Though he argues, like reader-response criticism, for the centrality of the reader, Iser differs from such reader-response critics as David Bleich or Stanley Fish in his belief that the text has an objective structure even if that structure must be completed by the reader. He claims that all texts create 'gaps' or 'blanks' which the reader must use his or her imagination to fill. It is in this interaction between text and reader that aesthetic response is created.

The major reader-response critics, such as Bleich and Fish, start from the premise that the object has no separate existence from the subject and they have explored the implications of this for literary criticism. Unlike Jauss's reception theory, reader-response criticism lays little stress on a work's original reception and in contrast to Iser it denies that the work embodies objective constraints on the reader.

David Bleich is associated with 'subjective criticism' and takes to an extreme the view that literary meaning is not to be found in texts but in readers. He is often associated with Norman N. Holland and the 'Buffalo school', but he is critical of Holland's emphasis on the 'transactive' relation between reader and text. Bleich places greater stress on the emotional response of the reader in determining how a text is read.

Stanley Fish's position has undergone considerable develop- ment since his important essay of 1970, 'Literature in the Reader: Affective Stylistics', in which he emphasised the temporal nature of the reading process and argued that the meaning of a literary text cannot be seen as separate from the reader's experience of it. In his later work he confronts the objection that a reader-based theory inevitably leads to relativism by arguing that totally subject- ive responses are impossible since they cannot exist in isolation from sets of norms, systems of thought etc. which are inter- subjective. Thus he argues that the subject–object dichotomy breaks down as there are no pure subjects and no pure objects. The object, including the literary text, is always a construct by the subject, or more exactly, by a group of subjects or what Fish calls an 'interpretive community'. Different sets of reading strategies and norms produce different communities of interpreters. Fish adopts the radical view that even such apparently objective fea- tures of literary texts as metrical form, rhyme scheme, and other types of patterning are the product of interpretative strategies.

FURTHER READING

David Bleich, 'Intersubjective Reading', *New Literary History*, 17 (1986), 401–21. (Reveals shift of emphasis in Bleich's position from 'subjective' to 'intersubjective'.)

——, *Subjective Criticism* (Baltimore, 1978).
Paul de Man, 'Introduction' to Jauss, *Toward an Aesthetic of Reception*, trans Timothy Bahti (Brighton, 1982).
Eugene H. Falk, *The Poetics of Roman Ingarden* (Chapel Hill, NC, 1981).
Stanley Fish, *Is There a Text in This Class? The Authority of Interpretive Communities* (Cambridge, Mass., 1980).
——, 'Why No One's Afraid of Wolfgang Iser', *Diacritics*, 11 (1981), 2–13. (Critique of Iser.)
Robert C. Holub, *Reception Theory: A Critical Introduction* (London, 1984).
Wolfgang Iser, 'Interview', *Diacritics*, 10 (1980), 57–74. (Iser confronts Norman N. Holland, Wayne C. Booth, and Stanley Fish.)
——, *The Act of Reading: A Theory of Aesthetic Response* (Baltimore, 1978).
Hans Robert Jauss, *Aesthetic Experience and Literary Hermeneutics*, trans. Michael Shaw (Minneapolis, 1982).
Robert R. Magliola, *Phenomenology and Literature* (West Lafayette, Ind., 1977).
Steven Mailloux, 'Reader-Response Criticism?', *Genre*, 10 (1977), 413–31.
K. M. Newton, *In Defence of Literary Interpretation: Theory and Practice* (London, 1986).
Susan Suleiman and Inge Crosman (eds), *The Reader in the Text: Essays on Audience and Interpretation* (Princeton, NJ, 1980).
Jane Tompkins (ed.), *Reader-Response Criticism: From Formalism to Post-Structuralism* (Baltimore, 1980).

38 HANS ROBERT JAUSS: 'LITERARY HISTORY AS A CHALLENGE TO LITERARY THEORY'

My attempt to bridge the gap between literature and history, between historical and aesthetic approaches begins at the point at which both [the Marxist and the Formalist] schools stop. Their methods conceive the *literary fact* within the closed circle of an aesthetics of production and of representation. In doing so, they deprive literature of a dimension that inalienably belongs to its aesthetic character as well as to its social function: the dimension of its reception and influence. Reader, listener, and spectator – in short, the factor of the audience – play an extremely limited role in both literary theories. Orthodox Marxist aesthetics treats the reader – if at all – no differently from the author: it inquires about

Reprinted from *Toward an Aesthetic of Reception*, trans. Timothy Bahti (Brighton, 1982), pp. 18–45.

his social position or seeks to recognize him in the structure of a represented society. The Formalist school needs the reader only as a perceiving subject who follows the directions in the text in order to distinguish the [literary] form or discover the [literary] procedure. ... Both methods lack the reader in his genuine role, a role as unalterable for aesthetic as for historical knowledge: as the addressee for whom the literary work is primarily destined. ...

...The historical life of a literary work is unthinkable without the active participation of its addressees. For it is only through the process of its mediation that the work enters into the changing horizon-of-experience of a continuity in which the perpetual inversion occurs from simple reception to critical understanding, from passive to active reception, from recognized aesthetic norms to a new production that surpasses them. The historicity of literature as well as its communicative character presupposes a dialogical and at once processslike relationship between work, audience, and new work that can be conceived in the relations between message and receiver as well as between question and answer, problem and solution. ... If the history of literature is viewed in this way within the horizon of a dialogue between work and audience that forms a continuity, the opposition between its aesthetic and its historical aspects is also continually mediated. Thus the thread from the past appearance to the present experience of literature, which historicism had cut, is tied back together.

The relationship of literature and reader has aesthetic as well as historical implications. The aesthetic implication lies in the fact that the first reception of a work by the reader includes a test of its aesthetic value in comparison with works already read. The obvious historical implication of this is that the understanding of the first reader will be sustained and enriched in a chain of receptions from generation to generation; in this way the historical significance of a work will be decided and its aesthetic value made evident. ...

From this premise, the question as to how literary history can today be methodologically grounded and written anew will be addressed in the following seven theses.

Thesis 1. A renewal of literary history demands the removal of the prejudices of historical objectivism and the grounding of the traditional aesthetics of production and representation in an aesthetics of reception and influence. The historicity of literature rests not on an organization of 'literary facts' that is established *post festum*, but rather on the preceding experience of the literary work by its readers.

... A literary work is not an object that stands by itself and that offers the same view to each reader in each period. It is not a monument that monologically reveals its timeless essence. It is much more like an orchestration that strikes ever new resonances among its readers and that frees the text from the material of the words and brings it to a contemporary existence. ... The coherence of literature as an event is primarily mediated in the horizon of expectations of the literary experience of contemporary and later readers, critics, and authors. Whether it is possible to comprehend and represent the history of literature in its unique historicity depends on whether this horizon of expectations can be objectified.

Thesis 2. The analysis of the literary experience of the reader avoids the threatening pitfalls of psychology if it describes the reception and the influence of a work within the objectifiable system of expectations that arise for each work in the historical moment of its appearance, from a pre-understanding of the genre, from the form and themes of already familiar works, and from the opposition between poetic and practical language.

My thesis opposes a widespread skepticism that doubts whether an analysis of aesthetic influence can approach the meaning of a work of art at all or can produce, at best, more than a simple sociology of taste. ...

A literary work, even when it appears to be new, does not present itself as something absolutely new in an informational vacuum, but predisposes its audience to a very specific kind of reception by announcements, overt and covert signals, familiar characteristics, or implicit allusions. It awakens memories of that which was already read, brings the reader to a specific emotional attitude, and with its beginning arouses expectations for the 'middle and end', which can then be maintained intact or altered, reoriented, or even fulfilled ironically in the course of the reading according to specific rules of the genre or type of text. The psychic process in the reception of text is, in the primary horizon of aesthetic experience, by no means only an arbitrary series of merely subjective impressions, but rather the carrying out of specific instructions in a process of directed perception, which can be comprehended according to its constitutive motivations and triggering signals, and which also can be described by a textual linguistics. ... The new text evokes for the reader (listener) the horizon of expectations and rules familiar from earlier texts, which are then varied, corrected, altered, or even just reproduced. ...

Thesis 3. Reconstructed in this way, the horizon of expectations of a work allows one to determine its artistic character by the kind and the degree of its influence on a presupposed audience. If one characterizes as aesthetic distance the disparity between the given horizon of expectations and the appearance of a new work, whose reception can result in a 'change of horizons' through negation of familiar experiences or through raising newly articulated experiences to the level of consciousness, then this aesthetic distance can be objectified historically along the spectrum of the audience's reactions and criticism's judgment (spontaneous success, rejection or shock, scattered approval, gradual or belated understanding).

The way in which a literary work at the historical moment of its appearance, satisfies, surpasses, disappoints, or refutes the expectations of its first audience obviously provides a criterion for the determination of its aesthetic value. The distance between the horizon of expectations and the work, between the familiarity of previous aesthetic experience and the 'horizontal change'[1] demanded by the reception of the new work, determines the artistic character of a literary work, according to an aesthetics of reception: to the degree that this distance decreases, and no turn toward the horizon of yet-unknown experience is demanded of the receiving consciousness, the closer the work comes to the sphere of 'culinary' or entertainment art [*Unterhaltungskunst*]. ... If, conversely, the artistic character of a work is to be measured by the aesthetic distance with which it opposes the expectations of its first audience, then it follows that this distance, at first experienced as a pleasing or alienating new perspective, can disappear for later readers, to the extent that the original negativity of the work has become self-evident and has itself entered into the horizon of future aesthetic experience, as a henceforth familiar expectation. The classical character of the so-called masterworks especially belongs to this second horizontal change; their beautiful form that has become self-evident, and their seemingly unquestionable 'eternal meaning' bring them, according to an aesthetics of reception, dangerously close to the irresistibly convincing and enjoyable 'culinary' art, so that it requires a special effort to read them 'against the grain' of the accustomed experience to catch sight of their artistic character once again. ...

Thesis 4. The reconstruction of the horizon of expectations, in the face of which a work was created and received in the past, enables one on the other hand to pose questions that the text gave an answer to, and thereby to discover how the contemporary reader could have viewed and understood the work. This approach corrects the mostly unrecognized norms of a classicist or modernizing understanding of art, and avoids the circular recourse to a general 'spirit of the age'. It brings to view the hermeneutic difference between the former and the current understanding of a work; it raises to consciousness the history of its reception, which mediates both positions; and it thereby calls into question as a platonizing dogma of philogical metaphysics the apparently self-evident claims that in the literary text, literature [*Dichtung*] is eternally present, and that its objective meaning, determined once and for all, is at all times immediately accessible to the interpreter.

The method of historical reception is indispensable for the understanding of literature from the distant past. When the author of a work is unknown, his intent undeclared, and his relationship to sources and models only indirectly accessible, the philological question of how the text is 'properly' – that is, 'from its intention and time' – to be understood can best be answered if one foregrounds it against those works that the author explicitly or implicitly presupposed his contemporary audience to know. ...

Thesis 5. The theory of the aesthetics of reception not only allows one to conceive the meaning and form of a literary work in the historical unfolding of its understanding. It also demands that one insert the individual work into its 'literary series' to recognize its historical position and significance in the context of the experience of literature. In the step from a history of the reception of works to an eventful history of literature, the latter manifests itself as a process in which the passive reception is on the part of authors. Put another way, the next work can solve formal and moral problems left behind by the last work and present new problems in turn. ...

Thesis 6. The achievements made in linguistics through the distinction and methodological interrelation of diachronic and synchronic analysis are the occasion for overcoming the diachronic perspective – previously the only one practiced – in literary history as well. If the perspective of this history of reception always bumps up against the functional connections between the understanding of new works and the significance of older ones when changes in aesthetic attitudes are considered, it must also be possible to take a synchronic cross-section of a moment in the development, to arrange the heterogeneous multiplicity of contemporaneous works in equivalent, opposing, and hierarchical structures, and thereby to discover an overarching system of relationships in the literature of a historical moment. From this the principle of representation of a new literary history could be developed, if further cross-sections diachronically before and after were so arranged as to articulate historically the change in literary structures in its epoch-making moments. ...

Thesis 7. The task of literary history is thus only completed when literary production is not only represented synchronically and diachronically in the succession of its systems, but also seen as 'special history' in its own unique relationship to 'general history'. This relationship does not end with the fact that a typified, idealized, satiric, or utopian image of social existence can be found in the literature of all times. The social function of literature manifests itself in its genuine possibility only where the literary experience of the reader enters into the horizon of expectations of his lived praxis, performs his understanding of the world, and thereby also has an effect on his social behavior. ...

It follows from all this that the specific achievement of literature in social existence is to be sought exactly where literature is not absorbed into the function of a *representational* art. If one looks at the moments in history when literary works toppled the taboos of the ruling morals or offered the reader new solutions for the moral casuistry of his lived praxis, which thereafter could be sanctioned by the consensus of all readers in the society, then a still-little-studied area of research opens itself up to the literary historian. The gap between literature and history, between aesthetic and historical knowledge, can be bridged if literary history does not simply describe the process of general history in the reflection of its works one more time, but rather when it discovers in the course of 'literary evolution' that properly *socially formative* function that belongs to literature as it competes with other arts and social forces in the emancipation of mankind from its natural, religious, and social bonds.

If it is worthwhile for the literary scholar to jump over his ahistorical shadow for the sake of this task, then it might well also provide an answer to the question: toward what end and with what right can one today still – or again – study literary history?

NOTES

1. On this Husserlian concept, see G. Buck, *Lernen und Erfahrung* (Stuttgart, 1967), pp. 64ff.

39 WOLFGANG ISER: 'INDETERMINACY AND THE READER'S RESPONSE'

If texts actually possessed only the meaning brought to light by interpretation, then there would remain very little else for the reader. He could only accept or reject it, take it or leave it. The fundamental question is, however, what actually does take place between text and reader? Is it possible to look into that relationship at all, or is not the critic simply plunging into a private world where he can only make vague conjectures and speculations? Is one able to express anything at all about those highly heterogeneous reactions that run between text and reader? At the same time it must be pointed out that a text can only come to life when it is read, and if it is to be examined, it must therefore be studied through the eyes of the reader. ...

If it were really true – as the author of a certain well-known essay on 'the Art of Interpretation' would have us believe – that the meaning is concealed within a text itself, one cannot help wondering why texts should indulge in such a 'hide-and-seek' with their interpreters; and even more puzzling, why the meaning, once it has been found, should then change again, even though the letters, words, and sentences of the text remain the same. ...

Shouldn't the interpreter in fact renounce his sanctified role of conveying meanings, if he wants to open up the possibilities of a text? His description of the text is, after all, nothing more than an experience of a cultured reader – in other words, it is only one of the possible realizations of a text. ...

... How can we describe the relationship between text and reader? ... The first step is to indicate the special qualities of a literary text that distinguish it from other kinds of text. The second step will be to name and analyze the basic elements of the cause of the response to literary works. Here we shall pay special attention to different degrees of what I should like to call indeterminacy in a text and the various ways in which it is brought about. ...

Let us come to our first step. How can we describe the status of a literary text? The first point is that it differs from any other text that presents an object which exists independent of the text. If a piece

Reprinted from *Aspects of Narrative, Selected Papers from the English Institute*, ed. J. Hillis Miller (New York, 1971), pp. 2–45.

of writing describes an object that exists with equal determinacy outside it, then the text is simply an exposition of the object. In Austin's terms, it is a 'constative utterance,' as opposed to a 'performative utterance,'[1] which actually creates its object. It goes without saying that literary texts belong to the second category. There is no concrete object corresponding to them in the real world, although of course they constitute their objects out of elements to be found in the real world. ...

... If a literary text presents no real objects, it nevertheless establishes its reality by the reader's participation and by the reader's response. The reader, however, cannot refer to any definite object or independent facts in order to judge whether the text has presented its subject rightly or wrongly. This possibility of verification that all expository texts offer is, precisely, denied by the literary text. At this point there arises a certain amount of indeterminacy which is peculiar to all literary texts, for they permit no referral to any identical real-life situation. ...

...The gaps of indeterminacy can be filled in by referring the text to real, verifiable factors, in such a way that it appears to be nothing more than a mirror-reflection of these factors. In this case it loses its literary quality in the reflection. Alternatively, the indeterminacy of a text may be so resistant to counterbalancing that any identification with the real world is impossible. Then the world of the text establishes itself as being in competition with the familiar world, a competition which must inevitably have some repercussions on the familiar one. In this case, the text may tend to function as a criticism of life.

Indeterminacy can also be counterbalanced at any given time in terms of the individual experience of the reader. He can reduce a text to the level of his own experiences, provided that he projects his own standards onto the text in order to grasp its specific meaning. This, too, is a counterbalancing of indeterminacy which disappears when the subjective norms of the reader guide him through the text. On the other hand, a text may conceivably contradict our own preconceptions to such a degree that it calls forth drastic reactions, such as throwing a book away or, at the other extreme, being compelled to revise those preconceptions. This also constitutes a way of removing indeterminacy which always permits the possibility of connecting one's own experience with what the text wants to convey. Whenever this happens, indeterminacy tends to disappear, because communication has occurred.

Such basic reactions clarify the status of the literary text: Its main characteristic is its peculiar halfway position between the world of real objects and the reader's own world of experience.

The act of reading is therefore a process of seeking to pin down the oscillating structure of the text to some specific meaning. So far, we have only described the literary text, as it were, from the outside. We must now, in a second step, mention certain important formal conditions which give rise to indeterminacy in the text itself. At once, we are confronted with the question as to what really is the substance of such a text, for it has no counterpart in the world of empirical objects. The answer is that literary objects come into being through the unfolding of a variety of views which constitute the 'object' in stages and at the same time give a concrete form for the reader to contemplate. We shall call such views 'schematized views', following a term coined by the Polish philosopher Roman Ingarden,[2] because every one of them sets out to present the object not in an incidental or even accidental way, but in a representative manner. How many of these views are necessary to give a clear idea of the literary object? Obviously, a large number, if one is to get a precise conception.

This raises a highly relevant problem: each single view will generally reveal only one representative aspect. It therefore determines the literary object, and at the same time it raises the need for a new determination. This means that a literary object never reaches the end of its many-faceted determinacy. ...

If we assume that the 'schematized views' form a basic characteristic of the literary text, nothing has thus far been said as to how they link up with one another. While they touch upon one another, the degree of connections is usually not stated, but has to be inferred. ... In other words, between the 'schematized views' there is a no-man's-land of indeterminacy, which results precisely from the determinacy of the sequence of each individual view. Gaps are bound to open up, and offer a free play of interpretation for the specific way in which the various views can be connected with one another. These gaps give the reader a chance to build his own bridges, relating the different aspects of the object which have thus far been revealed to him. It is quite impossible for the text itself to fill in the gaps. In fact, the more a text tries to be precise (i.e., the more 'schematized views' it offers), the greater will be the number of gaps between the views. Classic examples of this are the last novels of Joyce, *Ulysses* and *Finnegans Wake*, where the overprecision of the presentation gives rise to a proportionate increase in indeterminacy. ...

The indeterminate sections or gaps of literary texts are in no way to be regarded as a defect; on the contrary, they are a basic element for the aesthetic response. Generally, the reader will not

even be aware of such gaps – at least so far as novels up to the end
of the nineteenth century are concerned. Nevertheless, they are
not without influence on his reading, for the 'schematized views'
are continually connected with each other in the reading process.
This means that the reader fills in the remaining gaps. He
removes them by a free play of meaning-projection and thus by
himself repairs the unformulated connections between the particular views. This is borne out by the fact that a second reading of
a piece of literature often produces a different impression from
the first. ...

In this way, every literary text invites some form of participation
on the part of the reader. A text which lays things out before the
reader in such a way that he can either accept or reject them will
lessen the degree of participation as it allows him nothing but a
yes or no. Texts with such minimal indeterminacy tend to be
tedious, for it is only when the reader is given the chance to participate actively that he will regard the text, whose intention he
himself has helped to compose, as real. For we generally tend to
regard things that we have made ourselves as being real. And so it
can be said that indeterminacy is the fundamental precondition
for reader participation. ...

... Let us therefore, by way of concluding, examine the consequences of the facts we have outlined. First of all, we can say that
the indeterminate element of literary prose – perhaps even of all
literature – represents the most important link between text and
reader. It is the switch that activates the reader in using his own
ideas in order to fulfill the intention of the text. This means that
it is the basis of a textural structure in which the reader's part is
already incorporated. ...

In this respect, literary texts differ from those which formulate
a concrete meaning or truth. Texts of the latter kind are, by their
very nature, independent of the individual reader, for the
meaning or truth which they express exists independently of any
reader's participation. But when the most vital element of a
textual structure is the process of reading, it is forced to rely on
the individual reader for the realization of a possible meaning or
truth. The meaning is conditioned by the text itself, but only in a
form that allows the reader himself to bring it out.

...While the literary text has its reality not in the world of
objects but in the imagination of its reader, it wins a certain prece-
dence over texts which want to make a statement concerning
meaning or truth; in short, over those which claim or have an
apophantic character. Meanings and truths are, by nature,

influenced by their historical position and cannot in principle be set apart from history. The same applies to literature, too, but since the reality of a literary text lies within the reader's imagination, it must, again by nature, have a far greater chance of transcending its historical position. From this arises the suspicion that literary texts are resistant to the course of time, not because they represent eternal values that are supposedly independent of time, but because their structure continually allows the reader to place himself within the world of fiction. ...

... And precisely because the literary text makes no objectively real demand on its readers, it opens up a freedom that every one can interpret in his own way. Thus, with every text we learn not only about what we are reading but also about ourselves, and this process is all the more effective if what we are supposed to experience is not explicitly stated but has to be inferred. ... It is largely because of this fact that literary texts are so constructed as to confirm none of the meanings we ascribe to them, although by means of their structure they continually lead us to such projections of meaning. Thus it is perhaps one of the chief values of literature that by its very indeterminacy it is able to transcend the restrictions of time and written word and to give to people of all ages and backgrounds the chance to enter other worlds and so enrich their own lives.

NOTES

[Reorganised and renumbered from the original]

1. J. L. Austin, *How to Do Things with Words*, ed. J. O. Urmson (Cambridge, Mass., 1962), pp. 1ff.

2. See Roman Ingarden, *Das literarische Kunstwerk* (Tubingen, 1960), pp. 261ff.

40   DAVID BLEICH: 'THE SUBJECTIVE CHARACTER OF CRITICAL INTERPRETATION'

Part of the original energy of the New Criticism was a reaction against unsystematic 'Impressionism'. The aim was to present aesthetic discussions so that they would be more intellectually informative and less easily dismissible. Early New Critics wanted to show that knowledge about literature is really knowledge and not merely a record of fleeting personal observations. From one standpoint one cannot dispute this aim, since anything one knows about literature is knowledge. However it remains true that interpretive knowledge is different from the formulaic knowledge of the physical sciences both in its origins and its consequences.

Interpretive knowledge is neither deduced nor inferred from a controlled experience. Rather, it is constructed from the uncontrolled experience of the interpreter, and the rules of construction are only vaguely known by anyone observing the interpreter. The consequences of interpretation are not made up of a finite set of possible events which must logically follow from the interpretation. Rather, as is easily seen from the critical response to, say, Bradley's interpretations of Shakespeare, the events consequent to interpretive knowledge are in principle infinite and are determined only by the number and kind of people responding to Bradley. Yet, although interpretive knowledge does not behave like other knowledge, it would be silly to deny that it is still knowledge. ...

Nominally, critics and their audiences *assume* interpretive knowledge to be as objective as formulaic knowledge. The assumption of objectivity is almost a game played by critics, a necessary ritual to help maintain the faith that if criticism presents its knowledge in the same form as the exact sciences, it will have the same authority. If pressed, most critics will admit to the fallacy in this ritual, and they will point out that they believe in critical pluralism; i.e., many interpretations of the same work may obtain simultaneously. The way we actually treat interpretive knowledge, therefore, shows that it is *subjective*, that it is not a formulation of some unchanging 'objective' truth, but the motivated construction of someone's mind. While interpretive knowledge is still knowledge, it does not logically limit the range of response to it, and it cannot predict future events.

Reprinted from *College English*, 36 (1975), 739–55.

I will try to show that our understanding of the subjective character of interpretive knowledge derives from an epistemological discovery, made through psychoanalysis, to which Freud did not consciously subscribe until late in his career. ...

While Freud's discoveries about psychological functioning are distinct and unambiguous, his epistemology underwent change until it became as revolutionary as his discoveries. The orthodox psychoanalytic view retains Freud's original epistemology: the Newtonian, objectivist position. My own understanding of the therapeutic process follows a later and more implicit Freudian epistemology. ... The most important epistemological contribution of psychoanalysis is precisely the spectacular demonstration that *rationality is itself a subjective phenomenon.* ...

...The more comprehensive scientific attitude, discovered in this century in regard to both human and physical sciences, is the principle that from now on *the observer is always part of what is being observed.* The knowledge gained under the hitherto prevailing assumption of objectivity – i.e. that the observed is independent of the observer – is not hereby rendered invalid. Rather, its limits have now been defined by further knowledge. Just as more detailed knowledge of matter is no longer possible without taking into account the effect of observing subatomic matter, detailed knowledge of the mind is likewise not possible without taking into account the effects of observing one's own mind. ...

The purpose of this discussion of Freud's interpretive methods and attitudes was to present an originological justification for the principle of critical subjectivity. My point can be summarized briefly: the truth about something that requires an audience to gain reality is a different sort of thing than the truth about something that does not. The truth about the Newtonian Bible requires the faith of the reader; the truth of the acceleration of gravity does not. The truth about literature has no meaning independent of the truth about the reader. The truth of this essay will be decided by the community which reads it. ...

This is not to say that a text is not an object; the words can be counted and catalogued, their definitions can be traced. But such activity does not qualify as literary experience, nor does it qualify as 'criticism'. It is only the organization of perceptual data; it is *counting*, as distinct from *naming*. The major activities in the history of literary study are acts of naming, that is, of identifying values and making judgments of value. A judgment of meaning is a special form of a value-judgment, since it depends on the selective perception of the judge, which in turn is determined by the set of values which govern his life. These values are forces whose behaviors are determined by the rules of personality functioning and by the constraints of social existence. They are, to be brief, subjective. If a literary text is to be anything beyond a piece of 'sense data' it must come under the control of a subjectivity; either an individual's subjectivity or the collective subjectivity of a group. The only way a work of literature has consequential meaning is as a function of the mind of the reader. ...

Naturally, the work of literature is also an object. But it is different from most objects because it is a symbolic object. Unlike a table or a car, it has no function in its material existence. It looks like an object, but it is not. Whereas the existence of an apple does not depend on whether someone sees it or eats it, the existence of the book does depend on whether someone writes it and reads it. *A symbolic object is wholly dependent on a perceiver for its existence. An object becomes a symbol only by being rendered so by a perceiver.* The fallacy of the New Criticism is its assumption that a symbolic object is an 'objective' object. ...

This revised view of the interpretive process urges us to change our understanding of two major areas in matters of literary enterprise. It gives us a different view of the function and authority of those in literary professions, and it suggests a more consequential way of conceiving both the creation of literature and its role in the social and psychological economics of individuals.

With regard to the first area the view urges us to abandon the critical attitude of Northrop Frye, who conceived his task as trying to confer upon criticism the authority of the scientist. ...

Frye would like the traditional standards of scientific truth to apply to criticism. Indeed, by his own logic, they cannot apply, because in the twentieth century, the century of the social sciences, the standard of truth has changed. When the observer is part of the observed truth is no longer objective. ... The study of how words work must proceed under the principle of the involved observer, for there is no longer any such thing as a detached observer, least of all in the study of language, literature and art.

The standard of truth in literary matters can only devolve upon the community of students. The test of truth in critical interpretation is its social viability. Those interpretations accepted as 'true' achieve this status because they reflect an area of *common subjective value.* If a certain set or school of interpretations prevails, it is not because it is closer to an objective truth about art, but because it is a communally agreed-upon way to articulate certain commonly held subjective feelings about art at that time. ...

... For the author, the work of literature is a response to his life experience. For the reader, the interpretation is the response to his reading experience. This understanding of the literary transaction creates a new scale of values for the serious study of literature and literary experience. The personalities involved in the literary trans-action are of primary importance; the properties of the work of art, while necessary, are insufficient and of secondary importance. ... Ultimately, I accept Frye's view that criticism is a 'science', in the sense that it is the systematic study of aesthetic experience which produces new knowledge. But it is a science that began almost at the moment when the assumption of objectivity had proved no longer adequate. Close examination of the aesthetic experience has shown that the assumption in fact is not viable in our efforts to learn about this experience. Instead, our recognition of the subjective character of critical interpretation yields satisfying new understanding.

This recognition shows that the study of literature and art cannot proceed independently of the study of the people involved in the artistic transaction. The entity to be studied is either the re-lationship between perceiver and work, or between artist and work. No matter how much we may wish it, it is idle to imagine that we can avoid the entanglements of subjective reactions and motives. Our minds are built so that knowledge of ourselves is not only possible and desirable, but necessary. Our minds are at the root of our literary experiences. The study of art and the study of ourselves are ultimately a single enterprise.

41   STANLEY FISH: 'INTERPRETING THE *VARIORUM*'

What I am suggesting is that formal units are always a function of the interpretive model one brings to bear; they are not 'in' the text, and I would make the same argument for intentions. That is, intention is no more embodied 'in' the text than are formal units; rather an intention, like a formal unit, is made when perceptual or interpretive closure is hazarded; it is verified by an interpretive act, and I would add, it is not verifiable in any other way. This last assertion is too large to be fully considered here, but I can sketch out the argumentative sequence I would follow were I to consider it: intention is known when and only when it is recognized; it is

Reprinted from *Critical Inquiry*, 2 (1976), 478–85.

recognized as soon as you decide about it; you decide about it as soon as you make a sense; and you make a sense (or so my model claims) as soon as you can. ...

It seems then that the price one pays for denying the priority of either forms or intentions is an inability to say how it is that one ever begins. Yet we do begin, and we continue, and because we do there arises an immediate counter-objection to the preceding pages. If interpretive acts are the source of forms rather than the other way around, why isn't it the case that readers are always performing the same acts or a random succession of forms? How, in short, does one explain these two random successions of forms? How, in short, does one explain these two 'facts' of reading?: (1) the same reader will perform differently when reading two 'different' (the word is in quotation marks because its status is precisely what is at issue) texts; and (2) different readers will perform similarly when reading the 'same' (in quotes for the same reason) text. That is to say, both the stability of interpretation among readers and the variety of interpretation in the career of a single reader would seem to argue for the existence of something independent of and prior to interpretive acts, something which produces them. I will answer this challenge by asserting that both the stability and the variety are functions of interpretive strategies rather than of texts.

Let us suppose that I am reading *Lycidas*. What is it that I am doing? First of all, what I am not doing is 'simply reading', an activity in which I do not believe because it implies the possibility of pure (that is, disinterested) perception. Rather, I am proceeding on the basis of (at least) two interpretive decisions: (1) that *Lycidas* is a pastoral and (2) that it was written by Milton. (I should add that the notions 'pastoral' and 'Milton' are also interpretations; that is they do not stand for a set of indisputable, objective facts; if they did, a great many books would not now be getting written.) Once these decisions have been made (and if I had not made these I would have made others, and they would be consequential in the same way), I am immediately predisposed to perform certain acts, to 'find' by looking for, themes (the relationship between natural processes and the careers of men, the efficacy of poetry or of any other action), to confer significances (on flowers, streams, shepherds, pagan deities), to mark out 'formal' units (the lament, the consolation, the turn, the affirmation of faith, etc.). My disposition to perform these acts (and others; the list is not meant to be exhaustive) constitutes a set of interpretive strategies, which, when they are put into execution,

become the large act of reading. That is to say, interpretive strategies are not put into execution after reading (the pure act of perception in which I do not believe); they are the shape of reading,
and because they are the shape of reading, they give texts their
shape, making them rather than, as it is usually assumed, arising
from them. Several important things follow from this account:

1. I did not have to execute this particular set of interpretive
strategies because I did not have to make those particular interpretive (pre-reading) decisions. I could have decided, for
example, that *Lycidas* was a text in which a set of fantasies and
defenses find expression. These decisions would have entailed the
assumption of another set of interpretive strategies (perhaps like
that put forward by Norman Holland in *The Dynamics of Literary
Response*) and the execution of that set would have made another
text.

2. I could execute this same set of strategies when presented
with texts that did not bear the title (again a notion which is itself
an interpretation) *Lycidas, A Pastoral Monody.* ... I could decide (it
is a decision some have made) that *Adam Bede* is a pastoral written
by an author who consciously modeled herself on Milton (still
remembering that 'pastoral' and 'Milton' are interpretations, not
facts in the public domain); or I could decide, as Empson did,
that a great many things not usually considered pastoral were in
fact to be so read; and either decision would give rise to a set of
interpretive strategies, which, when put into action, would *write*
the text I write when reading *Lycidas*. (Are you with me?)

3. A reader other than myself who, when presented with
Lycidas, proceeds to put into execution a set of interpretive strategies similar to mine (how he could do so is a question I will take
up later), will perform the same (or at least a similar) succession
of interpretive acts. He and I then might be tempted to say that
we agree about the poem (thereby assuming that the poem exists
independently of the acts either of us performs); but what we
really would agree about is the way to write it.

4. A reader other than myself who, when presented with *Lycidas*
(please keep in mind that the status of *Lycidas* is what is at issue),
puts into execution a different set of interpretive strategies will
perform a different succession of interpretive acts. (I am assuming, it is the article of my faith, that a reader will always execute
some set of interpretive strategies and therefore perform some
succession of interpretive acts.) One of us might then be tempted
to complain to the other that we could not possibly be reading
the same poem (literary criticism is full of such complaints) and

he would be right; for each of us would be reading the poem he had made.

The large conclusion that follows from these four smaller ones is that the notions of the 'same' or 'different' texts are fictions. If I read *Lycidas* and *The Waste Land* differently (in fact I do not), it will not be because the formal structures of the two poems (to term them such is also an interpretive decision) call forth different interpretive strategies but because my predisposition to execute different interpretive strategies will *produce* different formal structures. That is, the two poems are different because I have decided that they will be. The proof of this is the possibility of doing the reverse (that is why point 2 is so important). That is to say, the answer to the question 'why do different texts give rise to different sequences of interpretive acts?' is that *they don't have to*, an answer which implies strongly that 'they' don't exist. Indeed it has always been possible to put into action interpretive strategies designed to make all texts one, or to put it more accurately, to be forever making the same text. Augustine urges just such a strategy, for example, in *On Christian Doctrine* where he delivers the 'rule of faith' which is of course a rule of interpretation. It is dazzlingly simple: everything in the Scriptures, and indeed in the world when it is properly read, points to (bears the meaning of) God's love for us and our answering responsibility to love our fellow creatures for His sake. If only you should come upon something which does not at first seem to bear this meaning, that 'does not literally pertain to virtuous behavior or to the truth of faith', you are then to take it 'to be figurative' and proceed to scrutinize it 'until an interpretation contributing to the reign of charity is produced'. ... Whatever one may think of this interpretive program, its success and ease of execution are attested to by centuries of Christian exegesis. It is my contention that any interpretive program, any set of interpretive strategies, can have a similar success, although few have been as spectacularly successful as this one. ...

The other challenging question – 'why will different readers execute the same interpretive strategy when faced with the 'same' text?' – can be handled in the same way. The answer is again that *they don't have to*, and my evidence is the entire history of literary criticism. And again this answer implies that the notion 'same text' is the product of the possession by two or more readers of similar interpretive strategies.

But why should this ever happen? Why should two or more readers ever agree, and why should regular, that is, habitual, differences in the career of a single reader ever occur? What is the explanation on the one hand of the stability of interpretation (at least among certain groups at certain times) and on the other of the orderly variety of interpretation if it is not the stability and variety of texts? The answer to all of these questions is to be found in a notion that has been implicit in my argument, the notion of *interpretive communities*. Interpretive communities are made up of those who share interpretive strategies not for reading (in the conventional sense) but for writing texts, for constituting their properties and assigning their intentions. In other words these strategies exist prior to the act of reading and therefore determine the shape of what is read rather than, as is usually assumed, the other way around. If it is an article of faith in a particular community that there are a variety of texts, its members will boast a repertoire of strategies for making them. And if a community believes in the existence of only one text, then the single strategy its members employ will be forever writing it. The first community will accuse the members of the second of being reductive, and they in turn will call their accusers superficial. The assumption in each community will be that the other is not correctly perceiving the 'true text', but the truth will be that each perceives the text (or texts) its interpretive strategies demand and call into being. This, then, is the explanation both for the stability of interpretation among different readers (they belong to the same community) and for the regularity with which a single reader will employ different interpretive strategies and thus make different texts (he belongs to different communities). It also explains why there are disagreements and why they can be debated in a principled way: not because of a stability in texts, but because of a stability in the makeup of interpretive communities and therefore in the opposing positions they make possible. Of course this stability is always temporary (unlike the longed for and timeless stability of the text). Interpretive communities grow larger and decline, and individuals move from one to another; thus while the alignments are not permanent, they are always there, providing just enough stability for the interpretive battles to go on, and just enough shift and slippage to assure that they will never be settled. The notion of interpretive communities thus stands between an impossible ideal and the fear which leads so many to maintain it. The ideal is of perfect agreement and it would require texts to have a status independent of interpretation. The fear is of interpretive anarchy, but it would only be realized if interpretation (text making) were completely random. It is the fragile but real consolidation of interpretive communities that allows us to talk to one another, but with no hope or fear of ever being able to stop.

In other words interpretive communities are no more stable than texts because interpretive strategies are not natural or universal, but *learned*. This does not mean that there is a point at which an individual has not yet learned any. The ability to interpret is not acquired; it is constitutive of being human. What is acquired are the ways of interpreting and those same ways can also be forgotten or supplanted, or complicated or dropped from favor ('no one reads that way anymore'). When any of these things happens, there is a corresponding change in texts, not because they are being read differently, but because they are being written differently.

The only stability, then, inheres in the fact (at least in my model) that interpretive strategies are always being deployed, and this means that communication is a much more chancy affair than we are accustomed to think it. For if there are no fixed texts, but only interpretive strategies making them; and if interpretive strategies are not natural but learned (and are therefore unavailable to a finite description), what is it that utterers (speakers, authors, critics, me, you) do? In the old model utterers are in the business of handing over ready made or prefabricated meanings. These meanings are said to be encoded, and the code is assumed to be in the world independently of the individuals who are obliged to attach themselves to it (if they do not they run the danger of being declared deviant). In my model, however, meanings are not extracted but made and made not by encoded forms but by interpretive strategies that call forms into being. It follows then that what utterers do is give hearers and readers the opportunity to make meanings (and texts) by inviting them to put into execution a set of strategies. It is presumed that the invitation will be recognized, and that presumption rests on a projection on the part of a speaker or author of the moves *he* would make if confronted by the sounds or marks he is uttering or setting down.

It would seem at first that this account of things simply reintroduces the old objection; for isn't this an admission that there is after all a formal encoding, not perhaps of meanings, but of the directions for making them, for executing interpretive strategies? The answer is that they will only *be* directions to those who already have the interpretive strategies in the first place. Rather than producing interpretive acts, they are the product of one. An author hazards his projection, not because of something 'in' the marks, but because of something he assumes to be in his reader. The very existence of the 'marks' is a function of an interpretive community, for they will be recognized (that is, made) only by its members. Those outside that community will be deploying a different set of interpretive strategies (interpretation cannot be withheld) and will therefore be making different marks.

So once again I have made the text disappear, but unfortunately the problems do not disappear with it. If everyone is continually executing interpretive strategies and in that act constituting texts, intentions, speakers, and authors, how can any one of us know whether or not he is a member of the same interpretive community as any other of us? The answer is that he can't, since any evidence brought forward to support the claim would itself be an interpretation (especially if the 'other' were an author long dead). The only 'proof' of membership is fellowship, the nod of recognition from someone in the same community, someone who says to you what neither of us could ever prove to a third party: 'we know'. I say it to you now, knowing full well that you will agree with me (that is, understand) only if you already agree with me.

X FEMINIST CRITICISM

One of the major developments in literary studies in the past twenty-five years or so has been the emergence of feminist criticism, at the level of both theory and practice. Initially feminist criticism reflected the political goals of feminism in that authors and texts were judged in accordance with how far they could be reconciled with feminist ideology. The 'images of women' school of feminist critics adopts this point of view and is particularly concerned with how women characters are represented in literature. Josephine Donovan is one of its leading exponents and in the article reprinted here argues that for feminist criticism there can be no separation between the aesthetic and the moral aspects of literary texts even if this means judging adversely works as central to Western civilisation as Homer's *Odyssey*, Dante's *Divine Comedy*, and Goethe's *Faust*.

Another important concern of feminist criticism is women's writing. Elaine Showalter advocates 'gynocriticism', in which the concerns of the woman as writer are central. She argues that the 'woman as reader' approach of critics such as those in the 'images of women' school is restrictive in that it concentrates on male views of women. In this essay she is also critical of the attempt by some feminist critics to reconcile Marxian or post-structuralist concepts with feminist theory. Elizabeth A. Meese, in contrast, argues that feminist literary criticism should make use of the ideas of a post-structuralist thinker such as Foucault and of French feminist theorists such as Luce Irigaray in attacking in political terms the ideology underlying the structures of authority intrinsic to male-dominated 'interpretive communities'.

Hélène Cixous is the most influential French feminist theorist. Language for her is the crucial area of concern and she believes that in order to resist the phallocentrism or intrinsic male dominance of culture women have to find their own linguistic space. Thus she posits the existence of an 'écriture féminine' or feminine writing which is derived from the mother rather than the father. This form of language, drawing on the mother–child relationship which exists within the unconscious but remains repressed as the result of the domination of male-centred language, subverts fixity and closure in language and celebrates free-play of signification. In the selection from her work reprinted here she argues against the rigidities of both conventional theory and conventional feminism. For her it is absurd to reject male writing and male theory but nevertheless the fact that the feminine body is different and that language is a translation which 'speaks through the body' gives women 'another universe of expression from men'.

FURTHER READING

Josephine Donovan (ed.), *Feminist Literary Criticism: Explorations in Theory* (Lexington, Kentucky, 1975).
Mary Eagleton (ed.), *Feminist Literary Theory: A Reader* (Oxford, 1986).
Maggie Humm, *Feminist Criticism* (Brighton, 1986).
Elaine Marks and Isabelle de Courtivron (eds), *New French Feminisms: An Anthology* (Brighton, 1981).
Juliet Mitchell, *Women: The Longest Revolution: Essays in Feminism, Literature and Psychoanalysis* (London, 1984).
Toril Moi, *Sexual/Textual Politics: Feminist Literary Theory* (London, 1985).
K. K. Ruthven, *Feminist Literary Studies: An Introduction* (Cambridge, 1984).
Elaine Showalter (ed.), *The New Feminist Criticism: Essays on Women, Literature and Theory* (New York, 1985).

42 JOSEPHINE DONOVAN: 'BEYOND THE NET: FEMINIST CRITICISM AS A MORAL CRITICISM'

While feminist criticism has diversified considerably in the past few years, I wish in this article to return to the 'images of women' approach that dominated feminist literary studies in the early 1970s and is still central to the pedagogy of Women's Studies in literature. Through the 'images of women' approach the critic determines how women characters are presented in literature. Usually the critic discovers that the images are *Other*, and therefore that the literature is alien. The task may be labeled 'negative criticism' if one wishes to adapt the dialectical terms of the Frankfurt school of Marxist criticism. It is 'negative' because the critic is in effect saying 'no' to reified perceptions, structures, and models that have historically denied full humanity to women. This means looking 'negatively' at much of Western literature. Here I wish to set down a theoretical moral basis for this critique.

Reprinted from *Denver Quarterly*, 17 (1983), 40–53.

Feminist criticism is rooted in the fundamental *a priori* intuition that women are seats of consciousness: are selves, not others. ... Women in literature written by men are for the most part seen as Other, as objects, of interest only insofar as they serve or detract from the goals of the male protagonist. Such literature is alien from a female point of view because it denies her essential selfhood. ...

The primary assumption a critic in the 'images of women' school must make is an evaluation of the *authenticity* of the female characters. Authenticity is another concept borrowed from the Existentialists, in particular Heidegger, who meant by it whether an individual has a self-defined critical consciousness, as opposed to a mass-produced or stereotypical identity. Sartre defined the latter as the *en-soi*, the *in-itself* or the object-self, as opposed to the authentic *pour-soi* or *for-itself*, which is the critical or reflective consciousness capable of forming projects.

The concept of authenticity in feminist criticism is therefore not a free-floating, 'impressionistic' notion, as has been suggested.[1] Judgments which evaluate a character's authenticity are rooted in the extensive body of Existentialist theory on the subject. Such judgments are made according to whether the character has a reflective, critical consciousness, where s/he is a moral agent, capable of self-determined action, whether, in short, s/he is a Self, not an Other. Such judgments enable the feminist critic to determine the degree to which sexist ideology controls the text. Sexist ideology necessarily promotes the concept of woman-as-object or woman-as-other. ...

Some films of Ingmar Bergman provide excellent if subtle examples of the phenomenon of aesthetic exploitation of women characters. *Cries and Whispers* (1972) is a film which one might, on first viewing, hail as a sensitive portrayal of the lives of four women. The extraordinary visual beauty of the film is seductive enough to promote this judgment. However, on reflection one comes to realize that the women are used aesthetically as if they were on the same level of moral importance as the red decor of their surroundings. ...

I am using *aesthetic* here in the sense given it at least since Kant, that of a disinterested appreciation of a phenomenon that exists as a discrete entity in space and time, which is pleasing within these or because of these spatio-temporal coordinates. As we shall see, I believe that the imputed divorce between aesthetics and morals which this view entails is specious, masking as it does ideological exploitation of female figures. ... Consequently an artist like Bergman can treat his female figures as objects within a spatio-temporal continuum that are of use only insofar as they fit into the total aesthetic vision he has fashioned. ...

The aesthetic dimension of literature and of film cannot be divorced from the moral dimension, as we have facilely come to assume under the influence of technique-oriented critical methodologies (New Criticism, for example). Since Aristotle, the aesthetic experience has in fact been understood as one which provides release, relief, catharsis, and the pleasure of wholeness. The events within this aesthetic frame may be horrible or violent but they are ultimately redeemed by the fact that they take their place within an order. This order cannot be a superficial order, i.e., it is not sufficient to simply frame a scene of grotesque suffering. It has to be placed within a moral order of great consequence. All the 'great works' of Western literature intend and depend upon a moral order. The events of the work take their place within an order that satisfied one's sense of justice or one's sense of irony, which itself requires a belief in an order beyond the events of the work.

When one identifies too closely with a character's suffering in a work of art, or when that suffering is exploited to the point where it breaks the boundaries of appropriateness within the moral context of the work, the aesthetic continuity is dislocated: the suffering cannot be justified, morally or aesthetically. ...

Much of our literature in fact depends upon a series of fixed images of women, stereotypes. These reified forms, surprisingly few in number, are repeated over and over again through much of Western literature. The objectified images have one thing in common, however; they define the woman insofar as she relates to, serves, or thwarts the interests of men.

In the Western tradition these stereotypes tend to fall into two categories, reflecting the endemic Manicheistic dualism in the Western world-view. Female stereotypes symbolize either the spiritual or the material, good or evil. Mary, the mother of Jesus, came through time to exemplify the ultimate in spiritual goodness, and Eve, the partner of Adam, the most sinister of evil physicality. The following diagram shows how this dualism is conceived:

spiritual	material
spirit/soul	body
virginal ideal	sex object
Mary	Eve
inspiration	seductress
good	evil

Under the category of the good-woman stereotypes, that is, those who serve the interests of the hero, are the patient wife, the mother/martyr, and the lady. In the bad or evil category are deviants who reject or do not properly serve man or his interests: the old maid/career woman, the witch/lesbian, the shrew or domineering mother/wife. Several works, considered archetypal masterpieces of the Western tradition, rely upon these simplistic stereotypes of woman. ...

These works, central to the Western tradition – the *Odyssey*, the *Commedia*, and *Faust* – do not present the 'inside' of women's experience. We learn little, if anything, of the women's own personal responses to events. They are simply vehicles for the growth and salvation of the male protagonist. The women are Other in Beauvoir's sense of the term, and therefore this literature must remain alien to the female reader who reads as a woman.

One can argue, of course, that a woman reader can suspend her femaleness and appreciate great works which have male protagonists (and objectified women) when the protagonists are wrestling with universal human problems. In other words, one can argue that one can transcend one's sex in appreciating a literary work. To some extent I believe that this is indeed possible. ...

The real question is not whether a woman *can* identify with the subjective consciousness or the self if it is male, but whether she *should*, given her own political and social environment. In other words, isn't it morally misleading to encourage a person who is barred from action to identify with an individual whose dilemma (in the case of Hamlet) is simply whether to act? Action, taking charge, is a choice that historically has been denied women and still is unavailable to them in many areas. Until, however, ideological socialization ceases, we as female readers cannot authentically transcend our sex. Such literature as treated in this article must remain alien. This does not mean that we should throw out or refuse to read these works, but that they should be read with perspective that recognizes the sexism inherent in their moral vision. ...

Feminist criticism is moral because it sees that one of the central problems of Western literature is that in much of it women are not human beings, seats of consciousness. They are objects, who are used to facilitate, explain away, or redeem the projects of men. Western projects of redemption almost always depend upon a salvific woman. On the other hand, in some Western literature women are the objects, the scapegoats, of much cruelty and evil. Much Western thought and literature has failed to come to grips with the problem of evil because it facilely projects evil upon woman or other hypostasized 'Others', such as the Jew, the Negro, thereby denying the reality of the contingent order.

Feminist criticism becomes political when it asserts that literature, academic curricula, and the standards of critical judgment should be changed, so that literature will no longer function as propaganda furthering sexist ideology. The feminist critic recognizes that literature is an important contributing element to a moral atmosphere in which women are derogated. ...

Linguistic analysis and semiological studies can tell us much about how cultural ideologies are expressed in literary form. But only when style is studied in the context of the author's or the culture's moral view of women can it be of feminist significance. Unfortunately much formalist analysis in the past has relied on the convenient divorce between values and aesthetics described above. For this reason it has been able to evade the central evaluative issue that criticism must face: that of the moral stature of the work.

Criticism, by ignoring central questions of content, has become dehumanized in the same way as modern art did when it gave way to exclusively formal concerns. ... Literature on its most profound level is a form of learning. We learn, we grow from the knowledge of life, of psychology, of human behavior and relationships that we discover in worthwhile works of art.

NOTE

[Reorganised and renumbered from the original]
1. See Stuart Cunningham, 'Some Problems of Feminist Literary Criticism', *Journal of Women's Studies in Literature*, 1 (1979), 159–78.

43   ELAINE SHOWALTER: 'TOWARDS A FEMINIST POETICS'

Feminist criticism can be divided into two distinct varieties. The first type is concerned with *woman as reader* – with woman as the consumer of male-produced literature, and with the way in which the hypothesis of a female reader changes our apprehension of a given text, awakening us to the significance of its sexual codes. I shall call this kind of analysis the *feminist critique*, and like other kinds of critique it is a historically grounded inquiry which probes the ideological assumptions of literary phenomena. Its subjects include the images and stereotypes of women in literature, the omissions and misconceptions about women in criticism, and the fissures in male-constructed literary history. It is also concerned with the exploitation and manipulation of the female audience, especially in popular culture and film; and with the analysis of woman-as-sign in semiotic systems. The second type of feminist criticism is concerned with *woman as writer* – with woman as the producer of textual meaning, with the history, themes, genres and structures of literature by women. Its subjects include the psychodynamics of female creativity; linguistics and the problem of a female language; the trajectory of the individual or collective female literary career; literary history; and, of course, studies of particular writers and works. No term exists in English for such a specialised discourse, and so I have adapted the French term *la gynocritique:* '*gynocritics*' (although the significance of the male pseudonym in the history of women's writing also suggested the term 'georgics').

The feminist critique is essentially political and polemical, with theoretical affiliations to Marxist sociology and aesthetics; gynocritics is more self-contained and experimental, with connections to other modes of new feminist research. ...

As we see in this analysis, one of the problems of the feminist critique is that it is male-oriented. If we study stereotypes of women, the sexism of male critics, and the limited roles women play in literary history, we are not learning what women have felt and experienced, but only what men have thought women should be. In some fields of specialisation, this may require a long

Reprinted from *Women Writing and Writing about Women*, ed. Mary Jacobus (London, 1979), pp. 25–40.

apprenticeship to the male theoretician, whether he be Althusser, Barthes, Macherey or Lacan; and then an application of the theory of signs or myths or the unconscious to male texts or films. The temporal and intellectual investment one makes in such a process increases resistance to questioning it, and to seeing its historical and ideological boundaries. The critique also has a tendency to naturalise women's victimisation, by making it the inevitable and obsessive topic of discussion. ...

In contrast to this angry or loving fixation on male literature, the programme of gynocritics is to construct a female framework for the analysis of women's literature, to develop new models based on the study of female experience, rather than to adapt male models and theories. Gynocritics begins at the point when we free ourselves from the linear absolutes of male literary history, stop trying to fit women between the lines of the male tradition, and focus instead on the nearly visible world of female culture. ...

... Before we can even begin to ask how the literature of women would be different and special, we need to reconstruct its past, to rediscover the scores of women novelists, poets and dramatists whose work has been obscured by time, and to establish the continuity of the female tradition. ... As we recreate the chain of writers in this tradition, the patterns of influence and response from one generation to the next, we can also begin to challenge the periodicity of orthodox literary history, and its enshrined canons of achievement. It is because we have studied women writers in isolation that we have never grasped the connections between them. When we go beyond Austen, the Brontës and Eliot, say, to look at a hundred and fifty or more of their sister novelists, we can see patterns and phases in the evolution of a female tradition which correspond to the developmental phases of any subcultural art. In my book on English women writers, *A Literature of their Own*, I have called these the Feminine, Feminist and Female stages. During the Feminine phases, dating from about 1840 to 1880, women wrote in an effort to equal the intellectual achievements of the male culture, and internalised its assumptions about female nature. The distinguishing sign of this period is the male pseudonym, introduced in England in the 1840s, and a national characteristic of English women writers. ... The feminist content of feminine art is typically oblique, displaced, ironic and subversive; one has to read it between the lines, in the missed possibilities of the text.

In the Feminist phase, from about 1880 to 1920, or the winning of the vote, women are historically enabled to reject the accommodating postures of femininity and to use literature to dramatise the ordeals of wronged womanhood. ...

In the Female phase, ongoing since 1920, women reject both imitation and protest – two forms of dependency – and turn instead to female experience as the source of an autonomous art, extending the feminist analysis of culture to the forms and techniques of literature. Representatives of the formal Female Aesthetic, such as Dorothy Richardson and Virginia Woolf, begin to think in terms of male and female sentences, and divide their work into 'masculine' journalism and 'feminine' fictions, redefining and sexualising external and internal experience. ...

In trying to account for these complex permutations of the female tradition, feminist criticism has tried a variety of theoretical approaches. The most natural direction for feminist criticism to take has been the revision, and even the subversion of related ideologies, especially Marxist aesthetics and structuralism, altering their vocabularies and methods to include the variable of gender. I believe, however, that this thrifty feminine making-do is ultimately unsatisfactory. Feminist criticism cannot go around forever in men's ill-fitting hand-me-downs, the Annie Hall of English studies; but must, as John Stuart Mill wrote about women's literature in 1869, 'emancipate itself from the influences of accepted models, and guide itself by its own impulses'[1] – as, I think, gynocritics is beginning to do. This is not to deny the necessity of using the terminology and techniques of our profession. But when we consider the historical conditions in which critical ideologies are produced, we see why feminist adaptations seem to have reached an impasse. ...

The new sciences of the text based on linguistics, computers, genetic structuralism, deconstructionism, neo-formalism and deformalism, affective stylistics and psychoaesthetics, have offered literary critics the opportunity to demonstrate that the work they do is as manly and aggressive as nuclear physics – not intuitive, expressive and feminine, but strenuous, rigorous, impersonal and virile. In a shrinking job market, these new levels of professionalism also function as discriminators between the marketable and marginal lecturer. Literary science, in its manic generation of difficult terminology, its establishment of seminars and institutes of post-graduate study, creates an élite corps of specialists who spend more and more time mastering the theory, less and less time reading the books. We are moving towards a two-tiered system of 'higher' and 'lower' criticism, the higher concerned with the 'scientific' problems of form and structure, the 'lower' concerned with the 'humanistic' problems of content and interpretation. And these levels, it seems to me, are now taking on subtle gender identities, and assuming a sexual polarity – hermeneutics and hismeneutics. Ironically, the existence

of a new criticism practised by women has made it even more possible for structuralism and Marxism to strive, Henchard-like, for
systems of formal obligation and determination. Feminists writing
in these modes, such as Hélène Cixous and the women contributors
to *Diacritics*, risk being allotted the symbolic ghettoes of the special
issue or the back of the book for their essays.

It is not because the exchange between feminism, Marxism and
structuralism has hitherto been so one-sided, however, that I
think attempts at syntheses have so far been unsuccessful. While
scientific criticism struggles to purge itself of the subjective, feminist criticism is willing to assert (in the title of a recent anthology) *The Authority of Experience.*[2] The experience of woman can
easily disappear, become mute, invalid and invisible, lost in the
diagrams of the structuralist or the class conflict of the Marxists.
Experience is not emotion; we must protest now as in the nineteenth century against the equation of the feminine with the irrational. But we must also recognise that the questions we most
need to ask go beyond those that science can answer. We must
seek the repressed messages of women in history, in anthropology, in psychology, and in ourselves, before we can locate the feminine not-said, in the manner of Pierre Macherey,[3] by probing the
fissures of the female text.

Thus the current theoretical impasse in feminist criticism, I
believe, is more than a problem of finding 'exacting definitions
and a suitable terminology', or 'theorizing in the midst of a struggle'. It comes from our own divided consciousness, the split in
each of us. We are both the daughters of the male tradition, of
our teachers, our professors, our dissertation advisers and our
publishers – a tradition which asks us to be rational, marginal and
grateful; and sisters in a new women's movement which engen-
ders another kind of awareness and commitment, which demands
that we renounce the pseudo-success of token womanhood, and
the ironic masks of academic debate. How much easier, how less
lonely it is, not to awaken – to continue to be critics and teachers
of male literature, anthropologists of male culture, and psychologists of male literary response, claiming all the while to be universal. Yet we cannot will ourselves to go back to sleep. As women
scholars in the 1970s we have been given a great opportunity, a
great intellectual challenge. The anatomy, the rhetoric, the
poetics, the history, await our writing. ...

...The task of feminist critics is to find a new language, a new
way of reading that can integrate our intelligence and our experience, our reason and our suffering, our scepticism and our vision.

This enterprise should not be confined to women; I invite Criticus, Poeticus and Plutarchus to share it with us. One thing is certain: feminist criticism is not visiting. It is here to stay, and we must make it a permanent home.

NOTES

[Reorganised and renumbered from the original]
1. J.S. Mill, *The Subjection of Women* (London, 1869), p. 133.
2. Lee Edwards and Arlyn Diamond (eds), *The Authority of Experience* (Amherst, Mass., 1977).
3. [Ed.] See Pierre Macherey, *A Theory of Literary Production*, trans. Geoffrey Wall (London, 1978).

44   ELIZABETH A. MEESE: 'SEXUAL POLITICS AND CRITICAL JUDGMENT'

In 'Literature as an Institution: The View from 1980', Leslie Fiedler cynically observes: 'We all know in our hearts that literature is effectively what we teach in departments of English; or conversely what we teach in departments of English is literature. Within that closed definitional circle, we perform the rituals by which we cast out unworthy pretenders from our ranks and induct true initiates, guardians of the standards by which all song and story ought presumably to be judged.'[1] The effects of this kind of exclusion are transparent: it places literature almost entirely in the service of white, male elite culture. ...

... In his collection of essays, *Is There a Text in this Class? The Authority of Interpretive Communities*, Stanley Fish presents a view of critical judgments as issuing from an interpretive community, which, when examined from a feminist perspective, provides a useful means of describing the nature of critical bias. Perhaps inadvertently, Fish helps us to see clearly what we have always intuited. A strong insider-outsider dynamic, taking the form of a gender-based literary tribalism, comes into play as a means of control. Critics who permit the possibility of variations in critical

Reprinted from *After Strange Texts: The Role of Theory in the Study of Literature*, ed. Gregory S. Jay and David L. Miller (Alabama, 1985), pp. 86–100.

interpretation, as opposed to those seeking the *Ur*-reading, immediately face the problem of closing ranks against the extremes of relativism in interpretation. Otherwise, the authority of the mainstream literary tradition could be seriously threatened. ... While it is true that Fish represents only one current in today's confluence, other critics who disagree with him in some respects seem to accept the concept of the authoritative community. ...

...We see that the 'interpretive community' is really the 'authoritative community'. Even though Fish regards criticism as an 'open category', we are forced to see it, like his version of community, as a closed system which excludes us from the arena of its authority. ...

Interpretive communities, like tribal communities, possess the power to ostracize or to embrace, to restrict or to extend membership and participation, and to impose norms – hence their authority. ...

...The more vigorously Fish argues to allay his colleagues' fears of rampant interpretive anarchy, the more clearly the feminist critic perceives the power held by members of this interpretive community. They control the admissibility of facts, texts, and evidence, as well as the norms constitutive of reasonableness in argumentation. Out of commitment to the illusion of objectivity, they miss an essential distinction that Camus apprehended: 'There are crimes of passion and crimes of logic. The boundary between them is not clearly defined.'[2]

Fish very cleverly catches all of us up in his critical net. Like it or not we all play the game because, for him, there is no other. Even if we reject the rules we are still participants, because the rules themselves include the rejection of the rules – an inauspicious position for those who are not members of the authoritative community. You become a member when the community makes you one, and not necessarily by virtue of how well you perform critical acts. The truth that Fish fails to disclose is that membership is a privilege (conferred by those in power) rather than a right (earned by skill).

Fish's work is useful to feminist critics because he redirects our attention, away from the mystique of the text – from arguments concerning 'facts', 'truth', 'beauty', and 'universality' – toward the more political considerations of how literary value is legislated and culture thereby shaped. Because he speaks as a member of the authoritative community whose arguments in any contest of persuasion are invested with undeniable value, if not validity, he can honestly claim that disputes are settled by persuasion, that there is no position of privilege, and that one's argument will be considered, if not accepted. In contrast, the trespassers find themselves on shifting ground – trained on the one hand to construct arguments from textual and contextual evidence which then have little impact, and, on the other, to avoid unseemly debates, in reality the fundamental ones, predicated upon 'extraliterary' assumptions concerning the nature of social and political reality, or the sexual politics of literary judgment. Ishmael Reed expresses similar frustration from the viewpoint of the black writer caught in the same system of judgment: 'Art is what white people do. All other people are "propagandists".'[3]

Feminist criticism is a monumental undertaking which involves changing the very structure/sex of knowledge, thereby attempting to liberate us from what Diana Hume George calls an 'operational model that artificially ... dualizes intellectual activity and sexuality'.[4] The problem confronting us is both epistemological and political – each equally significant and inseparable from the other. For years feminist critics have hedged on both counts, wanting to believe on the one hand in that 'theoretical equality', and fearing on the other the fragmentation that could result from definition and the articulation of methodology (an inchoate ideological map). Consciously or not, we have obscured the terms of the dispute, and with them the need to differentiate between criticism written by women and feminist criticism. Within feminist criticism, we have avoided both the political and the epistemological, as though there were no purpose in recapitulating the politics of gender (which threaten to separate women from men and from the institutions of culture). ...

Some proponents of poststructuralism, engaged in their own attack on the ideological character of discourse believe that criticism has finally freed itself of its orientation toward objectivity and universality. It is tempting to regard the poststructuralist position as pervasive, characteristic of criticism of the past decade. And yet, far from epitomizing critical activity today, poststructuralists have made only a beginning in their attack on the historically rooted traditions of criticism. ... Just as the masters are never obliged to learn the language of the slave, the hierarchy of critical communities will continue to resist feminist, black, and Marxist criticism as long as the power configuration upon which it rests remains undisturbed.

The records of the new and newly seen are accumulating in a swiftly mounting challenge to the old structures of knowledge. As Foucault suggests in *Power/Knowledge*, 'The essential political problem for the intellectual is ... that of ascertaining the possibility of constituting a new politics of truth. The problem is not changing people's consciousness – or what's in their heads – but the political, economic, institutional regime of the production of truth.'[5] In other words, prevailing paradigms reflect and are reflected in the current regime of truth. Truth does not hold an independent relationship to systems of power. It results from or is coincident with the very power which structures knowledge itself. Thus, our effort as feminist critics necessarily becomes highly political when approaching a paradigm from the outside. Foucault explains 'It's not a matter of emancipating truth from every system of power (which would be a chimera, for truth is already power) but of detaching the power of truth from the forms of hegemony, social, economic and cultural, within which it operates at the present time.'[6] Foucault's observation speaks directly to those functioning outside of the literary critical establishment. It is clear that those excluded from the terms of truth are the very ones who perceive the inadequacies of the paradigm and experience the sense of urgency required to address it. A diffusion of the experience of discontinuity, beyond the right of outsiders/trespassers, is needed before significant changes can occur. Such a generalized discomfort – the guilt or uncertainty that includes at least one novel by a woman in a course or invites feminist and other minority critics to the English Institute – marks the transitional phase toward paradigm revolution.

It has never been the obligation of literary critics, masked by the pretense of objectivity, to explicate the political origins and implications of their judgments. As a result, feminist critics need to question vigorously the methods and techniques of the inherited critical tradition. For example, Fish, in his notion of the interpretive (authoritative) community, proffers equality: literature is an open system, admitting any text (within reason); variations in interpretation are permitted (within reason); and persuasion is the means by which (reasonable) critics establish consensus. When he reinvests the authority for determining the limits of the reasonable in the profession as it is now constituted, Fish reinscribes the politics of exclusion he might have undone by defining literature as an open category and defending interpretive pluralism. But inherent in Fish's approach is the fact that the right reason and the power of determination are located where power and reason have always rested in Western civilization – within the community of elite white men. He thereby preserves theoretical access at the expense of actual change. It makes sense to suspect, as Marxist critics have always noted from their vantage point, that our conceptual frameworks mirror ideology. The principal task of feminist criticism, in providing a necessary re-vision of the politics of 'truth', is to make its own ideology explicit. If we seek to transform the structures of authority, we must first name them, and in doing so, unmask and expose them for all to see. As we forge a new criticism, our theories and assumptions must stay clear of a hegemonic role reversal that results from unending deconstructions of oppositions like male/female and insider/outsider, where the second term simply replaces the first in an infinite regression within an economy of oppression. The future of feminist criticism rests on defying the oppositional logic currently fostering the very concept of privilege.

In 'When Our Lips Speak Together', Luce Irigaray warns us of the failure to extricate ourselves from this phallogocentric system: 'If we continue to speak the same language to each other, we will reproduce the same story. Begin the same stories all over again. ... If we continue to speak this sameness, if we speak to each other as men have spoken for centuries, as they taught us to speak, we will fail each other.'[7] But the transformation of literature and criticism as cultural institutions demands a language of defiance rather than the silent complicity required of us for the perpetuation of phallogocentrism. Feminist criticism, if it is any good, is guaranteed to offend the mighty. This is essential to its value, a barometer of its ultimate effectiveness. A new politics, based not on negation but on the positive construction of woman through the solidarity of feminist practitioners, should yield a new theory as well as a new praxis.

NOTES

[Reorganised and renumbered from the original]

1. Leslie Fiedler, 'Literature as an Institution: The View from 1980', in *Opening Up the Canon, Selected Papers from the English Institute, 1979*, ed. Leslie Fiedler and Houston A. Baker, Jr (Baltimore, 1981), pp. 73–4.

2. Albert Camus, *The Rebel: An Essay on Man in Revolt*, trans. Anthony Bower (New York, 1956), p. 3.

3. Quoted in Richard Kostelanetz, *The End of Intelligent Writing: Literary Politics in America* (New York, 1974), p. 243.

4. Diana Hume George, 'Stumbling on Melons: Sexual Dialectics and Discrimination in English Departments', *Opening Up the Canon*, p. 109.

5. Michel Foucault, *Power/Knowledge: Selected Interviews and Other Writings, 1972–1977*, ed. Colin Gordon, trans. Colin Gordon et al. (New York, 1980), p. 133.

6. Ibid.

7. Luce Irigaray, 'When Our Lips Speak Together', trans. Carolyn Burke, *Signs*, 6 (1980), 69.

45 HÉLÈNE CIXOUS: 'CONVERSATIONS'

We are not outside theory in the seminar though I hope in a way we are above it. We use theoretical instruments, but we use them as aids, as a means of advancing further. This is not a way of repressing or obliterating theory but of giving it a place which is not an end in itself. What I most try to avoid is the turning of theory into an idol. We are not idolaters though neither are we ignorant. We have all undergone our programme of systematic theoretical initiation, but we have done this not to be confined by theory, but for theory to appear as what it is, useful and traversable.

Some years ago there was such an inflation of theoretical discourse in France that whole generations of students were arriving at university already terrorized by the monster. So much so that it was necessary to embark on a programme of theory just to prove to them that it wasn't a monster, but a discourse constituted amongst others which could help us get closer to the text. The problem was that theory was constituted within the institution as an end in itself, like a trophy. We have had to do battle against that.

The theoretical trend in France has been a negative criticism of meaning and representation. A text is neither representation nor expression. A text is beyond both representation – the exact reproduction of reality – and expression: it always says something other than it intends to say. The text is always more than the author wants to express or believes s/he expresses. As a result of fashionable theoretical practices, all this has been repressed. We have been in the phase of non-meaning, in the suspension, the exclusion of the message. This has had serious implications for reading in France. We began to read texts on a purely formal level. University practice is still very largely formal.

Fifteen years ago, Freud was prohibited in feminist circles, on the pretext that he was a misogynist. At the time I wondered how these feminists could possibly hope to get through life because everything had been invented by men. It was like saying, 'we can't go by plane because a woman didn't invent it'. Freud focused attention on the unconscious in an extraordinary series of discoveries. Do we behave as if the unconscious doesn't exist? We live in a post-Freudian, Derridean age of electricity and the aeroplane. So

Reprinted from *Writing Differences: Readings from the Seminar of Hélène Cixous*, ed. Susan Sellers (Milton Keynes, 1988), pp. 142–54.

let's do as modern people do, let's use the contemporary means of transport. We owe Freud the exploration of the unconscious. Freud learnt from the poets. In the network of relays, apprenticeships and schools, we need to know how to give everyone their place. Some of the poets we work on in the seminar didn't know about psychoanalysis, which doesn't stop them from being subject to psychoanalysis. At the same time, in their creation they are poetically beyond psychoanalysis. It's this 'poetically beyond' which is important to me. In the early stages of reading, we go much faster if we are in the analytic automobile, if we take Freud's plane. And we need to go quickly. We need to go quicker to begin with in order to go more slowly later on, to be able to take the time to meditate on the 'poetically beyond' which psychoanalysis can't deal with, philosophy can't deal with, because it escapes them, is stronger, more difficult, more complex, more alive. ...

The space we work in qualifies itself by the grouping together of many strangenesses. The texts we work on are strange either because of their language or because of what they say. What binds us together is our belief in the need to ensure that the essence of each strangeness is preserved.

The image this meeting of strangenesses evokes for me is one of movement. When I first encountered the texts of Clarice Lispector I remembered Celan's image of the bottle and the sea: the poem's journey to the reader. Reading Clarice, I witnessed this journey. I saw the map of the world crossed by a voice, a message.

Sometimes in the seminar I feel as if we were replying to the curse of Babel. The biblical curse was finding oneself prey to a multiplicity of languages but I see it as a blessing to be in the midst of so many languages. For languages say different things. And our multiple collectivity makes these differences – this infinite enrichment – apparent to us.

There is a passage in Blanchot where the narrator says 'I espoused him in his language'. What we try to do is to espouse a text in its language. When we translate a text, for example, we don't try to *reduce* it to French. We work to preserve the essence of each different language as it passes from one language to the other.

The work we do is a work of love, comparable to the work of love that can take place between two human beings. To understand the other, it is necessary to go in their language, to make the journey through the other's imaginary. For you are strange to me. In the effort to understand, I bring you back to me, compare you to me. I translate you in me. And what I note is your difference, your strangeness. At that moment, perhaps, through recognition of my own differences, I might perceive something of you.

This movement is like a voyage. Sometimes I have worked on countries poetically. Cambodia is an example. In my mind, I had an imaginary Cambodia composed of everything I had read. But, of course, nothing could render the actual experience of going to Cambodia which is something that passes through the body, through the senses, something which happens between Cambodia and me – my encounter with its smell, its space, the colours of its sky.

I have always thought how much I should like to be able to keep all the various stages of this journey. The pre-journey; the imaginary journey. All the preparations for the journey. The first encounter. The moment of discovery. Then everything we bring back from the encounter.

All these different stages are, in reality, the history of a text. And our reading must be a movement capable of following all the stages of this vast journey from one to the other, to me, to you.

I believe that in order to read – to translate – well, we have to undertake this journey ourselves. We have to go to the country of the text and bring back the earth of which the language is made. And every aspect is important, including the things we don't know, the things we discover. ...

Everything begins with love. If we work on a text we don't love, we are automatically at the wrong distance. This happens in many institutions where, in general, one works on a text as if it were an object, using theoretical instruments. It's perfectly possible to make a machine out of the text, to treat it like a machine and be treated by it like a machine. The contemporary tendency has been to find theoretical instruments, a reading technique which has bridled the text, mastered it like a wild horse with saddle and bridle, enslaving it. I am wary of formalist approaches, those which cut up structure, which impose their systematic grid.

If I set loving the text as a condition, I also set up the possibility that there will be people who will not love some of the text we work on. Some of us won't 'bite' into certain texts, certain texts won't mean anything to us. It doesn't matter. Others amongst us will be called by them and moved to reply.

There are thirty ways into a text. Reading together in this way we bring the text into play. We take a page and everyone comes individually towards it. The text begins to radiate from these approaches. Slowly, we penetrate together to its heart.

I choose to work on the texts that 'touch' me. I use the word deliberately because I believe there is a bodily relationship between reader and text. We work very close to the text, as close to the body of the text as possible; we work phonically, listening to the text, as well as graphically and typographically. Sometimes I look at the design, the geography of the text, as if it were a map, embodying the world. I look at its legs, its thighs, its belly, as well as its trees and rivers: an immense human and earthly cosmos. I like to work like an ant, crawling the entire length of a text and examining all its details, as well as like a bird that flies over it, or like one of Tsvetaeva's immense ears, listening to its music.

We listen to a text with numerous ears. We hear each other talking with foreign accents and we listen to the foreign accents in the text. Every text has its foreign accents, its strangenesses, and these act like signals, attracting our attention. These strangenesses are our cue. We aren't looking for the author as much as what made the author take the particular path they took, write what they wrote. We're looking for the secret of creation, the same process of creation each one of us is constantly involved with in the process of our lives. Texts are the witnesses of our proceeding. The text opens up a path which is already ours and yet not altogether ours. ...

Some years ago, at the height of the feminist campaigns, a number of women came to the seminar who asked me why there were texts on the annual programme by men. These women had been expecting an exclusively 'feminist' programme with texts written only by women. There has never been in the seminar opposition to or exclusion of one genre by another, one sex by the other.

We work on the mystery of human being, including the fact that humans are sexed beings, that there is sexual difference, and that these differences manifest themselves, write themselves in texts. The differences inscribe themselves in whatever is born from us.

Throughout the world there are differences. Differences of behaviour, differences in relation to living. There are choices. We have a preference for one way of behaviour rather than another because it allows us to live more fully, makes us happier. I prefer a behaviour which is capable of change, capable of taking risks, to a behaviour which is closed and conservative, and which resists any form of loss.

In our work, we are motivated by the inscription of these differences which cannot be contained by the labels man/woman, masculine/feminine. Difference transcends, it traverses everything that exists. It moves in a complex way through every expression, every creation, every (textual) production.

The title of last year's seminar was 'Bereavement and Benediction'. In our reading we traced the theme of bereavement, of how one mourns, how each individual goes through the process of mourning, the apprenticeship that the experience of bereavement represents from earliest childhood through all the stages of life. There is the baby's bereavement, the bereavement of severance, which is also severance for the mother. There are all the stages, all the transformations of the ordeal of bereavement and separation which we encounter in diverse forms throughout life. How do we live the ordeal? What do we make of it? Do we experience it as something negative or do we transform it into something positive? What does it give to writing? these are the questions we work on which we divide for the sake of convenience into 'masculine' and 'feminine'.

For it happens that these questions join with questions. The distinction between masculine cultural behaviour and feminine cultural behaviour, for example. These questions are the clichés of our time and hold everyone prisoner. Culturally the people whose apprenticeship to bereavement has created a relationship to it which is open and will allow for progress are women. This is because, culturally, women have been taught how to lose, they've been sent to the school of losing. But there are men who have learnt how to lose, who have been to the school of losing and who have come out victorious, transforming their loss into blessing. Some of them are our greatest poets. It's not a question of sex. It's a question of apprenticeship. Which school did you go to?

This year we have worked on texts which are wonderful songs, hymns of what there may be of beauty in the encounter with an inflicted bereavement. We have worked on Mandelstam, on Celan. What do we do when we lose the world, when language is stolen from us by a political regime, when we no longer have a country, when exile is our home? Both men and women have given us their answer.

It's true that I privilege what I would hope to be my answer. I would hope that even in the most extreme exile there will be a force greater than everything, a force which continues to sing: what Celan calls the *Singbarrest*, the singable remains. Even when there is nothing left but silence or the murmuring of despair, I believe there is still hope. Reading Etty Hillesum's diaries from inside the Nazi concentration camps, I am strengthened in my hope. There are texts which help us to believe.

This is where difference leads us. Even though the text carries in its body, in its flesh, the marks of the gender granted us at birth, it necessarily situates itself above these questions.

I don't believe a man and a woman are identical. The fact that men and women have the whole of humanity in common and that at the same time there is something slightly different, I consider a benediction. Our differences have to do with the way we experience pleasure, with our bodily experiences, which are not the same. Our different experiences necessarily leave different marks, different memories. The way we make love – because it isn't the same – produces different sensations and recollections. And these are transmitted through the text. I don't understand what people mean when they tell me these differences don't exist. I consider their belief censorious, repressive, deadly. These differences are simply a small part of the entirety of a human being.

As a writer, I regret we cannot go from one side to the other, from one body to another. I regret not being Tiresias. In ancient times, Tiresias was possible. Perhaps he will be again. But I'm not Tiresias. I can write about feminine pleasure, but I can't write about the masculine experience of it. There is a block.

I am not Tiresias. I am not God. I am only a woman, which is already a great deal. From the moment I say: 'I am only a woman', this reserve or opening inscribes itself in my text. This is the point I write from. It makes itself read. It doesn't run through everything because I'm also a human being. As Clarice Lispector says: 'I'm a woman, plus something else.' A part of me is specifically woman and the rest of me is human. It's the same for a man. These are the backgrounds of inscription, of thinking in the text, which are distinguishable from each other.

If I were to write a historical novel, what would it matter if I were a man or a woman? But if I write about love, then it does matter. I write differently. If I write letting something of my body come through, then this will be different, depending on whether I have experience of a feminine or masculine body.

I could write a thesis on the theme of giving birth in texts by women, it would be fascinating. It's a metaphor which comes easily to women, dictated by their experience. It's a metaphor Clarice Lispector uses, it's a metaphor I use. During childbirth a discovery is made inside the body. We can transpose the discovery, using it to understand moments in life which are analogous. A man will understand different things differently. Their bodies are sources of totally different images, transformations, expressions. ...

Language is a translation. It speaks through the body. Each time we translate what we are in the process of thinking, it necessarily passes through our bodies. If a woman disposes of her body (and I'm not talking about women who are alienated from their bodies, but about those who have a body which is theirs, who inhabit it, live in it), when she speaks, her words pass through it. This gives another universe of expression from men. We are not machines.

People often ask me: are there any great writers? It's a question I always have difficulty with because, of course, there are great writers: great technicians, great artists of writing, extraordinary acrobats of language. But I believe in the importance of the message in a text. Writers only begin to interest me if what they say has a relationship to humanity.

I believe the text should establish an ethical relation to reality as well as to artistic practice. I might summarize my definition of poetry as 'philosophic singing'. Philosophic reasoning, and, at the same time, the overflowing of the boundaries of philosophic discourse: making the river of poetry flow into the bed of philosophy. Some poetry, of course, doesn't have a message. There is poetry which is more musical than thoughtful. What I call poetry crosses the fertile field of philosophy in order to go beyond.

A few years ago, we subtitled our work in the seminar with the doublet 'poetry-politics'. This was in the attempt not to let poetry stray too far from reality, in the struggle to try to think politically via a poetic route.

As far as my own writing is concerned, my constant worry has been to try to find a footbridge, a way of crossing from a world so totally anti-poetic as the world of political actuality to a world of poetry. To ensure the bridge isn't cut. And very often I have had the feeling that all I can do is to note the difficulty, the virtual impossibility of passages. There were echoes, recollections of one world by the other, but I had difficulty finding the crossings.

History gives us lessons. The texts of Mandelstam, Celan, all those who were involved in violent political conflict, who were imprisoned in the concentration camps, are bearers of texts, suffering, heavy, impregnated with political reality.

But I don't believe we can play with the facts. Someone who has not been in a concentration camp cannot say what someone who has been imprisoned says. But one thing we who have escaped the camps can do is to make the effort to turn our thoughts towards those who are in captivity. The other thing is to try to find a language that corresponds to the reality of the camps.

This is a question which has haunted me. In every one of my
texts, through the troubles in Vietnam, Iran, the USSR – the list is
endless – my question has been: how can we talk about it? Can we
talk about it?. Who has the right to talk about it? What form must
our talking about it take? What form can we give to our outrage,
speaking about these things which are unspeakable, which take
away our breath?

One way is by inscribing the question, signifying our impotence, our obligation, our memory of what is happening.

Personally, I found the only way I could deal with politics –
poetically – was by changing genres.

Reading *The Hour of the Star* I realized what a revolution Clarice
Lispector underwent in order to get close to the other. In *The
Hour of the Star* Clarice Lispector asks the question of how to talk
of the other, how to leave space for the other: how to create the
other's space. And to answer her question, she literally transformed herself to the point of changing roles, changing sex.

Sometimes, in fiction, the answers are extreme. Because the
other in these cases is extreme. I have only been able to resolve
the question in an equivalent movement to Clarice's strategy
which consists in making the author I am fade to the point of dis-
appearing. I, the author, have to disappear so that you, so other,
can appear. My answer has come through writing for the theatre.

On the stage, I, the author, am no longer there, but there is
the other. And even the absolute other, the absolute stranger.

The author's 'I' should be the lightest, the most transparent
possible. I don't believe that this is a point we arrive at straight
away. The inaugural gesture of writing is always in a necessary relation to narcissism. When one begins to write, one is constantly
reminding oneself of the fact: 'I write'. Rimbaud is a good
example, his verse echoes with 'I', 'I', 'I' ... an absolutely
magnificent, exploded 'I'. It takes time for 'I' to get used to 'I'.
Time for the 'I' to be sure 'I' exists. Only then is there room for
the other.

My work now is child of the theatre, product of the theatre, but
I have had to go through all the various stages to come to this
point. I have had to change genres and I've only been able to do
that through working on the 'I'. And the work has taken time.

Perhaps 200 years ago, I would have written fiction like Kleist.
Kleist is theatrical. His fiction presents a stage. There is an agreement between the text and the reader which is comparable to
the one that exists between the play and the public. We open
the text and the play begins. That's how it's written. With a total

withdrawal of the author. But we can no longer write like Kleist. We no longer live in Kleist's time. We can't write now as people wrote then. We can't write in the age of the aeroplane as people wrote 200 years ago. We are in the age of the unconscious, of linguistic transformation. We could try to copy Kleist, of course, but if we did, what we wrote would be a reconstruction. Now that we have another language, we can't go backwards. We cannot rewrite the Bible as it has been written.

We always say the same thing. What changes is our way of saying it. A new effect is produced by the shift, the alteration in form.

This is what Clarice Lispector says in her story about love. We have loved in the same way ever since the world existed. And yet, of course, it's completely different because everyone reinvents their own version. The same is true of the text. When I read, what moves me is the finding of a new image, a new way of saying the most ancient and eternal truths. It's this novelty of expression which is extraordinary and which pays tribute to the incredible richness of the human imagination.

XI CULTURAL MATERIALISM AND NEW HISTORICISM

Cultural Materialism and New Historicism are forms of historicist criticism that take into account contemporary critical theory, particularly Foucauldian and neo-Marxian theory. The term 'cultural materialism' was formulated by Raymond Williams. Williams had long been interested in literature within its socio-economic context, but had stopped short of committing himself to a Marxian position. However, in his later writing he does characterise his work as Marxist though he continues to be critical of what he sees as the rigidities of earlier Marxist thinking. He modifies the latter by utilising the ideas of neo-Marxian theorists, notably Gramsci. For Williams, the relation between the economic base and the superstructure was much more complex than earlier Marxists believed. At any particular period different cultural forces are in play, with the dominant forces never attaining complete power but being resisted by reactionary or progressive forces. Williams argues that a materialist analysis of the relation between literature and its social determinants must take account of the complex nature of the social formation and his essay 'Dominant, Residual, and Emergent' attempts to create a model that avoids the determinism of earlier Marxism while still suggesting that products of the superstructure such as literature are conditioned by specific material forces and practices.

Williams's cultural materialism was particularly influential on British critics. In the USA New Historicism has been the equivalent of cultural materialism in Britain. Whereas contemporary Marxism mediated by figures like Williams and the cultural studies movement have been the main influences on British cultural materialists, American New Historicists have been more influenced by Foucauldian power and discourse theory and developments within social anthropology, particularly the work of Clifford Geertz. New Historicism has also tended to focus more on questions of form and textuality than cultural materialism, a situation that perhaps reflects its struggle with deconstruction for dominance within American literary criticism and theory. In Louis Montrose's essay, New Historicism is famously characterised chiastically as 'a reciprocal concern with the historicality of texts and the textuality of history'.

Both New Historicism and Cultural Materialism reject any privileging of literary texts over other forms of discourse, but whereas New Historicists tend to concentrate on texts contemporary with the literary texts discussed, Cultural Materialists often situate the literary text within a modern political context. Recent British cultural materialist theory has emphasised reading dissidence into texts. This concentration on dissidence was to a considerable extent a reaction to Stephen Greenblatt's new historicist essay, 'Invisible Bullets', which argued that though literary texts may communicate subversive ideas, the dominant culture tolerated such subversion and incorporated it within itself as it allowed a relatively harmless outlet for opposition to the dominant discourses of the culture. By distinguishing the dissident from the subversive Alan Sinfield argues that texts can overcome such containment and thus challenge dominant discourses.

FURTHER READING

Jonathan Dollimore and Alan Sinfield (eds), *Political Shakespeare: New Essays in Cultural Materialism* (Manchester, 1985).

Stephen Greenblatt, *Shakespearean Negotiations: The Circulation of Social Energy in Renaissance England* (Oxford, 1988). (Contains 'Invisible Bullets' essay.)

H. Aram Veeser (ed.), *The New Historicism Reader* (New York and London, 1994).

Raymond Williams, *Problems in Materialism and Culture: Selected Essays* (London, 1980).

46 RAYMOND WILLIAMS: 'DOMINANT, RESIDUAL, AND EMERGENT'

The complexity of a culture is to be found not only in its variable processes and their social definitions – traditions, institutions, and formations – but also in the dynamic interrelations, at every point in the process, of historically varied and variable elements. In what I have called 'epochal' analysis, a cultural process is seized as a cultural system, with determinate dominant features: feudal culture or bourgeois culture or a transition from one to the other. This emphasis on dominant and definitive lineaments and features is important and often, in practice, effective. But it then

Reprinted from *Marxism and Literature* (Oxford, 1977), pp. 121–6.

often happens that its methodology is preserved for the very different function of historical analysis, in which a sense of movement within what is ordinarily abstracted as a system is crucially necessary, especially if it is to connect with the future as well as with the past. In authentic historical analysis it is necessary at every point to recognize the complex interrelations between movements and tendencies both within and beyond a specific and effective dominance. It is necessary to examine how these relate to the whole cultural process rather than only to the selected and abstracted dominant system. Thus 'bourgeois culture' is a significant generalizing description and hypothesis, expressed within epochal analysis by fundamental comparisons with 'feudal culture' or 'socialist culture'. However, as a description of cultural process, over four or five centuries and in scores of different societies, it requires immediate historical and internally comparative differentiation. Moreover, even if this is acknowledged or practically carried out, the 'epochal' definition can exert its pressure as a static type against which all real cultural process is measured, either to show 'stages' or 'variations' of the type (which is still historical analysis) or, at its worst, to select supporting and exclude 'marginal' or 'incidental' or 'secondary' evidence.

Such errors are avoidable if, while retaining the epochal hypothesis, we can find terms which recognize not only 'stages' and 'variations' but the internal dynamic relations of any actual process. We have certainly still to speak of the 'dominant' and the 'effective', and in these senses of the hegemonic. But we find that we have also to speak, and indeed with further differentiation of each, of the 'residual' and the 'emergent', which in any real process, and at any moment in the process, are significant both in themselves and in what they reveal of the characteristics of the 'dominant'.

By 'residual' I mean something different from the 'archaic', though in practice these are often very difficult to distinguish. Any culture includes available elements of its past, but their place in the contemporary cultural process is profoundly variable. I would call the 'archaic' that which is wholly recognized as an element of the past, to be observed, to be examined, or even on occasion to be consciously 'revived', in a deliberately specializing way. What I mean by the 'residual' is very different. The residual, by definition, has been effectively formed in the past, but it is still active in the cultural process, not only and often not at all as an element of the past, but as an effective element of the present. Thus certain experiences, meanings, and values which cannot be expressed or substantially verified in terms of the dominant culture, are nevertheless lived and practised on the basis of the residue – cultural as well as social – of some previous social and cultural institution or formation. It is crucial to distinguish this aspect of the residual, which may have an alternative or even oppositional relation to the dominant culture, from that active manifestation of the residual (this being its distinction from the archaic) which has been wholly or largely incorporated into the dominant culture. ...

A residual cultural element is usually at some distance from the effective dominant culture, but some part of it, some version of it – and especially if the residue is from some major area of the past – will in most cases have had to be incorporated if the effective dominant culture is to make sense in these areas. Moreover, at certain points the dominant culture cannot allow too much residual experience and practice outside itself, at least without risk. It is in the incorporation of the actively residual – by reinterpretation, dilution, projection, discriminating inclusion and exclusion – that the work of the selective tradition is especially evident. This is very notable in the case of versions of 'the literary tradition', passing through selective versions of the character of literature to connecting and incorporated definitions of what literature now is and should be. This is one among several crucial areas, since it is in some alternative or even oppositional versions of what literature is (has been) and what literary experience (and in one common derivation, other significant experience) is and must be, that, against the pressures of incorporation, actively residual meanings and values are sustained.

By 'emergent' I mean, first, that new meanings and values, new practices, new relationships and kinds of relationship are continually being created. But it is exceptionally difficult to distinguish between those which are really elements of some new phase of the dominant culture (and in this sense 'species-specific') and those which are substantially alternative or oppositional to it; emergent in the strict sense, rather than merely novel. Since we are always considering relations within a cultural process, definitions of the emergent, as of the residual, can be made only in relation to a full sense of the dominant. Yet the social location of the residual is always easier to understand, since a large part of it (though not all) relates to earlier social formations and phases of the cultural process, in which certain real meanings and values were generated. In the subsequent default of a particular phase of a dominant culture there is then a reaching back to those meanings and values which were created in actual societies and actual situations in the past, and which still seem to have significance because they represent areas of human experience, aspiration, and achievement which the dominant culture neglects, under-values, opposes, represses, or even cannot recognize.

The case of the emergent is radically different. It is true that in the structure of any actual society, and especially in its class structure, there is always a social basis for elements of the cultural process that are alternative or oppositional to the dominant elements. One kind of basis has been valuably described in the central body of Marxist theory: the formation of a new class, the coming to consciousness of a new class, and within this, in actual process, the (often uneven) emergence of elements of a new cultural formation. Thus the emergence of the working class as a class was immediately evident (for example, in nineteenth-century England) in the cultural process. But there was extreme unevenness of contribution in different parts of the process. The making of new social values and institutions far outpaced the making of strictly cultural institutions, while specific cultural contributions, though significant, were less vigorous and autonomous than either general or institutional innovation. A new class is always a source of emergent cultural practice, but while it is still, as a class, relatively subordinate, this is always likely to be uneven and is certain to be incomplete. For new practice is not, of course, an isolated process. To the degree that it emerges, and especially to the degree that it is oppositional rather than alternative, the process of attempted incorporation significantly begins. ... The process of emergence, in such conditions, is then a constantly repeated, an always renewable, move beyond a phase of practical incorporation: usually made much more difficult by the fact that much incorporation looks like recognition, acknowledgement, and thus a form of *acceptance*. In this complex process there is indeed regular confusion between the locally residual (as a form of resistance to incorporation) and the generally emergent.

Cultural emergence in relation to the emergence and growing strength of a class is then always of major importance, and always complex. But we have also to see that it is not the only kind of emergence. This recognition is very difficult, theoretically, though the practical evidence is abundant. What has really to be said, as a way of defining important elements of both the residual and the emergent, and as a way of understanding the character of the dominant, is that *no mode of production and therefore no dominant social order and therefore no dominant culture ever in reality includes or exhausts all human practice, human energy, and human intention.* This is not merely a negative proposition, allowing us to account for significant things which happen outside or against the dominant mode. On the contrary it is a fact about the modes of domination, that they select from and consequently exclude the full range of human practice. What they exclude may often be seen as the personal or the private, or as the natural or even the metaphysical. Indeed it is usually in one or other of these terms that the excluded area is expressed, since what the dominant has effectively seized is indeed the ruling definition of the social.

It is this seizure that has especially to be resisted. For there is always, though in varying degrees, practical consciousness, in specific relationships, specific skills, specific perceptions, that is unquestionably social and that a specifically dominant social order neglects, excludes, represses, or simply fails to recognize. A distinctive and comparative feature of any dominant social order is how far it reaches into the whole range of practices and experiences in an attempt at incorporation. There can be areas of experience it is willing to ignore or dispense with: to assign as private or to specialize as aesthetic or to generalize as natural. Moreover, as a social order changes, in terms of its own developing needs, these relations are variable. Thus in advanced capitalism, because of changes in the social character of labour, in the social character of communications, and in the social character of decision-making, the dominant culture reaches much further than ever before in capitalist society into hitherto 'reserved' or 'resigned' areas of experience and practice and meaning. The area of effective penetration of the dominant order into the whole social and cultural process is thus now significantly greater. This in turn makes the problem of emergence especially acute, and narrows the gap between alternative and oppositional elements. The alternative, especially in areas that impinge on significant areas of the dominant, is often seen as oppositional and, by pressure, often converted into it. Yet even here there can be spheres of practice and meaning which, almost by definition from its own limited character, or in its profound deformation, the dominant culture is unable in any real terms to recognize. Elements of emergence may indeed be incorporated, but just as often the incorporated forms are merely facsimiles of the genuinely emergent cultural practice. Any significant emergence, beyond or against a dominant mode, is very difficult under these conditions; in itself and in its repeated confusion with the facsimiles and novelties of the incorporated phase. Yet, in our own period as in others, the fact of emergent cultural practice is still undeniable, and together with the fact of actively residual practice is a necessary complication of the would-be dominant culture.

47 LOUIS A. MONTROSE: 'PROFESSING THE RENAISSANCE: THE POETICS AND POLITICS OF CULTURE'

There has recently emerged within Renaissance studies, as in Anglo-American literary studies generally, a renewed concern with the historical, social, and political conditions and consequences of literary production and reproduction: The writing and reading of texts, as well as the processes by which they are circulated and categorized, analyzed and taught, are being reconstrued as historically determined and determining modes of cultural work; apparently autonomous aesthetic and academic issues are being reunderstood as inextricably though complexly linked to other discourses and practices – such linkages constituting the social networks within which individual subjectivities and collective structures are mutually and continuously shaped. This general reorientation is the unhappy subject of J. Hillis Miller's 1986 Presidential Address to the Modern Language Association. In that address, Miller noted with some dismay – and with some hyperbole – that 'literary study in the past few years has undergone a sudden, almost universal turn away from theory in the sense of an orientation toward language as such and has made a corresponding turn toward history, culture, society, politics, institutions, class and gender conditions, the social context, the material base.'[1] By such a formulation, Miller polarizes the linguistic and the social. However, the prevailing tendency across cultural studies is to emphasize their reciprocity and mutual constitution: On the one hand, the social is understood to be discursively constructed; and on the other, language-use is understood to be always and necessarily dialogical, to be socially and materially determined and constrained. ...

A couple of years ago, I attempted briefly to articulate and scrutinize some of the theoretical, methodological and political assumptions and implications of the kind of work produced since the late 1970s by those (including myself) who were then coming to be labelled as 'New Historicists.'[2] The focus of such work has been upon a refiguring of the socio-cultural field within which

Reprinted from *The New Historicism*, ed. H. Aram Veeser (New York and London, 1989), pp. 15–24.

canonical Renaissance literary and dramatic works were originally produced; upon resituating them not only in relationship to other genres and modes of discourse but also in relationship to contemporaneous social institutions and non-discursive practices. Stephen Greenblatt, who is most closely identified with the label 'New Historicism' in Renaissance literary studies, has himself now abandoned it in favor of 'Cultural Poetics,' a term he had used earlier and one which perhaps more accurately represents the critical project I have described.[3] In effect, this project reorients the axis of inter-textuality, substituting for the diachronic text of an autonomous literary history the synchronic text of a cultural system. As the conjunction of terms in its title suggests, the interests and analytical techniques of 'Cultural Poetics' are at once historicist and formalist; implicit in its project, though perhaps not yet adequately articulated or theorized, is a conviction that formal and historical concerns are not opposed but rather are inseparable.

Until very recently – and perhaps even now – the dominant mode of interpretation in English Renaissance literary studies has been to combine formalist techniques of close rhetorical analysis with the elaboration of relatively self-contained histories of 'ideas,' or of literary genres and topoi – histories that have been abstracted from their social matrices. In addition to such literary histories, we may note two other traditional practices of 'history' in Renaissance literary studies: one comprises those commentaries on political commonplaces in which the dominant ideology of Tudor–Stuart society – the unreliable machinery of socio-political legitimation – is misrecognized as a stable, coherent, and collective Elizabethan world picture, a picture discovered to be lucidly reproduced in the canonical literary works of the age; and the other, the erudite but sometimes eccentric scholarly detective work which, by treating texts as elaborate ciphers, seeks to fix the meaning of fictional characters and actions in their reference to specific historical persons and events. Though sometimes reproducing the methodological shortcomings of such older idealist and empiricist modes of historical criticism, but also often appropriating their prodigious scholarly labors to good effect, the newer historical criticism is *new* in its refusal of unproblematized distinctions between 'literature' and 'history,' between 'text' and 'context'; new in resisting a prevalent tendency to posit and privilege a unified and autonomous individual – whether an Author or a Work – to be set against a social or literary background. ...

Inhabiting the discursive spaces traversed by the term 'New Historicism' are some of the most complex, persistent, and unsettling of the problems that professors of literature attempt variously to confront or to evade: Among them, the essential or historical bases upon which 'literature' is to be distinguished from other discourses; the possible configurations of relationship between cultural practices and social, political and economic processes; the consequences of post-structuralist theories of textuality for the practice of an historical or materialist criticism; the means by which subjectivity is socially constituted and constrained; the processes by which ideologies are produced and sustained, and by which they may be contested; the patterns of consonance and contradiction among the values and interests of a given individual, as these are actualized in the shifting conjunctures of various subject positions – as, for example, intellectual worker, academic professional, and gendered domestic, social, political and economic agent. My point is not that 'The New Historicism' as a definable project, or the work of specific individuals identified by themselves or by others as New Historicists, can necessarily provide even provisional answers to such questions, but rather that the term 'New Historicism' is currently being invoked in order to bring such issues into play and to stake out – or to hunt down – specific positions within the discursive spaces mapped by these issues.

The post-structuralist orientation to history now emerging in literary studies may be characterized chiastically, as a reciprocal concern with the historicity of texts and the textuality of history. By *the historicity of texts*, I mean to suggest the cultural specificity, the social embedment, of all modes of writing – not only the texts that critics study but also the texts in which we study them. By *the textuality of history*, I mean to suggest, firstly, that we can have no access to a full and authentic past, a lived material existence, unmediated by the surviving textual traces of the society in question – traces whose survival we cannot assume to be merely contingent but must rather presume to be at least partially consequent upon complex and subtle social processes of preservation and effacement; and secondly, that those textual traces are themselves subject to subsequent textual mediations when they are construed as the 'documents' upon which historians ground their own texts, called 'histories.' As Hayden White has forcefully reminded us, such textual histories necessarily but always incompletely constitute in their narrative and rhetorical forms the 'History' to which they offer access.[4] ...

Recent invocations of 'History' (which, like 'Power,' is a term now in constant danger of hypostatization) often appear as responses to

– or, in some cases, merely as positivistic retrenchments against – various structuralist and post-structuralist formalisms that have seemed, to some, to put into question the very possibility of historical understanding and historical experience; that have threatened to dissolve history into what Perry Anderson has recently suggested is an antinomy of objectivist determinism and subjectivist free-play, an antinomy which allows no possibility for historical agency on the part of individual or collective human subjects.[5] 'Subject,' a simultaneously grammatical and political term, has come into widespread use not merely as a fashionable synonym for 'The Individual' but precisely in order to emphasize that individuals and the very concept of 'The Individual' are historically constituted in language and society. The freely self-creating and world-creating Individual of so-called bourgeois humanism is – at least, in theory – now defunct. Against the beleaguered category of the historical agent, contending armies of Theory now oppose the specters of structural determinism and post-structural contingency (the latter tartly characterized by Anderson as 'subjectivism without a subject' [*In the Tracks of Historical Materialism*, p. 54]): We behold, on the one hand, the implacable code, and on the other, the slippery signifier – the contemporary equivalents of Predestination and Fortune. I believe that we should resist the inevitably reductive tendency to constitute such terms as binary oppositions, instead construing them as mutually constitutive *processes*. We might then entertain the propositions that the interdependent processes of subjectification and structuration are both ineluctably social and historical; that social systems are produced and reproduced in the interactive social practices of individuals and groups; that collective structures may enable as well as constrain individual agency; that the possibilities and patterns for action are always socially and historically situated, always limited and limiting; and that there is no necessary relationship between the intentions of actors and the outcomes of their actions. Thus, my invocation of the term 'Subject' is meant to suggest an equivocal process of *subjectification*: on the one hand, shaping individuals as loci of consciousness and initiators of action – endowing them with *subjectivity* and with the capacity for agency; and, on the other hand, positioning, motivating, and constraining them within – *subjecting them to* – social networks and cultural codes that ultimately exceed their comprehension or control.[6]

'The Historicity of Texts and the Textuality of History': If such chiastic formulations are in fashion now, when the concept of referentiality has become so vexed, it may be because they figure forth from within discourse itself the model of a dynamic, unstable, and reciprocal relationship between the discursive and material domains.[7] This refiguring of the relationship between the verbal and the social, between the text and the world, involves a re-problematization or wholesale rejection of some prevalent alternative conceptions of literature: As an automomous aesthetic order that transcends the shifting pressure and particularity of material needs and interests; as a collection of inert discursive records of 'real events'; as a superstructural reflexion of an economic base. Current practices emphasize both the *relative* autonomy of specific discourses and their capacity to impact upon the social formation, to make things happen by shaping the subjectivities of social beings. Thus, to speak of the social production of 'literature' or of any particular text is to signify not only that it is socially produced but also that it is socially productive – that it is the product of work and that it performs work in the process of being written, enacted, or read. Recent theories of textuality have argued persuasively that the referent of a linguistic sign cannot be fixed; that the meaning of a text cannot be stabilized. At the same time, writing and reading are always historically and socially determinate events, performed *in* the world and *upon* the world by gendered individual and collective human agents. We may simultaneously acknowledge the theoretical indeterminacy of the signifying process and the historical specificity of discursive practices – acts of speaking, writing, and interpreting. The project of a new socio-historical criticism is, then, to analyze the interplay of culture-specific discursive practices – mindful that it, too, is such a practice and so participates in the interplay it seeks to analyze. By such means, versions of the Real, of History, are instantiated, deployed, reproduced; and by such means, they may also be appropriated, contested, transformed.

Integral to such a collective project of historical criticism must be a realization and acknowledgement that our analyses and our understandings necessarily proceed from our own historically, socially and institutionally shaped vantage points; that the histories we reconstruct are the textual constructs of critics who are, ourselves, historical subjects. If scholarship actively constructs and delimits its object of study, and if the scholar is historically positioned vis-à-vis that object, it follows that the quest of an older historical criticism to recover meanings that are in any final or absolute sense authentic, correct, and complete is illusory. Thus, the practice of a new historical criticism invites rhetorical strategies by which to foreground the constitutive acts of textuality that traditional modes of literary history efface or misrecognize. It also necessitates efforts to historicize the present as well as the past, and to historicize the dialectic between them – those reciprocal historical pressures by which the past has shaped the present and the present reshapes the past. In brief, to speak today of an historical criticism must be to recognize that not only the poet but also the critic exists in history: that the texts of each are inscriptions of history; and that our comprehension, representation, interpretation of the texts of the past always proceeds by a mixture of estrangement and appropriation, as a reciprocal conditioning of the Renaissance text and our text of Renaissance. Such a critical practice constitutes a continuous dialogue between a *poetics* and a *politics* of culture.

NOTES

[Reorganised and renumbered from the original]

1. J. Hillis Miller, 'Presidential Address 1986. The Triumph of Theory, the Resistance to Reading, and the Question of the Material Base,' *PMLA*, 102 (1987), 281–91; p. 283.

2. Louis Montrose, 'Renaissance Literary Studies and the Subject of History,' *English Literary Renaissance*, 16 (1986), 5–12. Much of that essay is subsumed and reworked in the present one.

3. The term 'new historicism' seems to have been introduced into Renaissance studies (with reference to cultural semiotics) in Michael McCanles, 'The Authentic Discourse of the Renaissance,' *Diacritics*, 10: 1 (Spring 1980), 77–87. However, it seems to have gained currency from its use by Stephen Greenblatt in his brief, programmatic introduction to 'The Forms of Power and the Power of Forms in the Renaissance,' a special issue of *Genre* (15: 1–2 [1982], 1–4). Earlier, in the Introduction to *Renaissance Self-Fashioning* (Chicago: Univ. of Chicago Press, 1980), Greenblatt had called his project a 'cultural poetics.' He has returned to this term in the introductory chapter of his recent book, *Shakespearean Negotiations: The Circulation of Social Energy in Renaissance England* (Berkeley and Los Angeles: Univ. of California Press, 1988). Here he defines the enterprise of cultural poetics as 'study of the collective making of distinct cultural practices and inquiry into the relations among these practices'; the relevant concerns are 'how collective beliefs and experiences were shaped, moved from one medium to another, concentrated in manageable aesthetic form, offered for consumption [and] how the boundaries were marked between cultural practices understood to be art forms and other, contiguous, forms of expression' (p. 5). I discuss the relevance of anthropological theory and ethnographic practice – specifically, the work of Clifford Geertz – to the study of early modern English culture in my review essay on *Renaissance Self-Fashioning*: 'A Poetics of Renaissance Culture,' *Criticism*, 23 (1981), 349–59.

4. On the constitutive discourse of the historian and the genres of history writing, see Hayden White, *Tropics of Discourse* (Baltimore: Johns Hopkins Univ. Press, 1978).

5. See the incisive Marxist critique of structuralism and post-structuralism in Perry Anderson, *In the Tracks of Historical Materialism* (Chicago: Univ. of Chicago Press, 1984), 32–55; and, for a Marxist critique of Anderson's own summary dismissal of Deconstruction, see Terry Eagleton, 'Marxism, Structuralism, and Post-Structuralism,' *Diacritics*, 15: 4 (Winter 1985), 2–12.

6. The process of subjectification as a seemingly uncontestable process of *subjecting to* is central to much of Michel Foucault's work: See, for example, 'The Subject and Power,' *Critical Inquiry*, 8 (1982), 777–95; and, for a Marxist critique, Peter Dews, 'Power and Subjectivity in Foucault,' *New Left Review*, no. 144 (March–April 1984), 72–95. Edward Said comments that 'Foucault's imagination of power is largely within rather than against it. ... His interest in domination was critical but not finally as contestatory, or as oppositional as on the surface it seems to be. This translates into the paradox that Foucault's imagination of power was by his analysis of power to reveal its injustice and cruelty, but by his theorization to let it go on more or less unchecked' ('Foucault and the Imagination of Power,' in *Foucault: A Critical Reader*, ed. David Couzens Hoy [Oxford: Basil Blackwell, 1986], pp. 149–55; p. 152).

I am indebted to the chapter, 'Agency, Structure,' in Anthony Giddens, *Central Problems in Social Theory* (Berkeley: University of California Press, 1979), 49–95. Also see the cogent formulation of 'experience' ('a process by which, for all social beings, subjectivity is constructed'), in Teresa de Lauretis, *Alice Doesn't: Feminism, Semiotics, Cinema* (Bloomington: Indiana University Press (1984): 'Through that process one places oneself or is placed in social reality, and so perceives and comprehends as subjective (referring to, even originating in, oneself) those relations – material, economic, and interpersonal – which are in fact social and, in a larger perspective, historical. The process is continuous, its achievement unending or daily renewed. For each person, therefore, subjectivity is an ongoing construction, not a fixed point of departure or arrival from which one then interacts with the world. On the contrary, it is an effect of that interaction ... and thus it is produced not by external ideas, values, or material causes, but by one's personal, subjective engagement in the practices, discourses, and institutions that lend significance (value, meaning, and affect) to the events of the world' (p. 159).

7. Compare Fredric Jameson's counter-Deconstructionist formulation of this relationship in terms of Marxism that is itself necessarily post-structuralist:

The type of interpretation here proposed is more satisfactorily grasped as the rewriting of the literary text in such a way that the latter may itself be seen as the rewriting or restructuration of a prior historical or ideological *subtext*, it being always understood that that 'subtext' is not immediately present as such, not some common-sense external reality, nor even the conventional narratives of history manuals, but rather must itself always be (re)constructed after the fact. ... The whole paradox of what we have here called the subtext may be summed up in this, that the literary work or cultural object, as though for the first time, brings into being that very situation of which it is also, at one and the same time, a reaction. ... History is inaccessible to us except in textual form. ... It can be approached only way of prior (re)textualization. ... To overemphasize the active way in which the text reorganizes its subtext (in order, presumably, to reach the triumphant conclusion that the 'referent' does not exist); or on the other hand to stress the imaginary status of the symbolic act so completely as to reify its social ground, now no longer understood as a subtext but merely as some inert given that the text passively or fantasmatically 'reflects' – to overstress either of these functions of the symbolic act at the expense of the other is surely to produce sheer ideology, whether it be, as in the first alternative, the ideology of structuralism, or, in the second, that of vulgar materialism. (*The Political Unconscious* [Ithaca: Cornell University Press, 1980], pp. 81–2).

For another Marxist consideration of and responses to recent theoretical challenges to historical criticism, see 'Text and History: Epilogue 1984' in Robert Weimann, *Structure and Society in Literary History*, expanded edn (Baltimore: Johns Hopkins University Press, 1984), pp. 267–323.

Introductions to materialist cultural theory include Raymond Williams, *Marxism and Literature*; Raymond Williams, *Culture* (London: Fontana, 1981); Janet Wolff, *The Social Production of Art* (London: Macmillan, 1981).

48 ALAN SINFIELD: 'READING DISSIDENCE'

The reason why textual analysis can so readily demonstrate dissidence being incorporated is that dissidence operates, necessarily, with reference to dominant structures. It has to invoke those structures to oppose them, and therefore can always, ipso facto, be discovered reinscribing that which it proposes to critique. 'Power relations are always two-way; that is to say, however subordinate an actor may be in a social relationship, the very fact of involvement in that relationship gives him or her a certain amount of power over the other,' Anthony Giddens observes.[1] The interinvolvement of resistance and control is systemic: it derives from the way language and culture get articulated. Any utterance is bounded by the other utterances that the language makes possible. Its shape is the correlative of theirs: as with the duck/rabbit

Reprinted from *Faultlines: Cultural Materialism and the Politics of Dissident Reading* (Oxford, 1992), pp. 47–51.

drawing, when you see the duck the rabbit lurks round its edges, constituting an alternative that may spring into visibility. Any position supposes its intrinsic *op*-position. All stories comprise within themselves the ghosts of the alternative stories they are trying to exclude.

It does not follow, therefore, that the outcome of the inter-involvement of resistance and control must be the incorporation of the subordinate. Indeed, Foucault says the same, though he is often taken as the theorist of entrapment. In *The History of Sexuality: An Introduction*, he says there is no 'great Refusal,' but envisages 'a plurality of resistances ... spread over time and space at varying densities, at times mobilising groups or individuals in a definitive way.' He *denies* that these must be 'only a reaction or rebound, forming with respect to the basic domination an underside that is in the end always passive, doomed to perpetual defeat.'[2] In fact, a dissident text may derive its leverage, its purchase, precisely from its partial implication with the dominant. It may embarrass the dominant by appropriating its concepts and imagery. For instance, it seems clear that nineteenth-century legal, medical, and sexological discourses on homosexuality made possible new forms of control; but, at the same time, they also made possible what Foucault terms 'a "reverse" discourse,' whereby 'homosexuality began to speak in its own behalf, to demand that its legitimacy or "naturality" be acknowledged, often in the same vocabulary, using the same categories by which it was medically disqualified.'[3] Deviancy returns from abjection by deploying just those terms that relegated it there in the first place. A dominant discourse cannot prevent 'abuse' of its resources. Even a text that aspires to contain a subordinate perspective must first bring it into visibility; even to misrepresent, one must present. And once that has happened, there can be no guarantee that the subordinate will stay safely in its prescribed place. Readers do not have to respect closures – we do not, for instance, have to accept that the independent women characters in Shakespearean comedies find their proper destinies in the marriage deals at the ends of those plays. We can insist on our sense that the middle of such a text arouses expectations that exceed the closure.

Conversely, a text that aspires to dissidence cannot control meaning either. It is bound to slide into disabling nuances that it fails to anticipate, and it cannot prevent the drawing of reactionary inferences by readers who want to do that. (Among other things, this might serve as a case against ultra-leftism, by which I mean the complacency of finding everyone else to be ideologically suspect.)

There can be no security in textuality: no scriptor can control the reading of his or her text. And when, in any instance, either incorporation or resistance turns out to be the more successful, that is not in the nature of things. It is because of *their relative strengths in that situation*. So it is not quite as Jonathan Goldberg has recently put it, turning the entrapment model inside out, that 'dominant discourses allow their own subversion precisely because hegemonic control is an impossible dream, a self-deluding fantasy.'[4] Either outcome depends on the specific balance of historical forces. Essex's rebellion failed because he could not muster adequate support on the day. It is the same with competence. Williams remarks that the development of writing reinforced cultural divisions, but also that 'there was no way to teach a man to read the Bible ... which did not also enable him to read the radical press.' Keith Thomas observes that 'the uneven social distribution of literacy skills greatly widened the gulf between the classes'; but he illustrates also the fear that 'if the poor learned to read and write they would become seditious, atheistical, and discontented with their humble position.'[5] Both may occur, in varying degrees; it was, and is, all to play for.

It is to circumvent the entrapment model that I have generally used the term *dissident* rather than *subversive*, since the latter may seem to imply achievement – that something *was subverted* – and hence (since mostly the government did not fall, patriarchy did not crumble) that containment must have occurred. 'Dissidence' I take to imply refusal of an aspect of the dominant, without prejudging an outcome. This may sound like a weaker claim, but I believe it is actually stronger insofar as it posits a field necessarily open to continuing contest, in which at some conjunctures the dominant will lose ground while at others the subordinate will scarcely maintain its position. As Jonathan Dollimore has said, dissidence may provoke brutal repression, and that shows not that it was all a ruse of power to consolidate itself, but that 'the challenge really *was* unsettling.'[6]

The implications of these arguments for literary criticism are substantial, for it follows that formal textual analysis cannot determine whether a text is subversive or contained. The historical conditions in which it is being deployed are decisive. 'Nothing can be intrinsically or essentially subversive in the sense that prior to the event subversiveness can be more than potential; in other words it cannot be guaranteed a priori, independent of articulation, context and reception,' Dollimore observes.[7] Nor, independently of context, can anything be said to be safely contained.

This prospect scandalizes literary criticism, because it means that meaning is not adequately deducible from the text-on-the-page. The text is always a site of cultural contest, but it is never a self-sufficient site.

It is a key proposition of cultural materialism that the specific historical conditions in which institutions and formations organize and are organized by textualities must be addressed. That is what Raymond Williams was showing us for thirty years. The entrapment model is suspiciously convenient for literary criticism, because it means that little would be gained by investigating the specific historical effectivity of texts. And, indeed, Don Wayne very shrewdly suggests that the success of prominent new historicists may derive in large part from their skills in close reading – admittedly of a far wider range of texts – which satisfy entirely traditional criteria of performativity in academic criticism.[8] Cultural materialism calls for modes of knowledge that literary criticism scarcely possesses, or even knows how to discover – modes, indeed, that hitherto have been cultivated distinctively within that alien other of essentialist humanism, Marxism. These knowledges are in part the provinces of history and other social sciences – and, of course, they bring in their train questions of historiography and epistemology that require theory more complex than the tidy post-structuralist formula that everything, after all, is a text (or that everything is theater. This prospect is valuable in direct proportion to its difficulty for, as Foucault maintains, the boundaries of disciplines effect a policing of discourses, and their erosion may, in itself, help to 'detach the power of truth from the forms of hegemony (social, economic and cultural) within which it operates at the present time' in order to constitute 'a new politics of truth.'[9]

Shakespearean plays are themselves powerful stories. They contribute to the perpetual contest of stories that constitutes culture: its representations, and our critical accounts of them, reinforce or challenge prevailing notions of what the world is like, of how it might be. 'The detailed and substantial *performance of a known model* of "people like this, relations like this", is in fact the real achievement of most serious novels and plays,' Raymond Williams observes;[10] by appealing to the reader's sense of how the world *is*, the text affirms the validity of the model it invokes. Among other things, *Othello* invites *recognition* that this is how people are, how the world goes. That is why the criteria of plausibility are political. This effect is not countered, as essentialist-humanists have long supposed, by literary quality; the more persuasive the writing, the greater its potential for political intervention.

The quintessential traditional critical activity was always interpretive, getting the text to make sense. Hence the speculation about character motivation, image patterns, thematic integration, structure: the task always was *to help the text into coherence.* And the discovery of coherence was taken as the demonstration of quality. However, such practice may feed into a reactionary politics. The easiest way to make *Othello* plausible in Britain is to rely on the lurking racism, sexism, and superstition in British culture. Why does Othello, who has considerable experience of people, fall so conveniently for Iago's stories? We can make his gullibility plausible by suggesting that black people are generally of a rather simple disposition. To explain why Desdemona elopes with Othello and then becomes so submissive, we might appeal to a supposedly fundamental silliness and passivity of women. Baffled in the attempt to find motive for Iago's malignancy, we can resort to the devil, or the consequence of skepticism towards conventional morality, or homosexuality. Such interpretations might be plausible; might 'work,' as theater people say; but only because they activate regressive aspects of our cultural formation.

Actually, coherence is a chimera, as my earlier arguments should suggest. No story can contain all the possibilities it brings into play; coherence is always selection. And the range of feasible readings depends not only on the text but on the conceptual framework within which we address it. Literary criticism tells its own stories. It is, in effect, a subculture, asserting its own distinctive criteria of plausibility. Education has taken as its brief the socialization of students into these criteria, while masking this project as the achievement by talented individuals (for it is in the program that most should fail) of a just and true reading of texts that are just and true. A cultural materialist practice will review the institutions that retell the Shakespeare stories, and will attempt also a self-consciousness about its own situation within those institutions. We need not just to produce different readings but to shift the criteria of plausibility.

NOTES

[Reorganised and renumbered from the original]

1. Anthony Giddens, *Central Problems in Social Theory* (London: Macmillan, 1979 p. 6. See further Raymond Williams, *Marxism and Literature* (Oxford: Oxford University Press, 1977), pp. 108–27; Fredric Jameson, 'Reification and Utopia in Mass Culture; *Social Text,* 1 (1979): 144–8; Colin Gordon, 'Afterword,' in Michel Foucault, *Power/Knowledge* (Brighton; Harvester, 1980).

2. Michel Foucault, *The History of Sexuality: Volume 1*, trans. Robert Hurley (New York: Random House, Vintage Books, 1980), pp. 95–6. Also, as Jonathan Culler has remarked, Foucault's exposure of the ubiquity of regulatory practices may itself be experienced as liberatory: Culler, *Framing the Sign* (Oxford: Blackwell, 1988), pp. 66–7.

3. Foucault, *History of Sexuality*, p. 101. See Jonathan Dollimore and Alan Sinfield, 'Culture and Textuality: Debating Cultural Materialism,' *Textual Practice*, 4, no. 1 (Spring 1990): 91–100, p. 95; and Jonathan Dollimore, 'Sexuality, Subjectivity and Transgression: The Jacobean Connection,' *Renaissance Drama*, n.s., 17 (1986): 53–82.

4. Jonathan Goldberg, 'Speculations: *Macbeth* and Source,' in Jean E. Howard and Marion F. O'Connor, *Shakespeare Reproduced* (London: Methuen, 1987), pp. 244, 247. See also Jonathan Goldberg, *Writing Matter: From the Hands of the English Renaissance* (Stanford: Stanford Univ. Press, 1990), esp. pp. 41–55.

5. Raymond Williams, *Culture* (Glasgow: Fontana, 1981), pp. 94, 110; Keith Thomas, 'The Meaning of Literacy in Early Modern England,' in Gerd Baumann (ed.), *The Written Word: Literacy in Transition* (Oxford: Clarendon Press, 1986), pp. 116, 118.

6. Jonathan Dollimore, 'Shakespeare, Cultural Materialism, Feminism and Marxist Humanism,' *New Literary History*, 21 (1990) 482. See also James Holstum, 'Ranting at the New Historicism,' *English Literary Renaissance*, 19 (1989), 189–225.

7. Jonathan Dollimore and Alan Sinfield (eds), *Political Shakespeare: New Essays in Cultural Materialism* (Manchester, 1985), p. 13; discussed in Dollimore and Sinfield, 'Culture and Textuality.' See also Alan Liu's argument that we need to consider not only subjects and representation, but action: Liu, 'Power of Formalism: The New Historicism', *English Literary History*, 56 (1989), 734–5.

8. Don Wayne, 'New Historicism,' in Malcolm Kelsall, Martin Coyle, Peter Garside, and John Peck (eds), *Encyclopedia of Literature and Criticism* (London: Routledge, 1990), pp. 801–2. See also Culler, *Framing*, p. 37; Carolyn Porter, 'History and Literature: After the New Criticism', *New Literary History*, 21 (1990), 255–6.

9. 'The Political Function of the Intellectual,' trans. Colin Gordon, *Radical Philosophy*, 17 (1977): 12–15, p. 14; see Eve Tavor Bannet, *Structuralism and the Logic of Dissent* (London: Macmillan, 1989), pp. 170–83.

10. Raymond Williams, *Marxism and Literature* (Oxford: Oxford Univ. Press, 1977) p. 209.

XII   NEW PRAGMATISM

New Pragmatism is not so much a theoretical position as a theoretically informed critique of theory in itself. Knapp and Michaels are clearly influenced by the work of Richard Rorty and Stanley Fish, and their critique also has some connections with the philosophy of Jean-François Lyotard. In 'Against Theory' they see the essentials of theory as 'the attempt to govern interpretations of particular texts by appealing to an account of interpretation in general'. For them theory can never legitimately stand outside practice. One of the interests of their essay is their defence of authorial intention in the determination of literary meaning despite its having been rejected by various critical schools: Russian Formalism, New Criticism, post-structuralism. For them any separation between meaning and intention is impossible, so understanding meaning is necessarily an attempt to recover the author's intention, though it could be argued that even if they are right the author's intention is not to be seen as necessarily an individual phenomenon but as shaped by such supra-individual forces as culture or history or ideology.

Knapp and Michaels argued that Stanley Fish had not taken his theory, or his anti-theory, far enough. Fish responded with the essay 'Consequences' in which he thoroughly aligned himself with a new pragmatist position. He argues that both he and Knapp and Michaels are committed to an anti-foundational-ist theory associated with Rortian anti-essentialism, though this is only a theory in the ironic sense that it is 'an argument against the possibility of theory'. Foundationalism asserts that there are beliefs that are foundational in that all other beliefs rest upon them and that these foundational beliefs cannot be questioned without threatening all beliefs. The dire consequences that foundationalists claim will result from anti-foundationalism can never happen according to Fish. There is no need to seek out rules or constraints or shared standards as all individuals are un-avoidably enmeshed in cultural practices that are inevitably rule-governed: the subject is always socially constrained and 'will always be guided by the rules or rules of thumb that are the content of any settled practice'.

FURTHER READING

Stanley Fish, *There's No Such Thing as Free Speech and it's a Good Thing, Too* (Oxford, 1994).

W. J. T. Mitchell, *Against Theory: Literary Studies and the New Pragmatism* (Chicago, 1985).

Richard Rorty, *Consequences of Pragmatism (Essays: 1972–80)* (Brighton, 1982).

49   STEVEN KNAPP AND WALTER BENN MICHAELS: 'AGAINST THEORY'

By 'theory' we mean a special project in literary criticism: the attempt to govern interpretations of particular texts by appealing to an account of interpretation in general. The term is sometimes applied to literary subjects with no direct bearing on the interpretation of individual works, such as narratology, stylistics, and prosody. Despite their generality, however, these subjects seem to us essentially empirical, and our argument against theory will not apply to them.

Contemporary theory has taken two forms. Some theorists have sought to ground the reading of literary texts in methods designed to guarantee the objectivity and validity of interpretations. Others, impressed by the inability of such procedures to produce agreement among interpreters, have translated that failure into an alternative mode of theory that denies the possibility of correct interpretation. Our aim here is not to choose between these two alternatives but rather to show that both rest on a single mistake, a mistake that is central to the notion of theory per se. The object of our critique is not a particular way of doing theory but the idea of doing theory at all.

Theory attempts to solve – or to celebrate the impossibility of solving – a set of familiar problems: the function of authorial intention, the status of literary language, the role of interpretive assumptions, and so on. We will not attempt to solve these problems, nor will we be concerned with tracing their history or surveying the range of arguments they have stimulated. In our view, the mistake on which all critical theory rests has been to imagine that these problems are real. In fact, we will claim such problems only

Reprinted from *Critical Inquiry*, 8 (1982), 723–42.

seem real – and theory itself only seems possible or relevant – when theorists fail to recognize the fundamental inseparability of the elements involved.

The clearest example of the tendency to generate theoretical problems by splitting apart terms that are in fact inseparable is the persistent debate over the relation between authorial intention and the meaning of texts. Some theorists have claimed that valid interpretations can only be obtained through an appeal to authorial intentions. This assumption is shared by theorists who, denying the possibility of recovering authorial intentions, also deny the possibility of valid interpretations. But once it is seen that the meaning of a text is simply identical to the author's intended meaning, the project of *grounding* meaning in intention becomes incoherent. Since the project itself is incoherent, it can neither succeed nor fail; hence both theoretical attitudes toward intention are irrelevant. The mistake made by theorists has been to imagine the possibility or desirability of moving from one term (the author's intended meaning) to a second term (the text's meaning), when actually the two terms are the same. One can neither succeed nor fail in deriving one term from the other, since to have one is already to have them both. ...

The issues of belief and intention are, we think, central to the theoretical enterprise; our discussion of them is thus directed not only against specific theoretical arguments but against theory in general. Our examples are meant to represent the central mechanism of all theoretical arguments, and our treatment of them is meant to indicate that all such arguments will fail and fail in the same way. If we are right, then the whole enterprise of critical theory is misguided and should be abandoned. ...

In debates about intention, the moment of imagining intentionless meaning constitutes the theoretical moment itself. From the standpoint of an argument against critical theory, then, the only important question about intention is whether there can in fact be intentionless meanings. If our argument against theory is to succeed, the answer to this question must be no. ...

We have argued that what a text means and what its author intends it to mean are identical and that their identity robs intention of any theoretical interest. A similar account of the relation between meaning and intention has recently been advanced by P. D. Juhl. According to Juhl, 'there is a logical connection between statements about the meaning of a literary work and statements about the author's intention such that a statement about the meaning of a work *is* a statement about the author's intention.'[1] ...

Like [E.D.] Hirsch, but at a further level of abstraction, Juhl ends up imagining the possibility of language prior to and independent of intention and thus conceiving intention as something that must be added to language to make it work. Like Hirsch, and like theorists in general, Juhl thinks that intention is a matter of choice. But where Hirsch recommends that we choose intention to adjudicate among interpretations, Juhl thinks no recommendation is necessary – not because we need never choose intention but only because our concept of a literary work is such that to read literature is already to have chosen intention.

Discussing the case of a 'poem' produced by chance ('marks on [a] rock' or 'a computer poem'), Juhl points out that there is 'something odd about *interpreting* [such a] "text."' However one might understand this text, one could not understand it as a representation of 'the meaning of a particular utterance.' We agree with this – if it implies that the random marks mean nothing, are not language, and therefore cannot be interpreted at all. ... Our point is that marks produced by chance are not words at all but only resemble them. For Juhl, the marks remain words, but words detached from the intentions that would make them utterances. ...

Juhl is right of course to claim that marks without intention are not speech acts, since the essence of a speech act is its intentional character. But we have demonstrated that marks without intention are not language either. Only by failing to see that linguistic meaning is always identical to expressed intention can Juhl imagine language without speech acts. To recognize the identity of language and speech acts is to realize that Juhl's prescription – when confronted with language, read it as a speech act – can mean nothing more than: when confronted with language, read it as language.

For Hirsch and Juhl, the goal of theory is to provide an objectively valid method of literary interpretation. To make method possible, both are forced to imagine intentionless meanings or, in more general terms, to imagine a separation between language and speech acts.[2] The method then consists in adding speech acts to language; speech acts bring with them the particular intentions that allow interpreters to clear up the ambiguities intrinsic to language as such. But this separation of language and speech acts need not be used to establish an interpretive method; it can in fact be used to do just the opposite. For a theorist like Paul de Man, the priority of language to speech acts suggests that all attempts to arrive at determinate meanings by adding intentions amount to a violation of the genuine condition of language. If theory in its positive or methodological mode rests on the choice of speech acts over language, theory in its negative or antimethodological mode tries to preserve what it takes to be the purity of language from the distortion of speech acts.

De Man's separation of language and speech acts rests on a mistake. It is of course true that sounds in themselves are meaningless. It is also true that sounds become signifiers when they function in language. But it is not true that sounds in themselves are signifiers; they become signifiers only when they acquire meanings, and when they lose their meanings they stop being signifiers. ... What reduces the signifier to noise and the speech act to an accident is the absence of intention. Conceiving linguistic activity as the accidental emission of phonemes, de Man arrives at a vision of 'the absolute randomness of language, prior to any figuration or meaning': 'There can be no use of language which is not, within a certain perspective thus radically formal, i.e. mechanical, no matter how deeply this aspect may be concealed by aesthetic, formalistic delusions.'[3] ...

For both Juhl and de Man, proper interpretation depends upon following a methodological prescription. Juhl's prescription is: when confronted with language, read it as a speech act. De Man's prescription is: when confronted with what seems to be a speech act, read it as language. ...

Intention cannot be added to or subtracted from meaning because meanings are always intentional; intention cannot be added to or subtracted from language because language consists of speech acts, which are also always intentional. Since language has intention already built into it, no recommendation about what to do with intention has any bearing on the question of how to interpret any utterance or text. ...

The aim of theory's epistemological project is to base interpretation on a direct encounter with its object, an encounter undistorted by the influence of the interpreter's particular beliefs. Several writers have demonstrated the impossibility of escaping beliefs at any stage of interpretation and have concluded that theory's epistemological goal is therefore unattainable. Some have gone on to argue that the unattainability of an epistemologically neutral stance not only undermines the claims of method but prevents us from ever getting any correct interpretations. For these writers the attack on method thus has important practical consequences for literary criticism, albeit negative ones.[4]

But in discussing theory from the ontological side, we have tried to suggest that the impossibility of method has no practical consequences, positive or negative. And the same conclusion has been reached from the epistemological side by the strongest critic of theoretical attempts to escape belief, Stanley Fish. ... Fish's attack on method begins with an account of belief that is in our view correct. The account's two central features are, first, the recognition that beliefs cannot be grounded in some deeper condition of knowledge and, second, the further recognition that this impossibility does not in any way weaken their claims to be true. ... Since one can neither escape one's beliefs nor escape the sense that they are true, Fish rejects both the claims of method and the claims of skepticism. Methodologists and skeptics maintain that the validity of beliefs depends on their being grounded in a condition of knowledge prior to and independent of belief; they differ only about whether this is possible. The virtue of Fish's account is that it shows why an insistence on the inescapability of belief is in no way inimical to the ordinary notions of truth and falsehood implicit in our sense of what knowledge is. The character of belief is precisely what gives us those notions in the first place; having beliefs just *is* being committed to the truth of what one believes and the falsehood of what one doesn't believe. ...

A realist thinks that theory allows us to stand outside our beliefs in a neutral encounter with the objects of interpretation; an idealist thinks that theory allows us to stand outside our beliefs in a neutral encounter with our beliefs themselves. The issue in both cases is the relation between objects and beliefs. For the realist, the object exists independent of beliefs, and knowledge requires that we shed our beliefs in a disinterested quest for the object. For the idealist, who insists that we can never shed our beliefs, knowledge means recognizing the role beliefs play in *constituting* their objects. Fish, with his commitment to the primacy of beliefs, chooses idealism: 'objects,' he thinks, 'are made and not found'; interpretation 'is not the art of construing but the art of constructing.'...

Theory, he thinks, can have no practical consequences; it cannot be lived because theory and practice – the truth about belief and belief itself – can never in principle be united. In our view, however, the only relevant truth about belief is that you can't go outside it, and, far from being unlivable, this is a truth you can't help but live. It has no practical consequences not because it can never be *united* with practice but because it can never be *separated* from practice.

The theoretical impulse, as we have described it, always involves the attempt to separate things that should not be separated: on the ontological side, meaning from intention, language from speech acts; on the epistemological side, knowledge from true belief. Our point has been that the separated terms are in fact inseparable. It is tempting to end by saying that theory and practice too are inseparable. But this would be a mistake. Not because theory and practice (unlike the other terms) really are separate but because theory is nothing else but the attempt to escape practice. Meaning is just another name for expressed intention, knowledge just another name for true belief, but theory is not just another name for practice. It is the name for all the ways people have tried to stand outside practice in order to govern practice from without. Our thesis has been that no one can reach a position outside practice, that theorists should stop trying, and that the theoretical enterprise should therefore come to an end.

NOTES

[Reorganised and renumbered from the original]

1. See P. D. Juhl, *Interpretation: An Essay in the Philosophy of Literary Criticism* (Princeton, NJ, 1980).

2. This distinction, in one form or another, is common among speech-act theorists. H. P. Grice, for example, distinguishes between 'location of the form "U (utterer) meant that ..."' and 'locations of the form "X (utterance type) means ..."' characterizing the first as 'occasion-meaning' and the second as 'applied timeless, meaning' (H. P. Grice, 'Utterer's Meaning, Sentence-Meaning and Word-Meaning,' in *The Philosophy of Language*, ed. Searle [London, 1971], pp. 54, 56). And Searle, citing Wittgenstein ('*Say* "it's cold here" and *mean* "it's warm here"') distinguishes between the mind and 'matter of intention'.

3. Paul de Man, 'The Purloined Ribbon,' *Glyph*, 1 (1977), 44, 41.

4. Negative theory rests on the perception of what de Man calls 'an insurmountable obstacle in the way of any reading or understanding' (*Allegories of Reading* [New Haven, Conn., 1979], p. 131). Some theorists (e.g. David Bleich and Norman Holland) understand this obstacle as the reader's subjectivity. Others (like de Man himself and J. Hillis Miller) understand it as the aporia between constative and performative language, between demonstration and persuasion. In all cases, however, the negative theorist is committed to the view that interpretation is as Jonathan Culler says, 'necessary error' (*The Pursuit of Signs* [Ithaca, NY, 1981], p. 14).

50   STANLEY FISH: 'CONSEQUENCES'

Nothing I wrote in *Is There a Text in This Class?* has provoked more opposition or consternation than my (negative) claim that the argument of the book has no consequences for the practice of literary criticism.[1] To many it seemed counterintuitive to maintain (as I did) that an argument in theory could leave untouched the practice it considers: After all, isn't the very point of theory to throw light on or reform or guide practice? In answer to this question I want to say, first, that this is certainly theory's claim – so much so that independently of the claim there is no reason to think of it as a separate activity – and, second, that the claim is unsupportable. Here, I am *in agreement* with Steven Knapp and Walter Benn Michaels, who are almost alone in agreeing with me and who fault me not for making the 'no consequences' argument but for occasionally falling away from it. Those who dislike *Is There a Text in This Class?* tend to dislike 'Against Theory' even more, and it is part of my purpose here to account for the hostility to both pieces. But since the issues at stake are fundamental, it is incumbent to begin at the beginning with a discussion of what theory is and is not.

'Against Theory' opens with a straightforward (if compressed) definition: 'By "theory" we mean a special project in literary criticism: the attempt to govern interpretations of particular texts by appealing to an account of interpretation in general.' In the second sentence the authors declare that this definition of theory excludes much that has been thought to fall under its rubric and especially excludes projects of a general nature 'such as narratology, stylistics, and prosody'. On first blush this exclusion seems arbitrary and appears to be vulnerable to the charge (made by several respondents) that by defining theory so narrowly Knapp and Michaels at once assure the impregnability of their thesis and render it trivial. I believe, on the contrary, that the definition is correct and that, moreover, it is a reformulation of a familiar and even uncontroversial distinction. In E.D. Hirsch's work, for example, we meet it as a distinction between general and local hermeneutics. 'Local hermeneutics,' Hirsch explains,

Reprinted from *Doing What Comes Naturally: Change, Rhetoric, and the Practice of Theory in Literary and Legal Studies* (Oxford, 1989), pp. 315–24.

consists of rules of thumb rather than rules. ... Local hermeneutics can ... provide models and methods that are reliable most of the time. General hermeneutics lays claim to principles that hold true all of the time. ... That is why general hermeneutics is, so far, the only aspect of interpretation that has earned the right to be named a 'theory.'[2]

By 'general hermeneutics,' Hirsch means a procedure whose steps, if they are faithfully and strictly followed, will 'always yield correct results';[3] 'local hermeneutics,' on the other hand, are calculations of probability based on an insider's knowledge of what is likely to be successful in a particular field of practice. ... A rule is formalizable: it can be programmed on a computer and, therefore, can be followed by anyone who has been equipped with explicit (noncircular) definitions and equally explicit directions for carrying out a procedure. A rule of thumb, on the other hand, cannot be formalized, because the conditions of its application vary with the contextual circumstances of an ongoing practice; as those circumstances change, the very meaning of the rule (the instructions it is understood to give) changes too, at least for someone sufficiently inside the practice to be sensitive to its shifting demands. To put it another way, the rule-of-thumb reader begins with a knowledge of the outcome he desires, and it is within such knowledge that the rule assumes a shape, becomes readable; the rule follower, in contrast, defers to the self-declaring shape of the rule, which then generates the correct outcome independently of his judgment. The model for the 'true' rule and, therefore, for theory is mathematics, for as John Lyons points out, if two people apply the rules of mathematics and come up with different results, we can be sure that one of them is mistaken, that is, has misapplied the rules.[4]

Thus understood, theory can be seen as an effort to govern practice in two senses: (1) it is an attempt to *guide* practice from a position above or outside it ..., and (2) it is an attempt to *reform* practice by neutralizing interest, by substituting for the parochial perspective of some local or partisan point of view the perspective of a general rationality to which the individual subordinates his contextually conditioned opinions and beliefs. ...

The argument *against* theory is simply that this substitution of the general for the local has never been and will never be achieved. Theory is an impossible project which will never succeed. It will never succeed simply because the primary data and formal laws necessary to its success will always be spied or picked out from within the contextual circumstances of which they are supposedly independent. The objective facts and rules of

calculation that are to ground interpretation and render it principled are themselves interpretive products: they are, therefore,
always and already contaminated by the interested judgments they
claim to transcend. The contingencies that are to be excluded in
favor of the invariant constitute the field within which what will
(for a time) be termed the invariant emerges. ...

This, then, is why theory will never succeed: it cannot help but
borrow its terms and its contents from that which it claims to transcend, the mutable world of practice, belief, assumptions, point of
view, and so forth. And, by definition, something that cannot
succeed cannot have consequences, cannot achieve the goals it
has set for itself by being or claiming to be theory, the goals of
guiding and/or reforming practice. Theory cannot guide practice
because its rules and procedures are no more than generalizations from practice's history (and from only a small piece of that
history), and theory cannot reform practice because, rather than
neutralizing interest, it begins and ends in interest and raises the
imperatives of interest – of some local, particular, partisan project
– to the status of universals.

Thus far I have been talking about 'foundationalist' theory (what
Knapp and Michaels call 'positive theory'), theory that promises to
put our calculations and determinations on a firmer footing than
can be provided by mere belief or unjustified practice. In recent
years, however, the focus of attention has been more on 'anti-foundationalist' theory (what Knapp and Michaels call 'negative
theory'), on arguments whose force it is precisely to deny the possibility (and even the intelligibility) of what foundationalist theory
promises. Anti-foundationalist theory is sometimes Kuhnian, sometimes Derridean, sometimes pragmatist, sometimes Marxist, sometimes anarchist, but it is always historicist; that is, its strategy is
always the one I have pursued in the previous paragraphs, namely,
to demonstrate that the norms and standards and rules that foundationalist theory would oppose to history, convention, and local
practice are in every instance a function or extension of history,
convention, and local practice. As Richard Rorty puts it: 'There are
no essences anywhere in the area. There is no wholesale, epistemological way to direct, or criticize or underwrite the course of
inquiry. ... It is the vocabulary of practice rather than of theory ...
in which one can say something useful about truth.'[5] (Notice that
this does not mean that a notion like 'truth' ceases to be operative,
only that it will always have reference to a moment in the history of
inquiry rather than to some God or material objectivity or invariant
calculus that underwrites all our inquiries.)

The fact that there are two kinds of theory (or, rather, theoretical discourse – anti-foundationalism really isn't a theory at all; it is an argument against the possibility of theory) complicates the question of consequences, although in the end the relationship of both kinds of theory to the question turns out to be the same. As we have seen, those who believe in the consequences of foundationalist theory are possessed by a hope – let us call it 'theory hope' – the hope that our claims to knowledge can be 'justified on the basis of some objective method of assessing such claims' rather than on the basis of the individual beliefs that have been derived from the accidents of education and experience.[6] Anti-foundationalist theory tells us that no such justification will ever be available and that therefore there is no way of testing our beliefs against something whose source is not also a belief. As we shall see, anti-foundationalism comes with its own version of 'theory hope,' but the emotion its arguments more often provoke is 'theory fear,' the fear that those who have been persuaded by such arguments will abandon principled inquiry and go their unconstrained way in response to the dictates of fashion, opinion, or whim. Expressions of theory fear abound (one can find them now even in daily newspapers and popular magazines), and in their more dramatic forms they approach the status of prophecies of doom. Here, for example, is Israel Scheffler's view of what will happen if we are persuaded by the writings of Thomas Kuhn:

Independent and public controls are no more, communication has failed, the common universe of things is a delusion, reality itself is made ... rather than discovered. ... In place of a community of rational men following objective procedures in the pursuit of truth, we have a set of isolated monads, within each of which belief forms without systematic constraints.[7]

For Scheffler (and many others) the consequences of anti-foundationalist theory are disastrous and amount to the loss of everything we associate with rational inquiry: public and shared standards, criteria for preferring one reading of a text or of the world to another, checks against irresponsibility, etc. But this follows only if anti-foundationalism is an argument for unbridled subjectivity, for the absence of constraints on the individual; whereas, in fact, it is an argument for the situated subject, for the individual who is always constrained by the local or community standards and criteria of which his judgment is an extension. Thus the lesson of anti-foundationalism is not only that external and independent guides will never be found but that it is unnecessary to seek them, because you will always be guided by the rules or rules of thumb that are the content of any settled practice, by the assumed definitions, distinctions, criteria of evidence, measures of adequacy, and such, which not only define the practice but structure the understanding of the agent who thinks of himself as a 'competent member.' That agent cannot distance himself from these rules, because it is only within them that he can think about alternative courses of action or, indeed, think at all. Thus anti-foundationalism cannot possibly have the consequences Scheffler fears; for, rather than unmooring the subject, it reveals the subject to be always and already tethered to the contextual setting that constitutes him and enables his 'rational' acts.

Neither can anti-foundationalism have the consequences for which some of its proponents *hope*, the consequences of freeing us from the hold of unwarranted absolutes so that we may more flexibly pursue the goals of human flourishing or liberal conversation. The reasoning behind this hope is that since we now know that our convictions about truth and factuality have not been imposed on us by the world, or imprinted in our brains, but are derived from the practices of ideologically motivated communities, we can set them aside in favor of convictions that we choose freely. But this is simply to imagine the moment of unconstrained choice from the other direction, as a goal rather than as an abyss. Anti-foundationalist fear and anti-foundationalist hope turn out to differ only in emphasis. Those who express the one are concerned lest we kick ourselves loose from constraints; those who profess the other look forward to finally being able to do so. Both make the mistake of thinking that anti-foundationalism, by demonstrating the contextual source of conviction, cuts the ground out from under conviction – it is just that, for one party, this is the good news and, for the other, it is the news that chaos has come again. But, in fact, anti-foundationalism says nothing about what we can now do or not do; it is an account of what we have always been doing and cannot help but do (no matter what our views on epistemology) – act in accordance with the standards and norms that are the content of our beliefs and, therefore, the very structure of our consciousness.

NOTES

[Reorganised and renumbered from the original]

1. See my *Is There a Text in This Class?: The Authority of Interpretive Communities* (Cambridge, Mass., 1980), p. 370. For a response to the 'no consequences' claim, see Mary Louise Pratt, 'Interpretive

Strategies/Strategic Interpretations: On Anglo-American Reader Response Criticism,' *boundary* 2, 11 (Fall–Winter 1982–83): 222.

2. E. D. Hirsch, Jr, *The Aims of Interpretation* (Chicago, 1976), p. 18. I should note here that while I agree in general with Steven Knapp and Walter Benn Michaels on what is and is not a theoretical enterprise, I think them mistaken in their choice of particular examples. Stylistics, narratology, and prosody are, it seems to me, paradigm instances of theory in the strong sense. As I have argued elsewhere (see *Is There a Text in This Class?* chapters 2 and 10), the entire project of stylistics is an effort to produce a taxonomy of observable formal features which can then be correlated in some mechanical or rule-governed way with a set of corresponding significances and/or effects. In short, if stylistics were ever to succeed (and I am certain that it will not), it would be an engine of interpretation, a method, a theory. One sure sign of a theoretical enterprise is the lengths its proponents will go in order to pursue it. It seems to me extremely unlikely that stylisticians would have built their formidable apparatuses and worked out their complex formulations only so as to be able to produce a new reading of James Joyce's 'Eveline.' The same goes for narratology and for prosody, at least in its transformational or Halle–Keyser version.

3. Hirsch, *The Aims of Interpretation*, p. 18.

4. See John Lyons, *Noam Chomsky*, rev. ed. (New York, 1978), p. 37.

5. Rorty, *Consequences of Pragmatism (Essays 1972–1980)* (Minneapolis, 1982), p. 162.

6. Keith Lehrer, *Knowledge* (Oxford, 1974), p. 17.

7. Israel Scheffler, *Science and Subjectivity* (Indianapolis, 1967), p. 19. For similar statements, see Hirsch, *The Aims of Interpretation*, pp. 152–5, and Owen M. Fiss, 'Objectivity and Interpretation,' *Stanford Law Review*, 34 (April 1982): 763.

XIII POSTMODERNISM

Though the term postmodernism seems to have been mainly used at first in a literary context, since the 1980s it has tended to be used in a much wider context, for example to characterise the culture of the late twentieth century in general. Probably the most influential proponent of postmodernism in this cultural sense is Jean-François Lyotard, especially in his book *The Postmodern Condition*. In that book he attacks the thought of Jürgen Habermas, a foundationalist who argued that the beliefs of the Enlightenment – ideals such as reason and progress – are the bases of modernity and who attacked those whom he saw as undermining them. For Lyotard postmodernity rejects such thinking. In particular Lyotard rejects what he calls the 'grand narratives' of progress and perfectability in favour of the contingent or the provisional: 'Simplifying to the extreme, I define *Postmodern* as incredulity toward metanarratives. ... Postmodern knowledge is not simply a tool of the authorities; it refines our sensitivity to differences and reinforces our ability to tolerate the incommensurable' (*The Postmodern Condition*, pp. xxiv–xxv).

Fredric Jameson is often thought of as a critic who attacks postmodernism from a Marxian standpoint. However, though he sees postmodernism as a socio-economic product, this does not lead him to condemn postmodernist art and literature in the way that a Marxist critic such as Lukács condemned modernism. Jameson finds value in many manifestations of the postmodern but nevertheless argues that it has to be understood as a cultural phenomenon emerging out of late capitalism.

Linda Hutcheon is not so much concerned with the cultural origins of postmodernism as with its poetics and develops Lyotard's characterisation of the postmodern in relation to literature and art. In particular she makes clear how postmodernism differs from modernism despite various common features, such as the use of pastiche, fragmentariness, a rejection of realist conventions. She suggests that whereas in a modernist like T. S. Eliot, 'one sensed a kind of wishful call to continuity beneath the fragmented echoing', for postmodernists pastiche and fragmentariness are seen as liberating. Totalising and ordering concepts are not merely regarded in a modernist manner as not available and therefore the subject of nostalgia; postmodernist artists deliberately set out to challenge and undermine them.

FURTHER READING

Peter Brooker (ed.), *Modernism/Postmodernism* (London, 1992).
Linda Hutcheon, *The Politics of Postmodernism* (London, 1989).
Fredric Jameson, *Postmodernism, or, The Cultural Logic of Late Capitalism* (London, 1991).
Jean-Francois Lyotard, *The Postmodern Condition: A Report on Knowledge* (Manchester, 1984).
Patricia Waugh (ed.), *Postmodernism: A Reader* (London, 1992).

51 FREDRIC JAMESON: 'POSTMODERNISM, OR THE CULTURAL LOGIC OF LATE CAPITALISM

The last few years have been marked by an inverted millenarianism, in which premonitions of the future, catastrophic or redemptive, have been replaced by senses of the end of this or that (the end of ideology, art, or social class; the 'crisis' of Leninism, social democracy, or the welfare state, etc., etc.): taken together, all of these perhaps constitute what is increasingly called postmodernism. The case for its existence depends on the hypothesis of some radical break or *coupure*, generally traced back to the end of the 1950s or the early 1960s. As the world itself suggests, this break is most often related to notions of the waning or extinction of the hundred-year-old modern movement (or to its ideological or aesthetic repudiation). Thus, abstract expressionism in painting, existentialism in philosophy, the final forms of representation in the novel, the films of the great *auteurs*, or the modernist school of poetry (as institutionalized and canonized in the works of Wallace Stevens): all these are now seen as the final, extraordinary flowering of a high modernist impulse which is spent and exhausted with them. The enumeration of what follows then at once becomes empirical, chaotic, and heterogeneous: Andy Warhol and pop art, but also photorealism, and beyond it, the 'new expressionism'; the moment, in music, of John Cage, but also the synthesis of classical and 'popular' styles found in composers like Phil Glass and Terry Riley, and also punk and new wave rock (the Beatles and the Stones now standing as the high-modernist moment of that more recent and rapidly evolving tra-

Reprinted from *New Left Review*, 146 (1984), 53–64.

dition); in film, Godard, post-Godard and experimental cinema and video, but also a whole new type of commercial film (about which more below); Burroughs, Pynchon, or Ishmael Reed, on the one hand, and the French *nouveau roman* and its succession on the other, along with alarming new kinds of literary criticism, based on some new aesthetic of textuality or *écriture*. ... The list might be extended indefinitely; but does it imply any more fundamental change or break than the periodic style- and fashion-changes determined by an older high-modernist imperative of stylistic innovation?...

   Nor should the break in question be thought of as a purely cultural affair: indeed, theories of the postmodern – whether celebratory or couched in the language of moral revulsion and denunciation – bear a strong family resemblance to all those more ambitious sociological generalizations which, at much the same time, bring us the news of the arrival and inauguration of a whole new type of society, most famously baptized 'post-industrial society' (Daniel Bell), but often also designated consumer society, media society, information society, electronic society or 'high tech', and the like. Such theories have the obvious ideological mission of demonstrating, to their own relief, that the new social formation in question no longer obeys the laws of classical capitalism, namely the primacy of industrial production and the omnipresence of class struggle. The Marxist tradition has therefore resisted them with vehemence, with the signal exception of the economist Ernest Mandel, whose book *Late Capitalism* sets out not merely to anatomize the historic originality of this new society (which he sees as a third stage or moment in the evolution of capital), but also to demonstrate that it is, if anything, a *purer* stage of capitalism than any of the moments that preceded it. I will return to this argument later; suffice it for the moment to emphasize a point I have defended in greater detail elsewhere, namely that every position on postmodernism in culture – whether apologia or stigmatization – is also at one and the same time, and *necessarily*, an implicitly or explicitly political stance on the nature of multinational capitalism today.

   A last preliminary word on method: what follows is not to be read as stylistic description, as the account of one cultural style or movement among others. I have rather meant to offer a periodizing hypothesis, and that at a moment in which the very conception of historical periodization has come to seem most problematical indeed. I have argued elsewhere that all isolated or discrete cultural analysis always involves a buried or repressed theory of historical periodization; in any case, the conception of the 'genealogy' largely lays to rest traditional theoretical worries about so-called linear history, theories of 'stages', and teleological historiography. In the present context, however, lengthier theoretical discussion of such (very real) issues can perhaps be replaced by a few substantive remarks.

One of the concerns frequently aroused by periodizing hypotheses is that these tend to obliterate difference, and to project an idea of the historical period as massive homogeneity (bounded on either side by inexplicable 'chronological' metamorphoses and punctuation marks). This is, however, precisely why it seems to me essential to grasp 'postmodernism' not as a style, but rather as a cultural dominant: a conception which allows for the presence and coexistence of a range of very different, yet subordinate features.

Consider, for example, the powerful alternative position that postmodernism is itself little more than one more stage of modernism proper (if not, indeed, of the even older romanticism); it may indeed be conceded that all of the features of postmodernism I am about to enumerate can be detected, full-blown, in this or that preceding modernism (including such astonishing genealogical precursors as Gertrude Stein, Raymond Roussel, or Marcel Duchamp, who may be considered outright postmodernists, *avant la lettre*). What has not been taken into account by this view is, however, the social position of the older modernism, or better still, its passionate repudiation by an older Victorian and post-Victorian bourgeoisie, for whom its forms and ethos are received as being variously ugly, dissonant, obscure, scandalous, immoral, subversive and generally 'anti-social'. It will be argued here that a mutation in the sphere of culture has rendered such attitudes archaic. Not only are Picasso and Joyce no longer ugly; they now strike us, on the whole, as rather 'realistic'; and this is the result of a canonization and an academic institutionalization of the modern movement generally, which can be traced to the late 1950s. This is indeed surely one of the most plausible explanations for the emergence of postmodernism itself, since the younger generation of the 1960s will now confront the formerly oppositional modern movement as a set of dead classics, which 'weigh like a nightmare on the brains of the living', as Marx once said in a different context. ...

What has happened is that aesthetic production today has become integrated into commodity production generally: the frantic economic urgency of producing fresh waves of ever more novel-seeming goods (from clothing to airplanes), at ever greater rates of turnover, now assigns an increasingly essential structural function and position to aesthetic innovation and experimentation. Such economic necessities then find recognition in the institutional support of all kinds available for the newer art, from foundations and grants to museums and other forms of patronage. Architecture is, however, of all the arts that closest constitutively to the economic, with which, in the form of commissions and land values, it has a virtually unmediated relationship: it will therefore not be surprising to find the extraordinary flowering of the new postmodern architecture grounded in the patronage of multinational business, whose expansion and development is strictly contemporaneous with it. That these two new phenomena have an even deeper dialectical interrelationship than the simple one-to-one financing of this or that individual project we will try to suggest later on. Yet this is the point at which we must remind the reader of the obvious, namely that this whole global, yet American, postmodern culture is the internal and superstructural expression of a whole new wave of American military and economic domination throughout the world: in this sense, as throughout class history, the underside of culture is blood, torture, death and horror.

The first point to be made about the conception of periodization in dominance, therefore, is that even if all the constitutive features of postmodernism were identical and continuous with those of an older modernism – a position I feel to be demonstrably erroneous but which only an even lengthier analysis of modernism proper could dispel – the two phenomena would still remain utterly distinct in their meaning and social function, owing to the very different positioning of postmodernism in the economic system of late capital, and beyond that, to the transformation of the very sphere of culture in contemporary society. ...

The exposition will take up in turn the following constitutive features of the postmodern: a new depthlessness, which finds its prolongation both in contemporary 'theory' and in a whole new culture of the image or the simulacrum; a consequent weakening of historicity, both in our relationship to public History and in the new forms of our private temporality, whose 'schizophrenic' structure (following Lacan) will determine new types of syntax or syntagmatic relationships in the more temporal arts; a whole new type of emotional ground tone – what I will call 'intensities' – which can best be grasped by a return to older theories of the sublime; the deep constitutive relationships of all this to a whole new technology, which is itself a figure for a whole new economic world system; and, after a brief account of postmodernist mutations in the lived experience of built space itself, some reflections on the mission of political art in the bewildering new world space of late multinational capital.

We will begin with one of the canonical works of high modernism in visual art, Van Gogh's well-known painting of the peasant shoes, an example which as you can imagine has not been innocently or randomly chosen. I want to propose two ways of reading this painting, both of which in some fashion reconstruct the reception of the work in a two-stage or double-level process.

I first want to suggest that if this copiously reproduced image is not to sink to the level of sheer decoration, it requires us to reconstruct some initial situation out of which the finished work emerges. Unless that situation – which has vanished into the past – is somehow mentally restored, the painting will remain an inert object, a reified end-product, and be unable to be grasped as a symbolic act in its own right, as praxis and as production. ...

How is it then that in Van Gogh such things as apple trees explode into a hallucinatory surface of colour, while his village stereotypes are suddenly and garishly overlaid with hues of red and green? I will briefly suggest, in this first interpretative option, that the willed and violent transformation of a drab peasant object into the most glorious materialization of pure colour in oil paint is to be seen as a Utopian gesture: as an act of compensation which ends up producing a whole new Utopian realm of the senses, or at least of that supreme sense – sight, the visual, the eye – which it now reconstitutes for us as a semi-autonomous space in its own right – part of some new division of labour in the body of capital, some new fragmentation of the emergent sensorium which replicates the specializations and divisions of capitalist life at the same time that it seeks in precisely such fragmentation a desperate Utopian compensation for them.

There is, to be sure, a second reading of Van Gogh which can hardly be ignored when we gaze at this particular painting, and that is Heidegger's central analysis in *Der Ursprung des Kunstwerkes*, which is organized around the idea that the work of art emerges within the gap between Earth and World, or what I would prefer to translate as the meaningless materiality of the body and nature and the meaning-endowment of history and of the social. ...

At any rate, both of these readings may be described as *hermeneutical*, in the sense in which the work in its inert, objectal form, is taken as a clue or a symptom for some vaster reality which replaces it as its ultimate truth. Now we need to look at some shoes of a different kind, and it is pleasant to be able to draw for such an image on the recent work of the central figure in contemporary visual art. Andy Warhol's *Diamond Dust Shoes* evidently no longer speaks to us with any of the immediacy of Van Gogh's footgear: indeed, I am tempted to say that it does not really speak to us at all. ...

There is therefore in Warhol no way to complete the hermeneutic gesture, and to restore to these oddments that whole larger lived context of the dance hall or the ball, the world of jetset fashion or of glamour magazines. Yet this is even more paradoxical in the light of biographical information: Warhol began his artistic career as a commercial illustrator for shoe fashions and a designer of display windows in which various pumps and slippers figured prominently. Indeed, one is tempted to raise here – far too prematurely – one of the central issues about postmodernism itself and its possible political dimensions: Andy Warhol's work in fact turns centrally around commodification, and the great billboard images of the Coca-cola bottle or the Campbell's Soup Can, which explicitly foreground the commodity fetishism of a transition to late capital, *ought* to be powerful and critical political statements. If they are not that, then one would surely want to know why, and one would want to begin to wonder a little more seriously about the possibilities of political or critical art in the postmodern period of late capital.

But there are some other significant differences between the high modernist and the postmodernist moment, between the shoes of Van Gogh and the shoes of Andy Warhol, on which we must now very briefly dwell. The first and most evident is the emergence of a new kind of flatness or depthlessness, a new kind of superficiality in the most literal sense – perhaps the supreme formal feature of all the postmodernisms to which we will have occasion to return in a number of other contexts. ...

The waning of affect is, however, perhaps best initially approached by way of the human figure, and it is obvious that what we have said about the commodification of objects holds as strongly for Warhol's human subjects, stars – like Marilyn Monroe – who are themselves commodified and transformed into their own images. And here too a certain (brutal) return to the older period of high modernism offers a dramatic shorthand parable of the transformation in question. Edvard Munch's painting *The Scream* is of course a canonical expression of the great modernist thematics of alienation, anomie, solitude and social fragmentation and isolation, a virtually programmatic emblem of what used to be called the age of anxiety. It will here be read not merely as an embodiment of the expression of that kind of affect, but even more as a virtual deconstruction of the very aesthetic of expression itself, which seems to have dominated much of what we call high modernism but to have vanished away – for both practical and theoretical reasons – in the world of the postmodern. The very concept of expression presupposes indeed some separation within the subject, and along with that a whole metaphysics of the inside and the outside, of the wordless pain within the monad and the moment in which, often cathartically, that 'emotion' is then projected out and externalized, as gesture or cry, as desperate communication and the outward dramatization of inward feeling. And this is perhaps the moment to say something about contemporary theory, which has among other things been committed to the mission of criticizing and discrediting this very hermeneutic model of the inside and the outside and of stigmatizing such models as ideological and metaphysical. But what is today called contemporary theory – or better still, theoretical discourse – is also, I would want to argue, itself very precisely a postmodernist phenomenon. It would therefore be inconsistent to defend the truth of its theoretical insights in a situation in which the very concept of 'truth' itself is part of the metaphysical baggage which poststructuralism seeks to abandon. What we can at least suggest is that the poststructuralist critique of the hermeneutic, of what I will shortly call the depth model, is useful for us as a very significant symptom of the very postmodernist culture which is our subject here.

Overhastily, we can say that besides the hermeneutical model of inside and outside which Munch's painting develops, there are at least four other fundamental depth models which have generally been repudiated in contemporary theory: the dialectical one of essence and appearance (along with a whole range of concepts of ideology or false consciousness which tend to accompany it); the Freudian model of latent and manifest, or of repression (which is of course the target of Michel Foucault's programmatic and symptomatic pamphlet *La Volonté de savoir*); the existential model of authenticity and inauthenticity, whose heroic or tragic thematics are closely related to that other great opposition between alienation and disalienation, itself equally a casualty of the poststructural or postmodern period; and finally, latest in time, the great semiotic opposition between signifier and signified, which was itself rapidly unravelled and deconstructed during its brief heyday in the 1960s and 70s. What replaces these various depth models is for the most part a conception of practices, discourses and textual play, whose new syntagmatic structures we will examine later on: suffice it merely to observe that here too depth is replaced by surface, or by multiple surfaces (what is often called intertextuality is in that sense no longer a matter of depth). ...

All of which suggests some more general historical hypothesis: namely, that concepts such as anxiety and alienation (and the experiences to which they correspond, as in *The Scream*) are no longer appropriate in the world of the postmodern. ...

Here too Munch's painting stands as a complex reflexion on this complicated situation: it shows us that expression requires the category of the individual monad, but it also shows us the heavy price to be paid for that precondition, dramatizing the unhappy paradox that when you constitute your individual subjectivity as a self-sufficient field and a closed realm in its own right, you thereby also shut yourself off from everything else and condemn yourself to the windless solitude of the monad, buried alive and condemned to a prison-cell without egress.

Postmodernism will presumably signal the end of this dilemma, which it replaces with a new one. The end of the bourgeois ego or monad no doubt brings with it the end of the psychopathologies of that ego as well – what I have generally here been calling the waning of affect. But it means the end of much more – the end for example of style, in the sense of the unique and the personal, the end of the distinctive individual brushstroke (as symbolized by the emergent primacy of mechanical reproduction). As for expression and feelings or emotions, the liberation, in contemporary society, from the older *anomie* of the centred subject may also mean, not merely a liberation from anxiety, but a liberation from every other kind of feeling as well, since there is no longer a self present to do the feeling. This is not to say that the cultural products of the postmodern era are utterly devoid of feeling, but rather that such feelings – which it may be better and more accurate to call 'intensities' – are now free-floating and impersonal, and tend to be dominated by a peculiar kind of euphoria to which I will want to return at the end of this essay.

The waning of affect, however, might also have been characterized, in the narrower context of literary criticism, as the waning of the great high-modernist thematics of time and temporality, the elegiac mysteries of *durée* and of memory (something to be understood fully as a category of literary criticism associated as much with high modernism as with the works themselves). We have often been told, however, that we now inhabit the synchronic rather than the diachronic, and I think it is at least empirically arguable that our daily life, our psychic experience, our cultural languages, are today dominated by categories of space rather than by categories of time, as in the preceding period of high modernism proper.

52   LINDA HUTCHEON: 'THEORIZING THE POSTMODERN'

What precisely, though, is being challenged by postmodernism? First of all, institutions have come under scrutiny: from the media to the university, from museums to theaters. Much postmodern dance, for instance, contests theatrical space by moving out into the street. Sometimes it is overtly measured by the clock, thereby foregrounding the unspoken conventions of theatrical time (see Pops, 1984, 59). Make-believe or illusionist conventions of art are often bared in order to challenge the institutions in which they find a home – and a meaning. ...

The important contemporary debate about the margins and the boundaries of social and artistic conventions (see Culler, 1983, 1984) is also the result of a typically postmodern transgressing of previously accepted limits: those of particular arts, of genres, of art itself. Rauschenberg's narrative (or discursive) work, *Rebus*, or Cy Twombly's series on Spenserian texts, or Shosaku Arakawa's poster-like pages of *The Mechanism of Meaning* are indicative of the fruitful straddling of the borderline between the literary and visual arts. As early as 1969, Theodore Ziolkowski had noted that the

new arts are so closely related that we cannot hide complacently behind the arbitrary walls of self-contained disciplines: poetics inevitably gives way to general aesthetics, considerations of the novel move easily to the film, while the new poetry often has more in common with contemporary music and art than with the poetry of the past. (1969, 113)

Reprinted from *Theorizing the Postmodern: Toward a Poetics* (New York and London, 1988), pp. 9–15.

The years since have only verified and intensified this perception. The borders between literary genres have become fluid: who can tell anymore what the limits are between the novel and the short story collection (Alice Munro's *Lives of Girls and Women*), the novel and the long poem (Michael Ondaatje's *Coming Through Slaughter*), the novel and autobiography (Maxine Hong Kingston's *China Men*), the novel and history (Salman Rushdie's *Shame*), the novel and biography (John Banville's *Kepler*)? But, in any of these examples, the conventions of the two genres are played off against each other; there is no simple, unproblematic merging. In Carlos Fuentes's *The Death of Artemio Cruz*, the title already points to the ironic inversion of biographical conventions: it is the death, not the life, that will be the focus. The subsequent narrative complications of three voices (first-, second-, and third-person) and three tenses (present, future, past) disseminate but also reassert (in a typically postmodernist way) the enunciative situation or discursive context of the work (see Chapter 5). The traditional verifying third-person past tense voice of history and realism is both installed and undercut by the others. In other works, like Italian writer Giorgio Manganelli's *Amore*, the genres of theoretical treatise, literary dialogue, and novel are played off against one another (see Lucente, 1986, 317). Eco's *The Name of the Rose* contains at least three major registers of discourse: the literary-historical, the theological-philosophical, and the popular-cultural (de Lauretis, 1985, 16), thereby paralleling Eco's own three areas of critical activity.

The most radical boundaries crossed, however, have been those between fiction and non-fiction and – by extension – between art and life. In the March 1986 issue of *Esquire* magazine, Jerzy Kosinski published a piece in the 'Documentary' section called 'Death in Cannes,' a narrative of the last days and subsequent death of French biologist, Jacques Monod. Typically postmodern, the text refuses the omniscience and omnipresence of the third person and engages instead in a dialogue between a narrative voice (which both is and is not Kosinski's) and a projected reader. Its viewpoint is avowedly limited, provisional, personal. However, it also works (and plays) with the conventions of both literary realism and journalistic facticity: the text is accompanied by photographs of the author and the subject. The commentary uses these photos to make us, as readers, aware of our expectations of both narrative and pictorial interpretation, including our naïve but common trust in the representational veracity of photography. ...

In addition to being 'borderline' inquiries, most of these post-modernist contradictory texts are also specifically parodic in their intertextual relation to the traditions and conventions of the genres involved. When Eliot recalled Dante or Virgil in *The Waste Land*, one sensed a kind of wishful call to continuity beneath the fragmented echoing. It is precisely this that is contested in post-modern parody where it is often ironic discontinuity that is re-vealed at the heart of continuity, difference at the heart of similarity (Hutcheon, 1985). Parody is a perfect postmodern form, in some senses, for it paradoxically both incorporates and challenges that which it parodies. It also forces a reconsideration of the idea of origin or originality that is compatible with other postmodern interrogations of liberal humanist assumptions (see Chapter 8). While *theorists* like Jameson (1983, 114–19) see this loss of the modernist unique, individual style as a negative, as an imprisoning of the text in the past through pastiche, it has been seen by postmodern *artists* as a liberating challenge to a definition of subjectivity and creativity that has for too long ignored the role of history in art and thought. ...

Another consequence of this far-reaching postmodern inquiry into the very nature of subjectivity is the frequent challenge to tra-ditional notions of perspective, especially in narrative and paint-ing. The perceiving subject is no longer assumed to a coherent, meaning-generating entity. Narrators in fiction become either dis-concertingly multiple and hard to locate (as in D.M.Thomas's *The White Hotel*) or resolutely provisional and limited – often under-mining their own seeming omniscience (as in Salman Rushdie's *Midnight's Children*). (See Chapter 10.) In Charles Russell's terms, with postmodernism we start to encounter and are challenged by 'an art of shifting perspective, of double self-consciousness, of local and extended meaning' (1980a, 192).

As Foucault and others have suggested, linked to this contesting of the unified and coherent subject is a more general questioning of *any* totalizing or homogenizing system. Provisionality and het-erogeneity contaminate any neat attempts at unifying coherence (formal or thematic). Historical and narrative continuity and closure are contested, but again, from within. The teleology of art forms – from fiction to music – is both suggested and transformed. The centre no longer completely holds. And, from the decentered perspective, the 'marginal' and what I will be calling (Chapter 4) the 'ex-centric' (be it in class, race, gender, sexual orientation, or ethnicity) take on new significance in the light of the implied recognition that our culture is not really the homogeneous monolith (that is middle-class, male, heterosexual, white, western) we might have assumed. The concept of alienated otherness (based on binary oppositions that conceal hierarchies) gives way, as I have argued, to that of differences, that is to the assertion, not of centralized sameness, but of decentralized community – another postmodern paradox. The local and the regional are stressed in the face of mass culture and a kind of vast global informational village that McLuhan could only have dreamed of. Culture (with a capital C and in the singular) has become cultures (uncapitalized and plural), as documented at length by our social scientists. And this appears to be happening in spite of – and, I would argue, maybe even because of – the homogenizing impulse of the consumer society of late capitalism: yet another postmodern contradiction.

In attempting to define what he called the 'trans-avant-grade,' Italian art critic Achille Bonito Oliva found he had to talk of differences as much as similarities from country to country (1984, 71–3): it would seem that the 'presence of the past' depends on the local and culture-specific nature of each past. The questioning of the universal and totalizing in the name of the local and particular does not automatically entail the end of all consensus. As Victor Burgin reminds us: '*Of course* moralities and histories are "relative", but this does not mean they do not *exist*' (1986, 198). Postmodernism is careful not to make the marginal into a new center, for it knows, in Burgin's words, that '[what] have expired are the absolute guarantees issued by over-riding metaphysical systems' (198). Any certainties we do have are what he calls 'positional,' that is, derived from complex networks of local and contingent conditions.

In this sort of context, different kinds of texts will take on value – the ones that operate what Derrida calls 'breaches or infractions' – for it is they that can lead us to suspect the very concept of 'art' (1981a, 69). In Derrida's words, such artistic practices seem 'to mark and to organize a structure of resistance to the philosophical conceptuality that allegedly dominated and comprehended them, whether directly, or whether through categories derived from this philosophical fund, the categories of esthetics, rhetoric, or traditional criticism' (69). Of course, Derrida's own texts belong solely to neither philosophical nor literary discourse, though they partake of both in a deliberately self-reflexive and contradictory (postmodern) manner.

Derrida's constant self-consciousness about the status of his own discourse raises another question that must be faced by anyone – like myself – writing on postmodernism. From what position can one 'theorize' (even self-consciously) a disparate, contradictory, multivalent, current cultural phenomenon? Stanley Fish (1986) has wittily pointed out the 'anti-foundationalist' paradox that I too find myself in when I comment on the importance of Derrida's critical self-consciousness. In Fish's ironic terms: 'Ye shall know that truth is not what it seems and *that* truth shall set you free.' Barthes, of course, had seen the same danger earlier as he watched (and helped) demystification become part of the *doxa* (1977, 166). Similarly Christopher Norris has noted that in textualizing all forms of knowledge, deconstruction theory often, in its very unmasking of rhetorical strategies, itself still lays claim to the status of 'theoretical knowledge' (1985, 22). Most postmodern theory, however, realizes this paradox or contradiction. Rorty, Baudrillard, Foucault, Lyotard, and others seem to imply that any knowledge cannot escape complicity with some meta-narrative, with the fictions that render possible any claim to 'truth,' however provisional. What they add, however, is that *no* narrative can be a natural 'master' narrative: there are no natural hierarchies; there are only those we construct. It is this kind of self-implicating questioning that should allow postmodernist theorizing to challenge narratives that do presume to 'master' status, without necessarily assuming that status for itself.

Postmodern art similarly asserts and then deliberately undermines such principles as value, order, meaning, control, and identity (Russell, 1985, 247) that have been the basic premises of bourgeois liberalism. Those humanistic principles are still operative in our culture, but for many they are no longer seen as eternal and unchallengeable. The contradictions of both postmodern theory and practice are positioned within the system and yet work to allow its premises to be seen as fictions or as ideological structures. This does not necessarily destroy their 'truth' value, but it does define the conditions of that 'truth.' Such a process reveals rather than conceals the tracks of the signifying systems that constitute our world – that is, systems constructed by us in answer to our needs. However important these systems are, they are not natural, given, or universal (see Chapter 11). The very limitations imposed by the postmodern view are also perhaps ways of opening new doors: perhaps now we can better study the interrelations of social, aesthetic, philosophical, and ideological constructs. In order to do so, postmodernist critique must acknowledge its own position as an ideological one (Newman, 1985, 60). I think the formal and thematic contradictions of postmodern art and theory work to do just that: to call attention to both what is being contested and what is being offered as a critical response to that, and to do so in a self-aware way that admits its own provisionality. In Barthesian terms (1972, 256), it is criticism which would include in its own discourse an implicit (or explicit) reflection upon itself.

In writing about these postmodern contradictions, then, I clearly would not want to fall into the trap of suggesting any 'transcendental identity' (Radhakrishnan, 1983, 33) or essence for postmodernism. Instead, I see it as an ongoing cultural process or activity, and I think that what we need, more than a fixed and fixing definition, is a 'poetics,' an open, ever-changing theoretical structure by which to order both our cultural knowledge and our critical procedures. This would not be a poetics in the structuralist sense of the word, but would go beyond the study of literary discourse to the study of cultural practice and theory. ...

A poetics of postmodernism would not posit any relation of causality or identity either among the arts or between art and theory. It would merely offer, as provisional hypotheses, perceived overlappings of concern, here specifically with regard to the contradictions that I see as characterizing postmodernism. It would be a matter of reading literature through its surrounding theoretical discourses (Cox, 1985, 57), rather than as continuous with theory. It would not mean seeing literary theory as a particularly imperialistic intellectual practice that has overrun art (H. White, 1978b, 261); nor would it mean blaming self-reflexive art for having created an 'ingrown' theory wherein 'specific critical and literary trends [have] buttressed each other into a hegemonic network' (Chénetier, 1985, 654). The interaction of theory and practice in postmodernism is a complex one of shared responses to common provocations. There are also, of course, many postmodern artists who double as theorists – Eco, Lodge, Bradbury, Barth, Rosler, Burgin – though they have rarely become the major theorists or apologists of their own work, as the *nouveaux romanciers* (from Robbe-Grillet to Ricardou) and surfictionists (Federman and Sukenick especially) have tended to do. What a poetics of postmodernism would articulate is less the theories of Eco in relation to *The Name of the Rose* than the overlappings of concern between, for instance, the contradictory form of the writing of theory in Lyotard's *Le Différend* (1983) and that of a novel like Peter Ackroyd's *Hawksmoor.* Their sequentially ordered sections are equally disrupted by a particularly dense network of interconnections and intertexts, and each enacts or performs, as well as theorizes, the paradoxes of continuity and disconnection, of totalizing interpretation and the impossibility of final meaning. In Lyotard's own words:

A postmodern artist or writer is in the position of a philosopher: the text he writes, the work he produces are not in principle governed by preestablished rules, and they cannot be judged according to a determining judgment, by applying familiar categories to the text or to the work. Those rules and categories are what the work of art itself is looking for. (1984, 81)

REFERENCES

Barthes, Roland (1972) *Critical Essays*, trans. Richard Howard, Evanton, Ill: Northwestern University Press.
—— (1977) *Image Music Text*, trans. Stephen Heath, New York: Hill and Wang.
Burgin, Victor (1986) *The End of Art Theory: Criticism and Postmodernity*, Atlantic Highlands, NJ: Humanities Press International.
Chenétier, Marc (1985) 'Charting Contemporary American Fiction: A View from Abroad', *New Literary History*, 16, 3:653–69.
Cox, Christoph (1985) 'Barthes, Borges, Foucault, Utopia', *Subjects/Objects*, 3:55–69.
Culler, Jonathan (1983, 1984) 'At the Boundaries: Barthes and Derrida' in Sussman, Herbert L. (ed.) *At the Boundaries*, Boston, Mass.: Northeastern University Press.
Derrida, Jacques (1981) *Positions*, trans. Alan Bass, Chicago, Ill: University of Chicago Press.
de Lauretis, Teresa (1985) 'Gaudy Rose: Eco and Narcissism', *SubStance*, 47: 13–29.
Fish, Stanley (1986) 'Critical Self-Consciousness or Can We Know What We Are Doing?', lecture, MacMaster University, Ontario.
Hutcheon, Linda (1985) *A Theory of Parody: The Teachings of Twentieth-Century Art Forms*, London and New York, Methuen.
Jameson, Fredric (1983) 'Postmodernism and Consumer Society', in Foster, Hal (ed.) *The Anti-Aesthetic: Essays on Modern Culture*, Port Townsend, Wash: Bay Press.
Lucente, Gregory L. (1986) *Beautiful Fables: Self-Consciousness in Italian Narrative from Manzone to Calvino*, Baltimore, Md and London: Johns Hopkins University Press.
Lyotard, Jean-François (1984) *The Postmodern Condition: A Report on Knowledge*, trans. Geoff Bennington and Brian Massumi, Minneapolis: University of Minnesota Press.
Newman, Charles (1985) *The Post-Modern Era: The Act of Fiction in an Age of Inflation*, Evanston, Ill.: Northwestern University Press.

Norris, Christopher (1985) *The Contest of Faculties: Philosophy and Theory After Deconstruction*, London and New York: Methuen.

Pops, Martin (1984) *Home Remedies*, Amherst: University of Massachusetts Press.

Radhakrishnan, Rajagoplan (1983) 'The Post-Modern Event and the End of Logocentrism', *boundary 2*, 12, 1:33–60.

Russell, Charles (1980) 'The Context of the Concept', in Garvin, Harry R. (ed.) *Romanticism, Modernism, Postmodernism*, Lewisburg, Pa: Bucknell University Press; London: Associated University Press.

—— (1985) *Poets, Prophets, and Revolutionaries: The Literary Avant-garde from Rimbaud through Postmodernism*, New York and Oxford: Oxford University Press.

White, Hayden (1978) *Tropics of Discourse: Essays in Cultural Criticism*, Baltimore, Md: Johns Hopkins University Press.

Ziolkowski, Theodore (1969) 'Toward a Post-Modern Aesthetics?' *Mosaic*, 2, 4:112–19.

XIV POST-COLONIAL CRITICISM

Post-colonial criticism emerged as a significant development in literary theory in the late 1980s. One can see its origins in such influential texts as Frantz Fanon's *The Wretched of the Earth*, Chinua Achebe's essay 'Colonialist Criticism', and Edward Said's *Orientalism*. Post-colonial critics and theorists attack the explicit or implicit claims made for Eurocentric art and literature as having universal application, thus relegating non-Western cultural forms to the margins. Said's *Orientalism* was particularly influential in exposing the biased representation of the Orient in Western writers, who either regarded it as an inferior 'Other' or projected onto it characteristics Westerners do not accept as typical of themselves, such as inhuman cruelty and pathological sensuality.

Post-colonial criticism tends to have a double focus: it concentrates either on the representation of the non-European in Western canonic literature or on writing from non-European cultural traditions, particularly writing from countries that have been colonised by Western nations. Cultural difference is therefore a central preoccupation of post-colonial critics and theorists. Edward Said's major work after *Orientalism, Culture and Imperialism*, is concerned with the relation between imperialism and Western art and culture. In the section from it included here he attacks the Eurocentrism of conventional conceptions of comparative literature. He argues, however, that this cultural imperialism does not serve the interests of Western literature and art. Not only is this to neglect or devalue non-European cultural forms but Western culture itself is devalued. He advocates what he calls a contrapuntal reading that plays off the Western and the non-Western against one another: 'As we look back at the cultural archive, we begin to reread it not univocally but *contrapuntally*, with a simultaneous awareness both of the metropolitan history that is narrated and of those other histories which (and together with which) the dominating discourse acts.' For him, 'Cultural experience or indeed every cultural form is radically, quintessentially hybrid.'

Homi K. Bhabha is a theorist who brings post-colonialist concerns into relation with contemporary critical theory in a quite radical way. His particular concern is with the construction of the subject and in the essay reprinted here he focuses on how the colonial subject as 'Other' is constructed as a stereotype in colonial discourse and how such discourse operates as an 'apparatus of power': 'The objective of colonial discourse is to construe the colonized as a population of degenerate types on the basis of racial origin, in order to justify conquest and to establish systems of administration and instruction.'

FURTHER READING

Bill Ashcroft et al. (eds), *The Empire Writes Back: Theory and Practice in Post-Colonial Literature* (London, 1989).
——, *The Post-Colonial Studies Reader* (London, 1994).
Homi K. Bhabha, *The Location of Culture* (London, 1994).
Edward W. Said, *Orientalism* (New York, 1978).
Gayatri C. Spivak, *The Post-Colonial Critic: Interviews, Strategies, Dialogues* (London, 1990).
Dennis Walder (ed.), *Literature and the Modern World* (Oxford, 1990). (Contains Achebe's 'Colonialist Criticism'.)
Robert J.C. Young, *Colonial Desire: Hybridity in Theory, Culture and Race* (London, 1994).

53   EDWARD W. SAID: 'OVERLAPPING TERRITORIES, INTERTWINED HISTORIES'

From long before World War Two until the early 1970s, the main tradition of comparative-literature studies in Europe and the United States was heavily dominated by a style of scholarship that has now almost disappeared. The main feature of this older style was that it was scholarship principally, and not what we have come to call criticism. No one today is trained as were Erich Auerbach and Leo Spitzer, two of the great German comparatists who found refuge in the United States as a result of fascism: this is as much a quantitative as a qualitative fact. ...

Behind such scholars was an even longer tradition of humanistic learning that derived from that efflorescence of secular anthropology – which included a revolution in the philological disciplines – we associate with the late eighteenth century and with such figures as Vico, Herder, Rousseau, and the brothers Schlegel. And underlying *their* work was the belief that mankind

Reprinted from *Culture and Imperialism* (London, 1993), pp. 50–72.

formed a marvellous, almost symphonic whole whose progress and formations, again as a whole, could be studied exclusively as a concerted and secular historical experience, not as an exemplification of the divine. Because 'man' has made history, there was a special hermeneutical way of studying history that differed in intent as well as method from the natural sciences. These great Enlightenment insights became widespread, and were accepted in Germany, France, Italy, Russia, Switzerland, and subsequently, England.

It is not a vulgarization of history to remark that a major reason why such a view of human culture became current in Europe and America in several different forms during the two centuries between 1745 and 1945 was the striking rise of nationalism during the same period. ...

What partly animated my study of Orientalism was my critique of the way in which the alleged universalism of fields such as the classics (not to mention historiography, anthropology, and sociology) was Eurocentric in the extreme, as if other literatures and societies had either an inferior or a transcended value. ...

Yet this narrow, often strident nationalism was in fact counteracted by a more generous cultural vision represented by the intellectual ancestors of Curtius and Auerbach, scholars whose ideas emerged in pre-imperial Germany (perhaps as compensation for the political unification eluding the country), and, a little later, in France. These thinkers took nationalism to be a transitory, finally secondary matter: what mattered far more was the concert of peoples and spirits that transcended the shabby political realm of bureaucracy, armies, customs barriers, and xenophobia. Out of this catholic tradition, to which European (as opposed to national) thinkers appealed in times of severe conflict, came the idea that the comparative study of literature could furnish a translational, even trans-human perspective on literary performance. ...

To speak of comparative literature therefore was to speak of the interaction of world literatures with one another, but the field was epistemologically organized as a sort of hierarchy, with Europe and its Latin Christian literatures at its centre and top. ...

Academic work in comparative literature carried with it the notion that Europe and the United States together were the centre of the world, not simply by virtue of their political positions, but also because their literatures were the ones most worth studying. When Europe succumbed to fascism and when the United States benefited so richly from the many émigré scholars who came to it, understandably little of their sense of crisis took root with them. *Mimesis*, for example, written while Auerbach was in exile from Nazi Europe in Istanbul, was not simply an exercise in textual explication, but ... an act of civilizational survival. It had seemed to him that his mission as a comparatist was to present, perhaps for the last time, the complex evolution of European literature in all its variety from Homer to Virginia Woolf. Curtius's book on the Latin Middle Ages was composed out of the same driven fear. ...

As *Mimesis* immediately reveals, however, the notion of Western literature that lies at the very core of comparative study centrally highlights, dramatizes, and celebrates a certain idea of history, and at the same time obscures the fundamental geographical and political reality empowering that idea. The idea of European or Western literary history contained in it and the other scholarly works of comparative literature is essentially idealistic and, in an unsystematic way, Hegelian. ...

The salutary vision of a 'world literature' that acquired a redemptive status in the twentieth century coincides with what theorists of colonial geography also articulated. In the writings of Halford Mackinder, George Chisolm, Georges Hardy, Leroy-Beaulieu, and Lucien Fevre, a much franker appraisal of the world system appears, equally metrocentric and imperial; but instead of history alone, now both empire and actual geographical space collaborate to produce a 'world-empire' commanded by Europe. ...

To their audience in the late nineteenth and early twentieth centuries, the great geographical synthesizers offered technical explanations for ready political actualities. Europe *did* command the world; the imperial map *did* license the cultural vision. To us, a century later, the coincidence or similarity between one vision of a world system and the other, between geography and literary history, seems interesting but problematic. What should we do with this similarity?

First of all, I believe, it needs *articulation* and *activation*, which can only come about if we take serious account of the present, and notably of the dismantling of the classical empires and the new independence of dozens of formerly colonized peoples and territories. We need to see that the contemporary global setting – overlapping territories, intertwined histories – was already prefigured and inscribed in the coincidences and convergencies among geography, culture, and history that were so important to the pioneers of comparative literature. Then we can grasp in a new and more dynamic way both the idealist historicism which fuelled the comparatist 'world literature' scheme and the concretely imperial world map of the same moment.

But that cannot be done without accepting that what is common to both is an elaboration of power. The genuinely profound scholarship of the people who believed in and practiced *Weltliteratur* implied the extraordinary privilege of an observer located in the West who could actually survey the world's literary output with a kind of sovereign detachment. Orientalists and other specialists about the non-European world – anthropologists, historians, philologists – had that power, and, as I have tried to show elsewhere, it often went hand in glove with a consciously undertaken imperial enterprise. ...

Without significant exception the universalizing discourses of modern Europe and the United States assume the silence, willing or otherwise, of the non-European world. There is incorporation; there is inclusion; there is direct rule; there is coercion. But there is only infrequently an acknowledgement that the colonized people should be heard from, their ideas known.

It is possible to argue that the continued production and interpretation of Western culture itself made exactly the same assumption well on into the twentieth century, even as political resistance grew to the West's power in the 'peripheral' world. Because of that, and because of where it led, it becomes possible now to reinterpret the Western cultural archive as if fractured geographically by the activated imperial divide, to do a rather different kind of reading and interpretation. In the first place, the history of such fields as comparative literature, English studies, cultural analysis, anthropology can be seen as affiliated with the empire and, in a manner of speaking, even contributing to its methods for maintaining Western ascendancy over non-Western natives, especially if we are aware of the spatial consciousness exemplified in Gramsci's 'southern question'. And in the second place our interpretative change of perspective allows us to challenge the sovereign and unchallenged authority of the allegedly detached Western observer.

Western cultural forms can be taken out of the autonomous enclosures in which they have been protected, and placed instead in the dynamic global environment created by imperialism, itself revised as an ongoing contest between north and south, metropolis and periphery, white and native. We may thus consider imperialism as a process occurring as part of the metropolitan culture, which at times acknowledges, at other times obscures the sustained business of the empire itself. The important point – a very

Gramscian one – is how the national British, French, American cultures maintained hegemony over the peripheries. How within them was consent gained and continuously consolidated for the distant rule of native peoples and territories?

As we look back at the cultural archive, we begin to reread it not univocally but *contrapuntally*, with a simultaneous awareness both of the metropolitan history that is narrated and of those other histories against which (and together with which) the dominating discourse acts. In the counterpoint of Western classical music, various themes play off one another, with only a provisional privilege being given to any particular one; yet in the resulting polyphony there is concert and order, an organized interplay that derives from the themes, not from a rigorous melodic or formal principle outside the work. In the same way, I believe, we can read and interpret English novels, for example, whose engagement (usually suppressed for the most part) with the West Indies or India, say, is shaped and perhaps even determined by the specific history of colonization, resistance, and finally native nationalism. At this point alternative or new narratives emerge, and they become institutionalized or discursively stable entities. ...

An example of the new knowledge would be the study of Orientalism or Africanism and, to take a related set, the study of Englishness and Frenchness. These identities are today analysed not as god-given essences, but as results of collaboration between African history and the study of Africa in England, for instance, or between the study of French history and the reorganization of knowledge during the First Empire. ...

Even the mammoth engagements in our own time over such essentializations as 'Islam', the 'West', the 'Orient', 'Japan', or 'Europe' admit to a particular knowledge and structures of attitude and reference, and those require careful analysis and research.

If one studies some of the major metropolitan cultures – England's, France's, and the United States', for instance – in the geographical context of their struggles for (and over) empires, a distinctive cultural topography becomes apparent. In using the phrase 'structures of attitude and reference', I have this topography in mind, as I also have in mind Raymond Williams's seminal phrase 'structures of feeling'. I am talking about the way in which structures of location and geographical reference appear in the cultural languages of literature, history, or ethnography, sometimes allusively and sometimes carefully plotted, across several individual works that are not otherwise connected to one another or to an official ideology of 'empire'.

In British culture, for instance, one may discover a consistency of concern in Spenser, Shakespeare, Defoe, and Austen that fixes socially desirable, empowered space in metropolitan England or Europe and connects it by design, motive, and development to distant or peripheral worlds (Ireland, Venice, Africa, Jamaica), conceived of as desirable but subordinate. And with these meticulously maintained references come attitudes – about rule, control, profit, and enhancement and suitability – that grow with astonishing power from the seventeenth to the end of the nineteenth century. These structures do not arise from some pre-existing (semi-conspiratorial) design that the writers then manipulate, but are bound up with the development of Britain's cultural identity, as that identity imagines itself in a geographically conceived world. Similar structures may be remarked in French and American cultures, growing for different reasons and obviously in different ways. ...

Reading and interpreting the major metropolitan cultural texts in this newly activated, reinformed way could not have been possible without the movements of resistance that occurred everywhere in the peripheries against the empire. ...

We live of course in a world not only of commodities but also of representation, and representations – their production, circulation, history, and interpretation – are the very element of culture. In much recent theory the problem of representation is deemed to be central, yet rarely is it put in its full political context, a context that is primarily imperial. Instead we have on the one hand an isolated cultural sphere, believed to be freely and unconditionally available to weightless theoretical speculation and investigation, and, on the other, a debased political sphere, where the real struggle between interests is supposed to occur. To the professional student of culture – the humanist, the critic, the scholar – only one sphere is relevant, and, more to the point, it is accepted that the two spheres are separated, whereas the two are not only connected but ultimately the same.

A radical falsification has become established in this separation. Culture is exonerated of any entanglements with power, representations are considered only as apolitical images to be parsed and construed as so many grammars of exchange, and the divorce of the present from the past is assumed to be complete. And yet, far from this separation of spheres being a neutral or accidental choice, its real meaning is as an act of complicity, the humanist's choice of a disguised, denuded, systematically purged textual model over a more embattled model, whose principal features would inevitably coalesce around the continuing struggle over the question of empire itself. ...

Cultural experience or indeed every cultural form is radically, quintessentially hybrid, and if it has been the practice in the West since Immanuel Kant to isolate cultural and aesthetic realms from the worldly domain, it is now time to rejoin them. This is by no means a simple matter, since – I believe – it has been the essence of experience in the West at least since the late eighteenth century not only to acquire distant domination and reinforce hegemony, but also to divide the realms of culture and experience into apparently separate spheres. Entities such as races and nations, essences such as Englishness or Orientalism, modes of production such as the Asiatic or Occidental, all of these in my opinion testify to an ideology whose cultural correlatives well precede the actual accumulation of imperial territories worldwide.

Most historians of empire speak of the 'age of empire' as formally beginning around 1878, with 'the scramble for Africa'. A closer look at the cultural actuality reveals a much earlier, more deeply and stubbornly held view about overseas European hegemony; we can locate a coherent, fully mobilized system of ideas near the end of the eighteenth century, and there follows the set of integral developments such as the first great systematic conquests under Napoleon, the rise of nationalism and the European nation-state, the advent of large-scale industrialization, and the consolidation of power in the bourgeoisie. This is also the period in which the novel form and the new historical narrative become pre-eminent, and in which the importance of subjectivity to historical time takes firm hold.

Yet most cultural historians, and certainly all literary scholars, have failed to remark the *geographical* notation, the theoretical mapping and charting of territory that underlies Western fiction, historical writing, and philosophical discourse of the time. ... The perfect example of what I mean is to be found in Jane Austen's *Mansfield Park*, in which Thomas Bertram's slave plantation in Antigua is mysteriously necessary to the poise and the beauty of Mansfield Park, a place described in moral and aesthetic terms well before the scramble for Africa, or before the age of empire officially began. As John Stuart Mill puts it in the *Principles of Political Economy*:

These [outlying possessions of ours] are hardly to be looked upon as countries ... but more properly as outlying agricultural or manufacturing estates belonging to a larger community. Our West Indian colonies, for example, cannot be regarded as countries with a productive capital of their own ... [but are rather] the place where England finds it convenient to carry on the production of sugar, coffee and a few other tropical commodities.

Read this extraordinary passage together with Jane Austen, and a much less benign picture stands forth than the usual one of cultural formations in the pre-imperialist age. In Mill we have the ruthless proprietary tones of the white master used to effacing the reality, work, and suffering of millions of slaves, transported across the middle passage, reduced only to an incorporated status 'for the benefit of the proprietors'. These colonies are, Mill says, to be considered as hardly anything more than a convenience, an attitude confirmed by Austen, who in *Mansfield Park* sublimates the agonies of Caribbean existence to a mere half-dozen passing references to Antigua. And much the same processes occur in other canonical writers of Britain and France; in short, the metropolis gets its authority to a considerable extent from the devaluation as well as the exploitation of the outlying colonial possession. ...

Lastly, the authority of the observer, and of European geographical centrality, is buttressed by a cultural discourse relegating and confining the non-European to a secondary racial, cultural, ontological status. Yet this secondariness is, paradoxically, essential to the primariness of the European; this of course is the paradox explored by Césaire, Fanon, and Memmi, and it is but one among many of the ironies of modern critical theory that it has rarely been explored by investigators of the aporias and impossibilities of reading. Perhaps that is because it places emphasis not so much on *how* to read, but rather on *what* is read and *where* is written about and represented. ...

What to read and what to do with that reading, that is the full form of the question. All the energies poured into critical theory, into novel and demystifying theoretical praxes like the new historicism and deconstruction and Marxism have avoided the major, I would say determining, political horizon of modern Western culture, namely imperialism. This massive avoidance has sustained a canonical inclusion and exclusion: you include the Rousseaus, the Nietzsches, the Wordsworths, the Dickenses, Flauberts, and so on, and at the same time you exclude their relationships with the protracted, complex, and striated work of empire. But why is this a matter of what to read and about where? Very simply, because critical discourse has taken no cognizance

of the enormously exciting, varied post-colonial literature produced in resistance to the imperialist expansion of Europe and
the United States in the past two centuries. To read Austen
without also reading Fanon and Cabral – and so on and on – is to
disaffiliate modern culture from its engagements and attach-
ments. That is a process that should be reversed.

But there is more to be done. Critical theory and literary historical scholarship have reinterpreted and revalidated major
swatches of Western literature, art, and philosophy. Much of this
has been exciting and powerful work, even though one often
senses more an energy of elaboration and refinement than a committed engagement to what I would call secular and affiliated criticism; such criticism cannot be undertaken without a fairly strong
sense of how consciously chosen historical models are relevant to
social and intellectual change. Yet if you read and interpret
modern European and American culture as having had something to do with imperialism, it becomes incumbent upon you
also to reinterpret the canon in the light of texts whose place
there has been insufficiently linked to, insufficiently weighted
towards the expansion of Europe. Put differently, this procedure
entails reading the canon as a polyphonic accompaniment to the
expansion of Europe, giving a revised direction and valence to
such writers as Conrad and Kipling, who have always been read as
sports, not as writers whose manifestly imperialist subject matter
has a long subterranean or implicit and proleptic life in the
earlier work of writers like, say, Austen or Chateaubriand.

Second, theoretical work must begin to formulate the relationship between empire and culture. ... Theoretically we are only at
the stage of trying to inventory the *interpellation* of culture by
empire, but the efforts so far made are only slightly more than
rudimentary. And as the study of culture extends into the mass
media, popular culture, micropolitics, and so forth, the focus on
modes of power and hegemony grows sharper.

Third, we should keep before us the prerogatives of the present
as signposts and paradigms for the study of the past. If I have
insisted on integration and connections between the past and the
present, between imperializer and imperialized, between culture
and imperialism, I have done so not to level or reduce differences, but rather to convey a more urgent sense of the interdependence between things. So vast and yet so detailed is
imperialism as an experience with crucial cultural dimensions,
that we must speak of overlapping territories, intertwined histories common to men and women, whites and non-whites, dwellers

in the metropolis and on the peripheries, past as well as present and future; these territories and histories can only be seen from the perspective of the whole of secular human history.

54 HOMI K. BHABHA: 'THE OTHER QUESTION: THE STEREOTYPE AND COLONIAL DISCOURSE'

An important feature of colonial discourse is its dependence on the concept of 'fixity' in the ideological construction of otherness.[1] Fixity, as the sign of cultural/historical/racial difference in the discourse of colonialism, is a paradoxical mode of representation: it connotes rigidity and an unchanging order as well as disorder, degeneracy and daemonic repetition. Likewise the stereotype, which is its major discursive strategy, is a form of knowledge and identification that vacillates between what is always 'in place', already known, and something that must be anxiously repeated ... as if the essential duplicity of the Asiatic or the bestial sexual licence of the African that needs no proof, can never really, in discourse, be proved. It is this process of *ambivalence*, central to the stereotype that my essay explores as it constructs a theory of colonial discourse. For it is the force of ambivalence that gives the colonial stereotype its currency: ensures its repeatability in changing historical and discursive conjunctures; informs its strategies of individuation and marginalization; produces that effect of probabilistic truth and predictability which, for the stereotype, must always be in *excess* of what can be empirically proved or logically construed. Yet the function of ambivalence as one of the most significant discursive and psychical strategies of discriminatory power – whether racist or sexist, peripheral or metropolitan – remains to be charted.

The absence of such a perspective has its own history of political expediency. To recognize the stereotype as an ambivalent mode of knowledge and power demands a theoretical and political response that challenges deterministic or functionalist modes of conceiving of the relationship between discourse and politics, and questions dogmatic and moralistic positions on the meaning

Reprinted from *The Sexual Subject: A Screen Reader in Sexuality* (London and New York, 1992), pp. 312–23.

of oppression and discrimination. My reading of colonial discourse suggests that the point of intervention should shift from the *identification* of images as positive or negative, to an understanding of the *processes of subjectification* made possible (and plausible) through stereotypical discourse. To judge the stereotyped image on the basis of a prior political normativity is to dismiss it, not to displace it, which is only possible by engaging with its *effectivity*; with the repertoire of positions of power and resistance, domination and dependence that constructs the colonial subject (both colonizer and colonized). I do not intend to deconstruct the colonial discourse to reveal its ideological misconceptions or repressions, to exult in its self-reflexivity, or to indulge its liberatory 'excess'. In order to understand the productivity of colonial power it is crucial to construct its regime of 'truth', not to subject its representations to a normalizing judgement. Only then does it become possible to understand the *productive* ambivalence of the object of colonial discourse – that 'otherness' which is at once an object of desire and derision, an articulation of difference contained within the fantasy of origin and identity. What such a reading reveals are the boundaries of colonial discourse and it enables a transgression of these limits from the space of that otherness.

The construction of the colonial subject in discourse, and the exercise of colonial power through discourse, demands an articulation of forms of difference – racial and sexual. Such an articulation becomes crucial if it is held that the body is always simultaneously inscribed in both the economy of pleasure and desire and the economy of discourse, domination and power. I do not wish to conflate, unproblematically, two forms of the marking – and splitting– of the subject nor to globalize two forms of representation. I want to suggest, however, that there is a theoretical space and a political place for such an *articulation* – in the sense in which that word itself denies an 'original' identity or a 'singularity' to objects of difference – sexual or racial. If such a view is taken, as Feuchtwang argues in a different context,[2] it follows that the epithets racial or sexual come to be seen as modes of differentiation, realized as multiple, cross-cutting determinations, polymorphous and perverse, always demanding a specific and strategic calculation of their effects. Such is, I believe, the moment of colonial discourse. It is the most theoretically underdeveloped form of discourse, but crucial to the binding of a range of differences and discriminations that inform the discursive and political practices of racial and cultural hierarchization. ...

The difference of colonial discourse as an apparatus of power will emerge more fully as this paper develops. At this stage, however, I shall provide what I take to be the minimum conditions and specifications of such a discourse. It is an apparatus that turns on the recognition and disavowal of racial/cultural/historical differences. Its predominant strategic function is the creation of a space for a 'subject peoples' through the production of knowledge in terms of which surveillance is exercised and a complex form of pleasure/unpleasure is incited. It seeks authorization for its strategies by the production of knowledges of colonizer and colonized which are stereotypical but antithetically evaluated. The objective of colonial discourse is to construe the colonized as a population of degenerate types on the basis of racial origin, in order to justify conquest and to establish systems of administration and instruction. Despite the play of power within colonial discourse and the shifting positionalities of its subjects (for example effects of class, gender, ideology, different social formations, varied systems of colonization and so on), I am referring to a form of governmentality that in marking out a 'subject nation', appropriates, directs and dominates its various spheres of activity. Therefore, despite the 'play' in the colonial system which is crucial to its exercise of power, colonial discourse produces the colonized as a social reality which is at once an 'other' and yet entirely knowable and visible. It resembles a form of narrative whereby the productivity and circulation of subjects and signs are bound in a reformed and recognizable totality. It employs a system of representation, a regime of truth, that is structurally similar to realism. And it is in order to intervene within that system of representation that Edward Said proposes a semiotic of 'Orientalist' power, examining the varied European discourses which constitute 'the Orient' as an unified racial, geographical, political and cultural zone of the world. ...

It is, on the one hand, a topic of learning, discovery, practice; on the other, it is the site of dreams, images, fantasies, myths, obsessions and requirements. It is a static system of 'synchronic essentialism', a knowledge of 'signifiers of stability' such as the lexicographic and the encyclopaedic. However, this site is continually under threat from diachronic forms of history and narrative signs of instability. And, finally, this line of thinking is given a shape analogical to the dreamwork, when Said refers explicitly to a distinction between 'an unconscious positivity' which he terms *latent* Orientalism, and the stated knowledges and views about the Orient which he calls *manifest* Orientalism.

Where the originality of this pioneering theory loses its inventiveness, and for me its usefulness, is with Said's reluctance to engage with the alterity and ambivalence in the articulation of these two economies which threaten to split the very object of Orientalist discourse as a knowledge and the subject positioned therein. He contains this threat by introducing a binarism within the argument which, in initially setting up an opposition between these two discursive scenes, finally allows them to be correlated as a congruent system of representation that is unified through a political-ideological *intention* which, in his words, enables Europe to advance securely and *unmetaphorically* upon the Orient. Said identifies the *content* of Orientalism as the unconscious repository of fantasy, imaginative writings and essential ideas; and the *form* of manifest Orientalism as the historically and discursively determined, diachronic aspect. This division/correlation structure of manifest and latent Orientalism leads to the effectivity of the concept of discourse being undermined by what could be called the polarities of intentionality.

This produces a problem with Said's use of Foucault's concepts of power and discourse. The productivity of Foucault's concept of power/knowledge lies in its refusal of an epistemology which opposes essence/appearance, ideology/science. *'Pouvoir/Savoir'* places subjects in a relation of power and recognition that is not part of a symmetrical or dialectical relation – self/other, master/slave – which can then be subverted by being inverted. Subjects are always disproportionately placed in opposition or domination through the symbolic decentring of multiple power relations which play the role of support as well as target or adversary. It becomes difficult, then, to conceive of the *historical* enunciations of colonial discourse without them being either functionally overdetermined or strategically elaborated or displaced by the *unconscious* scene of latent Orientalism. Equally, it is difficult to conceive of the process of subjectification as a placing *within* Orientalist or colonial discourse for the dominated subject without the dominant being strategically placed within it too. There is always, in Said, the suggestion that colonial power and discourse is possessed entirely by the colonizer, which is a historical and theoretical simplification. The terms in which Said's Orientalism is unified – the intentionality and unidirectionality of colonial power – also unify the subject of colonial enunication.

This is a result of Said's inadequate attention to representation as a concept that articulates the historical and fantasy (as the scene of desire) in the production of the 'political' effects of discourse. He rightly rejects a notion of orientalism as the misrepresentation of an Oriental essence. However, having introduced the concept of 'discourse' he does not face up to the problems it makes for the instrumentalist notion of power knowledge that he seems to require. ...

The strategic articulation of 'coordinates of knowledge' – racial and sexual – and their inscription in the play of colonial power as modes of differentiation, defence, fixation, hierarchization, is a way of specifying colonial discourse which would be illuminated by reference to Foucault's poststructuralist concept of the *dispositif* or apparatus. Foucault stresses that the relations of knowledge and power within the apparatus are always a strategic response to *an urgent need* at a given historical moment – much as I suggested at the outset – that the force of colonial discourse as a theoretical and political intervention, was the *need*, in our contemporary moment, to contest singularities of difference and to articulate modes of differentiation. Foucault writes:

the apparatus is essentially of a strategic nature, which means assuming that it is a matter of a certain manipulation of relations of forces, either developing them in a particular direction, blocking them, stabilising them, utilising them etc. The apparatus is thus always inscribed in a play of power, but it is also always linked to certain coordinates of knowledge which issue from it but, to an equal degree, condition it. This is what the apparatus consists in: strategies of relations of forces supporting and supported by, types of knowledge.[3]

In this spirit I argue for the reading of the stereotype in terms of fetishism. The myth of historical origination – racial purity, cultural priority – produced in relation to the colonial stereotype functions to 'normalize' the multiple beliefs and split subjects that constitute colonial discourse as a consequence of its process of disavowal. The scene of fetishism functions similarly as, at once, a reactivation of the material of original fantasy – the anxiety of castration and sexual difference – as well as a normalization of that difference and disturbance in terms of the fetish object as the substitute for the mother's penis. Within the apparatus of colonial power, the discourses of sexuality and race relate in a process of *functional overdetermination*, 'because each effect ... enters into resonance or contradiction with the others and thereby calls for a readjustment or a reworking of the heterogeneous elements that surface at various points'.[4]

There is both a structural and functional justification for
reading the racial stereotype of colonial discourse in terms of
fetishism.[5] My rereading of Said establishes the *structural* link.
Fetishism, as the disavowal of difference, is that repetitious scene
around the problem of castration. The recognition of sexual difference – as the precondition for the circulation of the chain of
absence and presence in the realm of the Symbolic – is disavowed
by the fixation on an object that masks that difference and re-
stores an original presence. The *functional* link between the
fixation of the fetish and the stereotype (or the stereotype as
fetish) is even more relevant. For fetishism is always a 'play' or
vacillation between the archaic affirmation of wholeness/similar-
ity – in Freud's terms: 'All men have penises'; in ours 'All men
have the same skin/race/culture' – and the anxiety associated
with lack and difference – again, for Freud 'Some do not have
penises'; for us 'Some do not have the same skin/race/culture'.
Within discourse, the fetish represents the simultaneous play
between metaphor as substitution (masking absence and difference) and metonymy (which contiguously registers the perceived
lack). The fetish or stereotype gives access to an 'identity' which is
predicated as much on mastery and pleasure as it is on anxiety
and defence, for it is a form of multiple and contradictory belief
in its recognition of difference and disavowal of it. This conflict of
pleasure/ unpleasure, mastery/defence, knowledge/disavowal,
absence/presence, has a fundamental significance for colonial
discourse. For the scene of fetishism is also the scene of the reactivation and repetition of primal fantasy – the subject's desire
for a pure origin that is always threatened by its division, for the
subject must be gendered to be engendered, to be spoken.

The stereotype, then, as the primary point of subjectification in
colonial discourse, for both colonizer and colonized, is the scene
of a similar fantasy and defence – the desire for an originality
which is again threatened by the differences of race, colour and
culture. My contention is splendidly caught in Fanon's title *Black
Skin White Masks* where the disavowal of difference turns the colonial subject into a misfit – a grotesque mimicry or 'doubling' that
threatens to split the soul and whole, undifferentiated skin of the
ego. The stereotype is not a simplification because it is a false representation of a given reality. It is a simplification because it is an
arrested, fixated form of representation that, in denying the play
of difference (which the negation through the Other permits),
constitutes a problem for the *representation* of the subject in
significations of psychic and social relations.

When Fanon talks of the positioning of the subject in the stereotyped discourse of colonialism, he gives further credence to my point. The legends, stories, histories and anecdotes of a colonial culture offer the subject a primordial Either/Or.[6] *Either* he is fixed in a consciousness of the body as a solely negating activity *or* as a new kind of man, a new genus. What is denied the colonial subject, both as colonizer and colonized, is that form of negation which gives access to the recognition of difference. It is that possibility of difference and circulation which would liberate the signifier of *skin/culture* from the fixations of racial typology, the analytics of blood, ideologies of racial and cultural dominance or degeneration. 'Wherever he goes,' Fanon despairs, 'the Negro remains a Negro' – his race becomes the ineradicable sign of *negative difference* in colonial discourses. For the stereotype impedes the circulation and articulation of the signifier of 'race' as anything other than its *fixity* as racism. We always already know that blacks are licentious, Asiatics duplicitous. ...

My anatomy of colonial discourse remains incomplete until I locate the stereotype, as an arrested, fetishistic mode of representation within its field of identification, which I have identified in my description of Fanon's primal scenes, as the Lacanian schema of the Imaginary. The Imaginary[7] is the transformation that takes place in the subject at the formative mirror phase, when it assumes a *discrete* image which allows it to postulate a series of equivalences, samenesses, identities, between the objects of the surrounding world. However, this positioning is itself *problematic*, for the subject finds or recognizes itself through an image which is simultaneously alienating and hence potentially confrontational. This is the basis of the close relation between the two forms of identification complicit with the Imaginary – narcissism and aggressivity. It is precisely these two forms of 'identification' that constitute the dominant strategy of colonial power exercised in relation to the stereotype which, as a form of multiple and contradictory belief, gives knowledge of difference and simultaneously disavows or masks it. Like the mirror phase 'the fullness' of the stereotype – its image *as* identity – is always threatened by 'lack'.

The construction of colonial discourse is then a complex articulation of the tropes of fetishism – metaphor and metonymy – and the forms of narcissistic and aggressive identification available to the Imaginary. Stereotypical racial discourse is a four-term strategy. There is a tie-up between the metaphoric or masking function of the fetish and the narcissistic object-choice and an opposing alliance between the metonymic figuring of lack and the aggressive phase of the Imaginary. A repertoire of conflictual positions constitutes the subject in colonial discourse. The taking up of any one position, within a specific discursive form, in a particular historical conjuncture, is thus always problematic – the site of both fixity and fantasy. It provides a colonial 'identity' that is played out – like all fantasies of originality and origination – in the face and space of the disruption and threat from the heterogeneity of other positions. As a form of splitting and multiple belief, the 'stereotype' requires, for its successful signification, a continual and repetitive chain of other stereotypes. The process by which the metaphoric 'masking' is inscribed on a lack which must then be concealed gives the stereotype both its fixity and its phantasmatic quality – the *same old* stories of the Negro's animality, the Coolie's inscrutability or the stupidity of the Irish *must* be told (compulsively) again and afresh, and are differently gratifying and terrifying each time.

In any specific colonial discourse the metaphoric/narcissistic and the metonymic/aggressive positions will function simultaneously, strategically poised in relation to each other; similar to the moment of alienation which stands as a threat to Imaginary plentitude, and 'multiple belief' which threatens fetishistic disavowal. The subjects of discourse are constructed within an apparatus of power which *contains*, in both senses of the word, an 'other' knowledge – a knowledge that is arrested and fetishistic and circulates through colonial discourse as that limited form of otherness, that form of difference, that I have called the stereotype.

NOTES

[Reorgsnised and renumbered from the original]
    1. Realizing that the question of woman's relation to castration and access to the Symbolic requires a very specific form of attention and articulation, I chose to be cautious till I had worked out its implications for colonial discourse. Second, the representation of class difference in the construction of the colonial subject is not specified adequately. Wanting to avoid any form of class determinism 'in the last instance' it becomes difficult, if crucial, to calculate its effectivity.
    2. Stephan Feuchtwang, 'Socialist, Feminist and Anti-racist Struggles', *m/f* (1980), no. 4, 41.
    3. Michel Foucault, 'The Confession of the Flesh', in *Power/Knowledge* (Brighton, Harvester Press, 1980), p. 196.
    4. Ibid., p. 195
    5. See Sigmund Freud, 'Fetishism' (1927) in *On Sexuality*, vol. VII, Pelican Freud Library (Harmondsworth, Penguin Books, 1981), p. 345ff;

Christian Metz, *Psychoanalysis and Cinema: the Imaginary Signifier* (London, Macmillan, 1982), pp. 67–78. See also Steve Neale, 'The Same Old Story: Stereotypes and Differences', *Screen Education* (Autumn–Winter 1979–80), nos. 32–3, 33–7.

6. Frantz Fanon, *Black Skin White Masks* (London, Paladin, 1970); see pp. 78–82.

7. For the best account of Lacan's concept of the Imaginary see Jacqueline Rose, 'The Imaginary', in Colin MacCabe (ed.), *The Talking Cure* (London, Macmillan, 1981).

INDEX